Crime and Spy Jazz
on Screen Since 1971

ALSO BY DERRICK BANG

*Crime and Spy Jazz on Screen, 1950–1970:
A History and Discography* (McFarland, 2020)

Vince Guaraldi at the Piano (McFarland, 2012)

Crime and Spy Jazz on Screen Since 1971
A History and Discography

Derrick Bang

Foreword by Pat Irwin

McFarland & Company, Inc., Publishers
Jefferson, North Carolina

LIBRARY OF CONGRESS CATALOGUING-IN-PUBLICATION DATA

Names: Bang, Derrick, author.
Title: Crime and spy jazz on screen since 1971 : a history and discography / Derrick Bang.
Description: Jefferson : McFarland & Company, Inc., Publishers, 2020. | Includes bibliographical references and index.
Identifiers: LCCN 2020012143 | ISBN 9781476681634 (paperback : acid free paper) ∞
ISBN 9781476639895 (ebook)
Subjects: LCSH: Motion picture music—History and criticism. | Jazz in motion pictures. | Jazz—History and criticism. | Crime films—History and criticism. | Spy films—History and criticism. | Television music—History and criticism. | LCGFT: Discographies.
Classification: LCC ML2075 .B29 2020 | DDC 781.5/42—dc23
LC record available at https://lccn.loc.gov/2020012143

BRITISH LIBRARY CATALOGUING DATA ARE AVAILABLE

ISBN (print) 978-1-4766-8163-4
ISBN (ebook) 978-1-4766-3989-5

© 2020 Derrick Bang. All rights reserved

No part of this book may be reproduced or transmitted in any form or by any means, electronic or mechanical, including photocopying or recording, or by any information storage and retrieval system, without permission in writing from the publisher.

Front cover images © 2020 Shutterstock

Printed in the United States of America

*McFarland & Company, Inc., Publishers
Box 611, Jefferson, North Carolina 28640
www.mcfarlandpub.com*

Table of Contents

Acknowledgments   vii
Foreword by Pat Irwin   1
Introduction   3

1. Do Your Thing: 1971   9
2. Blowin' Your Mind: 1972   29
3. Last Dance in Sausalito: 1973   46
4. Suite Revenge: 1974   66
5. So Smooth: 1975   83
6. God's Lonely Man: 1976   99
7. Bleak, Bad, Big City Dawn: 1977–78   109
8. That Old Feeling: 1979–81   122
9. Gumshoe Piano: 1982–84   133
10. Tequila Dreams: 1985–89   148
11. Freshly Squeezed: 1990–94   165
12. Chili Hot: 1995–99   178
13. Heartbroken: 2000–03   195
14. Sugar Plum Raid: 2004–2019   206

Epilogue   218
Appendix A: Instrument Abbreviations   221
Appendix B: Discography   222
Appendix C: Cover Artists, Compilation Albums and Box Sets   241
Chapter Notes   245
Bibliography   251
Index   253

Acknowledgments

When it comes to writing a book—*any* kind of book—the wisdom of Buzzy Linhart and Mark "Moogy" Klingman's 1973 hit song definitely resonates: You've got to have friends.

On top of which, one never knows the true depth of such kindness, until just such a friend graciously exerts an undisclosed amount of time and effort, while chasing down an obscure something-or-other. Such treasure hunts obviously are a lot easier in our modern era, but some things still elude digital search techniques. Actually, quite a few things ... at least, quite a few of the things *I* was looking for, while gathering the raw materials and data that ultimately led to the completion of this two-volume project.

Not that it began that way. When I initially pitched an analysis of film/television crime and action jazz to my obligingly intrigued editor, the resulting contract was for a single book of somewhere in the neighborhood of 125,000 words; I naïvely assumed said page count would be sufficient. That was four years ago, during which time I considered a combined total of roughly 1,000 movies and TV shows, ultimately discussing approximately 550 in brief or at considerable length. The result landed just shy of 600,000 words. Okay, fine; first drafts are overwritten. After some necessary pruning—and then additional judicious tightening—I wound up with 250,000 words. Trimming further would have cut into the "good stuff"; the text would have been compromised beyond repair, destroying the manuscript's design as a truly definitive study of this jazz subgenre.

The first note of thanks therefore goes to my editor, David Alff, and all others involved at McFarland, who agreed that the best solution was *not* to hack 'n' slash the manuscript to an all-but useless shadow of its former self, but to rewrite the contract for a two-volume set. Bless you all; my wife and I will name our subsequent cats and dogs after each and every one of you.

Moving on, many other people have been extraordinarily charitable with their time, expertise and patience, for which I'm profoundly grateful.

I couldn't have finished these books—heck, I couldn't have *started* them—without the research acumen of Scott McGuire, who constantly surprised me by ferreting out obscure recordings and video items from the most arcane sources. If somebody held a contest for sleuthing skills, I've no doubt he'd win.

Lee Riggs, of the UC Davis Shields Library, also deserves an enthusiastic shout-out for research assistance, and for door-to-door book check-out service. (Talk about getting spoiled...!)

Daniel Urazandi, of Bizarro World—an impressively diverse pop-culture shop, and our town's sole remaining DVD rental outlet—chased down quite a few obscure titles on my behalf. Much obliged.

A quick shout-out as well, to Thomas Film Classics (shop.thomasfilmclassics.com) and Robert's Hard to Find Videos (robertsvideos.com), for their amazing libraries of obscure films and television shows. Quite a few titles within these pages would have remained no more than tantalizing (and undiscussed) possibilities, absent their extensive catalogs.

A sweeping bow, tip o' the hat, and flourish of arms to Pat Irwin, for his generous introduction. Long may his impressively varied composing and performing career reign.

Lukas Kendall, of Film Score Monthly, spent two decades wrestling with Hollywood studios and major record labels, to bring soundtrack fans quality debuts and resurrections of beloved film and TV scores. He generously granted permission for many of the album covers that appear within these pages.

Roger Feigelson, of Intrada—a companion label similarly dedicated to the restoration of such music—was equally kind to allow the use of their album covers.

I occasionally use the word *indefatigable* in the subsequent text, to describe the select few composer/performers with the preternatural ability to produce stunning quantities of quality music despite absurdly tight scheduling constraints. The same term applies to journalist, author and lecturer Jon Burlingame, whom I've never met, but who absolutely deserves his reputation as America's leading writer on the subject of film and television music. He paved the way with wit, insight and thoughtful analysis—on top of which, he's fun to read—and his richly informative body of work is astonishing: commentary in all manner of publications (notably *Daily Variety* and *The Los Angeles Times*); detailed articles for the Film Music Society; lengthy oral history interviews on behalf of the Film Music Foundation and the Television Academy Foundation; enlightening liner notes for soundtrack reissues and debuts; and his three seminal books, *Sound and Vision: 60 Years of Motion Picture Soundtracks*, *TV's Biggest Hits* and *The Music of James Bond*. His oeuvre has been exceptionally helpful, and I humbly aspire to trail at the distant edge of his enormous shadow.

Needless to say, this book wouldn't exist without the brilliant individuals who *created* that which is described herein: the many scores of scorers (sorry, couldn't resist) who wrote and performed all of this great music. They've brought me *such* pleasure over the years, and I couldn't begin to cite them all … although a short list would include Elmer Bernstein, Henry Mancini, Edwin Astley, Quincy Jones, David Shire, John Barry, Earle Hagen and Lalo Schifrin. And Kenyon Hopkins and Nelson Riddle. Oh, Laurie Johnson and Mort Stevens. Jerry Goldsmith. Mike Post and Pete Carpenter. Did I mention Roy Budd? (Okay, stop. You get the idea.)

Finally, a bottomless pit of gratitude to my Constant Companion, Gayna: for her cheerful (well, mostly) willingness to proof-read the gargantuan first draft, and—even more so—for being such a good sport, while forced to *listen* to this stuff, over and over and *over* again, during these past four years. Greater love hath no spouse, and—believe me—that is *not* taken for granted. To borrow one of John Barry's James Bond title songs—lyrics by Tim Rice and Stephen Short—you're my "All Time High."

That said, this book and its companion volume, *Crime and Spy Jazz on Screen, 1950–1970: A History and Discography*, are dedicated to my father, whose great frustration—for many years—was that his baby-boomer son displayed a typical 1960s teenager's dismissive disinterest in jazz … until a concentrated exposure to Mr. Barry's early 007 scores, and Vince Guaraldi's anthems for Charlie Brown and the Peanuts gang, and a rapidly expanding diversity of jazz artists thereafter, put the kid on the proper path. (Dad was savvy enough to avoid using the "J-word"—not wanting to sabotage the evolving dynamic—until it was safe to do so.) He delighted in hearing the information and anecdotes that I dug up, as these two books took shape; he was captivated by occasional snatches of chapters-in-progress. My only regret, having now completed the journey, is that he didn't live long enough to see the results actually published. But I know—nonetheless—that he has been reading over my shoulder the entire time.

Foreword
by Pat Irwin

It's safe to say that on February 9, 1964, popular music changed forever. *All* music changed. *Everything* changed. The Beatles' debut performance on *The Ed Sullivan Show* drew an estimated 73 million viewers and touched countless more. TV could do that: It could bring millions and millions together, to watch a single performance at the same time.

I was one of the countless viewers inspired to pick up the electric guitar after seeing The Beatles on *Ed Sullivan*. But it was when I first heard the theme for *Goldfinger* that I knew how I wanted that electric guitar to sound. It wasn't long before I was tuning in to *The Man from U.N.C.L.E.*, *Mission: Impossible* and *Hawaii Five-O*, just to hear their opening themes. By the time I heard Lalo Schifrin's score for *Bullitt* and Isaac Hayes' *Theme from Shaft*, I was in deep. I was hooked for life.

Derrick covers this music in vivid detail. If you're a fan of soundtrack music, you might know it as "crime jazz"; sometimes it's "action jazz." Loosely speaking, this music sets the scene for secret agents, detectives, private investigators, cops and criminals. More than likely, there will be fast cars and heart-pounding chase sequences. And chances are, if your heart pounds just a little bit faster, it's because the soundtrack is pulling you a little bit closer to the action.

This volume covers 1971 through 2019. Film and television are given equal weight and respect, and not all of it comes from Hollywood or the major networks. And, strictly speaking, not all of it is jazz. To quote Derrick, "Some of my choices will be determined by historical context, or musicality, or simply because I wanted to include them." Chapters are organized chronologically; although some years are busier than others, there's plenty of exciting music being made, and plenty of crime jazz discoveries to be had.

In 1971, movies still were shown exclusively in theaters; to watch your favorite TV show, you had to tune in at a specific place and a set time. Musicians got together to record in same room. Scores were written out by hand, and synthesizers weren't yet replacing live musicians. Music was recorded to tape, and soundtracks were released on vinyl.

Derrick gives us much more than just a synopsis of what was recorded when and where, and it's not merely nostalgia. In 1971, Hayes' soundtrack for *Shaft* spent 60 weeks on *Billboard's* Hot 200 album chart and hit No. 1. Derrick introduces us to who played the distinctive hi-hat pattern, as well as who played the *wah-wah* guitar. We also glimpse inside a conversation between director Gordon Parks and Hayes, who was scoring a film for the first time. The year 1971 was also the one for *Dirty Harry*, with a score by Lalo Schifrin, and *The French Connection*, with its score by Don Ellis. These classics are covered with the same respect as *The Organization, The Anderson Tapes* and *Pretty Maids All in a Row*. TV had *Longstreet, Cannon, Monty Nash* and more. All with music that can be called crime—or action—jazz.

This book takes us from 1971 network television up through the advent of cable television and into the streaming era. Obscure box office failures are covered with the same enthusiasm as blockbuster movies. If it has a score that can be called crime or action jazz, it's in this book. I found myself returning to soundtracks that I know and love, and—in turn—getting lost inside of YouTube and Wikipedia explorations of music and composers, while making new discoveries.

This volume includes valuable information on killer scores by Quincy Jones, Dave Grusin and Jerry Goldsmith, as well as composers and shows that I learned about for the first time. I'm thrilled to discover TV episodes scored by favorite musicians and composers like Oliver Nelson and J.J. Johnson. And sure; I knew about Elmer Bernstein's classic crime jazz scores for *The Man with the Golden Arm* and *Sweet Smell of Success*, but I was happy to find out about his theme, and scores, for TV's *The Rookies*.

I still have that *Goldfinger* album—the vinyl sounds better than ever—but I've stopped trying to copy the sound of that guitar. Crime jazz has a hold on me to this day and doesn't seem like it'll let go anytime soon. Thanks, Derrick, for putting it all in a book. As he mentions in his Introduction, "Gather a group of friends or total strangers. Sit them in front of a good audio source and play the first few bars—just the first few bars—of John Barry's arrangement of the 'James Bond Theme,' or Lalo Schifrin's '*Mission Impossible* Theme.' Or Mort Stevens' '*Hawaii Five-O.*' Or Isaac Hayes' 'Theme from *Shaft*.' These recordings won't merely prompt recognition; listers will *smile*."—Definitely. Read on. Enjoy. Smile.

Pat Irwin (patirwinmusic.com) has lived and worked in New York City since the late 1970s. He composed the scores for Showtime's Nurse Jackie *and HBO's* Bored to Death, *as well as hundreds of cartoons, including* Rocko's Modern Life, Pepper Ann *and* SpongeBob SquarePants. *He was a founding member of two iconic NYC indie bands, The Raybeats and 8 Eyed Spy, and also was a longtime touring member of The B-52's.*

Introduction

Gather a group of friends or total strangers. Sit them in front of a good audio source and play the first few bars—*just* the first few bars—of John Barry's arrangement of the "James Bond Theme," or Lalo Schifrin's "*Mission: Impossible* Theme." Or Mort Stevens' "*Hawaii Five-O*." Or Isaac Hayes' "Theme from *Shaft*." These recordings won't merely prompt recognition; listeners will *smile*.

These tunes *resonate*. They evoke a time when watching a particular film or TV show involved *planning*: getting to the movie theater on time, or shuffling housework/homework/job responsibilities to park in front of the TV set during a given hour. (Today's 24/7 ability to watch such things on demand, no matter how convenient, eradicates the romance involved with booking and anticipating such an event, back in the day.)

So-called "crime and action jazz"—associated, for the purposes of this book, with detective, police, espionage, spy and *film noir* dramas and adventures—has produced some of the world's most iconic melodies. It's a genre rich with heritage, confined mostly to a "golden era" running from approximately the mid–1950s to the mid–1980s. At its peak, action jazz was *the* go-to choice for crowd-pleasing films and TV shows. Post–World War II generations who grew up with such stuff remember the music more than fondly; it often informs the soundtrack of their lives. Rock 'n' roll may have ruled during the later 1960s, but action jazz aficionados from roughly the same period—a little before, to a little after—can argue just as persuasively about the lasting impact of *their* obsession.

Thanks to increased awareness—our enhanced understanding, these days, of everything that goes into the making of a film or TV show—and the efforts of soundtrack specialty labels, such music is being resurrected and recognized to an exponentially increasing degree. Soundtrack fans in the 1960s were limited to LPs that generally contained no more than half of what a composer wrote for a given film or TV show. Worse yet, the "cues"—the individual musical segments—usually were freshly arranged into radio-friendly tracks, rerecorded with a different studio orchestra—often nowhere near as jazzy as the composer's original ensemble—and assembled *out of order* on the resulting album. (And *oh*, how true fans loathed hearing the music out of sequence!) These days, we can buy—or find, via all-encompassing bootlegs in the (ahem) gray areas of the Internet—actual full scores, as originally recorded, and tracked in the proper order. Heck, it's even possible to obtain scores that were rejected by directors or studios and subsequently replaced by somebody else's work. Imagine the fascination of a side-by-side comparison between Jerry Goldsmith's Academy Award–nominated score for 1974's *Chinatown* and Phillip Lambro's rejected score.

That's the enigma of artistic individuality. Hire a dozen composers to score the same film, and you'll get a dozen strikingly different musical tapestries.

Here and now, we soundtrack fans—and the subset of action jazz fans—live in a great era; there's *so* much more to be enjoyed, beyond the usual suspects. I've tried to hit them all: Acknowledgments of favorite films and TV shows. Reminders of others you've forgotten. Enthusiastic endorsements of many you've never heard of. All to be found within the subsequent pages.

But first...

What *is* jazz?

When asked, my father always gave the same two-word answer: "It *swings*."

Not a bad response, particularly in the context of this book. Crime, detective and spy jazz—action jazz—often *does* swing. The strong rhythmic foundation accelerates anticipation, tension and excitement. In the context of a TV show or film, the title theme becomes more memorable: the "earworm" phenomenon that producers and show runners crave. A carefully applied score can be just as crucial as the editing, to carry us through a narrative's highs and lows, its developing suspense and triumphant climaxes.

For the most part, so-called "free jazz"—generally bereft of rhythm and melody—isn't found in film or television scoring. It's too dissonant, weird and confrontational. If the music pulls you *out* of the story, then it's not being employed properly.

So, okay; let's establish a foundation of swing. That still covers a lot of territory. The pulse-quickening suspense jazz of 1974's *The Taking of Pelham One Two Three* is quite different than the groovy, attitude-laden funk and R&B of 1971's *Shaft*, which in turn couldn't be further from the bluesy sensuality of the cues that heighten the carnality and bad behavior found within 1981's *Body Heat*. All are jazz, as is a lot of stuff in between. All fit this book's brief, as do hundreds of others.

Bear in mind, a detailed discussion of jazz in *all* films and TV shows—and/or the scores of all *noir* and action epics—would require multiple volumes and a page count vastly beyond the scope of these two books. *Paris Blues* (1961) has a great Duke Ellington soundtrack, but it's a straight melodrama. Dave Grusin is responsible for much of what you'll find herein, but his great jazz score for 1989's *The Fabulous Baker Boys* isn't included; it's a romantic dramedy. Ditto his work on 1999's *Random Hearts* and 2001's *Dinner with Friends*. Ralph Burns' jazz score for 1974's *Lenny* is terrific, but biopics aren't in this book's brief. I love John Barry's score for 1998's *Playing by Heart*, but couldn't include it. Rolfe Kent's soft jazz touches in 2004's *Sideways* also didn't make the cut. Along with many, many others.

Jazz being a quintessential American art form, it's logical that most of the films and TV programs discussed herein emanate from the United States. But certainly not all: The United Kingdom is well represented, and some Western European films are too important to ignore. But arbitrary lines had to be drawn somewhere, lest this survey (again) become overwhelming. Ergo, don't take it personally if you don't find one of your favorite foreign films or TV shows in these pages. Such decisions resulted from practicality, not prejudice.

Even so, I fully expect to get a few outraged letters wondering how the heck I *possibly* could have neglected *that* classic (American or otherwise). Or *that* masterpiece. To which I can only reply, One tries one's best. And that's why God invented second editions. Suggestions are welcome, and I can be reached at this book's companion website: screenactionjazz.com.

All this said, some of my judgment calls are liable to raise eyebrows. *That* isn't crime/*noir*/action, you'll protest ... or *That* isn't even *jazz*. I plead guilty: Some of my choices will be determined by historical context, or musicality, or simply because I wanted to include them. My book, my rules.

* * *

Some essential terms:

- Title theme—the primary theme of a movie or TV show, generally heard behind the opening credits, and often repeated, perhaps in a different arrangement, during the end credits.
- Underscore—traditionally the music layered behind on-screen dialogue, although now more frequently referring to the bulk of a film or TV episode score: which is to say, everything except the title and end themes.
- Cue—a single portion of an underscore: a segment written for a specific scene or sequence.
- Motif—a brief series of notes that forms a core melody, from which the greater "whole" of a theme is constructed. The rising four notes that signal Tom Selleck's eyebrow-lifting grin are a primary motif of Mike Post's "Magnum P.I." theme.
- Leitmotif—a cue associated with a particular character, place or idea. John Williams' "The Imperial March" always accompanies bad behavior on the part of evil Empire villains, in the various *Star Wars* films.
- Ostinato—a phrase or motif that persistently repeats, somewhat in the manner of a vamp. Isaac Hayes' score for *Shaft* prompted a lot of composers to insert *wah-wah* guitar ostinatos.
- Stinger—a fleeting cue often associated with sudden on-screen action.
- Bumper—a short cue often designed to take the action out (or back in) between scenes (in a film), or between commercials (on television).
- Diegetic music—that which exists in the realm inhabited by the story's characters, often heard from a radio, juke box, phonograph player or live nightclub combo. In other words, the *dramatis personae* always hear diegetic music; sometimes they even perform it.
- Non-diegetic music—that which exists as underscore shading, to enhance or serve as counterpoint to on-screen action. We viewers hear non-diegetic music, but the *dramatis personae* do not.
- "Mickey-mousing"—the act of writing an underscore cue that precisely duplicates, in terms of mood and/or syncopation, the on-screen action. It's equivalent to a drummer needlessly hitting a rim shot to punctuate a comic's on-stage joke: in both cases, considered lazy and redundant.
- Tracking—building an underscore from a library of existing cues, as opposed to composing an entirely fresh score.
- Cover—a rerecording of an original tune or theme, often (but not always) by a different musician.

Most films are scored (composed) by a single individual—or sometimes a pair of collaborators—who handle everything: the main title, any necessary character themes, and all cues employed from the opening to closing credits. If the film generates a soundtrack album, that composer gets the name credit. Ergo, Jerry Goldsmith wrote the score for 1997's *L.A. Confidential*; he's the one credited on the resulting soundtrack album. He's also the one nominated for the Academy Award (which he lost to James Horner's non-jazz score for *Titanic*).

This model shifted in the 1980s and '90s, with the advent and rising popularity of electronic keyboards (synth) and "jukebox scores" built from period-specific or then-current pop/rock/rap/etc. tunes. Ensemble instrumental scores became unwelcome, as the film industry embraced the hyper-editing introduced by rock videos (helmed by individuals who, in many cases, went on to become film directors). We can thank John Williams—and *Star Wars*—for a herculean effort to stem that particular tide, and this will be discussed at greater length elsewhere in these pages.

Television shows were a different animal from the very beginning, in great part because of the far greater musical burden involved. While some early indefatigably creative composers followed the big-screen model, by scoring (almost) every episode of a TV series—Earle Hagen and Laurie Johnson come to mind—such individuals mostly vanished by the 1970s. (Mike Post and longtime partner Pete Carpenter are notable exceptions.) It became far more common for one person to help set a show's tone by writing the title theme and then scoring one or more early episodes, after which other composers took over.

By the 1970s, very few shows had the luxury—or budget—to request wholly original underscores for every single episode. The first half-dozen episodes might get original underscores from one or more composers, and their various cues—for car chases, fist fights, gun battles, suspenseful skulking, romantic overtures, whatever—would establish an ever-expanding library used to track subsequent episodes.

Starting in the 1980s, many shows warranted *only* an original title theme, and otherwise were sweetened solely by jukebox soundtracks. Action jazz all but vanished, particularly when many television programs began to abandon opening themes and title sequences (and you'll learn why in the subsequent pages). Many big-screen films similarly gravitated toward synth and jukebox scores. Today's music fans rarely have the opportunity that was so ubiquitous back in the day: to get sucked into a film or TV show by a killer opening theme.

* * *

An apology: Spoilers are inevitable. This study isn't merely a shopping list of composer, film and/or TV series credits; it's important to specify the music's *context*, in terms of how individual cues—and an overall score—augment (or, in some cases, damage) the on-screen action. Although every effort has been made to avoid the frivolous disclosure of plot surprises, it's impossible to discuss some of the following films and TV show episodes *without* doing so. Ergo, this isn't the book to read, if you're gonna get vexed by narrative revelations. *Mea maxima culpa.*

* * *

So:

In the beginning...

...on-screen jazz, as a dramatic musical component, was associated firmly with villainy, corruption, venality, murder, lust, vice, turpitude, lewdness, perversion, sensuality, indecency, carnality, profligacy, wantonness, lechery, drug use, prostitution, treachery, licentiousness, immorality, depravity, decadence, degeneracy, debasement, degradation, debauchery and any other deplorable behavior or criminal activity one could imagine (and could be shown—or merely hinted at—during an era when movies were subjugated sternly by the Motion Picture Production Code, and the nascent television industry was beholden to similarly prudish sponsors).

Jazz was "the devil's music." It had no business in the worship service of a film, screened within the temple of a movie theater, or viewed in the sanctuary of one's living room.

(As late as 1965, when Northern California–based jazz pianist Vince Guaraldi was preparing to debut the first Jazz Mass presented within the context of an American church service, the staff at San Francisco's Grace Cathedral—and most particularly the Rev. Charles Gompertz, who had facilitated the project—were excoriated by conservative individuals who were, in some cases, profoundly unhappy. "I got death threats: letters and telephone calls," Gompertz recalled, decades later. "They were scary. These people felt that I was bringing Satan into the church: bringing the music of the cocktail lounge—the den of sin and iniquity—into the holy and sacred precinct."[1])

Racism also had much to do with this vilification. In the eyes of many, immediately following World War II, jazz was synonymous solely with black musicians: Buddy Bolden, Duke Ellington, Sidney Bechet, Louis Armstrong, Fats Waller, Scott Joplin, Jelly Roll Morton, James P. Johnson, Earl "Fatha" Hines and countless other icons. That meant their music had no place in film and television, no matter *how* talented the performers were.

Comedies could cross that threshold, but only if the music were ridiculed to some degree. *Ball of Fire* (1941)—now recognized as one of director Howard Hawks' screwball classics, thanks to a brilliant script from Charles Brackett and Billy Wilder—managed to work in a conventional romance between Gary Cooper and Barbara Stanwyck, but only because college-educated Bertram Potts (Cooper) and his snooty professorial associates make fun of the jazz-laden criminal environment that Katherine "Sugarpuss" O'Shea (Stanwyck) hopes to flee. Absurdity blunted even the sharpest jazz-hued blade. The results were the same seven years later, when Hawks essentially remade the film with Danny Kaye and Virginia Mayo, once again working from a script by Wilder and new collaborator Thomas Monroe; the similarly burlesque *A Song Is Born* from 1948 features an even larger supporting cast of jazz band leaders and musicians, all playing themselves.

That, too, was another way around jazz's lamentable reputation. Unlike *Ball of Fire*, which merely dabbles with live performance, *A Song Is Born* is a true Hollywood musical. Jazz was more acceptable as a live presentation, even from the occasional black singer or musician ... as long as the ratio favored white stars and co-stars. (On top of which, unrepentant racists no doubt took solace from the fact that George Gershwin—as white as they came—practically invented the genre of orchestral jazz. Even if they had to overlook the fact that he was Jewish.)

Jazz therefore lost some of its pejorative overtones when it was *diegetic*, which is to say, "source" music: part of the soundtrack as performed by characters within the "story space" being presented. Diegetic is contrasted with *non-diegetic*, the latter referring to music emanating from some invisible "elsewhere," and designed to enhance a given scene's dramatic impact. Most film and TV scores are non-diegetic: It's understood, on the part of the viewer, that music's use is an often crucial element of what's being watched, which otherwise would feel "flat." We accept this, even though the reality of what's taking place—characters forever being shadowed by an invisible orchestra—is patently absurd. (To put it another way, we—viewers—hear non-diegetic music; the onscreen characters do not.) The cantina band—in the club where Luke Skywalker meets Han Solo, in *Star Wars*—delivers diegetic music; we see it being performed, while Luke and Han listen to it. When Luke blows the Death Star to smithereens, he does so to a triumphant blast from John Williams' non-diegetic underscore. Imagine how "empty" the latter sequence would be without this orchestral involvement.

In the eyes of post–World War II Hollywood/New York studios, and the audiences to whom they catered, jazz initially was restricted to the very narrow "sinful" applications cited, when it came to the non-diegetic scoring of a film or television show.

"Movies use jazz when someone steals a car," soundtrack composer Elmer Bernstein famously quipped, early in his career.[2]

Ironically, the arrival of rock erased the supposed immorality of jazz, which suddenly became quaintly conservative alongside the libertine acolytes of "sex, drugs and rock 'n' roll."

Clearly, attitudes changed; the film and television industries evolved. Beginning in the late 1950s, we relished roughly three decades of jazz glory in film and television, most excitingly in the genres of detective, espionage and spy thrillers. And while it's true that action jazz began to taper off in the 1970s—a trend that accelerated in the '80s and beyond—most years still offered some choice treats, as you'll discover.

As for *how* that shift occurred—how jazz rather suddenly became Hollywood's unloved stepchild—well, that's the story waiting to unfold on the subsequent pages.

1

Do Your Thing: 1971

Elmer Bernstein's aggressive, jazz-laden score for 1955's *The Man with the Golden Arm* triggered the soundtrack world's first tectonic shift; Henry Mancini struck next, with his swinging scores for television's *Peter Gunn*. Four years after that, John Barry's brass-heavy cues for James Bond similarly shook our senses. By the mid–1960s—back on the tube—the secret agents on *I Spy*, *The Man from U.N.C.L.E.* and numerous other imitators grooved to equally dynamic jazz cues from upstart "youngsters" such as Lalo Schifrin, Dave Grusin, Quincy Jones and Earle Hagen.

Action jazz fans' cups had runneth over for a decade. Could some other as-yet unknown jolt the soundtrack world *again*, in an unexpected way?

Absolutely. As the new decade dawned, a fresh name was on everybody's lips, thanks to the explosive rise of an entirely new film genre.

The Small Screen

Just as Raymond Burr's Robert Ironside refused to be limited by his wheelchair, insurance investigator Mike Longstreet wasn't about to let a little thing like blindness interfere with *his* profession. James Franciscus handles the title role in ABC's *Longstreet* with a compelling blend of stubborn pride and endearing vulnerability. He's always grateful for assistance from aide Nikki Bell (Marlyn Mason) and Pax, the white German Shepherd that serves as his seeing-eye dog. But scripters couldn't maintain this "gimmick" premise to the same degree that kept NBC's *Ironside* alive for eight seasons, so *Longstreet* lasted only a single 23-episode season, following its TV-movie pilot. The series also possesses a bit of cult cred, due to Bruce Lee's occasional appearances as a martial arts expert who teaches Mike how to defend himself in ways that don't rely on vision.

Oliver Nelson's title credits sequence succinctly recaps key events from the pilot film: Franciscus is introduced via a montage of activities easily enjoyed by sighted individuals, against a run of cheerful, midtempo flute couplets backed by bongos and gentle horn comping. A rising crescendo of portentous brass accompanies the murder attempt that leaves him alive but sightless. The theme's 3-3-5-3 motif is introduced via tasty piano against throbbing electric bass; the melody repeats via unison strings and rising brass elements while the credits appear. Strings supply a countermelody during a brief bridge, the bass maintaining a cool rhythmic beat; everything ultimately resolves into a rising brass crescendo. The end credits version is softer, allowing a flute to carry the bulk of the melody.

Episodes often open with—or find a reason to include—a late-night montage of jazz clubs as Mike wanders the streets of the French Quarter and other music-laden sections of

New Orleans. Episode titles appear against brief little swingers, and Nelson also supplies various arrangements of the title theme as underscore cues. He handled most episodes, subbing out a few to Benny Golson and Robert Drasnin. Jazz is the go-to choice for diegetic music heard from diner radios, or in restaurants and nightclubs. Only one episode—"Elegy in Brass"—is set entirely within the vibrant jazz world, when some rare and valuable instruments are stolen from the Crescent City Jazz Society; Nelson's work on this episode is particularly choice.

Sadly, no soundtrack album appeared.

Longstreet is blind; Ironside lost the use of his legs; Frank Cannon is ... fat.

Baby boomers and their parents certainly knew the voice. William Conrad played Marshal Matt Dillon during the 10-year run of radio's *Gunsmoke*; he also narrated the cliff-hanging exploits of Rocket J. Squirrel and Bullwinkle J. Moose during the 1959–64 television reign of *The Adventures of Rocky and Bullwinkle (and Friends)*. Conrad then provided just the right amount of world-weary irony while narrating the travails of poor Richard Kimble, in *The Fugitive*.

Conrad's huffing, puffing, middle-aged Frank Cannon is the last person most clients expect when seeking assistance; even so, his services don't come cheap. Expensive tastes—most notably in wine and fine cuisine—mandate high fees, but Cannon never leaves a customer unsatisfied. Formidable presence aside, Cannon is an old-school gumshoe who works a case with dogged persistence. Although the portly character could have been played as a joke, Conrad took the role quite seriously; his blend of empathy and shrewd deductive skills turned CBS' *Cannon* into a popular series during its five-year run.

Veteran television composer John Carl Parker, assigned to create a title theme for Conrad's unique character, responded with a droll anthem that opens with a vibrant three-note brass fanfare and then shifts to a pounding 4/4 melody introduced by jazz tuba. A sassy rhythmic bass line propels the theme, with unison horns picking up the melody—backed by shrill brass triplets—as Conrad and the episode's guest stars get their on-screen credits. The theme grows ever more ferocious while the orchestra climbs the scale, until concluding with a final three-note burst of shrieking brass. It's a terrific, instantly memorable theme, lamentably marred by the ubiquitous Quinn Martin Productions narrator.

Conrad wasn't wild about the theme when he first heard it. "He went to Quinn," recalled postproduction supervisor John Elizalde, "and told him, 'It's a caricature. It's too cartoony.' Quinn comes up to me. He says, 'What about that?' I said, 'Well, yeah, it *is* a caricature. It's perfect for Conrad.' Eventually, both Bill Conrad and Quinn wound up liking it. That was very unusual, giving Bill a theme like that. Very rarely did we assign musical themes to characters. Usually, you just wrote the music for the scenes."[1]

Conrad had the last laugh. After the first season, the title theme was modified, with unison reeds replacing the tuba. (It was sorely missed.)

Parker scored the pilot movie and nine episodes, including the series opener, "The Salinas Jackpot." He gets considerable mileage from that tuba, via whimsical dramatic cues, but also provides some suspenseful action jazz: most notably tense, drum-heavy swingers with strong sax elements, during lengthy car and foot chases. Both Tom Scott and Robert Drasnin handled four episodes; seven other composers contributed one, two or three each. All remaining episodes were tracked. Sadly, the underscores lost their jazz flavor as the seasons progressed.

No soundtrack album was produced, although the title theme was covered by the John Gregory Orchestra for a 1976 Philips 45. (The "Cannon's Theme" performed by the Cannonball Adderley Quintet, on a 1966 Capitol 45 single, is an entirely different piece of music.) Parker's title theme and two full underscores—the pilot film and "The Salinas Jackpot"—finally were digitized and released in 2019 as part of *The Quinn Martin Collection, Volume 1: Cop and Detective Series.*

Not all of the year's new detectives were "gimmick" characters. Arrogant, bull-headed Monty Nash, a top agent for the U.S. government's Department of Counter Intelligence, starred in a quintet of gritty espionage novels written by Richard Telfair between 1959 and '61. Nash was softened for a short-lived syndicated series that aired during the fall of 1971, with taciturn Harry Guardino a good fit for the character. But the show's low-budget limitations reduced Telfair's international-based espionage sagas to routine confrontations relating to domestic crime, racism, politics and the widening generation gap.

Monty Nash's dynamic title theme was a rare foray into dramatic scoring by Michael Lloyd, a prolific record producer, arranger, musician and songwriter. It's closer to surf rock than jazz; the melody also bears an eyebrow-lifting resemblance to P.F. Sloan and Steve Barri's "Secret Agent Man," sung so memorably by Johnny Rivers. Lloyd's theme plays over a montage of Guardino striding and riding through the streets of Washington, D.C., carrying his tricked-out attaché case, complete with telephone. This title theme and the jazzy episode underscores are performed by a cadre of session musicians known as "The Good Stuff," and the sobriquet is apt; many of the finger-snapping cues deliver a pleasant—if modest—touch of rhythmic swing.

The title theme, performed by The Good Stuff, was issued as a promo 45; that probably had more to do with Lloyd's industry connections than any expectation of radio station interest.

* * *

Over at NBC, somebody asked a smart question: Why introduce just one cool detective show when you can get better mileage by introducing three?

The NBC Mystery Movie was—by far—the most successful of the major networks' various umbrella shows, particularly since it debuted with a trio of solid entries: *Columbo*, *McCloud* and *McMillan and Wife*. The concept's success prompted NBC to divide and (hopefully) conquer further: Starting in the second season, those original three series anchored *The NBC Sunday Mystery Movie*, while three more new shows rotated within *The NBC Wednesday Mystery Movie*. But none of the midweek newcomers—or those that hastily replaced them—came close to the original trio's popularity. Beginning with the fourth season, NBC retreated back to the single Sunday timeslot.

Most of the individual entries came with their own music, which generally is forgotten; fans mostly think of Henry Mancini's "Mystery Movie Theme." This enigmatic melody plays against a silhouetted figure who strolls slowly toward the camera, waving a flashlight that highlights all of a given season's rotating characters, before finally showcasing that evening's entry. The theme begins with a slowly rising orchestral fanfare against a rolling rhythm section, after which the melody is seemingly "whistled," each refrain subsequently doubled by strings and horns. That captivating, instantly memorable "whistle" was created by jazz keyboardist Clare Fischer, soloing on a Yamaha YC-30 combo organ. (Fischer also was on board when Mancini expanded the theme for his 1972 album, *Big Screen/Little Screen*.)

The NBC Mystery Movie debuted on September 15 with *Columbo*, but this was by no means the rumpled detective's first appearance. The character—played by Bert Freed—was introduced in "Enough Rope," a July 1960 episode of the NBC summer replacement anthology series *The Chevy Mystery Show*. Scripters Richard Levinson and William Link then transformed their teleplay into a stage production titled *Prescription: Murder*, which starred 70-year-old Thomas Mitchell as Columbo; alas, Mitchell died before the play had a chance to conquer Broadway.[2] Undaunted, Levinson and Link built up their television credentials and then reintroduced Columbo—now with Peter Falk—in a TV-movie adaptation of *Prescription: Murder*, which aired February 20, 1968.

Dave Grusin's title theme accompanies credits superimposed over disturbing Rorschach images; the unsettling atmosphere is enhanced with sinister flutes and percussion instruments that climb the scale, developing into a cheeky swinger with a midtempo 3-6 brass motif. The melody yields to a veritable wall of horns against a rolling rhythm section; a final fanfare fades out as the credits segue to the on-screen action. Subsequent underscore cues build suspense with bowed bass, edgy flutes and shrieking strings, while the villain (Gene Barry) executes and then "stage dresses" his perfect murder; the climactic cue makes room for the dissonant sound of mashed piano keys, when the victim's hand drags against them. Falk's introduction is backed by a droll, mildly jazzy arrangement of the title theme. The rest of the score is mostly orchestral texturing, until reprises of the title theme surface during the lengthy jazz rhapsody that accompanies Columbo's final confrontation with the killer.

The telefilm failed to become a series, but NBC gave Levinson and Link a second shot three years later; a second telefilm—*Ransom for a Dead Man*—aired March 1, 1971. Falk's sophomore outing is scored by Billy Goldenberg, whose approach is softer, dominated by midtempo jazz waltzes and mischievous cues that better suit Falk's low-key, serio-comic approach to the character. ("Just one more thing…")

That film led to *The NBC Mystery Movie*. Goldenberg scored several first-season episodes of *Columbo*, including the iconic debut episode—"Murder by the Book"—directed by Steven Spielberg. Most composers would have established a musical "identity" for a new series, but *Columbo* wasn't designed that way. Every episode received a wholly original underscore, and each episode's villain—and the method of the crime—determined the nature of that score. Nor did Goldenberg ever write a cue specifically for Columbo. "There are characters in films that you do not musicalize," he explained. "They do it all for themselves. You can't make Columbo funny, because [Peter Falk] is doing it already in the acting. There's too much of the intellectual in *Columbo* to write music. He is his *own* music."[3]

During Lt. Columbo's initial seven-season run, the bulk of episode scores came from Goldenberg, Dick DeBenedictis, Bernardo Segall, Patrick Williams, Gil Mellé and John Cacavas. Very little could be considered jazz, and no official single or soundtrack album appeared. (That hasn't stopped enterprising fans from compiling bootleg "albums" readily available via the Internet.)

Falk revived his beloved character a decade later—on February 6, 1989—as one of the spokes of *The ABC Mystery Movie*, which rotated new episodes of *Columbo* with other series. They led to the intermittent release of 14 more telefilms, the last of which aired January 30, 2003. Falk's character still didn't have a title theme, and jazz was nonexistent in all later underscores.

The second spoke of the *NBC Mystery Movie* wheel also was "old news." Dennis Weaver's Deputy Marshal Sam McCloud, transplanted to New York City from his hometown of Taos, New Mexico, debuted February 17, 1970, in a TV-movie pilot titled *McCloud: Who Killed Miss USA?* The character was based—with a wink and a nod—on the role Clint Eastwood played in 1968's big-screen thriller *Coogan's Bluff* (see this book's companion volume).

1. Do Your Thing: 1971

The "range-hardy cowboy at odds with condescending big-city slickers" premise proved irresistible, and Weaver earned seven successful seasons: the first year as part of NBC's 1970–71 umbrella series unimaginatively titled *Four in One*, the latter six as part of the *NBC Mystery Movie*, beginning September 22, 1971.

McCloud's distinct title theme is a Western-hued cue written by David Shire, with reeds taking the melody against a rhythm section that has echoes (intentional or accidental) of David Rose's famed *Bonanza* theme. Shire also contributed underscores for the pilot film and all six first-season episodes, firmly establishing the cattle-punching twang that emphasizes McCloud's origins. Subsequent scoring assignments were handled by Stu Phillips, Dick DeBenedictis, Billy Goldenberg and others; jazz was rare. Beginning with the third season, Shire's title theme was abandoned in favor of a softer melody written by producer Glen A. Larson: an ill-advised decision wholly inappropriate to both character and show.

The final spoke of the *NBC Mystery Movie* wheel was created specifically for the series. *McMillan & Wife* features Rock Hudson and Susan Saint James as San Francisco Police Commissioner Stuart McMillan and his trouble-prone wife, Sally. The deliberately light tone, laced with plenty of flirty banter, is an update of the husband-and-wife investigators from earlier franchises such as *The Thin Man* and *Mr. and Mrs. North*.

McMillan & Wife belongs almost entirely to Jerry Fielding, who scored all but six of the 40 episodes; Luchi De Jesus handled the others. Fielding also wrote the title theme: a charming, midtempo jazz ballad with its 1-3-5 motif carried by gentle horns, against a countermelody played on synth. The theme builds to a soft climax via sets of four rising brass notes that generally resolve into the first underscore cue, as the on-screen action begins. The end credits arrangement is a bit peppier and brass-forward, without the keyboard countermelody. Fielding's underscore cues suit the series' blend of light comedy and occasional flashes of action; the pilot episode—"Once Upon a Dead Man"—lets him loose during a five-minute foot and bicycle chase through San Francisco's hilly streets. Sadly, subsequent episodes offer very little jazz.

* * *

Under better circumstances, Robert Hooks might have become the first black actor to anchor a prime-time TV drama series. Rising national consciousness provided the incentive; the big-screen popularity of Sidney Poitier's Virgil Tibbs added the lure of marketing success; and Hooks was a known quantity, having co-starred in ABC's 1967–69 cop series, *N.Y.P.D.* (see this book's companion volume). CBS therefore commissioned a pilot film—*Crosscurrent*—that stars Hooks as methodical San Francisco police inspector Lou Van Alsdale. Sadly, execs balked at the last moment; *Crosscurrent* was discarded on November 19, 1971, as a one-off via the network's *New CBS Friday Movie* slot. Hooks never had another shot at small-screen stardom.

The story begins with an unexplained murder on a San Francisco streetcar: a homicide unseen by any of the dozens of passengers, thanks to a distraction provided by three rowdy teenagers. Van Alsdale and his partner Pat Cassady (Jeremy Slate) catch the case; the victim turns out to be the son of wealthy shipping tycoon Frederick Cooper (John Randolph). The investigators soon have a multiplicity of suspects: Cooper's amiable business partner, McBride (Robert Wagner); a dangerous drug kingpin, Trench (Don Pedro Colley); an arrogant physician, Dr. Bedford (José Ferrer); and Cooper's waif-like daughter, Kathy (Carol Lynley).

Jerry Goldsmith contributed only four cues—main and end titles, and two interior action cues—and one of the latter went unused. All are propulsive, attention-demanding jazz: not very melodic, serving instead as intense action cues, their time signatures shifting after every eighth measure. The title theme is particularly arresting, the orchestration as sparse as the cues themselves: three keyboards (piano, harpsichord and Yamaha YC-30), three guitarists and seven percussionists.[4]

The diegetic cues—likely library music—are conventional jazz. An ironically cheerful flute/piano cue is heard over the morgue PA system, when Cooper identifies his son's body; bluesy sax drifts from a neighboring apartment, when Van Alsdale finds one of the boys who distracted the cable car passengers; lively, straight-ahead combo jazz fills the bar where the two cops find McBride shooting pool.

The sparse score finally was issued in 2007, on a disc dominated by Goldsmith's score for *The Last Run* and Dave Grusin's score for *The Scorpio Letters*.

Goldsmith put more effort into the 1971 telefilm *A Step Out of Line*, an unusually thoughtful heist drama that explores the circumstances that can drive otherwise good men to a reckless act. The San Francisco–based story focuses on three middle-age buddies fallen on hard financial times: Harry Connors (Peter Falk), an insurance analyst whose father needs dialysis; Joe Rawlins (Vic Morrow), a laid-off aerospace engineer with a fourth child on the way; and Art Stoyer (Peter Lawford), a filmmaker whose ambitions far outstrip the low-paying purgatory of mindless TV commercials. Harry's job grants him access to the security plans for a downtown Foreign Exchange Bank, along with knowledge of that institution's fat cash deposits. Joe has the technical skill to bypass the electronic security issues, and Art's contacts get them inside the building for the necessary reconnaissance. The heist isn't terribly clever, but the sequence nonetheless generates tension, as does the anxiety-laden aftermath.

Goldsmith's music blends textured, often anguished atmospheric cues with solid suspense jazz. Apprehensive drums, cymbals and strings introduce the title credits, after which Goldsmith's melancholy main theme—dominated by a 4-5 motif—emerges as a blues elegy heard first on solo trumpet, then repeated via strings. Reprises of this cue become ever more despondent: notably via solo sax, when Harry's wife has a chance for a raise, but only if she travels more; and as a morose source cue played by an unseen solo pianist, at the bar where Harry initially pitches his wild scheme to Joe.

Goldsmith contrasts these with a playful suspense cue—larkish piano and flute filigrees against midtempo percussion, bass and electric keyboard—when Harry takes the first step toward making the proposed crime a reality, by photocopying key security blueprints. Mischievous bass licks also shadow the three men, when they break into the bank. Once they've secured the loot, Goldsmith delivers a rhythmic, triumphant nod to his action cues from *Our Man Flint*: dynamic percussion, rising brass fanfares and a brief reprise of the main theme on electric guitar.

When Goldsmith's score finally was digitized in 2010, it became clear that director Bernard McEveety had overlooked several of Goldsmith's tastiest jazz tracks. They include "Ball Game Night," a jaunty arrangement of the main theme, with the melody taken by electric harpsichord and muted trumpets; and a terrific cue introduced by groovy bass ("The Safecrackers"), which builds into a rhythmic swinger and was intended as background for the entire five-minute heist.

Needless to say, not all telefilms are worth one's time. A lot of talent is wasted in *Mongo's Back in Town*, an anemic adaptation of a gritty 1969 thriller by violent felon Emil Richard Johnson, who enjoyed a career as a crime novelist while serving a lengthy sentence at Minnesota's Stillwater State Prison. Network TV restrictions prevented the adaptation from coming within spitting distance of the novel's street-level authenticity, and the film's brevity—73 minutes—compresses the plot to absurdity.

Mongo Nash (Joe Don Baker), hired by his gangster brother Mike (Charles Cioffi) to execute a rival, plods through rain-swept inner-city streets during the Christmas holiday, while trying to figure out *why* this particular hit is necessary. He picks up a naïve, newly arrived small-town girl (Sally Field) with big-city stars in her eyes; both run afoul of police investigator Pete Tolstad (Telly Savalas) and his junior partner, Gordon (Martin Sheen). The story concludes scarcely before it has a chance to start; the film is mildly worthwhile only as something of a test-run for Savalas' soon-to-be-famous role as Lt. Theo Kojak, whom Tolstad resembles in all but lollypop.

The December 10 telefilm marked the scoring debut of session keyboardist Michael Melvoin, whose efforts are dominated by the nervous, atmospheric synthesizer cues that shadow Baker's grim strolls amid pouring rain. Fleeting bursts of action jazz—trumpets against Emil Richards' percussion—attempt to build suspense when Mongo solves the key mystery and closes in on the person behind a string of murders. Melvoin delivers a final synth cue as the end credits unspool over Field's frozen features, her character wisely heading back home to West Virginia.

The Big Screen

Shaft—and its iconic Isaac Hayes soundtrack—weren't mere game-changers; both were no less than revolutionary. The film accelerated the blaxploitation subgenre into full gear, while Hayes' score became a smash best-seller, spending 60 weeks on *Billboard's* Hot 200 album chart, where it rose all the way to No. 1 on November 6, 1971. This success is particularly noteworthy in light of the soundtrack being a premium-priced double-album LP: quite rare for a primarily instrumental score. (The twin-LP *Star Wars* soundtrack was still six years in the future.) Indeed, *Shaft* was the first double-album of original studio recordings—of *any* kind—released by an R&B artist.[5] Hayes' "Theme from *Shaft*"—trimmed to fit onto a 45—occupied the No. 1 spot on *Billboard's* Hot 100 list for two weeks, November 20–27, during a 13-week run.

Hayes walked home with two Grammy Awards and the Academy Award for Original Song (but lost the Dramatic Score category to Michel Legrand's *Summer of '42*).

Hayes' music was a phenomenon.

The film it supports has become a bit creaky with age, but still entertains. John Shaft (Richard Roundtree), a New York–based private detective, is hired by Harlem crime boss Bumpy Jones (Moses Gunn) to find his kidnapped daughter. Bumpy sends Shaft in the direction of Ben Buford (Christopher St. John) and his fellow Black Panther-esque nationalists, but that's just jive; the actual culprits are rival Mafiosi looking to take over Bumpy's turf. Shaft deduces the double-cross, and—with help from Buford and his buddies—executes a bushel of Mafia thugs and rescues Bumpy's daughter.

"[Director] Gordon Parks sat down and talked to me about the character, because I'd never scored a movie," Hayes recalled. "He said, 'Isaac, just remember, when you write this music, zero in on the lead character, on his personality. He's a roving kind of character. He's relentless, and your music has to depict that.' So that's when I got the idea for the hi-hats, and made the guitar and all that stuff, and everything else followed."[6]

Given Hayes' inexperience, Parks and producer Joel Freeman insisted on a "tryout"

Isaac Hayes also hoped to *star* in *Shaft*. "I always wanted to act," he recalled, years later, in Rob Bowman's *Soulsville USA: The Story of Stax Records*. "I said, 'Okay, I'll do the score if you give me a shot at the lead role.' They agreed. I waited and waited and a couple of weeks passed, [but] they started shooting in New York [with] Richard Roundtree. I was crushed." Happily, not too crushed to renege on his agreement to compose the score.

with raw footage from three scenes: Shaft's debut, as he strides out of a subway; his subsequent stroll through Harlem; and a love scene with girlfriend Ellie (Gwenn Mitchell). Hayes responded with "Theme from *Shaft*," "Soulsville" and "Ellie's Love Theme"—to the great delight of all—and the assignment was his.[7]

Hayes then wrote and performed an impressively dense score that includes short bumpers, to bridge scenes, along with plenty of longer, full-blown melodies and songs. Parks, obviously recognizing the music's impact, grants Hayes' compositions considerable space; cues often run several minutes during mostly dialogue-less montages.

Hayes sets the mood immediately, when the film's title splashes across Roundtree's subway exit; the iconic main theme opens with drummer Willie Hall's hi-hat "ride pattern," accompanied by Charles Pitts' *wah-wah* funk guitar and Hayes' synthesizer. Rarely has an actor strutted New York's mean streets with such energetic musical verve; by the time the credits conclude, we know everything significant about this "black private dick who's a sex machine to all the chicks."

The mood softens when Shaft learns about the kidnapped girl; his client sheds tears while Hayes supplies a bluesy backdrop ("Bumpy's Lament") that suggests genuine feeling on the part of this vicious crime boss. That evening, Shaft and his regular gal enjoy each other's company against a sweetly sensual blend of vibes, guitar and percussion ("Ellie's Love Theme"). Rather amusingly, their coital climax is signaled by an earthy horn fanfare.

Tension later reigns in "Shaft's Cab Ride," as nervous percussion and strident trumpet blasts follow the detective's journey uptown, to his first meeting with Buford. After discovering where the kidnapped girl is being held, Shaft's full-scale assault is backed by furious action jazz that ultimately resolves into an instrumental reading of "Theme from *Shaft*," when the end credits appear.

Hayes expanded his dozen-plus themes into even groovier jazz compositions for the rerecorded double album. John Shaft was guaranteed to return (about which, more later).

In contrast, Sidney Poitier's third and final outing as Police Lt. Virgil Tibbs—*The Organization*—is both anticlimactic and something of a mess: a cheap, clumsily scripted crime thriller that feels like a TV movie with delusions of grandeur. The ham-fisted screenplay concerns idealistic San Francisco revolutionaries who steal a massive heroin shipment from a shadowy "Organization," hoping to expose the seemingly respectable businessmen who run the outfit; Tibbs gets caught in the middle.

On the other hand, jazz saxophonist/composer Gil Mellé's score is worth our attention. Whereas Quincy Jones supplied a lazy, bluesy insolence that mirrors the self-assured dignity with which Tibbs handles himself in the two earlier films (see this book's companion volume), Mellé goes for a grittier urban approach. Director Don Medford grants him plenty of space; the initial heist and several chase scenes run quite long and without dialogue, and Mellé takes full advantage.

He backs the heist with throbbing bass, electronic keyboard, electric guitar and occasional flute riffs; the cue builds to an explosive climax, at which point energized trumpets signal the title credits, when Tibbs and his fellow officers stroll onto the scene. Additional cool sequences include a lively percussion- and keyboard-driven waltz, when one of the revolutionaries waits on a busy sidewalk; and car and foot chases given additional intensity by Don Menza's sax and Mellé's double-time percussion and trumpet fanfares. The climax takes place within the Bay Area Rapid Transit (BART) tunnels that were under construction while this film was in production. Mellé begins this sequence with a noodly electronic keyboard theme backed by tambourine; he adds horns, plucked strings and electronic bass, and builds to a frantic drum, trumpet and keyboard finale.

A brief, nine-cue score that runs just under 27 minutes was released in 2010: nowhere near all the music used within the film, but the best we're likely to get. (Sadly, many of the session elements were lost or destroyed.)[8]

Quincy Jones likely passed on *The Organization* because he was busy elsewhere. First up was *The Anderson Tapes*, director Sidney Lumet's crackling adaptation of Lawrence Sanders' 1970 best-seller. This ingeniously mounted heist thriller was the first mainstream film to focus on the growing prevalence of citizen monitoring via security cameras and concealed recording devices, both illegal and judicially approved.

John "Duke" Anderson (Sean Connery) completes a 10-year prison stretch and immediately schemes to loot the six lavish units in one of New York City's wealthiest apartment buildings. His team includes shady antiques dealer Tommy Haskins (Martin Balsam); an electrical expert known only as The Kid (Christopher Walken); drivers Spencer and Everson (Dick Anthony Williams and Garrett Morris); and "Pops" (Stan Gottlieb), an aging ex-con Anderson befriended in prison. They're joined by "Socks" Parelli (Val Avery), a misfit thug assigned to the gang by Angelo (Alan King), the Mob boss backing the caper. Unknown to Duke, his actions are observed and recorded every step of the way: not because anybody is interested in him personally, but because various agencies and individuals—the FBI, the IRS, the Bureau of Narcotics and Dangerous Drugs (precursor to the DEA), and even a private detective—are, through sheer coincidence, monitoring the movements of everybody he contacts.

Most of the film proceeds without musical accompaniment, Lumet instead bridging scenes—and complementing the surveillance action—with the quaint electronic *bloops* and *bleeps* that suggested "computer activity" to 1970s audiences. But music nonetheless adds considerable sizzle to the narrative steak. Jones took the surveillance subtext as justification for a jazz/pop, Moog-based title theme which proves—without question—that a funk-fusion electronic score can swing. The main theme kicks in midway through the title credits, beginning with a soft, march-style drumbeat that backdrops the synthesizer melody. By the time the credits conclude, and the acoustic palette has expanded to include the entire ensemble, viewers are flat-out *excited*. No surprise, given an ensemble that includes Buddy Childers, Freddie Hubbard and Snooky Young (flugelhorn and trumpet); Wayne Andre and Garnett Brown (trombone); Hubert Laws (woodwinds); Jim Hall (guitar); Jimmy Smith (organ); Milt Jackson (vibraphone); Toots Thielemans (harmonica); Ray Brown (acoustic double bass); and Grady Tate (drums).

The next bit of music hits when Anderson sends his colleagues—immaculately dressed in "legitimate" guises—to case the six apartments. This stealth surveillance takes place against impish drum kicks and brushes, synth chords and some wickedly swinging walking bass. Smith weaves the title theme into a lovely organ solo, until walking bass powers the entire ensemble to triumphant intensity. Jones inserts another roaring version of the title theme when Anderson and the gang board the Mayflower moving van they've "borrowed" to transport their anticipated loot. The cue builds as they park, overpower the entryway concierge and begin the assault of each unit. At this point the music stops dead, while Lumet cleverly cuts back and forth between the heist in progress, and its bustling aftermath. The film concludes with a somber arrangement of the title theme: a melancholy reminder of everything that has gone wrong.

There wasn't enough music to fill a soundtrack album, but Jones does include a swinging arrangement of the title theme on his 1971 album, *Smackwater Jack*.

Happily, he played a far larger role in his final 1971 assignment.

Writer/director Richard Brooks' *$* (generally known as *Dollars*) is a frothy European romp that offers witty dialogue, considerable tension, and plenty of pizzazz from Jones' vibrant score: a mesmerizing blend of funk, jazz, soul, rock, gospel and even classical-era harpsichord, highlighted by Little Richard's bellowing delivery of the energetic title song, "Money Is." The result is all over the map stylistically, but the varied cues perfectly complement on-screen events.

Joe Collins (Warren Beatty) has played a *very* long con, as an American security consultant hired to enhance protective measures at the United World Bank in Hamburg, Germany. Joe has partnered with a pair of hookers—Dawn (Goldie Hawn) and Helga (Christiane Maybach)—who have identified three dodgy clients who routinely stuff their illicit cash into the bank's safe deposit boxes: a crooked Las Vegas attorney (Robert Webber); a U.S. Army sergeant (Scott Brady) with a black market sideline; and a ruthless drug smuggler dubbed Candy Man (Arthur Brauss). Joe concocts a brilliant scheme to empty those three safe deposit boxes, right under the nose of bank president Mr. Kessel (Gert Fröbe). The heist is a tautly edited, nail-biting sequence in its own right, but the best is yet to come: Joe and Dawn leave enough of a trail for Sarge and Candy Man to detect. The result: one of the best, longest and most exciting chase scenes ever lensed.

Music is minimal as the film opens. The title song finally debuts as diegetic music at the seedy strip club where Candy Man makes his deliveries on behalf of the coldly malevolent Granich (Wolfgang Kieling). A bit later, the Don Elliott Voices supply tension to suspenseful keyboard riffs and twitchy percussion, when Joe embarks on some late-night reconnaissance. The vocalese also adds sinister counterpoint to a cheerful melody that becomes jarringly ironic when Helga's body is found by police, Candy Man's suspicions having been aroused by her constant proximity. The lengthy heist unfolds without music; Jones then has fun with a mildly tense bit of percussion and horns, when Dawn—weighted down by a shopping bag bulging with cash—is helped out of the bank by the unsuspecting Kessel.

But Sarge and Candy Man aren't about to let this go; they combine forces and locate Joe and Dawn. The chase begins with fiddle maestro Doug Kershaw's furious solo, against double-time percussion, which cleverly simulates train sounds when Joe—burdened by a suitcase laden with cash—flees into a railway yard, Sarge and Candy Man mere steps behind. A swinging instrumental version of the title theme kicks in, as the chase continues: on and on and *on* and on. The cue accelerates and climbs the scale while the tension builds; Joe finally, eventually, exhaustedly seems doomed ... and then Brooks concludes this breathtaking third act with a one-two punch of unexpected twists.

Many of the shorter underscore cues are strung together on the soundtrack album's lengthy final cut, amusingly titled "Brooks' 50-Cent Tour (Main Title Collage)."

* * *

Back in San Francisco, Clint Eastwood and Lalo Schifrin made genre history.

The latter's spellbinding jazz score for *Dirty Harry* is as lean and mean as Eastwood's title character: throbbing explosions of bass and drums that signal suspense and *very* bad behavior by the story's infamously psychotic villain. Director Don Siegel uses music sparingly in this ground-breaking cop thriller, but every note counts; and Schifrin's quieter melodies and atmospheric cues are just as powerful as the more aggressive rhythms. It's one of his finest big-screen scores: a game-changing blast of angry jazz/funk on par with his (far different) work on *Bullitt* and *Cool Hand Luke*. The score's menacing undertone is achieved, in part, by Schifrin's frequent use of augmented fourths—also called tritones— which are notorious for their unpleasant, even unpalatable dissonance. "In the Middle Ages and the Renaissance," Schifrin explained, "the tritone was called '*diabolus in musica*' (the devil in music), and was sometimes forbidden. There was a story in which an organist was condemned to death if he played this interval. The augmented fourth was not allowed in four-part writing (the false relationship of the tritone). Nevertheless, this interval in our day and age is very useful for establishing tension."[9]

The story opens as a sniper coldly executes a young woman in a rooftop swimming pool. Schifrin heightens our anxiety with double-stroke kicking of ominous bass drums, the sharp staccato of snare drums, unsettling audio effects and even a bit of atonal vocalese: a dissonant yet hypnotic mélange that becomes the ongoing theme of the kill-crazy lunatic dubbed "Scorpio" (Andy Robinson).

"The whole object of the music, no matter what means are used, is to make a psychological contribution to the movie," Schifrin added. "I encountered the challenge of conveying the presence of a villain, Scorpio, who is a vicious mass murderer terrorizing the people of San Francisco. He is unpredictable, and at the beginning of the film, it seems he kills at random. I depicted his dangerous, almost invisible personality with the use of a female voice singing a haunting motif, accompanied by tune glasses and a water phone (an aluminum container of water, with rods attached). A player uses a cello bow to rub on the rods. The whole effect is very chilling, and creates a very uneasy feeling for the audience."[10]

Drums, bongos and a wicked walking bass signal Harry Callahan's subsequent entrance, against the title credits; strings and darkly nervous piano riffs help this rhythmic prologue build to an almost-melody delivered by rising strings, while he surveils the scene for clues. Additional piano riffs, a soupçon of Hammond B3 and bowed bass add a coda when he finds both a high-powered rifle shell casing and a rather nasty ransom demand. As exciting as this cue is, Schifrin and Siegel never intended it as a "Harry Callahan Theme." If Eastwood's character has an actual cue, it's the melancholy flute and electric piano dirge that debuts when—despite heroic effort on the detective's part—the lifeless body of another victim is pulled from the hole where Scorpio buried her. This theme reprises when the film concludes, Harry having "succeeded" at the cost of his own soul.

"It's sad," Schifrin acknowledged, referencing that theme, "but I tried to make it 'cool' sad. It had some pathos, but it's not hysterical, reflecting his attitude."[11]

The film initially failed to generate a soundtrack album, although Schifrin's reorchestrated, uptempo jazz-rock blend of the main title and Scorpio theme was released as a 45 single. A few score tracks popped up on compilation albums during the next several decades, but the full score wasn't issued until 2004. By then, Schifrin's jazz-rock arrangement of the title theme had become a staple on film/TV action jazz anthology CDs.

Eastwood's character—and Schifrin—were guaranteed to return (about which, more later).

Meanwhile, another of the composer's 1971 assignments was for a real jaw-dropper.

Finding heartthrob Rock Hudson in a tawdry sex comedy/thriller is disconcerting enough; seeing *Star Trek* creator Gene Roddenberry attached as scripter/producer qualifies as an out-of-body experience. *Pretty Maids All in a Row* was erotic French director Roger Vadim's attempt to penetrate the American film industry, and the result is an embarrassing bouillabaisse of dated flower-power slang, inept social commentary, bad acting and exploitatively bared flesh, stitched together by a couple of middle-aged guys pretending to understand the late–1960s sexual revolution.

Hudson stars as Michael "Tiger" McDrew, the football coach and guidance counselor at California's Oceanfront High School. Tiger spends most of his time shagging the school's sexually willing coeds, much to the envy of his young protégé, Ponce (John David Carson). This sexually repressed 17-year-old is ashamed of being a virgin, a problem solved when he catches the fancy of naïve substitute teacher Miss Smith (Angie Dickinson). Meanwhile, a growing number of the school's nubile cuties are turning up dead on campus; investigating Police Capt. Surcher (Telly Savalas) eventually realizes that all the victims have shared quality time with Tiger. Is he the serial killer, or could it be his equally voluptuous wife, Jean (Barbara Leigh)? Principal Proffer (Roddy McDowall)? Doofus Police Chief Poldaski (Keenan Wynn)? Or perhaps Ponce?

The film opens when Ponce arrives at school on a typical day, gazing hungrily at all the scantily dressed young women; the title credits appear against a forlorn pop ballad—"Chilly Winds"—performed by The Osmonds (whose squeaky-clean image was rather at odds with the film's salacious content). Most of Schifrin's subsequent underscore is atmospheric; the various cues employ jittery piano, Fender Rhodes, harp, low-register flute, bass and cimbalom to sinister effect, while the campus body count grows.

The frequent diegetic cues better reflect Schifrin's roots. A breezy jazz ballad with lovely piano and flute lines emanates from a radio in Tiger's office, when he persuades Miss

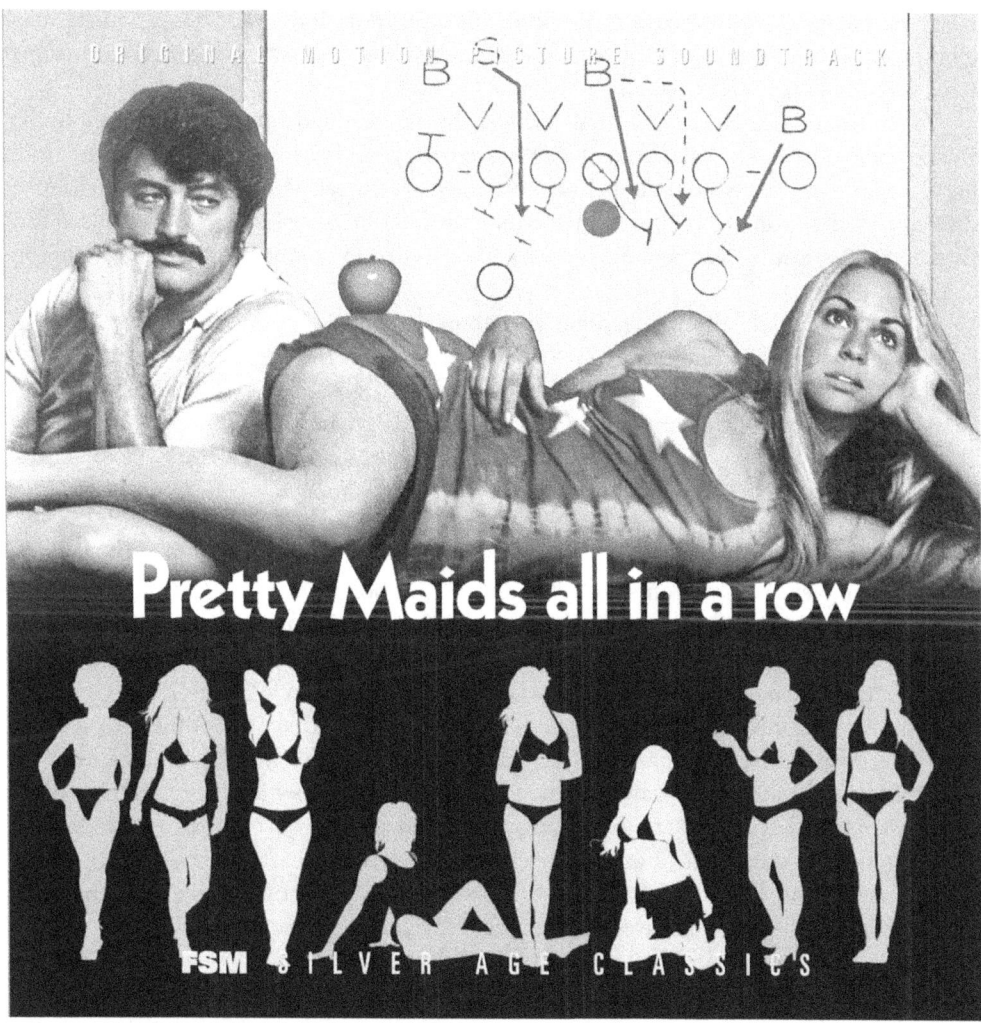

Gene Roddenberry based his screenplay for *Pretty Maids All in a Row* on the novel of the same title by erotica author Francis Pollini, and the film is reasonably faithful to its crude source (which is no compliment). The sexual promiscuity is hilarious by contemporary standards, but at least the plot is equal-opportunity, since high school kids of both genders are exploited (respectively) by teachers of the opposite sex (courtesy Film Score Monthly).

Smith to "help" Ponce. The eventual seduction, in her apartment, begins when she and the lad dance to a sensuous blend of drums, bass and muted trumpet, which blossoms into a slow, achingly sexy mélange of big band horns: a tune that emerges from her record player. The phonograph needle segues to another track, as they progress to a soapy bathtub encounter; the tempo becomes slightly faster, the big band trumpet line more mischievous, joined by some sparkling vibes. Tiger, meanwhile, is banging another coed in his car; their energetic coupling takes place against an impudent, uptempo fusion number that emanates from the radio: a vivacious swinger that grants ample exposure to Artie Kane's vibrant piano work. (Schifrin later expanded and rerecorded this cue as "Latin Slide," for his 1973 album *La Clave*.)

The soundtrack finally arrived in 2011; the primary attractions are the full-length jazz cues, including a few not heard in the film. "Campus Pop Source 2M1B" is a standout: a vibrant, Latin-hued big band swinger highlighted by plenty of horns, sassy sax and trumpet solos, against a cool salsa beat.

Don Ellis was a "mere" sideman when Schifrin included him in the ensemble that worked on 1968's *Bullitt*, but the avant-garde jazz trumpeter became a Hollywood force with his score for *The French Connection*. The taut, *cinema verité* script is based on Robin Moore's 1969 non-fiction book of the same title, which profiled the successful efforts of New York City detectives Eddie Egan and Sonny Grosso, who in 1962 made the then-largest heroin bust in U.S. history.

Director William Friedkin's slightly fictionalized narrative follows Jimmy "Popeye" Doyle (Gene Hackman) and Buddy Russo (Roy Scheider) as they get wind of a massive heroin shipment being mounted by local wise guy Sal Boca (Tony Lo Bianco); he has negotiated a deal with debonair drug smuggler Alain Charnier (Fernando Rey), based in Marseille. Things get more suspenseful when the crafty Charnier arrives in New York, accompanied by his pet assassin, Nicoli (Marcel Bozzuffi). By this time, Popeye is certain the drugs have entered the country ... but how?

Friedkin, seeking a composer whose work would reflect the jangly, down-and-dirty cacophony of New York's mean streets, turned to Ellis, best known at that time for a series of big-band albums laced with original tunes that bear wonderfully weird time signatures. He delivered sensational work for Friedkin, who used barely half of the composer's brassy, aggressively discordant 38 minutes of music. Friedkin preferred a "naturalistic" presentation that minimized—and even eliminated—music for great stretches of time.

"There was one chase scene," Ellis recalled, "when they're walking and stalking the guy, and it ends up in the subway, for which I used nine basses, which they told me was the most basses they'd ever used at Fox; and that turned out to be a sort of theme of the movie. For the main theme, the title, I used a very brutal sound with six trumpets, three of whom played quarter-tone horns. I got a very biting, spine-chilling dissonance by using the six in harmony, and then having three of them move into a quarter-tone thing."[12]

Ellis' work certainly catches one's attention, starting with the dissonant trumpets and throbbing woodwinds which accompany the stark title credits that shoot across the screen. We don't hear from Ellis again until the first time Doyle and Russo tail Sal; this cue is the memorable, propulsive 7/4 blend of bowed basses and edgy piano riffs that Ellis would reorchestrate and record as "Theme from *The French Connection*" on his 1972 album, *Connection*. This theme reprises during Doyle's patient tail of Charnier, starting at his hotel and continuing during a lengthy walk along New York's streets; Ellis augments the piano noodling with trumpet accents that climax when the Frenchman eludes our hero with a mocking wave of his fingers. Ellis' next significant contribution comes when Doyle and Russo carefully follow Sal's car to a dodgy part of the city: a "slow chase" that unfolds to a disconcerting blend of bowed strings, bongos and horn pops.

Ellis' avant-garde score remained unavailable until 2001, when it was paired it on a CD with the music from the movie's 1975 sequel.

The French Connection depicts the (more or less) authentic activities of real-world cops; *Chandler* puts a real-world author into a fictitious adventure much like those found in his books. Alas, the film is a mess; it benefits solely from star Warren Oates' reasonably convincing portrayal of the eponymous author. The narrative makes no sense—Chandler is hired to protect a missing government witness (Leslie Caron, as Katherine) being sought by various gangsters—and the dialogue is laughably overcooked. Chandler is offered this "protection" assignment by longtime buddy Bernie Oakman (Charles McGraw), who is betraying his friend as a favor to corrupt government agent Ross J. Carmady (Alex Dreier); he's in league with gangster Charles Kincaid (Mitchell Ryan). Matters build to an oceanside gun battle in picturesque Monterey, which drifts into an ambiguous conclusion.

George Romanis' score is a blend of "supper club" combo tracks and darker, despondent cues intended to reflect Chandler's world-weary languor. The film opens with melancholy sax and piano, which builds to an ominous trumpet fanfare and four-note motif as the credits conclude; this segues into a bluesy piano theme, when a reluctant Chandler accepts the case. A series of soft jazz cues—piano, sax, bass and flute—spot subsequent montages, while Chandler tracks Katherine to Monterey and then Carmel; a slow, quiet jazz waltz debuts when she and Chandler flirtatiously spar. Swinging action jazz backstops a car chase through Monterey's Cannery Row and, much later, a second pursuit that ultimately leads to the beach fracas.

No soundtrack album was issued, but Romanis did place his "Theme from *Chandler*" on a 45 single.

Meanwhile, Across the Pond...

The Persuaders! was the last of Britain's top-flight action/adventure television series, concluding a terrific decade that had begun with 1960's *Danger Man*. No expense was spared while courting two A-list stars—Roger Moore and Tony Curtis—and shooting episodes on location throughout Europe. When the ITV/ABC series debuted September 17, it also featured one of the coolest, most unusual—and most immediately striking—title themes ever written for a TV series on *either* side of the Atlantic. No surprise: It came from John Barry.

"The whole point about television," he explained, "is that you've got so little time. If a person's in the kitchen and they hear this in the living room, is it going to grab them? Are they going to say, 'What the hell is that?' I always went for a really intensely individual shot right off the top. You know: a sound that would grab you, very distinctive and memorable. And you have to capture that audience within, hopefully, the first four bars."[13]

His 70-second theme for *The Persuaders!* opens with a pair of seven piano chords, deceptively suggesting chamber music; this develops into a hypnotic blend of instruments playing the core 4-4-4-5 motif, against a throbbing rhythm section in slow waltz time. (It has the same "fuzz ambiance" as Barry's instrumental theme for 1969's *On Her Majesty's Secret Service*.) The *Persuaders!* theme intensifies as a dynamic title credits sequence "profiles" the lives of rags-to-riches American Danny Wilde (Curtis) and British aristocrat Lord Brett Rupert George Robert Andrew Sinclair (Moore).

Whenever Barry sought something unusual, he visited friend and colleague John Leach, who played the cimbalom for Barry's music in *The Ipcress File*. "If I wanted a strange sound, I went over to [John's] place. He had all these weird instruments; you couldn't get in the room for instruments!"[14]

Leach, picking up the story, explained that the melody was "built" from four overdubbed instruments. "The backing track was done. The first track we put down, Hugo [D'Alton] played mandolin, and I played cimbalom; on the second overdub, I played kantele and Hugo played mandola. John wrote the notes; if they weren't possible, I re-tuned the kantele and dropped them in."[15]

Unfortunately, the series can't match its attention-grabbing title theme. Although

Moore and Curtis have a lot of fun with ad-libbed banter, the core plots too frequently feel "lifted" from other action-oriented predecessors. The "exotic" European locations can't compensate for a growing sense of same old/same old. The orchestral underscores—almost all of them by Ken Thorne—are lamentably bland.

Barry's title theme became his final pop hit, spending 15 weeks on the British charts; it was covered by John Keating (Capitol) and Phil Tate (IDTA). The theme later enjoyed renewed life via alternative groups. The UK's postpunk Manchester band The Umbrella included a cover on its one-and-only vinyl EP, 1985's *Make Hell (for the Beautiful People)*. French/Tunesian pop star Lââm "borrowed" the melody for a protest ballad dubbed "Enfants Du Monde (Children of the World)," on her eponymous 2004 album. Finally, the French shoegaze/postrock project Les Discrets included a cover on its 2011 vinyl EP *Arctic Plateau*.

Elsewhere at ITV, Peter Wyngarde had been by far the most vibrant and popular presence in 1969's *Department S* (see this book's companion volume), so it was no surprise when his character earned his own series 18 month later. *Jason King* debuted September 15, 1971; little had changed, aside from his departure from official government work. King's efforts to remain a successful espionage author are interrupted constantly when he gets dragged into ill-advised adventures involving colorful villains and gorgeous women. The peril never is realistic, and Wyngarde swans through these escapades with the proper aristocratic *sang-froid*.

Laurie Johnson scored all 26 episodes. The title theme, one of his typically catchy, big band blasts of brass-heavy jazz, opens with a 1-1-3-3 background ostinato; this serves as countermelody to low-end horns that introduce the tune's 1-3-1-5 motif. The tempo is synchronized to foreground images of King typing away at a manuscript, while brief live-action clips show him skulking, smooching and skiing.

The underscores display the variety and atmosphere that Johnson brought to *The Avengers*: tense drum cues when bad guys are up to no good; sinister strings when King is in danger; sultry swing ballads when attractive women wander into the story; and exhilarating blasts of big band jazz—often flavored by electronic guitar and keyboard—for occasional action sequences. Many of the cues, particularly those employed as source music, run long and can be regarded as melodies in their own right.

Johnson issued an expanded arrangement of the title theme—with a perky organ solo dominating a new bridge—as a 45 single. No soundtrack appeared until 2009's double-disc *Jason King Original Soundtrack*, which includes the title theme and 77 other cues, alternate takes and unused bits.

* * *

British jazz pianist Roy Budd wrote a terrific score for *Get Carter*, and director Mike Hodges has long credited that music for adding just the right texture to his feature debut ... despite the fact that he used so little of it. Indeed, this brutal crime drama is mostly bereft of music, aside from the iconic title theme and several bits of source vocal pop, when the narrative dips into various clubs and sybaritic parties. It would be more accurate to say that the film gets its grim atmosphere from the *absence* of music: ironic, given the reputation the score has garnered.

Budd was a piano-playing child prodigy who performed in public at the age of 6, and by 16 was writing charts and heading trios and quartets in jazz clubs throughout London. His definitive trio featured Pete Morgan (bass) and Chris Karan (drums), and they performed together for roughly three decades.[16] Budd's fondness for cinema—and an extensive collection of soundtrack albums—prompted him to tackle film composing. "I used to go to the movies every day, and listen to how it worked," he once told Karan.[17] *Get Carter* was Budd's second film score—after 1970's *Soldier Blue*—and the one that put him on the soundtrack map.

The story, adapted from Ted Lewis' 1969 crime novel *Jack's Return Home*, is unflinchingly harsh. London-based gangster Jack Carter (Michael Caine) travels to his hometown of Newcastle, believing that his brother's sudden "accidental death" was anything but. Carter's relentless investigation confirms this suspicion; worse yet, his teenage niece has been forced into pornographic films by a consortium that includes Eric Paice (Ian Hendry), Albert Swift (Glynn Edwards), Cyril Kinnear (John Osborne) and Cliff Brumby (Bryan Mosley). Carter's enraged vengeance is shocking, particularly when handling the women at the fringes of these events. When the dust finally settles, the various bad guys have gotten their just desserts ... but Carter fares no better, ultimately put down like the rabid dog he has become.

Budd worked with a small ensemble, and the film's main theme would become iconic.

"What exactly inspired Roy to combine a Rhodes piano, harpsichord, double bass and tablas to be the sole ingredients of classic film theme is hard to say," observed Budd's manager, Jack Fishman, "but it certainly was original."[18]

"I played the electric piano and the harpsichord at the same time," Budd recalled, years

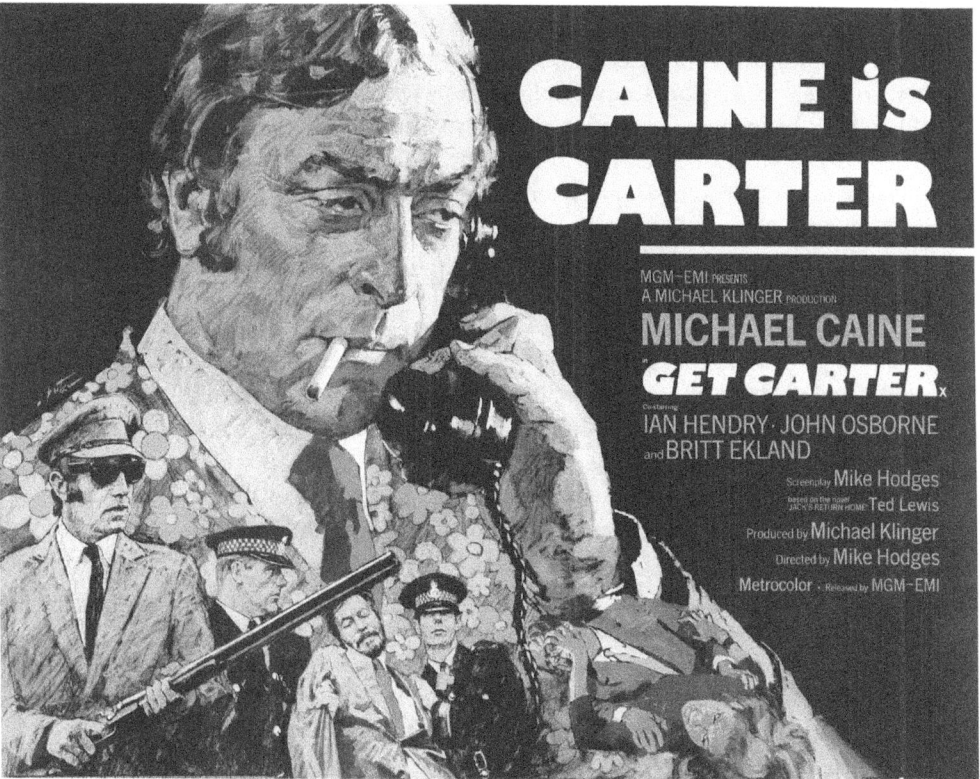

Almost half a century later, Michael Caine's portrayal of gangster Jack Carter remains one of the most cold-hearted bastards ever captured on film. Composer Roy Budd's title theme has become a staple of crime jazz anthology CDs: an honor he sadly didn't live to enjoy. He died of a fatal brain hemorrhage in 1993, at the youthful age of 46.

later. "At that time we didn't have the electronic wizardry we have nowadays, and I had to actually sit there. Uncomfortable, but it sounded pleasant."[19]

Budd and his combo recorded the score live, playing direct to the film as it was projected onto a huge screen.[20] A haunting solo harpsichord cue, backed by unsettling wind effects, accompanies our first glimpse of the immaculately dressed Carter; Caine's reptilian gaze is chilly, as he informs his London bosses that he's heading to Newcastle. The main theme debuts against the title credits, superimposed over Carter's train trip; Jeff Cline's bass and Karan's tablas back Budd's harpsichord treatment, the resulting 4/4 swinger deftly suggesting the disturbing activity to follow. Budd inserts a lively piano solo at the bridge, after which the keyboard and bass retreat, leaving only the slowing tablas to mimic the train's deceleration into Newcastle.

From this point forward, the limited bursts of music are confined to raucous pop/rock source tunes by Budd and Fishman, a lyricist/songwriter in his own right. The only other non-diegetic jazz theme—a fast-paced piano and drum cue—accompanies Carter's midstory encounter with Glenda (Geraldine Moffat), a free-spirited sybarite who turns out to be involved with the pornography ring. After that, the film proceeds with no underscore until the grim climax, set to a mournful solo harpsichord reprise of the main theme.

Budd's full score wasn't released until a 1998 prestige LP, with 22 tracks that alternate music with dialogue. It includes a few instrumental jazz tracks not in the film: the sleek, sultry "Something on My Mind"; and the mildly disturbing "Hallucinations." The title theme was covered by the synthpop band The Human League; and subsequently was sampled/riffed on recordings by Portishead, Massive Attack and other prog-rock groups. Budd's original arrangement also became a staple of crime jazz anthology CDs.

Elsewhere throughout England, James Bond's fans cheered the return of Sean Connery.

Even so, *Diamonds Are Forever* suffers from a relentlessly comic tone—a moon buggy, Jimmy Dean's spoof Howard Hughes, female bodyguards dubbed Bambi and Thumper—which, in hindsight, would have been far better suited to Roger Moore's reign. This burlesque approach dictated a less aggressive score from John Barry, with action jazz minimized in favor of humorous cues. It's not quite cartoon music—that would come later, with Moore's films—but *Diamonds Are Forever* does represent Bond's final fling with any of the hard-charging "spy jazz" that ignited an entire musical genre.

Barry nonetheless wrote another fantastic title song, delivered with robust sensuality by Shirley Bassey, behind Maurice Binder's erotic credits sequence. The tune opens with an explosion of brass and a repeating eight-note organ motif, symbolizing the eight facets of single-cut diamonds; Bassey's lusty pipes are backed by forceful drums, throbbing bass and brass fanfares. Instrumental arrangements crop up throughout the film, both as underscore for Bond's deepening relationship with reformed bad girl Tiffany Case (Jill St. John), and as diegetic music in some of the numerous Las Vegas settings. One contemplatively languid variation places the melody atop the familiar "James Bond Theme" bass line.

The precredits sequence is powered by a forceful, guitar-driven "James Bond Theme," during Bond's enraged hunt for Blofeld (Charles Gray). Following Binder's credits, Barry introduces the hypnotic cue that follows killers Wint and Kidd (Bruce Glover and jazz bassist-turned-actor Putter Smith) throughout the film: an enigmatic 4-4 sax and flute motif that repeats against equally mysterious percussion. The plot finds Bond assigned to infiltrate a diamond-smuggling operation that stretches from South Africa to Las Vegas; curiously, the stolen gems aren't turning up on the black market. Once in Vegas, Bond discovers that the diamonds have become the key component of a laser satellite that Blofeld intends to place into orbit, with the intention of destroying the nuclear weapons caches of countries that refuse to meet his ransom demands.

Many of the film's jazz cues are diegetic. A lovely cocktail combo arrangement of the title song, highlighted by sparkling piano and gentle brass elements, is heard in the Amsterdam hotel room where Bond first meets Tiffany. When he later flies to the States and links up with CIA buddy Felix Leiter (Norman Burton), the airport PA system delivers a saucy midtempo anthem fueled by an extremely dirty sax. A bold, brassy, big band swinger accompanies Bond's arrival at Las Vegas' Circus Circus, during a montage as he checks out the casino action and the gorgeous showgirls. Bond's brief splurge at a craps table is accompanied by a sparkling finger-snapper, with horns taking the melody against lyrical piano comping. This tune reappears later, during an amusing sequence when Tiffany catches Q (Desmond Llewelyn) gimmicking a row of slot machines.

Barry and Bond fans were annoyed by the soundtrack LP, which was engineered as an easy-listening, Las Vegas–style lounge album, skipping the best jazz and action cues in favor of softer orchestral numbers. Both the album and title song nonetheless enjoyed respectable runs in their respective *Billboard* charts. The preferred digital release finally arrived in 2003, with an additional 34 minutes that gives a far superior sense of the entire score.

Barry ceased his unbroken run as Bond's composer after *Diamonds Are Forever*, because his growing popularity found him busy with numerous other projects. The franchise remained strong during Roger Moore's seven-film run through 1985, but none of those scores can be considered jazz: not even those by Barry. Although he ultimately found time for five more 007 assignments, only one—his last, 1987's *The Living Daylights*—offers enough jazz to be discussed in these pages.

Sliding back to 1971, thriller/adventure author Alistair MacLean had become a serious pop-culture force by this time, with half a dozen of his popular novels made into (mostly) successful films. This gave him the clout to chaperone *Puppet on a Chain* by penning the screenplay, but the results leave much to be desired. Director Geoffrey Reeve hasn't any feel for action scenes or quieter character moments; he also has no idea how to integrate Piero Piccioni's tasty, strut-and-swagger score into the film.

The plot is little more than a thinly disguised polemic about the evils of heroin. Enigmatic American agent Paul Sherman (Sven-Bertil Taube) is sent to Amsterdam, which his government handlers have determined is the European source of drugs that have been flooding into the States. Sherman liaises with deep-cover colleague Maggie (Barbara Parkins), and the two gradually uncover a supply chain that involves doctored clocks, Bibles and colorful dolls. Our heroes' efforts are dogged by a mysterious assassin (Peter Hutchins), and all but dismissed by Col. De Graaf (Alexander Knox), Amsterdam's stuffy chief of police. All clues eventually lead to a sinister priest (Vladek Sheybal), and climax in a ludicrously protracted boat chase.

Piccioni's dynamic, heavily percussive score is dominated by energetic Hammond B3 cues, starting with a tough-as-nails title credits theme that opens with an orchestral blast of horns, then settles into groove-heavy 4/2-3 motifs backed by aggressive sax licks and thunderous percussion. Once in Amsterdam, Sherman's cat-and-mouse antics with a pursuing assassin unfold against throbbing, funk-laden bass and synth, augmented by psychedelic electric guitar: a cue repeated numerous times throughout the film, to accompany similar skulking activities. A slower arrangement backs Sherman's later attempt to confirm that a supposedly honest importer is up to no good.

Piccioni also contributes a few diegetic cues: a vibrant variation of the main theme, powered by some shrill sax, when Sherman eavesdrops on a clandestine meeting at a discothèque; and clichéd flutes and bongos, when he's taken to a "typical" marijuana den, laden with near-comatose young people. The soundtrack doesn't accelerate again until the freeze-frame final scene, which signals the end credits and a reprise of the pulsating big band title theme: horns and synthesizer blazing all the way to a climactic final chord.

The film deservedly bombed upon release, and the soundtrack album didn't appear until 2001. It's a peculiar beast. Although the 18 tracks encompass the bulk of Piccioni's music, most of the track *titles* are wholly inappropriate: designations apparently assigned randomly by somebody who hadn't watched the film.

Maclean had no better luck with *When Eight Bells Toll*, a limp attempt to ride the coattails of the Bond franchise. Anthony Hopkins swans unconvincingly through his starring role as British Treasury agent Philip Calvert, assigned with partner Hunslett (Corin Redgrave) to probe the hijacking of five cargo ships in the Irish Sea. Their investigation leads to the tiny port community of Torbay in the Scottish Highlands, location of the most recently hijacked ship: the *Nantesville*, loaded with £8 million in gold bullion. Clues point to well-respected tycoon and shipping magnate Sir Anthony Skouras (Jack Hawkins), who lives with his young wife, Charlotte (Nathalie Delon), aboard their luxury yacht *Shangri-La*. A few contrived skirmishes with low-level baddies later, Calvert is joined by his persnickety, London-based boss Sir Arthur Arnford-Jones (Robert Morley); together they invade a local castle at midnight (eight bells), to stymie the actual criminal masterminds.

Until bad reviews and poor box-office returns derailed such grandiose plans, producers Elliott Kastner and Jerry Gershwin intended this film to ignite a series of Philip Calvert spy thrillers[21]; their determination to duplicate the Bondian atmosphere apparently included a demand that soundtrack composer Walter Stott contribute a John Barry-esque title theme. Stott—better known as composer Angela Morley, following sex reassignment surgery in 1972—duly obliged, with a flamboyant, heavily percussive, brass-laden melody which begs for lyrics that remained unwritten. Additional action jazz cues also have the unmistakably bold Barry stamp: one that spots an early brawl between Calvert and a baddie; and a second heard during a thoroughly pointless cemetery melee, when Calvert gets beaten up by two nameless thugs. The rest of Stott's score is standard-issue orchestral strings and reeds.

No soundtrack LP was produced, although Stott's title theme proved popular enough, years later, to generate covers on a couple of compilation albums: John Wilson's *The Film & Television Music of Angela Morley*, and John Gregory's *Spies and Dolls*.

2

Blowin' Your Mind: 1972

With John Barry's film career expanding exponentially, he no longer had time for the small screen. His final assignment for an episodic television series debuted this year: a cool synthesizer/mandolin title theme for *The Adventurer*, a pallid production that scarcely deserved such a bold introduction each week.

On a slightly disturbing note—and ironic, given that the genre was established by Isaac Hayes' sumptuous jazz palette for *Shaft*—blaxploitation films began to minimize their instrumental score elements in favor soul and R&B vocals. Traditional soundtrack composers probably didn't regard this as a threat—at least, not yet—but such complacency wouldn't last long.

The Small Screen

If one young co-star is a draw, then three young stars would be even *more* popular, right? Just as 1968's *The Mod Squad* paired its three young adults with an older and more conservatively cynical "handler" (see this book's companion volume), *The Rookies*' three recent police academy graduates—Terry Webster (Georg Stanford Brown), Willie Gillis (Michael Ontkean) and Mike Danko (Sam Melville)—are supervised by Lt. Eddie Ryker (Gerald S. O'Loughlin), a gruff veteran openly contemptuous of the "kinder, gentler" law enforcement methods employed by his fresh-faced recruits. The ABC series enjoyed a healthy four-season run that began March 7.

Elmer Bernstein's dynamic title theme is highlighted by a killer sax solo, which perfectly matches the grimly melodramatic credits sequence. Bernstein opens with a powerful horn ostinato against *wah-wah* guitar, then shifts to an equally bold brass melody while the characters are introduced at a departmental shooting range. Vigorous sax takes over when a montage of police cars and gun-toting officers respond to unseen crises; the core melody—and brass counterpoint—return when the stars are credited, followed by a climactic orchestral chord as the three young stars race toward the camera.

Bernstein also scored a dozen episodes during the series' first two seasons; other assignments were handled by Jack Elliott, Allyn Ferguson, Shorty Rogers, Pete Rugolo, Mark Snow and Robert Drasnin. Very little of the interior music had the impact of Bernstein's title theme.

No soundtrack or single was released.

Music is a more vibrant presence in ABC's *The Streets of San Francisco*, thanks to the template established by Patrick Williams' sizzling title theme. The police procedural is one of the finer entries in the veteran/rookie mold, with career homicide detective Lt. Michael

Stone (Karl Malden) assigned alongside the younger and more impetuous Assistant Det. Steve Keller (Michael Douglas). The strong on- and off-camera bond between the two stars played a great part in the series' success, propelling it to five popular seasons after its September 16 debut. (Douglas left after the fourth season and was replaced by Richard Hatch's Inspector Dan Robbins.)

Williams' intense title theme is an urgent blast of funky urban jazz anchored by John Guerin's thumping drums, a clavinet, Carol Kaye's rhythm guitar and Tom Scott's tenor sax solo on the core 5-5 motif. The theme plays against a staccato montage of San Francisco scenery clips, edited so swiftly that it's impossible to register everything during a single viewing. As with all Quinn Martin productions, much of the theme is buried beneath a voice-over announcer.

"It was pretty hip for its time," Williams admitted. "I took a sound that I had used in some of the brass albums I had made in New York. To play the melody, there was a unison between the trumpets in the medium register, and the trombones in the high register. It had this real hot quality; the band loved to play it."[1]

The big band jazz ambiance extends to episode underscores, and Williams shared first season assignments with Scott, John Elizalde, Billy Byers and Robert Prince. "Bad guys up to no good" sequences often play as dialogue-less montages against peppy brass and/or sax rhythmic cues; the same is true of crime scene investigations and surveillance montages, whether on foot or by car. Vehicular chases prompt saucier uptempo swingers. Frequent visits to bars, restaurants and coffee shops—where Keller invariably embarrasses Stone by requesting tea—grant ample opportunities for softer jazz melodies performed by (usually) unseen soloists or combos. Very few episodes earned fresh scores after the first season; most were tracked with library cues.

The show failed to generate a soundtrack album, although Williams eventually expanded his title theme for a 1975 45 single; the arrangement is grittier and more forceful than what TV viewers heard each week, with a sizzling assault of unison horns and an electric keyboard bridge. It subsequently became a staple on crime and TV jazz anthology albums.

Police shows clearly were on the rise again, but the tube wasn't yet done with eccentric private investigators. *Banacek* kicked off NBC's *Wednesday Mystery Movie* on March 20, launched in the wake of its successful Sunday evening predecessor. George Peppard is sublime as Thomas Banacek, a suave, Boston-based freelance insurance investigator who specializes in seemingly impossible crimes, many of which can be considered locked-room mysteries: a valuable book that vanishes from a highly secure vault; a three-ton statue that seemingly evaporates into thin air; a football player who ceases to exist while playing a game being watched on national TV.

Billy Goldenberg's main theme is a gentle jazz waltz, with a soft woodwind melody backed by *wah-wah* guitar and tasty piano comping; it's heard against a title credits montage of Peppard rowing, strolling and driving around and among iconic regions of the Boston cityscape. The second-season arrangement runs a touch longer and displays more keyboard comping, a cheerful sax solo, and a countermelody during a fresh bridge. All underscores, alas, are bland orchestral shading.

No soundtrack album or single appeared, although John Gregory included a nifty cover on his 1976 Philips UK compilation album, *The Detectives*.

Not wanting to be left behind, ABC introduced a similar umbrella series rather dubiously titled *The Men*, which lasted only an undistinguished single season. The network commissioned Isaac Hayes to pen a jazzy wrap-around theme, and he certainly delivered. "Theme from *The Men*" is an explosion of catchy, funkified jazz, woefully edited down to a 40-second credits sequence dominated by breathy female vocalists who intone "the *mennnnnn*." It fleetingly introduces the three spokes of this action/adventure wheel: *Jigsaw*, with James Wainwright as a missing persons investigator; *The Delphi Bureau*, starring Laurence Luckinbill as a clandestine government researcher turned reluctant spy; and *Assignment: Vienna*, featuring Robert Conrad as an American expat based in the Austrian capital, who handles undercover work on behalf of the U.S. government. Hayes expanded his theme into a terrific four-minute groover for a 45 single; the arrangement features plenty of *wah-wah* guitar, along with lyrical brass elements and cool keyboard comping.

Assignment: Vienna debuted September 28. It's the only spoke with a notable jazz presence, due to Conrad's starring role as Jake Webster, whose "cover" is as the owner/proprietor of Jake's Bar & Grill; the cozy venue always features a tasty jazz combo. The music assignment went to Dave Grusin, who delivered network television's first series underscores dominated by the distinctive sound of a cimbalom. He handled three of the show's eight episodes, and many of his cues anticipate the cool percussive sound he'd soon use for the big screen's *Three Days of the Condor*. John Carl Parker scored two other episodes, and the remaining three were tracked.

Grusin's standout cue is the uptempo "Jake's Theme," a lyrical, midtempo ballad dominated by dynamic keyboard chops; an alternate arrangement recasts the tune as a soft jazz waltz, with the melody traded between sax and piano. It's often heard, albeit only briefly, as source music in Jake's Bar & Grill. Additional diegetic combo numbers include the gentle "Déjà Vu," boasting Tom Scott's lovely flute line; and the exciting "Montreal Express Blues," with Scott and Grusin wailing away on sax and piano, respectively. They're accompanied by Chuck Berghofer (bass) and John Guerin (drums).

Underscore cues involve larger ensembles, with percussionist Ken Watson handling the cimbalom work. Suspenseful snare drums and Eastern European inflections are present in many of Grusin's efforts for his debut episode—"The Last Target"—while other cues are saucy or languid arrangements of "Jakes' Theme." Grusin's second score—"Hot Potato"— features plenty of bongos, fuzz and *wah-wah* guitars, with unison horns adding tension and excitement.

By midseason, when neither *Assignment: Vienna* nor the other two spokes had registered much viewer interest, ABC dropped the wheel format and Hayes' theme; the three shows subsequently ran in month-long chunks, under their own identities. This gave Grusin the opportunity to transform "Jake's Theme" into a peppy, 50-second version for a new *Assignment: Vienna* title sequence.

No soundtrack album was produced, but 2010's box set *TV Omnibus: Volume One (1962–1976)* includes all three of Grusin's underscores and combo source cues, along with Parker's two underscores.

Although shows that feature detectives in contemporary settings are easier and less expensive to mount, every so often enterprising producers tried to return to the genre's period Hammett and Chandler origins. Case in point: NBC's *Banyon*.

The look is right, the setting is right, and the music is right. Robert Forster similarly is spot-on as former cop turned hard-luck private detective Miles C. Banyon, who trolls the mean streets of early Depression-era Los Angeles, handling cases from any client willing to pony up $20 per day. He maintains an uneasy relationship with police colleague Lt. Pete McNeil (Richard Jaeckel), and does far better with steady girlfriend Abby Graham (Julie

Gregg), who works as a nightclub chanteuse. Storylines deal with kidnappers, gangsters, murderers, extortionists and missing persons.

Banyon debuted as a telefilm that aired March 15, 1971. Leonard Rosenman drew that scoring assignment, but his music doesn't fit: too "modern," and definitely not appropriate for the 1930s. The film's subsequent transition to a weekly schedule occurred well over a year later, on September 15, 1972. Johnny Mandel provided a far superior title theme: a fast-paced big band swinger with a sassy, screaming clarinet solo that rises above unison horns, all playing against a staccato montage of action clips superimposed over graphic footprints, fingerprints, palm prints and—ultimately—images and credits for the cast and guest stars.

The setting—particularly the sequences involving Abby's nightclub work—encourages plenty of vintage jazz in the episode underscores.

Unfortunately, the series was a ratings failure, and Banyon solved his final case after only 15 episodes. None of the music has a presence beyond its television origins.

Banyon took viewers into the past; *Search* anticipated the future. Television's first weekly experiment with "spy-fi" began as a two-hour pilot film titled *Probe*—which aired February 11, 1972—and was retitled *Search* when it debuted as an NBC series later that year. (PBS already had a series titled *Probe*.) The action is based at World Securities Corp., a high-tech investigative outfit that equips its agents with miniature cameras, implanted audio receivers and telemetry units that monitor all field activity. WSC's "mission control" is headed by V.C.R. Cameron (Burgess Meredith) and senior medical technician Gloria Harding (Angel Tompkins). The primary *Search* agents—Hugh Lockwood (Hugh O'Brien), Nick Bianco (Tony Franciosa) and C.R. Grover (Doug McClure)—alternate assignments, with the three stars rotating episodes in the manner of *The Name of the Game*. Some adventures reflect the gadget-laden environment—pulse bombs, lunar samples, toxic bullets—but the rest are routine matters involving counterfeiting, kidnapping, blackmail and murder threats.

Dominic Frontiere handled the title theme and underscores for all 23 of the single-season episodes. The uptempo title cue relies overmuch on orchestral strings, but the primary melody comes from a tasty solo trumpet against swinging rhythm. The credits sequence employs the multicolored pixel graphics that suggested "computers" in the early 1970s and is well timed to the beats of Frontiere's theme; the music builds to a lively crescendo against a final split-screen montage of action clips.

The series was ahead of its time, but the scripts were too frivolous; it became more popular, decades later, as a retro relic. None of the music had a life beyond broadcast.

Made-for-TV movies initially began as prestige endeavors, but by the early 1970s most were potential series pilots or derivative action flicks. *Killer by Night* is both: an effort to find Robert Wagner a new series, following *It Takes a Thief*, and a low-rent retread of 1950's *Panic in the Streets*.

Dr. Larry Ross (Wagner), a communicable disease specialist at a Los Angeles hospital, attends a young woman who dies of diphtheria. Well aware of the potential for epidemic, Ross seeks help from the local police; unfortunately, the uncooperative Capt. George Benson (Greg Morris) is more concerned with a petty thief (Robert Lansing, as Claman) who killed two cops. No surprise: The cop-killer and Ross' diphtheria "index" (patient zero) turn out to be the same guy. The script is atrociously overcooked; Ross' frequent arguments with Benson are bad enough, but the poor doctor also gets static from live-in girlfriend Tracey (Diane Baker). Ah, but Ross gets his chance to become a hero, when at the climax he talks the by-now extremely sick Claman down from a potentially fatal confrontation with police.

Killer by Night was the first of Quincy Jones' five 1972 film scores. Lesser talents would have phoned in the results for this silly flick, but Jones took all of his assignments seriously, in part because he could design jazz scores that brought work to talented black musicians (who, at that time, still remained disproportionately underrepresented as Hollywood session players). His percussive title theme is a groove-laden, midtempo blues anthem with a dynamic beat; the melody is carried by muted trumpet, alongside nervous electric keyboard and guitar effects. Variations of this cue reprise throughout the film, the melody occasionally shadowed by harmonica riffs. Sharp-eared fans familiar with Jones' *oeuvre* will recognize several bars from his distinctive *Ironside* theme, when scores of police officers wait to see if Ross can persuade Claman to surrender.

Jones also composed a tender romantic ballad for Ross' quieter encounters with Tracey: a cue introduced on synthesizer, flute and harpsichord. An even softer arrangement later pops up as a diegetic cue heard from a phonograph, when compassionate cop Phil "Sharkey" Gold (Theodore Bikel) visits Tracey one evening. Other scenes boast incidental jazz riffs, such as a groovy blend of bass, guitar and harmonica, which accompanies Ross' initial visit to the diphtheria patient's apartment; and the dynamic blast of free jazz—heavy percussion, muted trumpet and impish woodwind touches—that anticipates the climax.

Jones' score finally was issued in 2011, paired on a disc with John Williams' score for *Nightwatch* (another failed TV pilot).

The Big Screen

The explosive success of *Shaft* launched dozens of blaxploitation imitators, most of which—as had been the case with Bond copycats—were low-budget quickies destined for rapid obscurity. A few, such as *Trouble Man*, endure due to the high-profile musicians enticed into scoring assignments. This humdrum crime thriller looks and sounds very much like an attitude-heavy retread of *Shaft*, which is no surprise; scripter John D.F. Black essentially repeats his own narrative template. *Trouble Man* would be long forgotten by now, were it not blessed with the sole film score by Motown R&B superstar Marvin Gaye.

The assignment came along just as Gaye became enchanted by the synthesizers that were becoming ubiquitous. He handles keyboards and drums and sings the title song; the resulting jazz/funk/R&B score is smooth as silk, although—arguably—it works better as a stand-alone album experience.

"I was listening to a great deal of Gershwin at the time, and I really wanted to do something great," Gaye recalled. "I was amazed at my concentration. It had never been this intense before. Working with the film images added to my inspiration."[2]

The plot finds Mr. T (Robert Hooks)—an inner-city private detective, pool hustler and go-to "fixer"—caught between rival gangs led by Big (Julius Harris) at one end of town, and partners Chalky (Paul Winfield) and Pete (Ralph Waite) at the other end. The latter two claim to need protection for their floating crap games, when in fact they intend to take down Big and frame Mr. T for the hit, leaving him to be arrested by surly LAPD Capt. Joe Marx (Bill Smithers). Fortunately, Mr. T is far too smart for such shenanigans.

A dramatic roll of drums kicks off the title song, as Gaye chuckles his way into the double-tracked vocal. This prologue montage is the film's highlight: Mr. T drives across Los Angeles, pausing in his apartment to "suit up," as Gaye allows the instrumental ensemble to crescendo. The first order of business is accepting a young hustler's challenge at the pool hall run by Jimmy (Bill Henderson). Two quick games are backed by diegetic cues emanating from the joint's radio: a jazz swinger fueled by a wall of brass, then a laid-back R&B anthem with plenty of synth and *wah-wah* guitars. A later visit with girlfriend Cleo (Paula Kelly) is backed by a sleepy, sultry melody built from horns, playful piano riffs and wickedly sexy sax. Gaye is equally adept at simple atmospheric cues: repeated sax or synth riffs that signal caution or danger; or the sad little piano and sax filigree heard when Mr. T phones Cleo to postpone a date.

Gaye ultimately unleashes a series of increasingly suspenseful jazz cues, when an angry Mr. T takes control during the blood-splattered third act. In the aftermath, sultry sax and a muted trumpet echo of the main theme back him, while he escorts yet another gorgeous young woman off the screen.

The soundtrack album is breathtaking. For openers, Gaye reworked his score cues into longer arrangements that give better exposure to Trevor Lawrence's superb sax work. The orchestrations are so far removed from their film score counterparts, as the tracks weave in and out of each other, that it's almost an entirely different experience.

"The *Trouble Man* film score was one of my loveliest projects," Gaye noted a few years later, with chilling prescience. "I enjoyed that job immensely; I enjoyed writing a film score. I'd love to do more. I'll probably be dead and gone before I get the probable acclaim from the *Trouble Man* album, the musical track, that I feel I should get."[3]

Mr. T had plenty of company, and *Shaft's Big Score* is the rare sequel that improves upon its predecessor. Richard Roundtree is more comfortable in the role, and the $2 million budget—considerably higher than the first film's $500,000—permitted superior production work and an exciting, action-packed climax. Isaac Hayes wasn't available to score this sophomore outing, although his presence is felt briefly; he also didn't allow the use of his iconic "Theme from *Shaft*." Returning director Gordon Parks instead assumed the musical reins, and the results certainly don't disappoint.

When Shaft's good friend Cal Asby is killed in an explosion, suspicion falls on the man's shifty partner in their combined insurance agency/funeral parlor, Johnny Kelly (Wally Taylor); he owes a lot of money to Italian mobster Gus Mascola (Joseph Mascolo). Shaft's misgivings are well placed; Kelly intended to settle his debt by stealing the considerable sum known to be in Asby's safe … but the money is gone. Stalling for time, Kelly offers partnerships with both Mascola and established Harlem gangster Bumpy Jonas (Moses Gunn), hoping the two rivals might kill each other. The scheme fails, and everybody is at each other's throats until the money is located where Cal hid it: in the coffin in which he later was buried. Shaft settles matters during a lengthy, action-packed battle against Mascola's minions.

The score differs from the gritty, street-level R&B that characterized Hayes' work on the first film. Parks slides more toward the lush, traditional swing of Count Basie or Duke Ellington … although you'd not expect that from the groovy title song ("Blowin' Your Mind"). It opens with pounding percussion, fuzz guitar, a smooth bass line and bad-ass lyrics—given cool bounce by vocalist O.C. Smith—and sounds like a second chapter to Hayes' title song.

The procession carrying Cal's coffin to its gravesite sways to a 4-4 strut highlighted by wailing sax and trumpet shading. Once Shaft is on the case, the investigation leads to the seductive Rita (Kathy Imrie); they flirt against a luxuriously erotic cue that opens with piano and vibes, before expanding with Ellington-esque strings and Freddie Hubbard's soft muted trumpet. Shaft later visits a nightclub dubbed Mother Ike's, and his prowl among the patrons is set against a new R&B groover from Isaac Hayes ("Type Thang") that perfectly captures the private eye's cool, feral allure. A terrific percussive theme boasting a vibrant horn solo slides into an instrumental reprise of the title theme, when Shaft later tails a car during the dead of night. All of this is prelude to the explosive finale, which Parks sets to an awesome chase cue in multiple movements (cheekily dubbed "Symphony for Shafted Souls"). Multiple cars, a speedboat and a helicopter get involved in this fracas, which builds to a literally explosive finale; keyboards and Hubbard's trumpet climb to a shrill crescendo that leaves viewers (and listeners) breathless.

The woefully abbreviated soundtrack album—barely 30 minutes of music—is dominated by O.C. Smith's three vocals and the "Symphony for Shafted Souls." The expanded digital release in 2008 is vastly superior.

John Shaft wasn't the only cool cat returning for a second round. *Cotton Comes to Harlem* (1970, see this book's companion volume) was popular enough to warrant a sequel, but the wincingly awful result put the final nail in the big-screen adventures of Coffin Ed and Grave Digger Jones. The first film may have turned them into comic cops, but *Come Back, Charleston Blue* makes them ludicrously stereotyped grotesques.

Grave Digger (Godfrey Cambridge) and Coffin Ed (Raymond St. Jacques) are confronted by a series of vicious murders that follow an intriguing pattern: All the victims are white criminals involved in the heroin trade. Each crime scene features a nasty calling-card: a blue-steel straight razor believed to belong to the legendary Charleston Blue, a long-dead vigilante who, back in the day, rid the neighborhood of all criminal elements. Somebody has resurrected this mythic champion, and evidence points to fashion photographer Joe Painter (Peter De Anda). He's dating Carol (Jonelle Allen), the feisty niece of Caspar Brown (Maxwell Glanville), an "Uncle Tom" errand boy for local Mafia don Frank Mago (Leonardo Cimino). After a series of mishaps and an ill-advised cemetery shoot-out, Grave Digger and Coffin Ed solve the case, with an assist from the regal "Her Majesty" (Minnie Gentry), who knew the actual Charleston Blue.

Music supervisor Quincy Jones gave the scoring assignment to jazz, blues and gospel singer/songwriter Donny Hathaway. Unfortunately, he had no concept of what a film score required, and the music is as uneven and unsatisfying as the film itself: a peculiar mix of old-timey jazz, Dixieland, big band swing and contemporary jazz/funk. A few cues reprise several times—not variations, but the *same exact cue*—and the repetition is quite noticeable.

Such weaknesses aside, high points include a society ballroom dance sequence, set against some slow, saucy big band swing in the classic Count Basie mold; a sleepy R&B cue that perfectly characterizes the neighborhood inhabitants starting their day early one morning; a great action cue—powered by dynamic horns—that fuels a sequence when a baddie blows up a warehouse; and the tense drumbeat and suspenseful horns that blossom into a cool funk cue, while Coffin Ed and Grave Digger tail a hearse that contains a highly suspicious casket.

The initial soundtrack album clumsily stitched many of Hathaway's short cues into single tracks: an ill-advised decision corrected by the 2007 digital reissue.

Although often included on lists of blaxploitation films, *Across 110th Street* doesn't warrant such placement; it's actually a bleak cop/crime drama, set against the social angst generated by the rising "black power" movement. The music is mostly soul; the score—and soundtrack album—give more weight to Bobby Womack's R&B vocals, than to J.J. Johnson's groove-laden instrumental tracks.

The story's parallel structure focuses on the upheaval taking place in early 1970s

Harlem, as African Americans demand more respect in all walks of life. In the local police precinct, racist Italian American cop Frank Mattelli (Anthony Quinn) bitterly resents his authority being superseded by newly arrived William Pope (Yaphet Kotto). On the criminal end, crime lord Doc (Richard Ward) is tired of being viewed as an underling to the Italian Mafia, personified by the similarly racist Nick D'Salvio (Tony Franciosa). The combustible twin dynamics explode when a Mafia-run Harlem "policy bank" is hit by three black freelancers—Jim Harris (Paul Benjamin), Joe Logart (Ed Bernard) and Henry Jackson (Antonio Fargas)—who slaughter seven men and make off with $300,000. They instantly become dead men walking; the question is whether old-school Mattelli and "college boy" Pope can find them, before they're butchered by D'Salvio and Doc.

Johnson's underscore includes numerous variations of the title song, but he also contributes a melancholy love theme for Harris and his girlfriend, Gloria (Norma Donaldson), when they imagine a happy, cash-fueled future that both know never will take place. This cue opens with contemplative synth riffs; the plaintive melody emerges on Hammond B3 and solo reeds, backed by gentle horns and Carol Kaye's tasty licks on acoustic double bass. When Logart is found by D'Salvio and his men, Johnson enhances the intensity with furious drums and frantic horns, the cue rising to a screaming climax when Logart races to the top of a building under construction ... and has nowhere to go.

The climactic melee kicks off when Harris—armed with a machine gun—tries to escape across Harlem rooftops. Johnson's lengthy cue for this brutal sequence is dominated by twitchy drums and jagged brass fanfares, with snippets of the main theme rising and falling amid the cacophony. The dismal aftermath is jolted by a final burst of violence and a freeze-frame, as the end credits roll against an even more mournful reprise of the love theme.

The soundtrack album is dominated by Womack's inappropriately cheerful vocals—given the film's grim tone—with only five tracks devoted to Johnson's contribution.

Quincy Jones' second score of the busy year complemented another cheeky heist thriller. Director Peter Yates' richly entertaining adaptation of *The Hot Rock* is highlighted by William Goldman's witty script, faithful to the plot and tone of Donald E. Westlake's 1970 caper novel. Robert Redford leads a top-flight assortment of well-cast scene stealers, and Jones assembled an equally stellar crew of jazz talent.

The New York City–based plot finds career criminal John Dortmunder (Redford) hired by United Nations diplomat Dr. Amusa (Moses Gunn) to "liberate" a fabulous gem—the Sahara Stone—on behalf of various African nations that regard it as sacred. The job appears simple, since the gem is being displayed in a museum with not-terribly-tight security. Dortmunder and his gang—locksmith Andy Kelp (George Segal), explosives expert Allan Greenberg (Paul Sand) and driver Stan Murch (Ron Leibman)—cleverly decoy the museum guards, gain access to the stone ... and then everything goes wrong. The increasingly harried Dr. Amusa winds up financing a series of supplementary heists, each with the goal of securing the same gem, which—thanks to fresh hiccups—eludes the gang every time.

Jones backs this whimsical caper with lighter versions of the "atmospheric jazz" he had composed for *$ (Dollars)*. He cleverly acknowledges the caper's cultural context by adding African-style percussion to a series of tension-laden cues. Most are heard when Dortmunder and his friends are in trouble or concocting fresh plans to retrieve the wayward diamond; the actual heist sequences remain unscored. Several cues also are adapted from the toe-tapping title credits theme, heard when Dortmunder is released from his most recent prison stretch. This tune opens with marching-style snare drums augmented by rhythmic bass and vocalese; the melody enters via Gerry Mulligan's tasty baritone sax. Electric keyboard introduces a countertheme during the bridge, and then the entire jazz crew resumes the core melody and brings the cue home.

Bobbi Porter's congas and bongos are backed by dissonant brass, reeds and African-hued percussion elements, while Dortmunder and Kelp case the museum, and then negotiate terms with Dr. Amusa. The score goes silent when the gang ingeniously penetrates the museum and snatches the gem, but their timing is off; a chaotic flight from the guards kicks off with furious bongos and alarmed brass riffs. After further complications, the gem winds up in a bank safe deposit box belonging to Greenberg's avaricious father, Abe (Zero Mostel). Fortunately, Dortmunder has one final ace to play. When he nervously walks out of the bank, gem in his pocket, Jones follows him with tentative percussion and Mulligan's slow reprise of the main theme; the tempo increases as Dortmunder clears the building and strolls down the sidewalk, his pace quickening in time to the music, a broad smile finally illuminating his face. Jones then shifts to some spirited *oom-pah* Dixieland twang, and the end credits scroll up the screen as each sideman gets a quick solo. In a respectful nod, the jazz soloists are credited right after the actors.

The soundtrack LP features just about all of Jones' music, with several tracks assembled from brief atmospheric cues. The album opens with a vocal version of the main theme—"Listen to the Melody," performed by the Ian Smith Singers—which isn't heard in the film. The 2018 Blu-ray includes an isolated score track.

The Hot Rock is frivolous; *The Getaway* is deadly serious. Based on a tough-as-nails 1958 Jim Thompson crime novel, the film became an enormous box-office hit that turned both director Sam Peckinpah and Steve McQueen into A-list superstars. It should have been composer Jerry Fielding's fourth big-screen collaboration with Peckinpah, following *The Wild Bunch*, *Straw Dogs* and *Junior Bonner*. He was delighted by Fielding's lean score, and he deemed it an integral part of the film; it previewed well, with the music drawing considerable praise. But McQueen was dissatisfied. He exerted pressure behind the scenes at the eleventh hour, and suddenly Fielding's score was dumped.[4] McQueen handed the assignment to his friend Quincy Jones, who had the daunting task of creating a full score in just two weeks. He also was limited to spotting only the scenes and sequences that Fielding had scored, since there was no time to reedit anything.

"Sam was delighted with the scoring on *The Getaway*," Fielding recalled. "Everybody was until Sam and Steve started having a war of some sort. And McQueen simply came in after I had finished the picture and rescored it. Sam did the best he could, and took out an ad in [*Daily Variety*]. But nothing changed. I got paid. But that wasn't why I wrote the music."[5]

The contemporary neo-*noir* thriller opens as career criminal Carter "Doc" McCoy (McQueen), serving time at Texas' Huntsville Prison, is denied parole. Unable to stand being cooped up, Doc sends his wife, Carol (Ali MacGraw), to cut a deal with Jack Benyon (Ben Johnson), a corrupt businessman with "influence" over the prison parole board. Doc is released, but at a price; Benyon wants him to mastermind the robbery of a local bank, for a split of the take. Doc and Carol are forced to accept two of Benyon's men—the homicidal Rudy (Al Lettieri) and greenhorn Frank (Bo Hopkins)—as part of the team. The robbery goes bad, although Doc and his team get away with the loot; Benyon, intending all along to double-cross him, orders Rudy to kill everybody else. Doc and Carol wind up on the run from cops, Benyon's various minions, and an enraged Rudy.

Jones' taut, lean score is effective both during the story's grim and suspenseful moments, and the calmer romantic scenes while Doc and Carol struggle to repair their estranged relationship. The title credits unfold against no music; Jones' score doesn't surface until after Doc is released, when he and Carol stroll in a park and then impulsively jump, fully clothed, into a nearby lake. The film's love theme debuts here: a tender jazz ballad dominated by Toots Thielemans' sensitive harmonica melody and backed by Dennis Budimir's guitar and Clare Fischer's synthesizer.

The atmosphere then become tense—supplemented by Harvey Mason's percussive effects, Dave Grusin's keyboard noodling, Ray Brown and Chuck Rainey's bass plucking, and the Don Elliott voices—when Doc lays out the planned bank job, with Rudy already exuding raw malevolence. Later, when Doc and Carol have fled, Jones supplies jittery cues for a sidebar sequence when she loses their satchel of money to a train station con artist. A twitchy blend of harmonica and percussion tracks Doc's seemingly impossible task of finding this guy and getting the money back. Similarly edgy cues back the climactic confrontations with Rudy and Benyon's goons.

The irony, all these years later, is irresistible: The entirety of Jerry Fielding's rejected score for *The Getaway* is readily available as an album, whereas Quincy Jones' replacement score—which accompanied the film—still awaits release. How often does *that* happen? (courtesy Film Score Monthly).

Jones' score was too spare to warrant a soundtrack album, although the love theme—now titled "Faraway Forever"—was released as a 45 single. Fielding's unused score cues survived and were released in 2005. The distinction is readily apparent: Fielding's work is light and "feathery," whereas Jones' efforts have a harder edge that better suits the story's grimmer elements.

Fielding was treated more respectfully on *The Mechanic*, a well-paced thriller that fueled Charles Bronson's rise to action-hero stardom. He plays Arthur Bishop, a veteran assassin who methodically researches his "marks" to deliver a result that—to the outside world—looks like death by misadventure or natural causes. Trouble arises when Bishop mentors the much younger Steve McKenna (Jan-Michael Vincent), a smugly amoral thrill-seeker who gets off on the suffering of others. Bishop's upper-echelon mob bosses resent this apprenticeship; betrayal and double-crosses lead to an unexpected—and unexpectedly swift—climax.

Fielding's score favors unsettling, percussion-driven texture and atmosphere. Two solid action cues spot deftly executed chase sequences, but they aren't really jazz. The prominent diegetic music is classical; Bishop listens to Beethoven while researching each new target. That being the case, the film's inclusion would be unwarranted here ... were it not for the score's 2007 release. The disc includes six diegetic cues that are solid big band jazz, which prompts the obvious question: Where are they in the movie? Answer: quite hard to find.

Perhaps 15 seconds of the cheerful, Latin-esque "Baja Band—Mexico Jazz" can be heard, *very* faintly, from behind a closed apartment door toward the film's beginning. "The Party" and "Beach House Jump," both keyboard- and electric guitar-driven acid jazz, serve as background music when McKenna's equally shallow friends throw a sybaritic party.

The 2014 Blu-ray includes a complete isolated score track.

Crime novelist Ed McBain was lucky enough to see three of his early 87th Precinct police thrillers—*Cop Hater*, *The Mugger* and *The Pusher*—made into solid (if low-budget) *noir* thrillers between 1958 and '60. It's therefore surprising that *Fuzz* is the only other

Composer Jerry Fielding's two best big band jazz cues were left behind when *The Mechanic* was released: a saucy, slow-tempo swinger titled "Let's Get Together Again," with a trumpet-driven main theme; and the faster-paced "Romping," which boasts vibrant horns, along with choice flute and piano solos. Both are available on the soundtrack album (courtesy Intrada Inc.).

American big-screen feature adapted from what became an enormously popular 55-book series. McBain's script excessively condenses his book's ingenious overlapping storylines, and director Richard A. Colla's tone occasionally veers toward slapstick, but the ensemble cast remains true to the chaos that frequently envelops the overworked police precinct of McBain's books. The film also benefits from Dave Grusin's propulsive, funk-laden jazz score; the music's intensity often compensates for the jokey touches.

A couple of ongoing cases become sidebars when the squad receives a phone call from an extortionist who promises to kill the city parks commissioner unless a $5,000 ransom is paid. The threat isn't taken seriously, until the parks commissioner *is* killed; a fresh extortion note then promises to kill the deputy mayor unless a $50,000 ransom is paid. The scheme is being masterminded by the "Deaf Man" (Yul Brynner), the precinct's ongoing *bête noire* in McBain's book series. Detectives Steve Carella (Burt Reynolds), Meyer Meyer (Jack Weston), Bert Kling (Tom Skerritt), Arthur Brown (James McEachin) and Andy Parker (Steve Ihnat) work through various leads, assisted by visiting detective Eileen McHenry (Raquel Welch), on loan to help catch a park rapist.

Grusin's exhilarating title theme debuts over the subway journey that brings Det. McHenry to the precinct; her trip is accompanied by funkified percussion, swinging bass and a driving 6-6-8-6 flute melody backed by suspenseful brass. Music always is absent during the many interior precinct sequences; Grusin's touches are limited to the outside world. Lazy bass and reeds follow Carella, dressed as a bum, when he tries to draw out a pair of lethal arsonists; twitchy treble piano and bass riffs later accompany McHenry's solo assignment, when she successfully entices the park rapist; plenty of groove-laden percussion and electric guitar follow the Deaf Man's gang, when they case the city mayor's mansion. Sheer coincidence ultimately brings multiple cases together, granting the cops several unexpected victories. They head back to the precinct as the end credits roll against Dinah Shore's bluesy rendition of the Billie Holiday classic "I'll Be Seeing You."

No soundtrack album emerged, and the score is unlikely to surface; the masters are believed lost.[6] Tenor sax legend Gene Ammons covered the title theme on his 1973 Prestige album, *Big Bad Jug*, turning the cue into a slow, 16-bar groover with a new 8-bar bridge.

Prime Cut is a notoriously lurid crime thriller from director Michael Ritchie and scripter Robert Dillon: an economical exercise in sexist sadism that couldn't possibly be made today. The bare-bones story finds Chicago enforcer Nick Devlin (Lee Marvin) sent to Kansas City, where slaughterhouse owner Mary Ann (Gene Hackman) has been neglecting to send the syndicate's share of his drug and prostitution side ventures. Mary Ann and his deranged brother Weenie (Gregory Walcott) have a habit of turning unwanted visitors into sausage; they also kidnap innocent local women and "sell" them, stripped naked, from cattle pens. One such waif, dubbed Poppy (Sissy Spacek, in an ill-advised acting debut), touches Nick's heart; his determination to rescue her complicates matters while subsequently dealing with Mary Ann and his hick gunsels.

Ritchie apparently had little use for Lalo Schifrin's score, which is barely evident throughout most of the film. That changes abruptly during the third act's climactic melee, when Nick and his associates play cat-and-mouse with Mary Ann's thugs in a massive field of sunflowers; Schifrin enhances this suspenseful sequence with propulsive action jazz right out of his *Bullitt* and *Dirty Harry* playbook. This musical intensity continues when Nick successfully penetrates Mary Ann's lair, leading to a thoroughly satisfying finale. In the aftermath, Nick and Poppy head back to Chicago, where he has promised to introduce her to big-city ways; the end credits roll against a cue in Schifrin's Americana mode, evoking his work on *Cool Hand Luke*.

The score was insufficient to warrant a soundtrack album, although a few isolated cues—ripped from DVDs—are easy to find via the Internet.

* * *

Although best known for his high-concept science-fiction novels, one of Michael Crichton's earliest books is a detective thriller. Concealed behind the pseudonym Jeffry Hudson, he published *A Case of Need* in 1969, the same year he graduated from Harvard Medical School. Production on the big-screen adaptation, *The Carey Treatment*, was notoriously acrimonious; the completed film was removed from director Blake Edwards' control and savagely edited down to 101 minutes, leaving essential exposition on the cutting-room floor. Even so, the narrative remains engaging.

Pathologist Peter Carey (James Coburn) begins a new job at a Boston Hospital, where he's reunited with longtime friend Dr. David Tao (James Hong). The latter is arrested for murder after the hospital head's 15-year-old daughter dies following a botched abortion; Tao is known to clandestinely perform this still-illegal procedure. But the medical details of the girl's death raise too many questions, on top of Carey's refusal to believe that his friend—a skilled surgeon—could have butchered any patient so badly. The subsequent inquiry makes the cocky, arrogant Carey look and sound like an outspoken, Chandler-esque private dick in lab whites, rather than anything remotely resembling a doctor.

The film marked the Hollywood debut of British soundtrack composer Roy Budd, whose cool jazz score conceals some of the story's expository lapses. Trumpet fanfares herald the main theme, powered by ferocious drums that back a melody traded between electric keyboard, flutes and sizzling strings. Carey and hospital dietician Georgia Hightower (Jennifer O'Neill) enjoy a double date with David and his wife at a club that boasts an off-camera piano trio, playing a delicious bit of slow blues; Carey's subsequent interludes with Georgia are accompanied by a gentle piano melody that reprises as the film proceeds. Budd delivers more aggressive action cues as the story demands, particularly during Carey's appalling treatment of the dead girl's roommate. Later, when Carey zeroes in on the actual killer(s), Budd's cues become more orchestral and textured; jazz doesn't return until the end credits reprise of the uptempo main theme.

Budd's score finally was digitized in 2005, in a double-CD "Crichton package" that includes Fred Karlin's score for 1973's *Westworld*, and Jerry Goldsmith's score for 1978's *Coma*. The *Carey Treatment* segment includes plenty of nifty jazz cues heard only briefly during the film or left behind after the hack-and-slash editing.

Crichton's literary star was ascending just as Helen MacInnes' fame was receding. Her brand of romance-soaked spyjinks simply didn't translate well to the big screen, and *The Salzburg Connection* is by far the worst of a bad lot. The script makes no sense, with its multiplicity of agents, double agents and triple agents, all working for a plethora of countries; it's impossible to separate the friendlies from the enemies.

The bizarre plot finds vacationing American lawyer Bill Mathison (Barry Newman) sucked into the deadly pursuit of a long-hidden chest that contains dangerous World War II documents, which could expose former Nazis who've "blended" throughout the world. He winds up trying to protect Anna (Anna Karina), wife of the free-lance photographer who recovers the chest from the bottom of an Austrian lake; he and various other vaguely identified individuals are killed by ... well, that's difficult to say. Additional duplicity and mild romantic tension are supplied by Elissa Lang (Karen Jensen), supposedly a young American traveling to celebrate her university graduation, but actually a KGB spy who ultimately betrays *her* colleagues. (Maybe. Perhaps.)

The scoring assignment went to Academy Award-winning composer Bronislau Kaper, a longtime Hollywood veteran lured out of semi-retirement; this became his final big-screen credit. The majority of his music is symphonic, as befits the film's travelogue approach, but Kaper does supply some mildly stimulating jazz here and there, in a (fruitless) effort to heighten ham-fisted suspense sequences. Some gently swinging percussion, bass and brass enliven Mathison's first brush with peril, when he's unknowingly pursued by a baddie; the most dynamic burst of jazz enhances a car chase, when Anna is kidnapped and Mathison hijacks another vehicle to follow. The final bit of action jazz comes during a mountain-climbing assault, spotted with a cue that sounds like something Henry Mancini could have written for TV's *Peter Gunn*.

No soundtrack album appeared.

Meanwhile, Across the Pond...

As the new decade progressed, Britain's love affair with whimsical espionage shows such as *The Avengers* and *Jason King* waned, in favor of more realistic, hard-hitting dramas. The ITV police procedural *New Scotland Yard* focuses on Det. Chief Superintendent John

Kingdom (John Woodvine), who with Det. Sgt. Alan Ward (John Carlisle) tackles a variety of contemporary, issue-oriented crimes that frequently lead to ambiguous conclusions: Was a confession forced, and therefore inadmissible in court? Was police brutality involved? *New Scotland Yard* was one of the first dramas to alter the perception of the British copper: away from the friendly, paternal "bobby" typified by the character Jack Warner played for two decades, in *Dixon of Dock Green*; and more toward the conflicted plain-clothes detective sometimes willing to turn rogue in the pursuit of justice.

The series ran four seasons after its April 22 debut, the final one with replacement characters DCS Clay (Michael Turner) and Det. Sgt. Dexter (Clive Francis). The peppy 45-second title theme plays over a swiftly edited montage of London, while a police vehicle navigates the city streets: first during daylight hours, then abruptly shifting to nighttime. The melody's 1-4-2 motif, delivered by unison brass, initially sounds cheerful. But after a few reprises, a rising crescendo of horns follows the vehicle as it approaches the show's title, seemingly painted on the street. The shift to late-night pursuit signals another rising brass crescendo; three concluding fanfares climb the scale when the final image freezes on the iconic rotating sign that identifies New Scotland Yard.

That theme and the show's minimal underscores were drawn from the Standard Music Library, which had been created in 1968 by London Weekend Television (ITV) and the Bucks Music Group, specifically to supply themes and cues for all manner of audio-visual productions.[7] As a result, no musicians are credited on this series, which is rather unfair to Max Harris; the *New Scotland Yard* title theme is an abbreviated arrangement of his frisky jazz tune "Eurocrat," absent its toe-tapping introduction and swinging brass bridge. It can be found on library compilation albums such as Codename Music's 2001 release, *Girl in a Suitcase*.

Harris remains mostly unknown, which certainly isn't the case with John Barry. His sleek title theme is about the only highlight of *The Adventurer*, an inept spy series that debuted September 29 and limped through a single ITV season; the scripts are incomprehensible. Star Gene Barry was imported to facilitate sales in the American market, but—approaching his mid–50s—he's much too old to be credible as a jet-setting secret agent posing as a movie star, who catches the fancy of every young lovely who crosses his path.

That said, John Barry's title theme is mesmerizing in a manner similar to what he did with *The Persuaders*: in this case, a hypnotic melody delivered by synthesizer and mandolin, against a pulsating rhythm section so low that—given the proper surround-sound equipment—it would rattle the walls. The theme is built around an introductory 5-8 motif, followed by a trio of 1-3 passages; this plays against the usual montage of the show's star doing spy-type stuff ... like scowling at paperwork. Barry had nothing to do with the unremarkable underscores, all of which are credited to Paul B. Clay. The series didn't generate a soundtrack LP, although Barry did expand his title theme for a Polydor single; that version is included on the 2009 digital rerelease of his album, *Americans*. The original TV title and end credits arrangements are featured on Network's 2009 two-disc set, *The Music of ITV*.

The Adventurer's half-hour episodes always feel like longer storylines arbitrarily ripped into unfathomable shreds, but that isn't the case with ATV's *The Protectors*, one of Britain's final half-hour action/espionage dramas. British composer, arranger, conductor and musician John Cameron brings a lot of swinging pizzazz to the series: something of a welcome home for former U.N.C.L.E. agent Robert Vaughn, who stars as London-based American Harry Rule, head of a team of private investigators specializing in the security of innocents. The firm's international flavor is characterized by Harry's cohorts. The Contessa Caroline di Contini (Nyree Dawn Porter), based in Italy, is an expert in art fraud; Frenchman Paul Buchet (Tony Anholt), a researcher and gadget whiz, resides in Paris. Dangerous missions take the trio all over the world: seeking a concealed cluster of former Nazis; preventing the kidnapping of a president; locating a scientist who has disappeared with a biological weapon; trying to stop a deranged Vietnam war veteran before he kills somebody; and so forth. The engaging show ran two seasons after its September 29 debut.

The vibrant title song—"Avenues and Alleyways," sung by Tony Christie—is heard during the *end* credits montage. A full-length version of the tune became a minor hit during a four-week run on the British pop charts in early 1973. Cameron delivers a swinging instrumental arrangement for the opening credits montage, which blends fleeting action footage with clips of Vaughn's Harry at home, enjoying breakfast alongside his faithful dog. Cameron's instrumentation and a driving rhythm section are far more dynamic than the simplistic melody, built mostly from numerous reprises of a 1-1-3 motif.

Given the accelerated pace at which stories are introduced and build to a climax, Cameron's underscore cues are an important means of bridging scenes and conveying the passage of time. He's equally adept at saucy big band swingers; gentle bossa nova ballads highlighted by tasty saxes or flutes; fast-paced blasts of brass for action sequences; sultry lounge instrumentals; funky groovers backed by *wah-wah* guitar riffs; and even rowdy jazz/rock dance tunes heard as diegetic music in the frequently visited discothèques.

The show didn't initially produce a soundtrack album, but Cameron finally got long-overdue respect with the 2009 release of *The Protectors: Original Soundtrack*, a sumptuous five-disc set containing all of the series' 364 cues. Unlike the similar sets for *Danger Man* and *The Saint*, where Edwin Astley's atmospheric cues quickly become repetitive, Cameron's efforts offer a great deal more variety, and in many cases can be appreciated as melodies in their own right.

* * *

On the big screen, Johnny Keating's third and final score was written for *Innocent Bystanders*, a spy thriller adapted by James Mitchell from his 1969 novel. Although a serious genre entry, the muddled script requires a road map to track the various intelligence entities and individuals who do or don't like each other, seemingly at random, from one moment to the next. Despite this, Keating's swinging orchestral score definitely gives the action a propulsive lift.

John Craig (Stanley Baker) is a veteran agent for a clandestine British Intelligence branch run by the stuffy Loomis (Donald Pleasance). Craig's age is showing, and he finds it hard to keep up with disrespectful younger colleagues Royce (Derren Nesbitt) and Benson (Sue Lloyd). Craig is offered one last shot at job relevance: to locate and retrieve scientist Aaron Kaplan (Vladek Sheybal), who recently escaped from a Russian gulag and is believed to be hiding somewhere in Turkey. Unfortunately, Kaplan also is wanted by all sorts of other people: Loomis' American counterpart, Blake (Dana Andrews); various KGB agents; and an organization of Russian Jews infuriated by the fact that Kaplan betrayed his comrades during the aforementioned escape. The torturous mission roams from London to New York, then to Turkey and Cypress, and Craig is double-crossed by friend and foe alike; his only "ally" is Miriam Loman (Geraldine Chaplin), a reluctant hostage who eventually falls in love with her captor.

The score's primary cue is an instrumental version of "What Makes the Man," a Keating song eventually given a bluesy vocal spin by Norman "Hurricane" Smith. The tune otherwise propels various car chases and action scenes, in exhilarating arrangements that favor guitar, percussion and a rowdy bank of horns; a frequent trumpet fanfare evokes (deliberately?) John Barry's introductory blast of horns for his *Thunderball* title theme. Other notable cues include propulsive action jazz choreographed to Craig's huffing, puffing efforts to best Royce and Benson during training sessions; a lyrical melody played on jazz flute, and backed by soft strings and woodwinds, as Miriam grows fond of her rough and rugged companion; and the exhilarating musical rush, powered by guitar- and trumpet-fueled gusto, which erupts during the climactic shoot-out at a luxurious cliffside home.

No soundtrack album or single emerged.

Roy Budd's equally stimulating blasts of vibrant orchestral jazz similarly grant *Fear Is the Key* more zest than it deserves. Having become a cult fave in 1971's *Vanishing Point*, thanks to the film-length car chase he led in a Dodge Challenger R/T, it's no surprise that Barry Newman soon found himself in another audaciously choreographed vehicular pursuit. This one screams through the swampland, back roads and sandy beaches of Louisiana, with Newman piloting a Ford Gran Torino while wreaking havoc with the police cars in his wake. Not long after the title credits, *Fear Is the Key* roars into this breathtaking 10-minute sequence, which gets additional *oomph* via split-second timing to Budd's exhilarating symphony of percussion and brass. Sadly, although director Michael Tuchner's subsequent drama faithfully follows the 1961 Alistair MacLean novel on which it's based, the rest of the film is as flat and lifeless as its characters.

The complex plot begins when drifter John Talbot (Newman) kicks up a fuss in a small Louisiana town, gets arrested and then escapes from his courtroom trial with a hostage in tow (Suzy Kendall). All of this turns out to be subterfuge: a means of persuading the villainous Vyland (John Vernon) that Talbot is equally larcenous. Once made a member of the gang, Talbot learns that Vyland is supervising some sort of salvage operation that involves a submersible anchored at an oil platform off the Louisiana coast. But even this isn't the actual reason for Talbot's presence, which only becomes clear during the claustrophobic climax.

Budd's title theme is built from a repeating 3-6 motif backed by sultry sax and trumpet riffs. (The cue has a slightly mournful quality that ultimately makes sense during the story's climactic revelations.) The musical backdrop to the aforementioned car chase begins with anticipatory percussion, then kicks into full throttle while Talbot and a terrified Sarah tear up the countryside; frantic trumpet fanfares, savage bass licks and throbbing drums yield to Ronnie Scott's sensational sax solo. Later, after Talbot has ingratiated himself with the gang, he briefly slips away to report his progress to waiting associates; Budd spots this clandestine rendezvous with a tense blend of percussion and Tubby Hayes' jazz flute. Everything builds to a confrontation aboard the submersible; somber strings and Hayes' flute clock approaching death by oxygen deprivation, and then—in an unsatisfying rush—the film just sort of stops. Budd delivers a final variation of the main theme when the end credits roll.

Two diegetic cues stand out: a bluesy little tune with a country-twang edge, dominated by Budd's savage keyboard work, and heard from a campsite radio; and a faster jazz melody—again allowing Budd to show off his awesome chops—emanating from a drive-in coffee shop's PA system.

The soundtrack album is highlighted by full-length arrangements of the two diegetic cues—"Louisiana Ferry" and "Bayou Blues"—and the 10-minute jazz symphony that powers the lengthy car chase. Unfortunately, the latter track is marred by sound effects: the car's ignition turning over, screeching tires, police sirens and occasional collisions. (Who *makes* a production decision that daft?)

Elsewhere in the World

Writer/director Jean-Pierre Melville's *Un Flic* (released in the States as *Dirty Money*) is a profound disappointment, coming from a filmmaker with so many terrific *noir* entries on his résumé. This lackluster, by-the-numbers drama is betrayed by a limited budget and a derivative plot; worse yet, the improbable heist sequence is ruined by too many establishing shots of a model train and toy helicopter. (Seriously? In 1972?) Melville also abuses Michel Colombier's fine score, overlooking several great jazz cues likely intended as diegetic music.

The investigation of a botched bank robbery falls to Commissaire Edouard Coleman (Alain Delon), a world-weary cop who derives some joy from visits to a nightclub run by his friend Simon (Richard Crenna); the club's hostess, Cathy (Catherine Deneuve), loves both men. Edouard has been gathering information about a heroin shipment scheduled to be sent out of the country via the night express train from Paris to Lisbon, and he hopes to bust the courier en route. As it happens, Simon—who masterminded the failed bank robbery—intends to steal the same drugs shipment. The heist is successful, but Edouard deduces his friend's involvement. Simon, holed up in a hotel with two heroin-laden suitcases, arranges for Cathy to collect him; Edouard arrives simultaneously, and the two men confront each other on an empty city street while she watches, frozen, in her parked car.

Colombier's score blends sleek combo jazz cues with melancholy orchestral passages and a few sad piano solos, the latter enhancing the film's atmosphere of misery and impending tragedy. This becomes clear during Edouard's first visit to the nightclub, when he sits at the piano and plucks out a lovely, wistful solo. The somber cues are offset by a series of solid jazz swingers, starting with the quartet number heard briefly on a car radio—the melody traded between muted trumpet and lazy piano—as Simon and his accomplices prepare to rob the bank. Unfortunately, we can barely hear the music against the ambient roar of pelting rain and gusting wind; this is typical of Melville's careless handling of Colombier's more vibrant cues.

No soundtrack album accompanied the film's release, although two instrumental cues appeared on a 45 single. Colombier's full score finally earned release in 2013, paired on a disc with Georges Delerue's work on 1963's *L'Aîné des Ferchaux*. The *Un Flic* highlights are two lovely cues left unused by Melville: "Nightclub, trois heures du matin," a sexy ballad with the melody traded between acoustic piano and electric keyboard; and chanteuse Isabelle Aubert's smoky torch song—"C'est ainsi que les choses arrivent (That's How Things Happen)"—which is backed by a soulful trumpet quartet.

3

Last Dance in Sausalito: 1973

Mike Post was a youthful rock 'n' roll songwriter/producer when he bumped into 55-year-old jazz trombonist/arranger Pete Carpenter at an industry golf tournament, resulting in an immediate personal and professional bond. "[It was] the best partnership that this town has ever known," Post recalled. "We worked together 18 years, and wrote approximately 1,800 hours of television together. We never had a contract; we never had a handshake; we never had an argument; we never had an unkind word between us. All of his friends thought that he was carrying me; all of my friends thought that I was carrying him. I never knew who wrote what; he never gave a damn who wrote what."[1] The partnership ended only because Carpenter died of lung cancer in October 1987.

Their impact over the next two decades would be *huge*.

The Small Screen

By the early 1970s, Joseph Wambaugh had become synonymous with intelligent police dramas. He was 11 years into his career with the Los Angeles Police Department when his debut novel, 1971's *The New Centurions*, became a popular best-seller. Two books later, he created NBC's *Police Story*, still one of the medium's most rigorously authentic depictions of rank-and-file law enforcement officers. The show was a critical hit; it also revived the anthology format, as most episodes are one-off dramas. The series began with a pilot film that aired March 20; it was picked up on a weekly basis that autumn. Semi-regular two-hour telefilms continued after the initial four-season run.

Jerry Goldsmith scored the pilot film and most first-season episodes, establishing a hard-edged musical template subsequently replicated by (primarily) Richard Markowitz, Richard Shores and Robert Drasnin. Since every episode is a self-contained minimovie, almost all first- and second-season entries earned original underscores. That said, the series' documentary-style approach eschewed conventional non-diegetic scoring, and there's no title theme; each episode's credits are superimposed over the introductory action, while an off-camera police dispatcher rattles off a series of alerts, messages and requests for assistance. Goldsmith's gritty main theme plays at length only during the end credits, with *wah-wah* guitar and a rhythmic bass ostinato backing the midtempo anthem: a mildly somber melody carried by woodwinds until a final jarring, four-note explosion of brass that feels like gunfire.

Variations of this theme are sprinkled throughout the pilot film and episode underscores; tempo and instrumentation vary according to dramatic requirements. Most other cues are brief bits of orchestral shading and atmospheric texture, although Goldsmith occasionally slides into quasi-jazz. This pattern holds throughout the series, regardless of composer; unlike most TV shows, it simply wouldn't have felt right for these characters to be followed by an invisible orchestra.

No soundtrack album appeared until 2000, with a disc that features Goldsmith's main theme and underscore cues for the pilot film, along with a dozen "library variation cues" arranged and conducted by Shores.

Wambaugh's cops may not have moved to music, but ABC's *Toma* has plenty of melodic snap. Post and Carpenter began their partnership with this gritty, fact-based police drama; it's adapted from the life and career of David Toma, a lone wolf undercover detective with the Newark, New Jersey, police department. Star Tony Musante brilliantly conveys the man's agitated intensity, along with a talent for submerging himself in master-of-disguise personas that allow him to cozy up to drug dealers, gangbangers and sketchy types from every level of the criminal hierarchy.

Jerry Goldsmith scored a staggering number of film and television scores during a career that lasted half a century, and concluded only with his death in 2004. He earned a whopping 18 Academy Award nominations, winning only once, for 1976's *The Omen*; he also won five of his seven Emmy Award nominations (Photofest).

Pete Rugolo scored the spring 1973 pilot film, giving the character and setting an urban funk ambiance; this served as a template for Post and Carpenter, when the series debuted later that year.

Their *Toma* title theme opens with a cow bell that takes eight beats, at which point *wah-wah* guitars—and a pounding 4/4 rhythm section—back a bold brass melody with a 1-1-4-2 motif. Unlike many TV themes, this one doesn't beat a single motif to death; the unison brass fanfare blossoms into a multilayered melody with swinging counterpoint, against clips of Musante in a variety of disguises. The final crescendo of guitar and brass is breathtaking, and absolutely "street." Post and Carpenter adopted a "less is more" approach to underscores; tone and instrumentation are predominantly swinging, inner-city grooves, with softer orchestrations for quieter, intimate moments. Occasional harmonica licks anticipate what the duo soon would write for *The Rockford Files*; action sequences earn throbbing cues fueled by unison horns.

No single or soundtrack LP emerged.

Despite its popularity, *Toma* ran only a single season; Musante was unwilling to commit to an ongoing role. ABC flirted with the notion of recasting the show's lead; what eventually emerged, half a year later, was a sorta/kinda new series—*Baretta*—that satisfied everybody's expectations.[2]

Toma relied on disguises; Telly Savalas' New York Police Lt. Theodore "Theo" Kojak made lollipops as hip as his natty suits and signature endearment—"Who loves ya, baby?"—during five seasons of CBS' *Kojak*. A pair of TV movies followed in 1985 and '87, along with a quintet of telefilms in 1989 and '90.

The character was introduced in March 1973, in the acclaimed TV docudrama *The Marcus-Nelson Murders*. Billy Goldenberg scored this film, and he remained part of the package when Kojak and his lollipops turned into weekly must-see TV, starting October 24, but the show's title theme—despite a solid rhythm section and *wah-wah* guitar—is surprisingly bland. Goldenberg delivered an even more string-heavy arrangement after the show had become a hit. John Cacavas handled the lion's share of episode underscores, which flirt only occasionally with jazz.

As the fifth season dawned, Cacavas wrote a new title theme to stall the ratings slide. Although boasting a much bolder use of brass, this fresh tune suffers from the pernicious presence of aggressive *thump-thump* disco elements which, by 1977, had become pervasive. Willie Bobo's cover of Goldenberg's original theme (Blue Note) is an eyebrow-lifting blend of disco and R&B; far better arrangements came from across the pond, courtesy of John Gregory (Philips) and Ray Davies (DJM).

The show was rebooted in 2005 on the USA Network, but disinterest killed this update after only nine episodes. Ving Rhames handled the lollipop with appropriate 'tude, but the scripts—and music—didn't speak to viewers.

CBS came late to the "wheel" format, with a single-season Tuesday evening timeslot that rotated between telefilms, a small-screen adaptation of *Shaft*, and James Stewart's eight-episode run as a small-town West Virginia defense attorney, in *Hawkins*. Although the latter's music favors folksy, homespun Americana texturing that matches Stewart's slow-talking, laid-back performance, mention must be made of Jerry Goldsmith's title theme: an uptempo swinger dominated by a driving rhythm section, a twangy, then-new Minimoog analog synthesizer, and an endearingly catchy melody introduced by reeds, and repeated by sparkling brass.

Richard Roundtree's take-no-prisoners private investigator was bowdlerized when brought to television; under no circumstances could the "bad muthah sex machine to all the chicks" do his usual "thang" without violating network censorship standards. The producers kept Roundtree and Isaac Hayes' iconic title theme—albeit without any lyrics—but this small-screen *Shaft* limped along for only seven episodes after its October 9 debut, since the character was tamed into utter blandness. His wardrobe is "upgraded" to tailored suits that his big-screen counterpart wouldn't be caught dead in, and—furthering the insult—Shaft maintains a comradely relationship with a white police lieutenant (Ed Barth).

On the other hand, this Shaft's soundtrack is as cool as ever. The assignment went to Johnny Pate, a one-time jazz bassist who had blossomed into a go-to producer and arranger in the Chicago R&B and soul movement. He was fresh from his work on *Shaft in Africa*, which had hit theaters four months earlier. Pate ensured a continuity of groovy jazz that is faithful to Hayes, and far funkier—and grittier—than most of the whitewashed screen action. Quotes from Hayes' theme are ubiquitous during brawls, car chases and establishing montages: often via inventive arrangements, unexpected tempos and clever combinations of instruments. Pate wrote full scores for the first three episodes; the remaining four are partially or fully tracked. Hypnotic *wah-wah* guitar licks are as ubiquitous as Roundtree himself; each episode also finds an excuse for the staccato 5-6 brass fanfare. Pate similarly excels at sultry brass and sax ballads for romantic encounters with obliging "chicks."

No soundtrack appeared until 2008's three-disc *Shaft Anthology: His Big Score and More!*, which includes every cue Pate wrote and arranged for Shaft's TV adventures.

John Shaft wasn't the only African American detective introduced to TV viewers this year, although few remember his kinder, gentler rival. *Tenafly* lasted only four episodes after its October 10 debut, becoming one of the failed spokes in NBC's *Mystery Movie* wheels. James McEachin is note-perfect as Harry Tenafly, a happily married suburban family man who works as one of many field agents at corporate-styled Hightower Investigations. Much of the show's charm derives from the contrast between Tenafly's amiably harried home life, and the shrewd intelligence and instincts with which he solves his cases.

Gil Mellé's title theme is a terrific little swinger that begins with a mocking muted trumpet statement, while Tenafly navigates front yard kid clutter during a typical morning, while trying to back out of the driveway; the cue blossoms into a saucy anthem—playing over the show's opening act, rather than within a distinct credits sequence—with the melody carried by unison horns against a lively rhythm section. Reeds supply a brief countermelody until the horns resume, with the theme fading out after a final plaintive bleat from the muted trumpet. Melle also handled the underscores, which are sparse but offer the same jazz pep. His music had no life beyond broadcast.

Networks always seek new gimmicks, and CBS' *Barnaby Jones* was the first of many "geezer detectives" who simultaneously ambled onto TV screens during the 1973–74 season, alongside Billy Jim Hawkins (James Stewart), Wade Griffin (Lorne Green) and Ernesta and Gwendolyn Snoop (Helen Hayes and Mildred Natwick). Unlike most of the others, ol' Barnaby gets some jazz-inflected swagger courtesy of a peppy title theme from Jerry Goldsmith, who also scored the pilot episode.

The series begins when Barnaby abandons retirement and resumes his former career as a private investigator, to track down the man who killed his son, who had taken over the family detective business. Once back in the saddle, Barnaby decides that retirement was premature; support is provided by grieving daughter-in-law Betty (Lee Meriwether), who becomes his full-time assistant. The CBS show's eight-season run rarely veered from an investigative approach that relies heavily on Barnaby's sharp perception and amiably homespun decorum, the latter deceiving smug culprits much the way Peter Falk's Columbo lulls *his* suspects into a false sense of superiority.

Goldsmith's title theme opens with a blast of French horns against an exhilarating rhythm section, and then introduces the core 9-8 motif via six alto flutes. (The music is far more exciting than the dull credits sequence that "builds" the show's title, in the manner of a jigsaw puzzle coming together.) A shorter end credits arrangement concludes with a final blast of horns; a harpsichord is prominent in Goldsmith's underscore cues, many based on the title theme. Well over two dozen composers followed Goldsmith, but the series' tone and approach rarely warranted anything beyond basic orchestral texturing.

Goldsmith's title theme and underscore—along with a second episode underscore by Bruce Broughton—finally were digitized and released in 2019, as part of *The Quinn Martin Collection, Volume 1: Cop and Detective Series*.

Writer/producer Stephen J. Cannell's *Chase* is a failed attempt at a concept he developed far more successfully years later, with *The A-Team*. This earlier NBC show's title refers both to primary character Chase Reddick (Mitchell Ryan), who heads an "unorthodox" team of cops within the Los Angeles Police Department; and the fact that each episode features high-octane chases involving anything with an engine. Reddick's colleagues initially include K-9 Sgt. Sam MacCray (Wayne Maunder), former Vietnam War chopper pilot Norm Hamilton (Reid Smith), hot-rod enthusiast Steve Baker (Michael Richardson) and motorcycle racer Fred Sing (Brian Fong). When the series failed to catch, a midseason makeover replaced the latter three with comparatively "ordinary" cops Ed Rice (Gary Crosby) and Tom Wilson (Craig Gardner).

Oliver Nelson's bold title theme opens with a double-time rhythm section and then introduces a 2-4-10 motif via unison strings and horns; reprises are punctuated by rapid brass fanfares. The theme is more or less synchronized to a montage of fast-moving vehicles, intercut with tight close-ups of the stars, all of them hilariously grim. Nelson also supplied most of the show's original underscores; the frequent chases prompt plenty of sizzling action jazz cues, often highlighted by funkified *wah-wah* guitar.

Alas, the series couldn't chase good ratings, and Nelson's music vanished after the single disappointing season.

His jazz chops also weren't given much of a workout in *The Alpha Caper*, a modest made-for-TV heist flick intended as the pilot for an anthology series to be called *Crime*, which would have followed a supposedly foolproof criminal endeavor from start to an unexpectedly flawed conclusion.[3] The series didn't sell, although ABC aired the film on October 6; it remains mildly noteworthy for its modestly clever script, and the swinging cues that Nelson inserts during the third act.

After veteran parole officer Mark Forbes (Henry Fonda) is ordered into an undesired retirement after four decades of loyal service, he angrily masterminds an audacious heist with the assistance of his favorite ex-cons: Mitch (Leonard Nimoy), Scat (James McEachin) and Tudor (Larry Hagman). The target: a heavily guarded armored truck transporting millions of dollars in gold bullion from one downtown Los Angeles vault to another. The scheme is reasonably shrewd, and the successful execution takes place under the noses of the massive police escort. Alas, nobody anticipates the simple traffic accident that spoils the almost perfect getaway.

Nelson's primary theme is a 7-7 motif repeated throughout the film; it's introduced as a clarinet lament when Mark learns that he won't be allowed to stay on the job. Music touches are minimal during the first and second act, but then the story gets some juice from a solid combo swinger heard when the gang drives a decoy sanitation truck into the bowels of the concrete-lined Los Angeles river basin. After the successful heist, Mark arranges to convert the gold bars into cash. As the story builds to its ironic finale, jazz flute takes the melody; this builds to a suspenseful crescendo when the men drive their gold-laden van through downtown streets—careful to maintain the speed limit—until the unexpected traffic mishap.

None of the music endured beyond the film. Nelson subsequently focused on episode scores for *Ironside* and *The Six Million Dollar Man* until he died unexpectedly of a heart attack in October 1975, at the youthful age of 43.

Lalo Schifrin's fans will recognize his touch on *Hunter*, an espionage film also intended as a pilot for a proposed series from producer Bruce Geller, of *Mission: Impossible* fame.[4] Sadly, Schifrin didn't seem very motivated; his work doesn't go beyond occasional suspense cues built from bass, brass and percussion. Only the end credits offer a fleeting taste of what could have blossomed into a jazzy action cue.

Professional "chameleon" David Hunter (John Vernon) is hired by the National Security Bureau (NSB) to determine why one of their top men, Alain Praetorious (Steve Ihnat), killed his fellow agent and best friend. Evidence points to nefarious activity at Tanner, a chemical weapons plant where Praetorious is soon to become chief of security. Hunter spends weeks "becoming" Praetorious, after which he assumes the man's role at Tanner and smokes out the enemy agents who brainwashed the actual NSB operative. This discovery comes just as Tanner personnel are about to dump canisters of a deadly biochemical gas into the ocean (!), to prevent it ever being used. The bad guys have other plans: to release the gas and wipe out all life in the northeastern United States (!!).

Schifrin's best contributions come early, while Tanner meticulously studies how to become Praetorious; these montages are backed by sleek suspense cues. A bit of action jazz also accompanies Tanner's climactic struggle to prevent the gas from being released. Schifrin's signature touch is most evident during a couple of diegetic bossa nova cues performed by an off-camera combo at a restaurant where Hunter flirts with his associate (Sabrina Scharf).

As with *The Alpha Caper*, the music had no life beyond its broadcast on January 9, 1973.

The Big Screen

Schifrin had a busy year, with seven feature assignments. The first proved iconic.

Warner Bros. became the first major American film studio to co-produce a martial arts film, a bold venture that yielded a classic—*Enter the Dragon*—which immediately made Bruce Lee an A-list celebrity ... despite his having died a month before the film's release. The action-packed stunt work aside, *Enter the Dragon* also is remembered fondly for Schifrin's exhilarating score.

He couldn't help feeling that the assignment was predestined. Shortly after beginning work, he lunched with Lee at the Warner Bros. Studio executive commissary. "[He was] excited to meet me," Schifrin recalled. "I was impressed by the fact that he was in such impressive shape. He told me that he practiced with a rigorous discipline in his dojo in Hong Kong, to the rhythm of my *Mission: Impossible*."[5]

The plot is simple: Lee's character (also named Lee) is sent to obtain evidence of a reclusive crime lord's drug and prostitution endeavors, in the guise of a participant in the man's high-profile martial arts tournament, held on his private island. The visiting champions include two Americans: Roper (John Saxon), a gambling addict in debt to the Mob; and Williams (Jim Kelly), a Vietnam War veteran. Their host, Han (Shih Kien), proves to be *quite* malevolent, as are his two bodyguards, Oharra (Robert Wall) and Bolo (Bolo Yeung). Lee's activities don't remain clandestine for long, leading to plenty of preliminary skirmishes and a furious martial arts climax.

Schifrin's main theme, introduced against a travelogue montage of Hong Kong locations, kicks off with hypnotic, *Shaft*-style percussion, blasts of brass and (we assume) Lee's piercing battle cries. These resolve into an Asian-inflected synthesizer melody over the same relentless rhythm, with background shading by *wah-wah* guitar and organ; horns take over as the theme concludes with a roaring, six-note orchestral statement. The story's first action sequence is a flashback, when a monk reveals—to a dismayed Lee—how his younger sister Su Lin (Angela Mao) died, while fleeing from half a dozen thugs led by Oharra. While she runs, evades and fights gallantly against overwhelming odds, Schifrin spots this lengthy melee with rapid rhythmic figures—trombones, piano and timpani—and a singsong, deceptively larkish melody that serves as ironic counterpoint to Su Lin's peril.

"The three tenor trombone clusters are based on the Chinese pentatonic scale YU," Schifrin explained. "The bass trombone plays the tonic (E flat, G flat, A flat, B flat, D flat). The two timpani, bongos, congas, temple blocks and drum set play *agitato ad libitum* (agitated, at liberty)."[6]

Han initially seems generous. When given the choice of a concubine for the evening, Williams is listening to a funky blend of Hammond B3 and *wah-wah* guitar on his headset (a groovy cue heard only briefly in the film but presented at length on the soundtrack album). Roper, in turn, beds Tania (Ahna Capri); their lovemaking takes place against a gentle ballad highlighted by sensuous jazz flute and muted trumpet. Han's surface benevolence vanishes when the undercover mission is exposed, leading to a chaotic melee that begins when Lee and Roper furiously fend off Han's guards; the odds are evened when scores of the island's prisoners join the fray. Schifrin spots this chaos with alternating rapid-fire percussion and blasts of brass, echoes of the earlier Su Lin cue, and an ominous 2-2 motif that climbs the scale. Lee's long-anticipated fight against Han climaxes in a room of mirrors; Schifrin augments this creepy setting with atmospheric strings and the tinkly, unsettling tune glasses that he used in *Dirty Harry*.

Before *Enter the Dragon*, Bruce Lee was best known to American viewers for his co-starring work in television's *The Green Hornet* and *Longstreet*. Lee's dynamic presence notwithstanding, the film also is fondly remembered for its exciting Lalo Schifrin score, which blends his suspenseful *Dirty Harry*-style cues—characterized by insistent percussion and *wah-wah* guitar elements—with traditional Chinese instruments and music.

The initial soundtrack LP was infuriatingly short, at just shy of 26 minutes; the remastered 1998 digital release runs a vastly superior 57 minutes. Over time, the album sold more than 500,000 copies and earned Schifrin a gold record.

Despite his fame, several of Schifrin's action scores remain unreleased: particularly regrettable in the case of *Charley Varrick*. This taut little crime thriller gives Walter Matthau a rare opportunity to star as an antihero who emerges as the *de facto* "good guy," because he's more decent than everybody else. The film gets considerable lift from Schifrin's sleek score, with its emphasis on piano, brass, tabla, pamba and cimbalom.

Charley (Matthau) is a former stunt pilot-turned-crop duster and part-time bank robber. The film opens as he, his wife, Nadine (Jacqueline Scott), and two accomplices (Harman and Al, played by Andy Robinson and Fred Scheiwiller) hold up a bank in the bucolic rural town of Tres Cruces, New Mexico. Although Charley and Harman get away with the vault's contents, Nadine and Al don't survive the unexpected shoot-out with police. Once back at Charley's trailer-park home, he and Harman get a second shock: Instead of the anticipated $10,000 to $20,000, they've netted $765,118. Charley realizes that the bank must've been laundering money for the Mob, which means big trouble. Mafia hit man Molly (Joe Don Baker) is sent to recover the cash, while Charley tries to figure a way out of this mess.

The title credits unfold over a leisurely montage of Tres Cruces; Schifrin complements these rural images with lyrical piano riffs. A cheerful flute solo adds early morning bounce; the cue accelerates slightly as the entire orchestra joins in, amid trumpet fanfares. The serenity is shattered when the bank hold-up goes down, against a propulsive action cue that opens with ba-da-ba-*bum*-da-da-*bum* runs of single-note, low-register piano keys. Jagged horn blasts accompany a close-up of patrol cops unholstering their guns, and then everything descends into chaos. Schifrin shifts to a percussive, fast-paced action cue when the gang roars off, propelled by more rapid keyboard notes.

Most of the second act warrants only fleeting atmospheric cues, as sidebar characters come and go—sometimes fatally—but Schifrin does have fun with a brief, swinging "strip anthem" that accompanies Molly's visit to a cathouse. Schifrin's theme for Charley finally debuts in the third act: a tabla-driven action cue that develops into a marvelous blend of percussion, horns and strings. The upbeat melody implies that Charley may have figured out a solution to this catastrophe. A reprise of the "bank heist" theme later accompanies his departure with most of the loot; Schifrin celebrates this triumph with a cheerful cue that slowly fades into silence.

Only two underscore cues have been released thus far—Varrick's character theme and the "Bank Robbery" cue—as part of Aleph's 2012 box set, *Lalo Schifrin: My Life in Music*.

Wherever TV writer/producer Bruce Geller went, Schifrin wasn't far behind. Geller directed only one big-screen film: the impudent *Harry in Your Pocket*, which gives star James Coburn another opportunity to exercise his signature blend of suave sophistication and snarky humor. The script approaches its topic—a pickpocket "wire mob"—with the same level of meticulous detail that Geller brought to every episode of *Mission: Impossible*; in a sense, this film is the criminal response to that spy series.

The story begins in Seattle's Union Station, while Sandy Coletto (Trish Van Devere) observes the clumsy antics of amateur pickpocket Ray Houlihan (Michael Sarrazin). Circumstance throws the two of them together—Sandy apparently at loose ends—and she tags along when Ray "interviews" with Casey (Walter Pidgeon), the recruiter for a wire mob run by Harry (Coburn). The newcomers are outfitted with posh wardrobes, then trained by Harry and Casey in the methods of the pickpocketing craft. As the quartet grifts during travels from Seattle to Victoria, B.C., and then Salt Lake City, Ray grows impatient; he also chafes at Harry's obvious designs on Sandy. Everything comes to a boil in Salt Lake City, where Casey's arrest prompts Harry into reckless behavior.

Schifrin's gentle jazz score is both impertinent and nostalgic, imbuing these characters with a touch of soulful despair. Most cues lean toward gentle, piano-based ballads; uptempo big band jazz is present mostly as diegetic cues. The film gets its mournful heart from Schifrin's primary theme: a lyrical, wistful melody dominated by a piano ostinato of rising 4-4 patterns.

Harry's jaunty theme debuts as an upbeat swinger heard on the radio in his luxurious hotel penthouse: a lush arrangement with the melody handled by vibes, backed by gentle brass fanfares. The first non-diegetic jazz cues spice a captivating "training" montage, when Harry and Casey cruise a Seattle park, trying to build some skill into Ray's fumbling fingers; Schifrin spots this sequence with a toe-tapping, flute-driven jazz shuffle, with jaunty harpsichord and piano riffs. Once Ray is deemed ready, Schifrin cuts to a hard-charging suspense cue; percussion, walking bass and vibes grant sophistication to the ease with which Harry and the others relieve hapless Seattle citizens of their wallets. Later, a celebratory restaurant dinner is backed by the venue's unseen combo, which performs a cheerful vibes swinger followed by a lush romantic ballad. The musical palette turns darker once the quartet hits Salt Lake City, and Schifrin's subsequent cues become ominously suspenseful.

The film's 33-track score wasn't issued until 2011.

Shifrin's highest-profile score of the year arrived on Christmas Day, with the inevitable sequel to *Dirty Harry*. *Magnum Force* is much more tastelessly violent and sexist than its predecessor; that aside, the film gets significant momentum from a sizzling score that establishes the primary themes destined to unify the rest of the series. Director Ted Post opens with a close-up of Harry's .44 magnum; the title credits blast onto the screen against a sizzling, bass- and percussion-heavy arrangement of what henceforth becomes Harry's main theme, with a mixed chorus supplying a 2-2-2 melodic ostinato against a wall of brass. Thundering horns add emphasis during a short bridge, after which the orchestra builds to an emphatic finale.

To soften Harry's anti-establishment tendencies, this sequel confronts him with a more lethal squad of vigilante cops who appoint themselves judge, jury and executioners, while ridding San Francisco of "bad elements." Four such killings occur during the first two acts; each is scored with ominous, martial snare drums and twitchy brass riffs, with "whispering" synth delivering *very* slow nods to Harry's 2-2-2 theme. Sidebar action scenes receive unique cues, as with the droll blend of bongos and walking bass, when Harry impersonates an airline pilot to handle two gun-toting hijackers. Schifrin also includes several reprises of the first film's "melancholy theme," debuting here via solo electric keyboard, after Harry saves his partner Early (Felton Perry) from being killed by convenience store robbers. Schifrin's more striking jazz touch climaxes when Harry confronts the remaining rogue cops atop one of the "retired" aircraft carriers then berthed at Western Richmond's Castro Point. Harry's triumph is bittersweet, and he begins a dejected stroll from the scene as the end credits appear against a lengthy electric keyboard arrangement of the "melancholy theme."

The full 22-track score didn't debut until 2005. The disc includes several unused cues: most notably "Potrero Hill," a vibrant bit of jazz/funk with a wicked brass melody, perhaps intended as nightclub source music.

Harry Callahan would return again, albeit with a new jazz accompanist (about which, more later).

The blaxploitation fad, meanwhile, kept accelerating.

Having rid Harlem's mean streets of pimps, drug pushers and other assorted low-lifes, *Shaft in Africa* finds the tough-talkin' private dick—again played by Richard Roundtree—

hired by Ethiopian royalty, to infiltrate and shut down a noxious operation that kidnaps young African men for slave labor in Europe. Scoring duties went to Johnny Pate.

The story begins as Ethiopian embassy officials put Shaft through a few grueling physical tests, to determine his strength and endurance. Once trained to impersonate a native-speaking itinerant laborer, he's flown to Addis Ababa to surveil the smuggling operation from within. The operation's secrecy is blown from the start; Shaft endures repeated attempts on his life, all ordered by the cultured Amafi (Frank Finlay), ringleader of the criminal enterprise. After witnessing so much brutality, an increasingly enraged Shaft works his way up the food chain to a thoroughly satisfying final confrontation with Amafi.

Pate opens the film with a blast of brass, *wah-wah* funk and lively keyboard chops, when Shaft's early morning routine is interrupted by well-dressed apartment intruders. The cue includes a nod to the subsequent title credits theme, "Are You Man Enough," sung with zest by Motown's celebrated Four Tops. Tribal drums later accompany Shaft's arrival in Addis Ababa; Pate expands this cue into a percussion-heavy trumpet arrangement of the title theme. Incessant drums and anxious flute/clarinet solos follow Shaft's initial contact with the slave smugglers. He and his fellow Africans then endure a desert journey to the port where they'll be stuffed into the hold of a tanker ship bound for Europe. But Shaft gets a bonus; smokin' electric guitar, sensuous flute and Hammond B3 riffs highlight an unlikely romantic interlude with Amafi's thrill-seeking girlfriend, Jazar (Neda Arneric). After reaching France, a horrific accident kills many of the migrants, sending Shaft into a fury. Screaming horns follow his explosive arrival at Amafi's lair; the cue builds to a triumphant brass roar when imprisoned migrants are freed, and—in a bit of fitting poetic justice—deal with Amafi themselves.

The soundtrack album proved quite popular, and—over time—many of Pate's vibrant jazz/funk cues were sampled by dozens of rap and hip-hop artists, including Tuff Crew, Diddy and Jay-Z.

Shaft would return, but not for quite awhile (about which ... well, you know).

The blaxploitation trend coincided with the decade's kung fu craze, so the two occasionally overlapped. Former football star Fred Williamson's laid-back charm does a lot to overcome the incomprehensible plot in *That Man Bolt*. The martial arts fight scenes are reasonably well staged, but the film is a laughable disaster in every other respect; that includes its weak score from up-and-comer Charles Bernstein. Too many of his cues are repetitive, as if edgy rhythm and *wah-wah* guitars alone are enough to turn up the funk.

The story begins in Hong Kong, where professional courier Jefferson Bolt (Williamson) is hired to bring $1 million in cash—stuffed into a single suitcase—to Mexico City, by way of Los Angeles. He survives an attack in L.A. and then detours to Las Vegas, for reunions with longtime girlfriend Sam (Teresa Graves) and casino buddy Connie (Jack Ging); both come to bad ends. Bolt discovers that the money might be counterfeit; then again, it might be genuine. Circumstances send him back to Hong Kong, where he runs afoul of goons belonging to debonair crime lord Kumada (Masatoshi Nakamura). Various skirmishes follow; Bolt perseveres.

Bernstein's title credits theme—a trifling synth melody over heavy rhythm and *wah-wah* guitar—debuts as the sweaty, bare-chested Williamson practices his martial arts chops. This cue recurs during most of the subsequent action scenes, over an equally monotonous 5-4 bass motif; the rest of the score relies on atmospheric synth, low-end bass and sinister percussion. Once Bolt returns to Hong Kong, a bit of brass highlights his late-night invasion of Kumada's refinery operation; it's spectacularly fire-bombed during a Jeep chase that gains momentum from some cool action jazz. Then it's back to atmospheric basics during climactic confrontations with Kumada and his lethal martial arts lieutenant, Spider (Ken Kazama).

No soundtrack album emerged, although a bootleg score is fairly easy to find.

Early blaxploitation entries focused on male stars, but it was only a matter of time before equally bad-ass women grabbed a slice of the action. *Coffy* is one of the genre's most emblematic examples; its rage-against-the-(white)-man scenario is larded with a particularly lurid blend of nudity and gory violence. These grisly sensibilities emerge immediately, when Coffy (Pam Grier) blows off a drug pusher's head with a shotgun. Despite such crude touches, Grier makes a plucky heroine who wrestles with her conscience while seeking vengeance against those responsible for destroying her younger sister's mind with contaminated heroin. Her amateur investigation eventually leads to King George (Robert DoQui), a flamboyant pimp connected to Mafia boss Arturo Vitroni (Allan Arbus), who funnels drugs into the city. Despite some potentially fatal stumbles, Coffy ultimately achieves her desired revenge.

The music assignment went to veteran funk, soul and jazz composer/vibes player Roy Ayers, and it remained his sole film score. His slinky vibes work dominates many of the cues, which echo Isaac Hayes' sassy funk and *wah-wah* guitar.

The film opens with an uptempo roar of piano, organ and brass, all against a hypnotic 2/2 beat: background music in the noisy nightclub where Coffy spots and teases her first target to his gruesome demise. This prologue is followed by the title theme, "Coffy Is the Color," a redundant soul anthem chanted by Ayers, Denise Bridgewater and Wayne Garfield. Aside from instrumental reprises of that song, the film's most frequent cue is a smooth, bouncy swinger with a repeating 5-6 motif on vibes and electric piano, against sassy bass licks and midtempo percussion; it's generally used as background for the numerous young women who pop up as hookers and call girls. When things eventually turn serious, Ayers supplies suspenseful action jazz as Coffy cleverly gets away from Vitroni's lethal lieutenant (Sid Haig) and a pair of corrupt cops; their effort to recapture her is spotted with staccato drumming, a repetitive four-note bass lick, and twitchy blasts of brass.

The film makes room for several songs, most notably the

Director Jack Starrett opted not to use several cues by co-composers Carl Brandt and J.J. Johnson: "Emdee," a moody, somewhat mysterious trumpet theme that sounds like it should have spotted some stealthy reconnaissance; "Ambush," a frantic action cue clearly intended for a sequence when Cleo is pinned down by a sniper; and the sweetly sultry, flute-fueled "Cleo and Reuben Love Theme." All are present on the soundtrack album (courtesy Film Score Monthly).

groovy "King George," with Ayers crooning Mephistophelian lyrics that perfectly convey this peacockish character's swagger.

The reorchestrated soundtrack album includes several cues that didn't make it into the film. The slow-burn "Coffy Sauna" obviously was written for a sex scene, and the salacious "Exotic Dance" is dominated by gentle horns and wicked guitar licks.

Cleopatra Jones is a rarity in the blaxploitation genre: a comparatively family-friendly action flick with no nudity, a strong anti-drug message, and restrained violence. The approach is high camp: an over-the-top blend of *Shaft* and the James Bond series, with Tamara Dobson's Cleo introduced as a take-charge special agent appointed by no less than the U.S. president. She invariably dresses in knockout runway goddess outfits and lavish furs, which—somehow—never interfere with her martial arts moves.

The story opens in Turkey, while Cleo oversees the destruction of a massive poppy field that belongs to a Los Angeles–based drug queen dubbed Mommy (Shelley Winters). Infuriated by the loss of $30 million worth of drugs, Mommy "arranges" to have the local police raid a community home for recovering drug addicts that is run by Cleo's lover, Reuben (Bernie Casey). When Cleo learns of this vile behavior by corrupt, racist cops, she returns to Southern California. She easily evades ambushes by Mommy's underlings, while sparring with Doodlebug (Antonio Fargas), a midlevel drug lord hoping to take over Mommy's turf. Everything climaxes in a wrecking yard, where Cleo ultimately hurls Mommy to her death. None of this can be taken seriously, but the displays of proud feminism and community spirit ring strong and true.

Soul singer Joe Simon performs the title theme; its rhythmic, four-beat backing ostinato is far more memorable than the melody and its silly lyrics. Indeed, that four-beat motif reprises throughout the film, often signaling an action scene. Composer Carl Brandt supplies several trumpet-fueled action cues: notably a lively R&B swinger when Cleo arrives in Los Angeles, and surprises Mommy's goons by jumping them from the luggage carousel; and a tasty, percussion-laden groove that kicks off the wrecking yard finale, then bursts into tension-laden horns and *wah-wah* guitar, while Cleo, Reuben and their neighborhood posse handle Mommy and her thugs. Co-composer J.J. Johnson's soul-laden diegetic cues are lazier and more laid back. Sultry flute, percussion and Hammond B3 are heard when Cleo slides a cassette into her car stereo; *wah-wah* guitar and Hammond B3 trade the melody of a down 'n' dirty tune emanating from the radio at the restaurant, where Cleo arranges to get help from brothers Matthew and Melvin (Albert Popwell and Caro Kenyatta, both martial arts masters). Johnson is equally adept at fast-paced action jazz; he spots a lengthy car chase with an exciting variation of the title theme, powered by plenty of congas, bongos, bass and blasts of trumpet.

The soundtrack album blended reorchestrated versions of the instrumental cues with the title song and two other Millie Jackson soul vocals used as diegetic music; the 2010 digital expansion includes more instrumental cues as bonus tracks.

With so many bad guys running around on the big screen, it's fortunate that plenty of movie cops were on hand as well, to keep them in line.

The Laughing Policeman, loosely adapted from the Edgar Award-winning 1968 crime novel by Swedish authors Maj Sjöwall and Per Wahlöö, is a solid police procedural that gives Walter Matthau one of his best dramatic roles. The story begins with the gruesome mass murder of nearly every passenger on a late-night bus; one of the victims is off-duty San Francisco police detective Dave Evans, partner to veteran homicide detective Jake Martin (Matthau). He becomes convinced that this catastrophe somehow relates to a long-festering cold case: the murder of Teresa Camarero, which Jake believed—but couldn't prove—was committed by the woman's husband (Albert Paulsen). Jake and new partner Leo Larsen (Bruce Dern) spend the bulk of the film with the grinding routine of dogged police work. Their grumpy, ill-fitting relationship is overstated at times, and more enlightened sensibilities have dated the lurid view of the "deviant" behavior at the root of the case, but the tension remains high while the story builds to its taut climax.

The Laughing Policeman was an unusual assignment for TV/film composer Charles Fox, best known for dramas and comedies. In keeping with the film's street-level authenticity, Fox and director Stuart Rosenberg hold the non-diegetic cues to a minimum. Jake's theme is prominent: a melancholy, small combo lament with a sax melody against gentle piano comping. The paucity of underscore cues notwithstanding, the film is laden with diegetic music emanating from bars, clubs and (most frequently) Jake's car radio. He favors 1940s big band jazz, and Fox supplies covers of "Ain't We Got Fun," "Blue Moon," "Big Noise from Winnetka" and many other classics.

"When Stuart [Rosenberg] was doing preparation for the film," Fox recalled, years later, "he spent days riding in a squad car, [and] the detective that he rode along with had his car radio set to a station that only played forties-era big band music. When it came time to score our film, that was a stylistic point of reference that he wanted to continue for Matthau's character."[7]

No soundtrack album appeared, but in 1977 Fox's main theme was covered by the New World Symphony on a 45 single, paired with his title theme for the TV series *Wonder Woman*.

While plans percolated for a follow-up to *The French Connection*, that film's producer—Philip D'Antoni—turned director to mount a quasi-sequel. *The Seven-Ups* also is set in New York City, with Roy Scheider reprising his *French Connection* character, Buddy Russo. He now heads the Seven-Ups, an elite NYPD squad allowed to employ off-book tactics to bring down mobsters. Buddy gets many of his valuable tips from Vito (Tony Lo Bianco), a low-level gangster who trades on their long relationship as childhood friends. Unfortunately, Vito is secretly running his own scam, using information gleaned from Buddy to kidnap and ransom upper-echelon mob bosses. The dynamic unravels when one of Buddy's squad is killed, at which point he connects the dots, leading to several violent confrontations.

As a producer, D'Antoni had supervised *Bullitt*, well known—as with *The French Connection*—for a memorable car chase. Wanting to up his own game, D'Antoni orchestrated a midfilm vehicular pursuit for *The Seven-Ups*, which has become the stuff of cinematic legend.

Jazz trumpeter Don Ellis came along for the ride, although he wasn't the filmmakers' first choice. Johnny Mandel completed a full score that was rejected—"They wanted a jazz score," Mandel recalled, "but I just didn't see it that way"[8]—at which point the hastily hired Ellis supplied an entirely new, nervous-making score based solely on percussion and atonal, discordant strings. Much of this music is low, faint and almost subliminal. Ellis signals this tone with a twitchy, pulsing title theme—screaming strings and bowed basses—that plays against stark white credits on a black screen. Steel drums and echo effects evoke disorientation, when one of the mob bosses is kidnapped; a frantic bowed bass signals the doomed cop's plight, when he is discovered by mob goons and stuffed into the trunk of a car. The lengthy car chase is left unscored. The eventual resolution, when Buddy confronts Vito, is elegiac and regretful: Even though the Seven-Ups have triumphed, it's a pyrrhic victory, because Buddy has lost his childhood friend.

No soundtrack album appeared until a 2007 digital release paired Ellis' music with Johnny Mandel's score for *The Verdict*. An expanded 2018 release also includes Mandel's complete unused score for *The Seven-Ups*.

Not all 1973 movie cops were honorable. Charles Bronson's vicious, racist Det. Lou Torrey in *The Stone Killer* makes Clint Eastwood's Harry Callahan look like a saint, and the film's fascist undertone is quite distasteful. The script has almost nothing to do with John Gardner's *A Complete State of Death*, the 1969 novel on which the film supposedly is based. In the hands of director Michael Winner, the narrative becomes a tawdry, excessively violent cartoon with a horrific body count. The only worthwhile element is Roy Budd's vigorous jazz/funk score: one of his best … and, in Winner's hands, one of the most ill-treated. The director chopped and clumsily stitched chunks of different cues, repeated some passages to an absurd degree, and completely ignored Budd's intended placement of themes designed for specific scenes.

Much of composer Don Ellis' efforts in *The Seven-Ups* are atmospheric cues that affect us subconsciously. There are no distinct themes, as was the case with his work on *The French Connection*, and this score barely qualifies as jazz; it's mostly texture, much like Urs Furrer's intentionally grainy cinematography (courtesy Intrada Inc.).

Torrey bounces back and forth between police precincts in New York and Los Angeles, trying to find a pattern to seemingly random slayings of midlevel Mafia gangsters and Vietnam veterans unable to cope with civilian life. Unknown to Torrey and his colleagues, aging Mafia don Al Vescari (Martin Balsam) has long nursed a plot to avenge the 1931 mass murder of his old-world Sicilian colleagues, executed by the Lucky Luciano/Meyer Lansky organized crime faction. Vescari's goal: the mass slaughter of current Jewish and (mainstream) Italian syndicate dons, thus putting Mafia control back in Sicilian hands. To maintain secrecy while this plan proceeds, Vescari and his associates have shunned Mafia hit men, instead hiring disgruntled Vietnam vets delighted by a fresh opportunity to employ their lethal skills.

Budd's title credits cue opens with bright staccato bursts of horns and percussion—an attention-grabbing style favored by TV news programs—and then settles into the 1-4 motif of Torrey's theme, with the melody delivered by synth as a wall of brass adds background color. Horns scream during the bridge, with a hard 2/2 drumbeat adding pizzazz. Variations of this theme are sprinkled throughout the film, during action sequences and Torrey's visits with former New York cop buddies. The plot's war veteran connection gives Budd an excuse to season several cues with military-style marching drums, which often segue to reprises of Torrey's 1-4 theme. Budd pulls out all the stops—throbbing percussion, suspenseful low-end piano riffs and insistent brass—during a frenetic vehicular chase. The film climaxes with a wretchedly excessive, multivehicle smash-up and mass gunfight involving Torrey and scores of cops in a basement parking garage, spotted with angry drums, screaming strings and staccato explosions of brass.

Because one of the midlevel bad guys—Paul Koslo, as Alfred—is a trombone player who loves big band jazz, the film grants ample space to jazz-flavored diegetic cues. Torrey's dogged effort to find Alfred involves chats with the employees at several record stores catering to jazz; the first is awash in a big band cut, while the second offers bluesy, Fender Rhodes-driven funk. That interview leads to a jazz club, where a house band (amazingly!) rehearses the same organ-laden funk heard in the record store. After getting sent to yet another club, Torrey finally finds Alfred blowing a trombone solo amid some uptempo swing by the house band.

The initial soundtrack LP left a few of the diegetic jazz tunes behind; they were resurrected for 1999's digital rerelease. Highlights include the funky "Black Is Beautiful" and the cool, bossa-oriented "Down Downtown." The 2017 Blu-ray includes an isolated score track, and late 2019 brought an enhanced digital score with numerous alternate takes and bonus tracks.

Director Peter Yates' *The Friends of Eddie Coyle*, adapted from George V. Higgins' 1972 novel about Boston's Irish-American underworld, gets its dramatic juice from Robert Mitchum's impeccably shaded performance as the titular character. He's a weary, working-class gangster grown tired of carrying water for his employers, who dreams of retiring to Florida like the upper-echelon mobsters who've somehow evaded federal prosecution. As the story begins, Eddie is caught between a rock and a hard place: trying to avoid a prison stretch by cooperating with ATF agent Dave Foley (Richard Jordan); while also raising money by supplying guns to a brazen, daylight bank-robbing gang led by Jimmy Scalise (Alex Rocco). The sad truth is that progress has left Eddie behind; the future belongs to younger, sassier and bolder crooks.

When it came to music, Yates knew precisely what he wanted. "[*Eddie Coyle*] really needed a jazz score, because it was the hardness of the film, and the whole feeling was like a jazz piece."[9] He turned to Dave Grusin, whose edgy, minimalist cues aptly complement these

Much of Dave Grusin's score for *The Friends of Eddie Coyle* favors twitchy, nervous-making cues that employ strings, flutes and low bass riffs to heighten the film's ominous suspense and increasing sense of danger (courtesy Film Score Monthly).

street-level gangsters. The main theme begins softly, as a bank manager leaves home for work, unaware that he's being watched by Scalise and his gang; percussion kicks the theme into a solid groove when the film's title appears. Grusin's somewhat forlorn electronic keyboard riffs then yield to a dynamic, funk-oriented cue as the manager arrives at his bank and takes receipt of an armored car delivery of cash. At which point, the carnage erupts.

Grusin's most dynamic cue belongs to Jackie Brown (Steven Keats), from whom Eddie has been getting his guns. He's introduced via uptempo, percussion-driven boogie: a boldly vivacious cue that reflects Jackie's brash, energetic behavior, and is a striking contrast to the despondent themes that shadow Eddie. Another deliciously funky, even faster cue can be heard later—faintly, as radio source music—when Eddie delivers some guns to the house Scalise shares with his girlfriend.

Grusin's score remained unreleased until 2012, when paired with his work on 1975's *Three Days of the Condor*. The disc reveals the degree to which Yates minimized his use of Grusin's music in *Eddie Coyle*; several cues were severely abbreviated or left behind entirely.

Donald E. Westlake's unstoppable antihero Parker returned in *The Outfit*, and Robert Duvall is thoroughly satisfying in the role, albeit saddled with yet another name change: Earl Macklin. After getting out of prison and reuniting with girlfriend Bett (Karen Black), he learns that his brother Eddie has been killed by the crime "Outfit" of the film's title. Macklin puts a $250,000 price tag on reparation; various levels of Outfit lieutenants refuse to pay, with predictable results. Top boss Mailer (Robert Ryan), understandably irritated, orders Macklin killed. This proves difficult, particularly when Macklin teams up with an equally capable buddy, Jack Cody (Joe Don Baker). Everything builds to a climactic assault on Mailer's heavily guarded mansion.

Jerry Fielding's score occasionally evokes his recent work on *The Mechanic*. Highlights include the exciting jazz march that propels Macklin's resolute stride down a hotel hallway, prior to robbing an Outfit-backed poker game. A subsequent raid on an Outfit-backed finance company unfolds against a cool 5/4 cue; the ensuing heist of an Outfit casino is choreographed to a funky riff with an echo of Quincy Jones. The climactic invasion of Mailer's mansion plays out against a taut blend of jazz and quasi-classical riffs: Fielding at his mood-enhancing best.

Unfortunately, Fielding's music was treated with considerable contempt by director John Flynn, who chops off many cues and—in some cases—inserts stuff from an entirely different composer! The most notorious example occurs early on, when Eddie's wife tries to phone him. The soft solo piano elegy heard behind this sequence is a cue from some other project by Roy Budd.

No soundtrack album appeared until 2002. Hearing Fielding's cues in their entirety makes Flynn's creative choices even more inept; the director squandered a score that clearly would have enhanced his film.

On the gumshoe front, *Shamus* relies almost entirely on Burt Reynolds' roguish charm, which makes this clumsy PI thriller more entertaining than it deserves. Director Buzz Kulik and scripter Barry Beckerman try for the Raymond Chandler vibe, with an assortment of eccentric characters and a plot that starts with a diamond heist and then—bewilderingly—blossoms into the illegal black-market sale of U.S. military ordnance. Reynolds' Shamus McCoy stumbles from one confrontation to the next with neither rhyme nor reason. His bedroom hijinks are far more engaging, along with the light comic relief provided by his four-legged feline companion, played by 9Lives' famed Morris the cat.

Jerry Goldsmith's droll score is highlighted by the slow jazz waltz that plays behind the hilarious title credits sequence: arguably the film's best part, as a hung-over McCoy stumbles out of bed (on his pool table) and searches for clothes, coffee and toothpaste. A whimsical piano melody plays against cool percussion effects, with soft flute providing counterpoint; a bit of *wah-wah* guitar slides into the mix during the melody's reprise. Kulik makes ample use of this theme, most notably with a warmer, romantic arrangement heard when McCoy gets between the sheets with a suspect's sexy sister (Dyan Cannon). Goldsmith also supplies fast-paced action jazz during a tumultuous sequence that begins in a warehouse, where McCoy finds crates of military guns, and continues during a furious sequence as he's pursued by a gaggle of gunsels. This climactic chase is backed by a percussive synth cue that sounds very much like Goldsmith's work on the two Derek Flint films.

No soundtrack album was produced, and we're not likely to get one; the original tapes are believed lost. The title theme finally showed up as one track of the 2012 compilation CD, *The Jerry Goldsmith Collection Volume One: Rarities*.

Speaking of Chandler, 1953's *The Long Goodbye* was the penultimate of his seven completed Philip Marlowe novels; it's also one of the author's most morose and semi-autobiographical works. When finally brought to the big screen, it proved an awkward fit with idiosyncratic director Robert Altman, whose quirky style is wholly at odds with Chandler's *noir* sensibilities. Altman and scripter Leigh Brackett dragged Marlowe into their present era, retaining his anachronistic 1950s moral code as a deliberate contrast to the 1970s' hippy-dippy "free love" attitudes.

The case begins when Marlowe (Elliott Gould) agrees to drive longtime friend Terry Lennox (Jim Bouton) to Tijuana. Once back in Los Angeles, Marlowe is arrested by police detectives who believe he helped Lennox kill his wife, Sylvia. That charge evaporates three days later, when Mexican authorities reveal that Lennox committed suicide. While trying to make sense of this, Marlowe is hired by Eileen Wade (Nina van Pallandt) to find her alcoholic, self-destructive husband, Roger (Sterling Hayden); he's traced to a fancy detox hospital run by the mildly sinister Dr. Verringer (Henry Gibson). Just as Marlowe begins to realize that Roger and Eileen Wade are more than casual acquaintances with the late Terry and Sylvia Lennox, the situation is complicated further by Marty Augustine (Mark Rydell), a sociopathic gangster from whom Terry apparently stole $350,000. These incongruent elements resolve more through caprice than investigative talent on Marlowe's part.

Altman's concept of the film's music proved equally eccentric. He hired John Williams and made a very precise request: that the entire score be built from numerous variations of the *same single cue*. Williams duly wrote a melancholy song with lyricist Johnny Mercer, appropriately titled "The Long Goodbye," which was recorded by several vocalists—Morgan Ames, Clydie King, Irene Kral and Jack Sheldon—for use as radio and location diegetic cues. Williams also created half a dozen instrumental arrangements for distinctly different combos, depending on mood and setting; one version is a smooth piano trio, with Williams at the keyboard. Other delectable versions are performed by the Dave Grusin Trio: first as a midtempo swinger with plenty of playful piano noodling; and later at a slower, more thoughtful pace, with Grusin's keyboard work sounding more contemplative.

"The music was a terrific idea—entirely Bob's," Williams recalled. "He said, 'Wouldn't it be great if there was one song, this omnipresent piece, played in all these different ways?' We would go into a dentist's office or an elevator, and there would be this ubiquitous and irritating music playing. It was threaded through, kind of like an unconscious wallpapering technique. I think it's completely unique. I don't think anyone has tried it quite the same way before or since."[10]

The film's melodic monotony initially made a soundtrack LP dubious, from a marketing standpoint, but a full digital version finally arrived in 2015.

Sophisticated gentleman thieves hearken back well over a century, most famously with E.W. Hornung's lighthearted stories about amateur cracksman A.J. Raffles. Few modern takes on this breezy formula are smoother than director Bud Yorkin's *The Thief Who Came to Dinner*. The film's incandescent glow emanates from the pairing of Ryan O'Neal and Jacqueline Bisset, and their flirty charisma gains additional sparkle from Henry Mancini's playful score: a sumptuous echo of the gentle jazz he wrote for Pete 'n' Edie, back in the *Peter Gunn* days.

The story kicks off as disenchanted computer programmer Webster McGee (O'Neal) impulsively decides to become a cat burglar. His first target—mildly corrupt businessman Gene Henderling (Charles Cioffi)—produces long-term benefits: Webster blackmails

Henry Mancini wrote numerous character cues for *The Thief Who Came to Dinner*, including a melody for the title character's ex-wife (Jill Clayburgh), who is dismayed by the fact that her former husband now seems far more exciting than the dull corporate drone to whom she once was married. Her theme is sad and slow: a simple synth and flute melody that reflects her forlorn resignation, when he gently insists that she's no longer part of his life (courtesy Film Score Monthly).

himself into Gene's aristocratic social circle, thereby gaining inside knowledge of the best moments to rob Houston's well-heeled upper class. Webster also meets vivacious Laura Keaton (Bisset), and they become lovers. His signature indulgence of leaving a chess piece at each crime prompts insurance investigator Dave Reilly (Warren Oates) to encourage *Houston Post* chess editor B. Zukovsky (Austin Pendleton) to challenge the thief to a match: a comic touch that becomes increasingly hilarious, when Webster employs his programming skills to enhance his half of the game. Reilly soon zeroes in on Webster as the likely "chess burglar," and everything builds to the ambitious heist of precious gems from a well-guarded museum exhibit.

The Thief Who Came to Dinner is one of Mancini's first big-screen scores to incorporate the synth and electronic elements with which he had dabbled on television, with his title themes for *The NBC Mystery Movie* and his own syndicated *Mancini Generation* series. He wasn't entirely comfortable with this brave new world: "There was a tendency in the beginning, especially in TV scoring, to go pretty heavy on it," he recalled. "The hardest thing is to find out what these things can do. So I'm constantly listening and getting demonstrations of the various instruments, to find out how I can use them. ... But then sometimes I listen back to the electronic sounds I used in the beginning, and I wonder: What the hell was *that*? What was I thinking?"[11]

Such concerns aside, Mancini delivers the goods on *Thief*. The gently swinging score effectively blends electronics and cocktail jazz and is anchored by a terrific main theme that opens with soft bongos, conga drums and sly Fender bass licks as the title credits appear. Clavinet and a Yamaha synthesizer introduce the melody, granting Webster's on-screen activities a "techie" atmosphere that suits his programming background. The melody segues smoothly to a slower second movement; keyboards and bass trade licks when Webster scopes out his first target—Henderling's house—while disguised as a plumber. This theme reprises during subsequent heist sequences, and it most notably anchors the veritable jazz rhapsody, in several movements, that spots the climactic museum caper.

Mancini also delivers a playful cue when Dave attempts to tail Webster's car; the bouncy assortment of brass, lively drums and mischievous synth features a wicked sax solo. Laura gets a sleek, languid and sexy theme; the relaxed synth melody is backed by gentle drums and romantically sweeping strings. Diegetic cues include some soft trumpet- and organ-driven jazz/pop, heard on a car radio while a couple of teenagers neck, not realizing that their vehicle is blocking Webster's escape.

Rather than reorchestrate the film cues for the soundtrack album—as was his frequent practice—Mancini let his score cues stand on their own. Intriguingly, his arrangement of the title theme for the simultaneous 45 single *is* different, with the melody shaded by a harmonic vocal chorus not heard in the film. His full score wasn't released until 2009, on a disc that includes three additional diegetic cues and demo versions of both "Love Theme for Laura" and "Ryan's Theme" (an early arrangement of the main theme).

Elsewhere in the World

Riz Ortolani merely flirted with jazz in 1967's *Tiffany Memorandum*, but he delivered the goods for *Si può essere più bastardi dell'ispettore Cliff?* (which roughly translates to *Can Anyone Be More of a Bastard than Inspector Cliff?*, and was retitled *Mafia Junction*, when released in the States). Director/co-scripter Massimo Dallamano's nasty crime/erotic thriller finds corrupt American narcotics officer Inspector Cliff (Ivan Rassimov) playing three criminal gangs against each other, to grant himself a $1 million payday *and* stroll into the sunset with "escort girl" Joanne (Stephanie Beacham).

Beirut-based criminal "Mamma the Turk" (Patricia Hayes) has long partnered with London crime boss Morell (Ettore Manni), whose "International Escort Service" actually is a kinky sex operation that films politicians and other high-placed men to blackmail them for cash or "favors." Cliff goes undercover as an enforcer for rival crime boss Marco (Giacomo Rossi Stuart), which puts him in conflict with Mamma's chief assassin, Gamble (Luciano Catenacci). Subsequent double- and triple-crosses revolve around a Chinese statue containing heroin, which an American ambassador (Cec Linder) has been blackmailed into transporting via diplomatic channels.

Ortolani's saucy title theme kicks off with a rhythmic 1-2-1-2 ostinato on drums and low brass, while piano supplies a funkified counterpoint; unison brass introduces the 1-1-3 melody. Brass and piano riff all over the place, as the background rhythm rises in volume; the resulting jazz strut perfectly characterizes the smug, amoral Inspector Cliff. This theme reprises frequently, often when Cliff coldly executes one or more adversaries. Ortolani contributes some terrific action jazz when Mamma and one of her psychotic sons drive rapidly through the hillside highways outside of Beirut, chortling over a pursuing car that has little hope of catching them; the rhythm-heavy cue sounds a lot like early Lalo Schifrin, with unison horns punctuating a throbbing beat.

On a gentler note, a sweet combo number—tasty muted trumpet carries the theme, backed by guitar, bass and drums—surfaces as diegetic music a few times, most notably when heard over the International Escort Service's PA system. A more salacious ballad—a muted trumpet positively dripping with lust—plays against the film's most torrid love scene.

No soundtrack LP coincided with the film's release, although an Italian 45 single features the title theme and the cue heard during Cliff and Joanne's sex scene. A full 20-track digital score finally debuted in 2018.

4

Suite Revenge: 1974

Pure chance turned this into one of cinema's best years for action jazz scores, with superlative efforts coming from Roy Budd, Jerry Fielding, Herbie Hancock and David Shire, among others

Unfortunately, this bounty was undercut by the nascent rise of a sound soon to be known as disco, destined to have a seriously deleterious impact on film and TV scoring.

The Small Screen

Mike Post and Pete Carpenter's first collaboration with creator/producer Steve Cannell—*Toma*—may have stalled at first base, but they hit the next one out of the park. NBC's *The Rockford Files* was an immediate success, and ultimately ran six popular seasons after its September 13 debut. The Post/Carpenter title theme subsequently enjoyed a healthy 16-week run on *Billboard's* Top 100 chart, during the spring and summer of 1975.

Jim Rockford (James Garner) is a pardoned ex-con turned low-key, Los Angeles–based private investigator who specializes in missing persons, cold cases, blackmail and minor insurance scams. Although Rockford's investigations generally conclude successfully, dodgy clients and his tendency to get stiffed on fees result in a modest income that barely allows him to maintain the beachfront mobile home that doubles as his office. He avoids fights and prefers not to carry his gun, which spends most of its time in a cookie jar. Friends include his father Rocky (Noah Beery, Jr.), sympathetic LAPD Sgt. Dennis Becker (Joe Santos), lawyer and semi-permanent girlfriend Beth Davenport (Gretchen Corbett) and shifty ex-con Angel Martin (Stuart Margolin).

Each episode begins with an amusing, threatening or just plain daft message left on Rockford's answering machine, after which the title theme kicks off against a series of stills showing a frequently woebegone Rockford at work and play.

"Cannell said Garner's from Oklahoma, so [Rockford] is a little Southern," Post recalled. "His father's a trucker. Doesn't want to get in a fight; doesn't want to get his ass kicked. There's something about him that has his hand on his hip, and has a wry sense of himself. So I came back and said 'Harmonica. Nobody's done a blues harmonica thing on TV. But we're [also] gonna use Dobro: this bluegrass instrument that has sass to it. And electric guitar. It's gonna be funky.'" He and Carpenter sat down, mapped it out, and decided to add "a chamber group on steroids: two flutes, two French horns, two trombones ... a weird little orchestra. And [we added] a Mini-moog, which had a sound of its own."[1]

The result shades more toward pop than jazz, but there's no denying the irresistible thumping rhythm and cheerfully insistent melody shared by synth and harmonica. The theme kicks off with a four-beat on drums and builds—with a little help from the horns—to an impudent electric guitar interlude and a final three-note orchestral climax. Post and Carpenter tweaked the arrangement over time, softening the tempo and granting more "space" to the guitar in later seasons. They also contributed fresh and impressively dense underscores to all but a few of the show's 123 episodes: twangy harmonica texturing; brass-forward variations of the title theme; dynamic rhythmic cues and suspenseful action jazz for car chases, brawls and other perilous encounters; and mournful downward spirals of synth and harmonica when Rockford (so frequently) is left with egg on his face.

Although nothing from the voluminous *Rockford* underscore library has been released through official channels, enterprising fans have filled the void with home-grown collections of cues, which are easy to find on the Internet.

Between November 1994 and April 1999, Garner revived *Rockford* for a series of two-hour films. Post scored those as well, granting posthumous co-credit to Carpenter. Post freshened the title theme for each one: adding thundering drums that deliver a powerful two-beat, or a synth line with more echo; slowing the tempo or introducing some acoustic piano; and even tweaking the melody itself.

Jim Rockford wasn't 1974's only long-suffering private sleuth. *Harry O* is one of the rare triumphant efforts to drag a Chandler-esque gumshoe into the modern world, and its success owes much to the world-weary crankiness that David Janssen brings to the title role of Harry Orwell. Philosophical voice-overs suit this guy, who never got over the frustration and anger of having lost his job as a San Diego cop, after being shot in the back. The injury impedes his physical abilities, making foot chases and brawls ill-advised; his unreliable Austin-Healey often forces Harry to rely on the public bus system. Cases aren't frequent enough to keep him financially secure, and—although he always solves them—the resolutions often are less than ideal. Down-time is spent fixing up a boat—dubbed *The Answer*—that has little chance of becoming sea-worthy.

The character debuted in a pair of telefilms: *Such Dust as Dreams Are Made On*, which aired March 11, 1973; and *Smile, Jenny, You're Dead*, which followed on February 3, 1974. Aside from Janssen's character, neither film has continuity with the subsequent series. The first film was scored by Richard Hazard; the second went to Billy Goldenberg, who was retained for the title theme and several first-season underscores when Harry gained his own series in the autumn of '74.

Goldenberg ultimately provided three arrangements of the title theme, as the series was reshaped over time. The initial version is a striking jazz anthem that opens with a powerful 6-4 blast of brass; this segues to a woodwind melody built from alternately rising and falling three-note passages, with background horns providing a countermelody. The woodwind motif repeats, each reprise bookended by the same 6-4 brass fanfare; the melody takes place against a series of clips that feature the obviously damaged Harry doing his best to navigate San Diego's streets.

To boost low ratings, ABC "adjusted" the show midway through the first season. Harry was moved to a Los Angeles beach house, off the Pacific Coast Highway; unaccommodating police Lt. Manny Quinlan (Henry Darrow) was replaced by the similarly irascible Lt. K.C. Trench (Anthony Zerbe). The show's tone became lighter, and Harry's demeanor softened a bit; he also gained a sorta-kinda girlfriend next door, in the form of stewardess Sue (Farrah Fawcett-Majors). Most striking, however, is the miraculous fact that the bullet wound no longer hinders his ability to run, jump and bust through doors like anybody else.

Goldenberg's fresh arrangement of the title theme isn't quite as vibrant. The tempo is slower; the sparkling 6-4 fanfares are absent, although the horns still provide a countermelody against the rising and falling triplets, with a stronger focus on strings. The rhythmic swing element is more pronounced, with an electric guitar adding some twang.

Season two found Goldberg delivering yet another, softer arrangement of the title theme against a much more stylish title credits sequence, which borrows the full-screen text graphics pioneered by *Name of the Game*. Electric guitar is more prominent, as it introduces the melody against delicate percussion. A synth keyboard takes over for the rising and falling triplets, against a double-time rhythm section.

Season one and two underscores—whether by Goldenberg or the composers who followed him—are dominated by conventional orchestral cues and sinister strings, with only occasional nods toward soft jazz (usually echoes of the title theme).

The show didn't generate a soundtrack LP or single.

Banyon may have failed two seasons earlier, but Quinn Martin wasn't willing to abandon the concept of a Depression-era private detective. CBS' *The Manhunter* has the same noteworthy characteristics—a good premise, solid production values, a persuasive sense of the era, and a nifty jazz title theme and underscores—but suffers from ill-advised casting. Boyishly amiable Ken Howard simply isn't right for a role that demands the taciturn determination of grim-faced performers such as Charles Bronson or Clint Eastwood. As a result, the handsomely mounted show—which began with a pilot film on February 26, 1974—didn't last beyond the single season which followed that autumn.

The setting is small-town Cleary, Idaho, in 1934; ex-Marine Dave Barrett (Howard) has just returned from military service in China, to find that the Depression has wreaked havoc with his family's financial stability. A local bank robbery goes badly awry—Dave loses both an ex-girlfriend and his beloved dog—and he vows to bring the killers to justice. After succeeding, he realizes that catching notorious gangsters for the reward money could be an excellent means of keeping the family farm afloat.

The scoring assignment went to veteran clarinetist and saxophonist Duane Tatro, known for stints with bands fronted by Stan Kenton and Mel Tormé, and as the composer of his one and only swing LP: 1956's well-received *Jazz for Moderns*. Tatro subsequently gravitated toward television, and *The Manhunter* was his only solo assignment; he gives the show a strong blend of period jazz and Americana.

"The most fun I ever had was with *The Manhunter*," he recalled. "I got to stretch out musically. I had sort of a 12-toned score, which was very helpful in creating edgy music and slipping into country themes. We used a lot of guitars. I used a gut-string guitar on the pilot, interrupted it with an orchestra when they'd get to a roadblock. The series theme came from the theme I'd written for Ken Howard's character in the pilot. It combined country with a contemporary sound."[2]

Guitars are indeed prominent in Tatro's title theme; so is the aggressively growling piano that anchors an agitated rhythm section. The melody doesn't immediately emerge from the cacophony of brass and reeds, and—when it does—the motif is as twitchy as the rest of the cue. The theme plays against a montage of sepia-hued photographs that evoke the era, with additional clips appearing in fat arrows that point toward and away from the four points of the compass. Brass flourishes then synch to all four arrows as they emanate from a close-up of Howard. Tatro's underscore cues often employ harmonica and accordion against tasty jazz orchestration, to evoke the Americana ambiance.

The series and Tatro's music have slipped into obscurity, although the title theme finally popped up in 2019's *The Quinn Martin Collection, Volume 1: Cop and Detective Series.*

4. Suite Revenge: 1974

Made-for-TV movies often continued to be stealth pilots for potential TV shows, and *Night Games* is a perfect example. The amiable legal whodunit aired March 16, 1974, returning Barry Newman to the role of Tony Petrocelli, a Harvard-educated, big-city defense lawyer who sets up practice in Arizona's small, cowboy-hatted community of Sam Remo. (Newman originated the role in 1970's *The Lawyer*, loosely based on the 1954 Sam Shepard murder trial.) *Night Games'* ratings were high enough to persuade NBC to embark on a series, and the new show—*Petrocelli*—debuted later in 1974, ultimately running a respectable two seasons.

The pilot film gets considerable bounce from Lalo Schifrin's western-hued jazz score. The main theme is a captivating minijazz symphony: It opens with a catchy blend of mouth harp and noodly piano riffs, then adds an attention-demanding blast of percussion, bass and horns as Petrocelli appears on screen, while driving to the Sam Remo courthouse in his rattle-trap truck. Suspenseful bongos and horns make a strong statement and then retreat, the cue softening to a gentle harmonica melody; piano riffs add color as a montage introduces our hero's wife (Susan Howard, as Maggie) and the home they're building, just outside of town. Aggressive drums kick in again, as jazz flute takes over the melody; sizzling strings and horns add tension when the montage expands to include action-packed scenes of the drama to come. The cue builds to a dynamic finale: Synthesizer and bass lend additional pizzazz, and then—instead of the final orchestral blast everybody expects—Schifrin impishly goes the other way, concluding with a wistful harmonica and mouth harp quote.

Flute-, harmonica- and keyboard-driven variations of that theme are frequent as the film progresses, most often as "bumpers" which accompany the fade out/fade ins that originally marked the commercial breaks. Schifrin also works in some sassy piano jazz, heard as a diegetic cue in the bar where we first meet Pete Ritter (Albert Salmi), Tony's resourceful investigator. The story concerns Petrocelli's effort to defend wealthy socialite Pauline Hannigen (Stefanie Powers), accused of having murdered her philandering husband.

Schifrin was retained for the subsequent series, and he supplied rich underscores for 18 of the 22 first-season episodes; his attention to jazz-inflected detail is evident throughout. (Almost all second-season episodes are tracked.) Schifrin reworked his original title theme for its new weekly appearance: an arrangement that is more "mainstream orchestral," and not quite as swinging as the pilot film version. Even so, the Schifrin-style drums are unmistakable, as are the "breaking news"-style jazz strings.

Sadly, none of his music endured beyond broadcast.

* * *

ABC's *Get Christie Love!* should win an award for most title themes within the shortest time period: During a brief seven months, the series went through three sets of composers, while an equal number of executive producers attempted to transform the struggling series into a hit. Their failure was surprising, since the initial pilot film—which ran January 22, 1974—pulled respectable ratings and was well-timed to cash in on Hollywood's blaxploitation phase. The subsequent show's cancellation also was unfortunate from an historical standpoint, since Teresa Graves was the first black actress to anchor a prime-time American network drama; she deserved better.

Graves' spunky charm as undercover LAPD cop Christie Love notwithstanding, her series suffered the same fate as television's attempt at *Shaft*: Both are too bland, homogenized and *nice*.

The series debuted September 11 with a title theme and underscores by Luchi De Jesus, who in the 1970s supplemented his work on network shows with numerous big-screen blaxploitation hits: *Slaughter*, *Detroit 9000* and *Black Belt Jones*, among others. He seemed the perfect choice for this new series, and his underscores are laden with swaggering urban jazz grooves and *wah-wah* guitar. That said, De Jesus' title theme is a *serious* miscalculation: a mawkish, horribly overproduced disco ballad with a mixed chorus chanting inane lyrics highlighted by almost a dozen refrains of the phrase "Get Christie Love." Viewers likely changed channels before the tune finished.

As midseason approached, the title tune was jettisoned in favor of a jazzier instrumental by Jack Elliott and Allyn Ferguson. Unfortunately, it's also dominated by a disco-hued rhythm section; any semblance of melody is buried beneath frequent bursts of brass. It lasted only two episodes (!) before being yanked and replaced by theme No. 3, this one from Stu Phillips and new executive producer Glen A. Larson. This vigorous big band jazz cue has everything its predecessors lacked: a growling urban groove, a pulsating beat—no trace of disco—and a memorable melody that develops properly, includes a sly key change, and builds to a nifty brass climax. This theme also supports a far better credits sequence, which showcases Graves' character as a determined and multitalented woman of action, rather than a mere runway model.

Alas, it was too little, too late. Love closed her final case on April 4, 1975, taking Graves' career with it; she never acted again. None of the show's three title themes made any subsequent appearances.

NBC had much better luck with *its* ground-breaking female cop.

Several episodes of its anthology series *Police Story* served as pilots, the most significant of which was a March 1974 installment starring Angie Dickinson as an undercover officer; she parlayed the role into *Police Woman*, which debuted on September 13. The series ran four seasons, becoming the first *successful* hour-long prime-time American drama with a woman in a starring role. Dickinson's "Pepper" Anderson answers to the Los Angeles Police Department's Sgt. Bill Crowley (Earl Holliman), head of a Criminal Conspiracy Unit that includes Pete Royster (Charles Dierkop) and Joe Styles (Ed Bernard).

Mort Stevens' kick-ass title theme runs a close second to his iconic *Hawaii Five-O* anthem. The *Police Woman* cue opens deceptively, with a slowly descending synth wail—mimicking a siren—against a quiet drumbeat. When this reaches the bottom of the scale, an explosion of brass kicks off a swinging keyboard riff that introduces the 1-1-3 melody on strings—frequently interrupted by more brass elements—against (in Stevens' words) "a heavy Brazilian beat."[3] The theme plays over a series of clips of Dickinson in action, and in revealing outfits; the cue then builds to a climactic orchestral rise and a final flurry of horns.

Stevens also scored the debut episode ("The End Game") and established a jazz template that perfectly suits the action-oriented show, given scripts that always involve chases, fights and violent exchanges of gunfire. Softer, come-hither swing ballads are employed for Pepper's sultry undercover identities. Stevens ultimately contributed a dozen original underscores; his final assignment, a holiday-themed fourth season episode titled "Merry Christmas Waldo," includes a gorgeous jazz arrangement of "Silent Night." Fellow composers Richard Shores, Pete Rugolo, Jerry Fielding and others followed his musical lead, when scoring their episodes. Alas, no soundtrack album appeared.

Stevens' title theme got a lot of cover action, by Tony Camillo's Bazuka (A&M), Henry Mancini (RCA Victor), The Ventures (UA), the John Gregory Orchestra (Mercury), and Ray Davies (DJM). Two decades later, BSX issued a downloadable single of an arrangement Stevens must've made while *Police Woman* was airing, but—for some reason—opted not to release. It's quite faithful to his television version, with an electric guitar solo fueling a fadeout.

Police Woman occasionally succumbed to silly scripts, but ABC's *Chopper One* was relentlessly inane. Dominic Frontiere's jazzy title theme is the sole notable feature of this thoroughly ridiculous adventure show, which was one of America's last network half-hour action dramas. Hunky Jim McMullan and Dirk Benedict are game enough as California-based chopper officers, but they can't inject any credibility into their often moronic dialogue; the writers and directors paid far more attention to the Bell 206 Jetranger than to its human inhabitants.

Even so, Frontiere's boisterous title theme is a hoot, opening with pounding drum rolls and brass fanfares, then sliding into a hard-charging synth melody punctuated by a *lot* of brass ostinatos. It certainly primed viewers for excitement, which made the subsequent 29-minute letdown that much more disappointing. The series lasted only 13 episodes after its January 17 debut, and Frontiere's theme faded into similar obscurity.

ABC did no better with *The Death Squad*, a pallid made-for-TV movie that aired January 8 and blatantly ripped off Clint Eastwood's second Dirty Harry outing, *Magnum Force* (although the notion of a clandestine inner circle of corrupt cops wasn't terribly original to begin with). Robert Forster stars as Eric Benoit, an honest detective tasked with infiltrating a "death squad" of precinct cops who've appointed themselves judge, jury and executioners, whenever blatantly guilty criminals go free as a result of courtroom technicalities. The dialogue is trite, the storyline patently obvious, and the pacing ridiculously accelerated.

The film's numerous deficiencies notwithstanding, Dave Grusin's funk-laden score is worth a listen; the thumping percussion and bass twang clearly anticipate his upcoming work for the big screen's *Three Days of the Condor*. His title theme for *Death Squad* is a groovy blend of electric keyboard and bass, highlighted by flute flourishes. Grusin doesn't bother with character themes; most interior cues are little more than atmospheric bridges between scenes. A few nonetheless stand out: a blast of percussion and bass guitar during a furious chase montage; and a gentle, sweetly romantic melody when Forster has a flirty first encounter with co-star Michelle Phillips.

No soundtrack album emerged.

The Big Screen

Chinatown is one of Hollywood's best-ever detective *noirs*, but it almost didn't make these pages; for the most part, Jerry Goldsmith's memorable score isn't jazz. The bulk of the music is orchestral shading, with distinct atonal classical touches, and he intended as much:

"The producers always talked about providing a period sound, but I didn't want to approach it that way. I felt that would be redundant, given what was on the screen. The unorthodox orchestral scoring came to me after seeing the picture; it just called for a tapestry of sound."[4]

"The first score for the film [by Phillip Lambro] had been rejected, and I was called in at the last minute to rescue it; I wrote the score in 10 days, which was pretty speedy. [Producer] Bob Evans wanted to know how I 'heard' the score, so I said, I hear four pianos, four harps, strings, two percussion, and he said 'Oh, I like that.' So, having spoken myself into this trap, it became a very interesting combination of instruments to write for."[5]

The result nonetheless warrants mention because of the film's achingly bluesy main theme, introduced over art deco title credits: as gorgeous a piece of balladic jazz as ever has been composed, and given its soulful edge by Uan Rasey's dreamy, heartfelt solo trumpet work. Goldsmith earned one of the film's many Academy Award nods, but he lost to Nino Rota and Carmine Coppola, for *Godfather Part II* (a fate shared with almost all the other *Chinatown* nominees).

Robert Towne's complex original story blends classic Hollywood *noir* with a fictitious retelling of the contentious, early 20th century California water wars that led to the expansion of Los Angeles. Private investigator J.J. "Jake" Gittes (Jack Nicholson) initially is hired to determine whether a Los Angeles Department of Water and Power engineer is having an affair. When the man turns up dead, Jake slowly uncovers evidence of a massive conspiracy involving Northwest Valley land ownership;

As explained in the liner notes for Intrada's 2016 prestige rerelease of Jerry Goldsmith's score for *Chinatown*, in many cases his cues employed a "prepared piano," with objects inserted among the strings, to dampen and resonate the sound in strange ways, giving the notes a heavy, percussive quality that matches the film's ambiance (courtesy Intrada Inc.).

the wasteful release of great quantities of reservoir water, despite an ongoing drought; and the stealthy machinations of the murdered man's former partner, the powerful and wealthy Noah Cross (John Huston). Additional intrigue is supplied by Evelyn Mulwray (Faye Dunaway), whose involvement with the case—and Cross—proves *quite* sticky.

Director Roman Polanski uses music sparingly, but to brilliant effect, often during montage sequences. The story's dramatic impact is powered throughout by Goldsmith's primary theme, which doubles as the romantic ballad that eventually unites Jake and Evelyn.

"I was trying to get inside the characters," Goldsmith recalled, "and the opening theme became a period piece with more updated harmonies. The jazziness came about because of the trumpet player interpreting it as a blues, which was very nice."[6]

The initial soundtrack LP blended nine score tracks with three period solo piano diegetic cues; the 2016 digital rerelease features both the reorchestrated LP tracks and Goldsmith's 20 original score cues.

Lambro's rejected score was released in 2012. The track titles make it fairly easy to recreate the soundtrack experience that might have been: another fascinating example of alternate universe choices.

It suddenly seemed like every Hollywood actor wanted to be a cop or private investigator. John Wayne traded his horse for a contemporary detective's badge during a couple of his final movies, with eyebrow-raising results; the aging Duke simply isn't credible as a hard-charging, lone wolf cop in an urban thriller. *McQ* is compromised further by its conservative political views, with Wayne's character and various cop colleagues frequently ridiculing and/or trash-talking youthful protestors, women's lib, "hippie scum" and undefined "militants."

The contrived plot finds Seattle police detective Lon "McQ" McHugh (Wayne) pursuing shipping magnate and drug dealer Manny Santiago (Al Lettieri), suspected of orchestrating the execution of numerous cops. McQ's loose-cannon approach doesn't sit well with homicide supervisor Edward Kosterman (Eddie Albert), who orders the feisty detective to back off; McQ responds by quitting and teaming up with local private eye Pinky Farrell (David Huddleston). Everything builds to a climactic car chase and shoot-out along the damp sand of a foggy ocean beach, involving McQ, Santiago and his men, along with a "surprise" villain who is no surprise at all.

Elmer Bernstein scored many of Wayne's westerns, and therefore was a logical choice for *McQ*'s musical tapestry. Most of his cues are limited to orchestral shading, but Bernstein deserves credit for his riveting title theme; it debuts during a brief prologue, with a lazy electric flute introducing the melody over a cool *ba-bump* strut. *Wah-wah* guitar adds some funk as the opening credits roll, but this is only a teasing taste of Bernstein's theme; it's best used—in full-blown, big-band glory—during action sequences, notably when McQ pursues a laundry van that he believes contains illegal drugs. Bernstein spots this vehicular chase with all manner of funk and jazz shading, while McQ takes his beloved Pontiac Firebird Trans Am through maneuvers that echo the iconic chase in *Bullitt*. After the climactic gun battle, the end credits roll to a final reprise of this main theme, trumpets blaring against thumping, full-blown percussion.

No soundtrack album appeared until 2003.

By the mid–1970s, novelist Elmore Leonard was transitioning from his early-career Western focus to the quirky crime sagas for which he'd soon become famous. *Mr. Majestyk* straddles both genres; it also boasts the intriguing characters and unfortunate coincidences that make his stories so compelling. Mostly, though, we admire Charles Bronson's Vince Majestyk because he's an honorable, working-class

Comparing *McQ*'s soundtrack album with the film reveals that director John Sturges extracted only fragments of numerous cues and eliminated some entirely. One unused treat is "Garden Party," a pleasant jazz cue intended as source background music when John Wayne's character visits his ex-wife, who is hosting an outdoor gathering; the melody is taken by horns and woodwinds, with gentle comping by piano and guitar (courtesy Film Score Monthly).

watermelon farmer: an uncomplicated guy who just wants to get his 160-acre crop harvested, to stave off bankruptcy, but has the bad luck to run afoul of a particularly vicious mob hit man.

Charles Bernstein's score is a welcome step up from his uneven work on 1973's *That Man Bolt*. He blends his jazz roots with bluegrass and south-of-the-border elements that deftly suit the film's setting and characters. The catchy acoustic result gets much of its eccentric pizzazz from the use of a Greek bouzouki and an Indonesian ektara.

"The music needed to touch a lot of bases," Bernstein admitted. "It's set in Colorado. That dusty, Mexican migrant environment is very much a character in the picture, then add to that the suspense and the chases. But the most important thing for [producer Walter Mirisch] was that *Mr. Majestyk* would have a musical voice that didn't sound like other action scores. The music has a larger burden with somebody like Charles Bronson, because his emotions are so hidden. The score has to make us understand what's motivating him."[7]

Majestyk's troubles begin when, having hired some Mexican migrant workers led by part-time union organizer Nancy Chavez (Linda Cristal), he returns home to confront a small-time thug (Paul Koslo) who heads a "field labor protection" racket. Majestyk disposes of him with no difficulty, but then gets arrested and jailed for assault, where he encounters mob enforcer Frank Renda (Al Lettieri). Majestyk unintentionally runs afoul of this hardened killer, who swears lethal revenge. The police, seeing an opportunity to catch Renda in the act, release Majestyk as bait. The stoic hero resumes his harvest, but when one of his best friends is badly injured by Renda and his goons, Majestyk decides to settle the matter via his training as a former U.S. Army Ranger instructor and Vietnam War veteran.

The film's credits unspool against a terrific action theme. Dynamic percussion and drums support Tony Terran's tasty trumpet melody, while Tommy Morgan's harmonica comps gently in the background. The theme suggests regret and resignation, as befits the title character's reluctant embrace of violence as a last resort. Oddly, director Richard Fleischer doesn't use this as Majestyk's primary character theme, relying instead on a cue that opens with sleek guitar work, and then expands with an even more melancholy trumpet melody.

"The use of solo trumpet underlines his singularity, and his inner, unshakeable nobility," Bernstein explained. "It also has a sense of military resolve in its voice, as well as loneliness, both of which reflect Majestyk's character."[8]

Once Majestyk is forced into action, his thoroughly credible reconnaissance—clandestinely sussing out where the bad guys are hiding—is given suspenseful, crowd-pleasing snap by fast-paced bongos, tense percussion and twitchy guitar, bouzouki and harmonica. The final confrontation—with Renda and his remaining associates holed up in an isolated cabin, while Majestyk prowls the surrounding grounds—is spotted by tense percussion, random bongo bursts and an eight-note guitar motif.

No soundtrack album appeared until 2009, on a disc that includes a few unused cues. These include "Chasing the Chase," an exciting blast of percussion that would have been perfect for a climactic car/truck chase; and "Majestyk's Land," a slightly calmer variation of the title theme that Bernstein probably intended for the end credits.

Mr. Majestyk is an entertaining B-flick, but the lurid *Death Wish* made Bronson a superstar.

As many quite talented musicians have learned over the years, developing a film score can be a uniquely intense—and frustrating—process that isn't for the faint of heart. Despite his name success with 1966's *Blow-Up* (see this book's companion volume), Herbie Hancock was unhappy with the result; he waited almost a decade before tackling another big-screen score. Director Michael Winner's adaptation of Brian Garfield's 1972 vigilante novel is notoriously tawdry, but Hancock had no regrets this time; the film gave him an opportunity to compose, perform, arrange *and* conduct what turned into an ambitiously complex jazz score. He alternates between piano, Fender Rhodes, ARP Odyssey, Hohner D-6 Clavinet and a few other electronic keyboards. Many of the resulting cues are jittery, nervous "texture music," intended to heighten Bronson's unsettling surrender to vengeance, when he becomes dissatisfied with the impotent police response to the brutal murder/rape of his wife and daughter.

Once Bronson's Paul Kersey embraces his inner bad self, his search for scumbags—and calm execution of same—unfolds against an exciting jazz backdrop. Hancock's themes unapologetically stoke the fires of our own voyeuristic blood lust; the resulting minisymphony, dubbed *Suite Revenge: Striking Back, Riverside Park, The Alley, Last Stop, 8th Avenue Station* on the soundtrack album, runs almost 10 minutes of pure, heart-pounding pleasure. And yet that isn't the score's most memorable cue. The takeaway tune is the calmer and gentler "Joanna's Theme," which reprises every time Kersey thinks about his dead wife.

"Toward the end of composing for *Death Wish*, I was just completely wiped out," Hancock recalled. "I still needed to write one of the most important parts: a piece for an emotional scene where Bronson's character is recalling his murdered wife. Michael Winner was really anxious for me to nail it. I was anxious, too, as this scene was the movie's emotional core. Finally, at the last moment, I came up with a melody and a chord structure that sounded haunting and heart-wrenching. I wrote out the parts and then hurried to get into the studio with the orchestra, to record it. When we finished.... I walked into the booth to listen to the take, and Michael came in, too. As the engineer played it back, I looked over to see Michael's response—and he had tears in his eyes."[9]

The tune's foundation is classic 1970s funk, but Hancock's melancholy keyboard work achieves just the right effect. In a movie laden with gratuitous excess, the most powerful emotional moment comes when Kersey checks his mail, a few weeks after the initial assault; he finds a packet of photos taken during the Hawaiian trip that he and his wife enjoyed, before they returned to New York. Hancock's wistful melody perfectly punctuates this moment, suggesting the soul-crushing grief that Bronson's stone-cold features can't convey on their own.

* * *

The aftermath of 1972's Watergate crisis prompted a flurry of surveillance/conspiracy thrillers, none more quietly creepy than writer/director Francis Ford Coppola's *The Conversation*. Although the film didn't make much noise during its initial release, the U.S. paranoia quotient has increased exponentially during the post–Edward Snowden era; Coppola's disturbing parable now seems uneasily prophetic.

San Francisco–based surveillance expert Harry Caul (Gene Hackman) is assigned by a shadowy "director" to record a conversation between a young couple (Cindy Williams and Frederic Forrest) during their lunchtime stroll in Union Square. As Harry fine-tunes the results, he becomes convinced that the couple is in danger, quite likely from the people who hired him; this possibility evokes unhappy memories of an earlier New York operation, when some of Harry's clandestine recordings resulted in three people being murdered. Subsequent encounters merely enhance Harry's suspicions, until he finally learns the truth: an epiphany that makes him fear for his *own* safety.

Rising film and TV composer David Shire was married to Coppola's sister Talia at the time, and the three hung out a lot while the filmmaker was shaping *The Conversation*; it was easy for Coppola to offer the scoring assignment to his brother-in-law. In a departure from the standard scoring process—where a composer usually gets involved only after the picture is in postproduction—Coppola instructed Shire to create solo piano pieces that would evoke Harry Caul, as Shire *imagined* him.

"Francis said 'I don't want you to do an electronic score, even though it's about an electronic eavesdropper," Shire recalled, "and I don't want a big orchestra. I want a solo piano score. I'm going to give you five titles—they're not scenes in the movie—and I want you to write short piano pieces about each one."[10] Shire dutifully wrote five thematic sketches and then played them for Coppola; he fell in love with the third one, which blossomed into a primary theme.

"Because I began before the film had been shot, I had a rare opportunity to have the score evolve alongside the creation of the film," Shire continued. "I attended the first day of rehearsal

"[Sound editor] Walter [Murch] turned what could have been a score that started to get boring," Shire acknowledged, during an interview included as a bonus feature in *The Conversation*'s 2011 Blu-ray re-issue, "because it was just piano, into something that had subtle variety, by feeding the piano to the mixing board, so he could vary the texture of the piano. As [Gene Hackman's character] got more and more tormented, the piano got more modulated, and the piano sound got more weird ... until, at the end, the score became electronic" (courtesy Intrada Inc.).

with the cast, when everyone sat around a table and read the shooting script, and I was on location when a number of scenes were shot. I am a firm believer that the unconscious mind does a great deal of the seminal work. The more precisely and vividly the unconscious can be seeded, the juicier and more abundant the fruit that one eventually is able to pick."[11]

Shire ultimately composed a series of cues that he initially performed on his own "poorly tuned" piano and preserved with a Wollensack tape recorder. Although sound editor Walter Murch "sweetened" these original cues—and Shire later rerecorded them on a Steinway grand, under optimal conditions in a Paramount studio—Coppola preferred the unsettling wow and flutter of the initial home recordings, feeling they enhanced Harry's withdrawn isolation and growing paranoia.

When not absorbed by his surveillance tapes and mixing consoles, Harry unwinds by playing his sax alongside jazz LPs. It's an exercise in frustration: His mindset is so rigorously structured—he's so cut off from his own emotions—that he cannot "let loose" and *swing* like the musicians he shadows. This internal conflict manifests in Shire's piano cues. The left hand plays a structurally precise, classically oriented, Chopin nocturne-esque backdrop, while the right hand delivers freer, bluesier runs: subtly haunting, often not so much a melody, as a *feeling*. Shire's primary theme debuts after Harry completes the initial surveillance assignment; it's a haunting pair of quiet, six-note motifs carried by the right hand, which develop into elaborate runs and trills while the left hand comps gently in the background.

Shire's predominantly solo piano score is accompanied by his Ellington-esque, uptempo combo jazz, which serves as the diegetic phonograph music when Harry plays along with his sax. Alas, he's ultimately denied the pleasure he derives from such music. When the film concludes—Harry's already fragile reliance on personal sanctuary completely shattered—he blows jagged, discordant notes from his sax, no longer trying for melody.

"It was a remarkable collaboration," Shire admitted, decades later. "I thought that was the way *all* movies were done, on that level!"[12]

Fans were denied the subtle delights of Shire's score until its 2001 digital release. The sole bonus track is a luscious version of the main theme, arranged for soprano sax, clarinet, bass clarinet, guitar and vibes. It's much too cheerful and "full" to have been appropriate for poor Harry's psychological disintegration.

Shire was given more instrumental freedom with his sensational action score for director Joseph Sargent's suspenseful big-screen adaptation of Morton Freedgood's 1973 thriller novel, *The Taking of Pelham One Two Three*. Screenwriter Peter Stone crafted a superb central character in Transit Authority Police Lt. Zachary Garber, molded to fit star Walter Matthau's curmudgeonly screen presence and signature slow takes.

The bulk of the film unfolds in real time, as four disguised men board one of New York City's downtown-bound subway trains; they refer to each other only as Mr. Blue (Robert Shaw), Mr. Green (Martin Balsam), Mr. Grey (Hector Elizondo) and Mr. Brown (Earl Hindman). They produce submachine guns and separate the lead car from the rest of the train. Blue then contacts the city's subway command center, demanding a random of $1 million to be delivered within one hour; the entire mess lands in Garber's lap. Aside from trying to maintain calm during the ongoing conversations with Blue, Garber also must deal with trigger-happy SWAT teams; an impotent mayor fearing voter backlash; and angry transit colleagues who resent the negotiation efforts. Most crucially, Garber can't figure out the big question: How do the hijackers expect to get away?

"I spent weeks trying to work toward a sound that captured the jazz feel and excitement of New York," Shire recalled, "and yet the sinisterness that went with a thriller."[13]

David Shire cut his teeth in 1969 and '70, scoring episodes of television's *McCloud* and *The Virginian*. The one-two punch of *The Conversation* and *The Taking of Pelham One Two Three* in 1974 quickly transformed him into an A-list film composer, and his career continues to this day. He earned two Academy Award nominations, and won for co-writing (with Norman Gimbel) "It Goes Like It Goes," the title song from 1979's *Norma Rae* (Photofest).

Shire ultimately developed his score—most notably the forceful main theme—in the manner of Arnold Schoenberg's 12-tone compositional structure.

"It was a difficult problem to solve. I knew I wanted dissonant jazz that was coherent and yet original, and didn't sound like watered-down Lalo Schifrin or Quincy Jones."[14]

Inspiration came in an unexpected flash.

"I finally thought about writing a tone row that would automatically be jazzy. So I found one that contained only characteristic jazz intervals: minor second, major seventh, minor third, major sixth. It was a great epiphany moment."[15]

The resulting main theme grabs viewers by the throat from the moment its heavily percussive, two-note bass line blasts onto the screen, with a bank of horns handling the pulsating, atonal melody. Low horns and saxes trade jagged notes that build into a catchy melody which plays over the stark title credits. The theme fades as the film begins; music remains absent until Blue and his colleagues take command of the subway car, backed by a slow, throbbing march of rolling snare drums, jagged low brass and a vaguely defined clarinet melody. Heavy percussion drives a tense, 7/4 variation of the primary theme, during an energetic montage that shows the $1 million in ransom bills counted, assembled and bundled into a sack that's tossed into a waiting police car. Shire's quieter cues are equally effective, as with the disturbing piano riffs and muted bursts of brass that accompany one victim's doomed walk down the track.

The story's lengthy epilogue transforms the narrative into an investigative procedural that concludes with Matthau's all-time best *gotcha!* expression, at which point a slower reprise of the main theme signals the end credits.

Shire's score remained unreleased until it was digitized in 1996. The album includes a few unused cues, notably "Dolowitz Takes a Look/Dolowitz Gets Killed," intended for an early sequence when a transit supervisor unwisely charges down the tunnel. It's a great jazz cue—impudent walking bass and electric guitar, with sparkling piano and trumpet—but probably too jovial for the action it was intended to support.

Some mysteries are too convoluted for their own good, and that's certainly true of *The Midnight Man*. Composer Dave Grusin obviously wasn't inspired, because his score is strictly by the numbers; the cues are divided between ominous atmospheric shading and instrumental arrangements of a bluesy ballad, "Come on Back Where You Belong."

Burt Lancaster stars as Jim Slade, a former Chicago policeman recently paroled after a prison stretch for shooting the guy he found sleeping with his wife. Slade lands in a quiet South Carolina town, where longtime buddy Quartz (Cameron Mitchell) has arranged a job as night watchman at nearby Jordan College. Slade learns that somebody stole several session tapes from the college counselor: a crime that badly upsets a young woman who turns up dead. Local Sheriff Casey (Harris Yulin) and his deputy, Virgil (Richard Winterstein), regard Slade with suspicion, since he was the last person to see the woman alive. Potential suspects include a lecherous, Bible-quoting janitor (Charles Tyner); the woman's sorta-kinda boyfriend (William Lancaster); and her father (Morgan Woodward), a powerful state senator. Slade can't help getting sucked into the case, which blossoms into blackmail and multiple murders.

Grusin's score is dominated by harmonica, used to gut-bucket excess during scenes that involve a gaggle of hillbilly thugs. Otherwise, most of the film's suspense sequences are spotted by moody harmonica, synthesizer, percussion and bass guitar. A few funky, uptempo R&B cues are employed for more aggressive action scenes.

No soundtrack album appeared, although Yvonne Elliman's vocal reading of "Come on Back Where You Belong" was released as a promo 45.

Grusin's touch is equally subtle in *The Yakuza*. Honor and betrayal co-exist in this modern *noir*, set amid the strong traditions of Japan's criminal underworld. Director Sydney Pollack takes a thoughtful approach, with the stiff formality of numerous character dynamics inexorably leading to an action-laden climax. Pollack gave the scoring assignment to Grusin: the first of what would become 10 big-screen collaborations.

Los Angeles–based retired detective Harry Kilmer (Robert Mitchum) is hired by longtime friend George Tanner (Brian Keith) to mediate a "problem" with Japanese *yakuza* gangster Tono (Eiji Okada). The latter has kidnapped Tanner's daughter and her boyfriend; Kilmer flies to Japan and saves them with the help of Tanaka Ken (Ken Takakura). He owes a debt of *giri*—a lifelong obligation—because the American saved his sister Eiko (Keiko Kishi) and her daughter, while stationed as an MP in Tokyo during the post–World War II occupation. The rescue is successful, but an enraged Tono vows vengeance against both men; matters are complicated further by Kilmer's long-unresolved bond with Eiko. Everything climaxes in a suspenseful melee at Tono's gangster-laden compound.

Dave Grusin's score for *The Yakuza*—most cues replete with flutes, chimes and gongs—strongly favors Japanese instruments and influences. Very little can be considered jazz: only one melancholy underscore theme, and a couple of terrific combo numbers heard faintly as diegetic cues (courtesy Film Score Monthly).

The film's primary theme—one of few Western-sounding cues—is a lyrical jazz ballad that characterizes the love and lost opportunities shared by Harry and Eiko. The tender melody is anchored by Bud Shank's luxurious alto sax, backed by gentle strings and percussion. Once the two estranged lovers reunite, their memories are rekindled while wordlessly paging through a scrapbook: a poignant sequence enhanced by a haunting solo piano cue. The first diegetic cue arrives when Ken crosses a street en route to an underworld parley. We hear a fleeting excerpt of a midtempo, funk-laden melody, presumably emanating from a nearby restaurant, which bears the classic Grusin sound: Hammond B3, electric guitar riffs and soft sax licks. Later, Kilmer and Ken consider strategy during a late-night walk along similarly quiet Tokyo streets; *very* faint snatches of a slow, bluesy, sax- and piano-driven swinger drift through the air.

The long-awaited soundtrack, released in 2005, includes lengthy versions of those two diegetic cues: "Shine On" and "Bluesy Combo."

After having jump-started the blaxploitation genre with John Shaft, director Gordon Parks seemed an ironic choice for *The Super Cops*, a cartoonish depiction of two white New York City rookie cops-turned-plainclothes detectives. Real-world Dave Greenberg and

Robert Hantz earned the nicknames "Batman and Robin" for their impressive string of unorthodox drug busts in Brooklyn's notorious Bedford-Stuyvesant neighborhood, a saga also recounted via breathless hyperbole in L.H. Whittemore's 1973 book of the same title. Although time has dimmed the heroic depiction of Greenberg and Hantz, *The Super Cops* remains a modestly entertaining action flick shot on location during New York's prerecovery low point.

The film also boasts one of Jerry Fielding's most entertaining action jazz scores: a smorgasbord of terrific swing, funk and exhilarating big band cues. The title credits unspool against a snappy militaristic march, as a montage reveals New York's mean streets to be a veritable war zone between thugs and overwhelmed cops. Eager newbies Greenberg (Ron Leibman) and Hantz (David Selby) are stuck in menial jobs until the former befriends Sara (Sheila Frazier), a stripper-turned-hooker who helps "educate" him in the way of the streets. Fielding supplies a terrific pair of diegetic cues for their sleazy, dive bar meetings: a fast-paced, funk-laden, sax-driven dance number followed by a slow, sultry blend of guitar, electronic keyboards and dirty trumpet.

Jerry Fielding was busy in 1974. In addition to *The Super Cops*, he scored two other big-screen films, three made-for-TV movies, and between one and five episodes each for a quartet of television shows, including *Hawkins* and *Police Woman* (courtesy Film Score Monthly).

Once the hero-wannabes start making progress, a pell-mell rooftop chase is accompanied by the sort of vibrant, suspenseful action jazz that had become Fielding's trademark. The boys inevitably anger the Hayes brothers (Charles Turner, Ralph Wilcox and Al Fann), who control the local heroin trade; the situation turns dire, but (naturally) everything works out all right. Parks concludes with a dramatized reenactment of the press conference where the actual Greenberg and Hantz were extolled by NYPD Commissioner Patrick V. Murphy; Fielding celebrates the moment with a jubilant, horn-fueled reprise of the march-like main theme.

No soundtrack album arrived until 2006, when Fielding's score was paired with Oliver Nelson's work on 1970's *Zig Zag*.

Meanwhile, Across the Pond...

Roy Budd *owned* British thriller scores in 1974.

Michael Caine's overly stoic performance isn't quite right for *The Black Windmill*, adapted from Clive Egleton's 1973 novel, *Seven Days to a Killing*. The story demands emotional nuance, but Caine reprises the chill, clinical persona that worked far better in *Get Carter*. Even so, *The Black Windmill* is a solid, intelligent and well-paced spy thriller.

The story opens as midlevel British intelligence officer John Tarrant (Caine) attempts to infiltrate a band of arms smugglers who are supplying weapons to Northern Ireland terrorists. Annoyed gang leader McKee (John Vernon) responds by kidnapping Tarrant's young son David, demanding a ransom of £500,000 in uncut diamonds: precisely the items that Tanner's prissy boss, Harper (Donald Pleasance), has earmarked for another task. This bespeaks a mole in MI6, and Harper begins to wonder if Tarrant staged the kidnapping himself. This suspicion blossoms further when McKee and his sexy girlfriend, Ceil (Delphine Seyrig), plant evidence to suggest that she was having an affair with Tarrant. Now surrounded by enemies on all sides, Tarrant's only trustworthy ally is his estranged wife, Alex (Janet Suzman), who rises to the occasion while he tries to locate their son on his own.

There's no trace of Budd's jazz chops as the film opens; the title credits are displayed via tranquil children's alphabet blocks, while a boys' chorus sings the hymn-like "Mother Nature." The mood shifts savagely when Budd and percussionist Chris Karan deliver a glissando of ominous drums and keyboard riffs, which builds to a throbbing burst of action jazz that accompanies McKee's nasty kidnapping of Tarrant's son. Sleek walking bass powers a subsequent swinger, when McKee and Ceil break into Tarrant's flat to take and plant the incriminating photos. Action jazz remains prevalent as the noose tightens, although Budd's softer themes are equally effective: particularly the melancholy piano and string lament heard when Tarrant quietly confides in Alex.

Two sizzling jazz anthems appear as diegetic cues. A funk-laden strut, with plenty of sassy 4/4 drum work, unison horns and electronic keyboard, is heard from a portable radio that Tarrant turns to high volume, to foil an eavesdropping bug planted in his flat. The second is a roaring trio number, with Budd's lightning-quick piano chops echoed by some equally slick bass licks; it's used as the tune McKee listens to on a portable cassette player, when he meets Tarrant for the first time.

The soundtrack album finally appeared in 1999.

Budd's tense jazz score also enhances the suspense in *The Internecine Project*, a devious espionage thriller adapted from Mort W. Elkind's novel *Internecine*. At an economical 89 minutes, the film is a bravura, breathless experience.

Respected American university professor Robert Elliot (James Coburn), based in London, has been selected to chair the U.S. President's Economic Advisory Committee. Nobody knows that Elliot has long been in the hip pocket of an ethically reprehensible multinational corporation, or that his career has benefited from dirty tricks and industrial espionage handled by his network of four cleverly placed confederates. Elliot decides to eliminate all loose ends by devising a round-robin plan of split-second timing, where during a single evening all four of his associates will kill each other: mild-mannered Foreign Office stalwart Alex Hellman (Ian Hendry), upper-echelon gentleman's club masseur Bert Parsons (Harry Andrews), high-class call girl Christina Larsson (Christiane Krüger) and military research scientist David Baker (Michael Jayston).

The film's primary melody is a love theme: a rhythmic, sinuous blend of percussion, strings, vibes and synthesizer, heard each time Elliot's machinations are distracted by former paramour Jean Robertson (Lee Grant). Tasty diegetic cues include a small-combo melody emanating from Christina's record player, as one of her "clients" departs; and a wistful piano trio arrangement of the love theme, heard in a restaurant while Elliot and Jean enjoy what she doesn't yet realize will be their final night together.

The film's lengthy second half is dominated by the unfolding scheme, which Elliot clocks from his study as his four soon-to-be-deceased acolytes phone in each completed step. Much of this sequence plays without dialogue, the suspense built and maintained by John Shirley's sharp editing and Budd's sinister cues. He relies on three repeating motifs, all on Jeff Clynes' bowed bass: a 4-6 note combination; a climbing run of eight notes; and a s-l-o-w rising and falling triad, backed by cimbalom, percussion and twitchy piano riffs. As the scheme builds toward the first execution, Budd increases the tempo to runaway intensity; everything seems to be going down precisely as Elliot planned. Until it doesn't.

No soundtrack album appeared until a chunk of Budd's score was digitized for the 1999 compilation CD, *Roy Budd: Foxbat/The Internecine Project/Something to Hide*. The seven tracks include the short movements of the jazz symphony that dominates the film's second half. *Internecine* finally earned its own full score album in late 2019.

Alas, neither Budd nor Michael Caine could save *The Marseille Contract* (aka *The Destructors*).

Although obviously intended as an adventure thriller in the Alistair MacLean mold, the film is a mess. Budd's mildly ethnic score is badly used by director Robert Parrish, who has no facility for spotting an action movie.

U.S. Drug Enforcement Agent Steve Ventura (Anthony Quinn), assigned to France, has lost numerous colleagues in his effort to bring down drug baron Jacques Brizard (James Mason). Ventura therefore hires suave contract killer Johnny Deray (Caine) to assassinate Brizard. Deray penetrates the drug lord's well-guarded estate by romancing the man's daughter, Lucienne (Maureen Kerwin), but Brizard nonetheless decides that Johnny is a liability. This leads to a tepid third act, when Ventura and Deray team up to bring Brizard down. The film's best action sequence arrived much earlier: a flirty race along twisty mountain roads between Deray, in an Alfa Romeo Montreal, and Lucienne, driving a Porsche 911S: a vehicular duel that's more exhilarating than any of the "serious" peril that follows.

Budd's title credits theme is a cacophony of keyboard noodling, Chris Karan's twitchy percussion—plenty of cimbalom and tablas—and Paul Fishman's electronic effects. The film's primary theme debuts a few scenes later, when a brief sax quote introduces a haunting piano ballad with a 7-7 motif. It debuts while Ventura watches his (married) lover walk down the street outside his apartment. Once Deray is hired for his lethal assignment, he drives to Marseille; his subsequent "chance" meeting with Lucienne, during their playful car chase, is nearly ruined by a lamentable spotting choice. The sequence plays against a weirdly inappropriate, circus-style carousel melody; one cannot *imagine* what Parrish was thinking.

The score regains its suspenseful edge with uptempo, funk-laden action music—energetic piano and percussion—when Deray dodges bad guys and police officers, first in a van and then on a motorcycle. Explosions of horns, strings, drums and growling low-end piano runs spot the climactic finale, when Ventura and Deray surprise Brizard and his men. Budd's best jazz touches actually are diegetic cues: a soft, luscious bit of bossa nova heard from a car radio, when Deray meets Lucienne at a yacht club; and plenty of big band dance swing performed by an ensemble at a charity gala.

The eventual 1999 soundtrack album is rather odd. Many tracks are identified only by their spotting titles—"MC/M2," "MC/M9" and so forth—and the arrangements are significantly different than what's heard in the film. Were it not for multiple arrangements of the primary theme, a casual listener would be hard-pressed to acknowledge that this *is* the film score.

5

So Smooth: 1975

The blaxploitation craze began to wane almost as quickly as it started. Although a diminishing number of films would continue to trickle into theaters until the end of the decade, this was the subgenre's final big year, and the last time an entry is cited in these pages … until post–1970s homages such as 1988's *Action Jackson* and the 2000 remake of *Shaft*.

The Small Screen

Some terrific title themes are recognized the moment they're performed; others endure a difficult childbirth.

After the loss of *Toma*, ABC scrambled to revise, reconfigure or replace what they knew was a can't-miss concept. The result, *Baretta*, can be viewed as "*Toma* lite": another police drama about an unorthodox plainclothes detective with a flair for disguises. Robert Blake's scruffy Anthony Vincenzo "Tony" Baretta is more likable, and a *lot* more playfully eccentric; he drives a rusted-out 1966 Chevy Impala dubbed "The Blue Ghost," and shares his dilapidated apartment with a cockatoo named Fred. Baretta is more comfortable consorting with the amiable low-lifes at Ross' Billiard Academy, than with his fellow officers at the 53rd precinct; he's also famous for signature phrases such as "Don't do the crime, if you can't do the time."

That admonishment originated in the title song composed by Dave Grusin and singer/songwriter/producer Morgan Ames, which is where the story gets interesting.

Blake encouraged his good friend Ames to write a song. Unfortunately, she turned up at the studio recording session—where Grusin and numerous other musicians waited—armed only with a brief, gospel-flavored couplet.

"As I recall, [Grusin] passed out blank paper to the band, [and] went to the piano and started doing his magic," Ames acknowledged. "I know he did write it in his head, driving to Universal."[1]

Grusin's improvised theme structurally supported Ames' couplet; this, in turn, uncorked her creative juices. She arrived at a second recording session with a set of impertinent lyrics that cleverly fit Grusin's funk-laden melody. (She has insisted, however, that Grusin deserves credit for "Don't do the crime/if you can't do the time.") The resulting tune, "Keep Your Eye on the Sparrow," was recorded by session vocalist Jim Gilstrap. Anybody with an ounce of sense would have smelled a hit single.

But not Universal Studios execs, who rejected the song. "They said you can't open a 'white' show with a black singer," Ames lamented.[2]

(We pause for sighs, head shakes and heavenward glances.)

Which is why, when the series debuted on January 17, the sleek title credits sequence was accompanied by an *instrumental* version of the Grusin/Ames song. Gilstrap's vocal track was replaced by an overdubbed electric guitar that *isn't properly synched to the melody*. It's still a cool theme, with a helluva rhythm section and brass elements anchored by wild percussion instruments, some of them sounding like a cockatoo; fortunately, the wobbly guitar yields to unison horns when the melody repeats and builds to its final orchestral flourish. The end credits' shortened arrangement adds a tasty jazz flute and eschews that intrusive electric guitar.

Grusin also scored the first two episodes, although he quickly grew disenchanted. "We had one week between episodes," he kvetched. "Then I'd come in on Monday to look at the next episode, go home, and start writing. After the experience of doing scores for *Baretta*, I refused to write for TV ever again."[3] His displeasure notwithstanding, the underscore cues for those two episodes are excellent, with the drama and action complemented by plenty of fusion "street jazz." Tom Scott subsequently took over, delivering roughly 30 original underscores during the show's four-season run. He also laced his episodes with urban funk, seductively rhythmic ballads and plenty of action jazz.

However…

Blake, Grusin and Ames had the last laugh. *Baretta* was a quick hit, which gave its star enough clout to insist that the title theme be resurrected as originally conceived. The vocal was rerecorded by Sammy Davis Jr. and—just like that—the tune became the bluesy pop sensation it should have been in the first place. Merry Clayton's take-no-prisoners Ode cover—with a cool sax bridge—stayed on *Billboard's* Hot 100 chart for nine weeks, peaking at No. 45 on September 20. Davis' mildly disco-fied version (20th century) went to No. 1 in Holland and Sweden but failed to chart in the States. Additional covers came from Rhythm Heritage (ABC), El Chicano (MCA), double bassist Ron Carter (Kudu) and jazz guitarist Earl Klugh (Blue Note). Grusin, not wanting to be left behind, included the tune on his 1976 album, *Discovered Again!*

The I've-got-your-back "bromance" subgenre of buddy-cop shows began with ABC's *Starsky & Hutch* pilot film on April 30, 1975, followed by its series debut that autumn. The action is set in fictitious Bay City, California, where detectives David Michael Starsky (Paul Michael Glaser) and Kenneth Richard "Hutch" Hutchinson (David Soul) roar around in a bright red Ford Gran Torino. The street-smart Starsky is intense and impetuous, in contrast to the laid-back and intellectual Hutch. They get much of their information from flashy, jive-talking informant Huggy Bear (Antonio Fargas).

The show has a strong musical component, with underscores by jazz heavyweights such as Shorty Rogers, J.J. Johnson and Mundell Lowe. Rather oddly, executive producers Aaron Spelling and Leonard Goldberg ordered fresh title themes for each of the show's four seasons.

The pilot film boasts a suspenseful, hard-edged jazz score by Lalo Schifrin, with plenty of urban funk: *wah-wah* guitars, throbbing electric bass, unexpected blasts of brass, and his signature tune glasses and water phone. Schifrin also inserts a sultry, midtempo big band swinger as a diegetic cue, when the guys visit a lap dance club. The film climaxes with an exciting chase sequence that earns a melodramatic, uptempo 4/4 cue with a unison horn and string melody, against a pounding four-note rhythm ostinato. This cue was extracted and repurposed as the title theme for season one; it plays against a tightly edited series of action clips featuring Glaser and Soul. Schifrin also provided underscores for two episodes, but his busy schedule precluded any more involvement with the series.

Jazz saxophonist Tom Scott was commissioned to deliver a fresh theme when the second season commenced; his get-down-funky, synth-heavy tune ("Gotcha!") is the one with which the show is most frequently associated. Everybody remembers the four rising couplets that introduce the core melody, along with the sleek acoustic piano and electric guitar licks that comp in the background, all rising to an explosive three-note climax.

But as the second season drew to a close, "[The producers decided] they didn't like that one," laughed Mark Snow, who'd been working on *The Rookies* for the same production company, "so they said, Why don't *you* take a shot. So I thought about *Mission: Impossible*, and I remembered that the rhythm was some kind of weird 5/4, and I thought that [would be] a cool idea, with a synthesizer as the lead instrument."[4]

His theme is more ambitious than a steady 5/4, with a rhythmic dum-*da*/dum-*da*-da ostinato backing a synth melody constructed of descending couplets; reprises are interrupted by pairs of four-note horn fanfares. It's a complex piece of music: quite memorable for its twisty delivery. Snow also became the series' most prolific composer, with 16 underscores to his credit.

"[My theme] lasted a year," Snow concluded, with a rueful smile, "and then someone said, Well, let's go back to Tom Scott's version."[5]

Scott responded with a slower, gentler arrangement of his theme; the familiar synth melody is all but lost beneath electric guitar riffs, a pulsating two-beat rhythm section and cool piano comping.

His original version is the one that made waves. He expanded it for a totally groovy Ode/Epic single; it features Richard Tee's wicked piano chops and Scott's wailing sax solo during an extended bridge. Notable covers came from The Ventures (UA) and Rhythm Heritage (ABC). The latter occupied the bottom of *Billboard*'s Hot Soul Singles for seven weeks, peaking at No. 93 on November 5, 1977. A decade later, the UK's James Taylor Quartet delivered a lengthy cover; that one and Scott's original have become ubiquitous on crime/spy jazz anthology albums.

Starsky and Hutch leaped to the big screen in 2004, for a Ben Stiller/Owen Wilson spoof that had nothing to do with the TV series, although Theodore Shapiro's otherwise colorless score does include updated arrangements of Scott's title theme.

Some action shows are remembered primarily for their themes: definitely the case with *S.W.A.T.* The aggressively violent ABC series didn't last long after its debut on February 24, 1975, although it likely introduced sheltered, small-town viewers to the Special Weapons and Tactics squads that had begun operating as the paramilitary arm of conventional big-city police forces, in response to the riots and counterculture protests that erupted nationally in the 1960s and early '70s. Vietnam veteran Lt. Dan "Hondo" Harrelson (Steve Forrest) heads the show's squad of younger, gung-ho officers; the team tackles cop killers, vengeful escaped convicts, assassins, weapons dealers, hostage crises and anything else requiring a lot of ordnance and stunt doubles.

The show was the first television assignment for fledgling film composer Barry De Vorzon, who was flummoxed after viewing the debut episode. "How do you write a hit about a S.W.A.T. team? I spent a week trying … and I finally gave up. So, the next best thing, I [decided to] give [the producers] *the* most exciting main title. At the time, television themes were brassy, big band and jazzy; I brought in a contemporary approach, with a *wah-wah* guitar and some rockin' drums. And I thought I came up with something pretty exciting."[6]

The theme definitely catches one's attention. It opens with a sound effect—a synth imitating a squealing siren—that segues to a *Shaft*-like preamble, while young officers grab guns and hustle into the rear of a waiting van. The rhythm section catches fire as the show's title expands onto the screen against a blast of horns, followed by the signature motif: four descending brass triplets, then a fifth ascending triplet, all against thundering rhythm and percussion. De Vorzon then confounds expectations by introducing an even *more* powerful brass countermelody, as the show's stars leap fences, crash through windows, and rappel down the sides of buildings. The rhythm section rises again, backing a climactic brass triplet when the van screeches to a halt and freezes in front of the camera.

At which point, viewers finally catch their breath.

De Vorzon supplied original underscores for roughly half of the first-season episodes, although most cues are orchestral texturing and string-laden suspense.

Rhythm Heritage gave the title theme a disco-hued bridge on a lively cover for an ABC single; it spent 24 weeks on *Billboard's* Hot 100 chart, and went all the way to No. 1 on February 28, 1976: the first time a prime-time TV theme had topped the singles pop chart since Bill Hayes' 1955 rendition of "The Ballad of Davy Crockett."

Decades later, the "failed" show became an even more violent 2003 big-screen feature starring Samuel L. Jackson and Colin Farrell; Elliot Goldenthal's synth score ignored the TV theme. The series returned to television in 2017, with a fresh cast and plenty more attitude; the title theme—although credited to series composer Robert Duncan—is a kick-ass handling of De Vorzon's original. (Inexplicably, he isn't acknowledged for it.) By this point, the theme also had become an obligatory track on crime and action show anthology albums.

Fortunately, not all 1975 TV cop shows were violent eye candy.

Two years earlier, Joseph Wambaugh and NBC had made television history with what is recognized as the first network miniseries: a four-part adaptation of his novel *The Blue Knight*. The story takes a sympathetic, first-person approach to veteran LAPD street cop William "Bumper" Morgan's final week on the job, in anticipation of his upcoming retirement. William Holden's delicately nuanced starring performance earned one of the miniseries' several Emmy Awards. Nelson Riddle eschewed his swing roots for a melancholy main theme and similarly forlorn underscore, which reflect the mixed feelings of a good man about to walk away from the job that has defined his life.

CBS revived the character for a telefilm on May 9, 1975; it served as a pilot for a series that debuted that December. George Kennedy took over the title role, and Bumper's "final week on the job" telescoped to encompass a single season of 24 weekly dramas. Henry Mancini assumed the musical chores for the pilot film, which boasts one of his career's most luxuriously bluesy torch instrumentals: a dreamy, midtempo melody ("Bumper's Theme") that opens as unison horns climb several scales to introduce a 2-3-2 motif, before yielding to brief solos on trumpet, sax and keyboards. Reprises of the core motif, by the unison horns, build to an achingly poignant orchestral finale.

Unfortunately, CBS execs apparently worried that this theme wasn't "commanding" enough for the subsequent series, which instead was assigned a superficially dynamic—but wholly uninspired—action cue that blends ho-hum clips of Kennedy against a tight close-up of Bumper's patrolman's badge. (Mancini's theme was retained for the end credits.) Episode underscores favored routine orchestral shading and suspense cues. None of Riddle's work emerged from the initial miniseries, but Mancini included an expanded arrangement of "Bumper's Theme" on his 1976 album, *The Cop Show Themes*.

Bumper Morgan would have enjoyed sharing a beer with Alex "Bronk" Bronkov.

Perennial big-screen heavy Jack Palance is cleverly cast against type as this thoughtful, pipe-smoking police investigator, who quietly strives to eradicate organized crime elements in Southern California's fictitious Ocean City. He has a cat, to which he's allergic; he also spends considerable time caring for his emotionally shattered teenage daughter, confined to a wheelchair in the wake of an accident that killed her mother (Bronk's wife). Palance puts a lot of not-quite-concealed pain into his performance, making Bronk a damaged soul not entirely able to adjust to the "new normal" of his everyday life.

Lalo Schifrin complemented Palance's performance with a gentle, mildly forlorn acoustic piano title theme and underscore for the CBS pilot film, which aired April 17, 1975. When *Bronk* debuted as a weekly series in September, Schifrin gave the theme a massive overhaul. Although he retained the somber solo piano melody that shadows the tight close-up that tracks across items on Bronk's desk, Schifrin then shifts to saucy action jazz, while the camera rises and catches Palance staring into the empty barrels of his gun. Those six circular chambers fill with a montage of clips that identify Palance and his co-stars, while unison horns belt out a 5-3 ostinato, against vibrant drums. The theme then emerges via seemingly "distant" brass: a complex melody that opens with a 1-1/1-1/6 motif but then wanders in unexpected directions.

Schifrin also scored two of the single season's early episodes; the rest were handled by Jacques Urbont, George Romanis and Robert Drasnin, all of whom maintained the pilot film's emotionally freighted atmosphere. Aside from Schifrin's revised title theme, nothing could be characterized as jazz; no album or single appeared.

* * *

Donald Hamilton's fans couldn't catch a break.

Dean Martin's big-screen "adaptations" of the Matt Helm novels are spy-spoof travesties (see this book's companion volume), and the character didn't fare any better on the small screen. As portrayed by Tony Franciosa, Helm is a former spy from a nebulous government agency known only as "The Machine," now settled into a new career as a run-of-the-mill TV detective. Absolutely nothing about *Matt Helm* is noteworthy, save (perhaps) for its music.

The show debuted with a telefilm that aired May 7, 1975; it was scored by Jerry Fielding, who "recycled" his title theme from 1970's *Hunters Are for Killing*. It's pretty much the same cue: a jaunty, mixed-meter swinger with a brash brass melody against cool rhythm. It kicks off the title credits sequence, which freezes the show's title against Franciosa's resolute features, while he motors his cute red sports car on a freeway. Fielding's subsequent underscore cues are equally cool, highlighted by propulsive action jazz for various skirmishes and car chases.

Fielding was otherwise occupied when *Matt Helm* became a weekly ABC series that September. Mort Stevens supplied a new and even jazzier title theme, which opens with the thunderous ostinato drum rolls he made famous with *Hawaii Five-O*. Electric guitar riffs and brass fanfares add color after a few measures, then unison low-end horns introduce the dominant 1-1-3 motif. Stevens also supplied the debut episode's underscore, which includes dynamic action cues that also hearken back to his *Five-O* stuff; subsequent episodes are scored by Jerrold Immel, Richard Shores and Richard Hazard, all of whom mirror the jazz template established by Fielding and Stevens.

Neither the music nor Franciosa's charm could save a series blighted by uninspired scripts. *Matt Helm* vanished quickly.

Things went better for one of literary fiction's most famous amateur sleuths.

Eagle-eyed Ellery Queen's final weekly television appearance—after three earlier runs in the 1950s—came with an eponymous NBC series. The show is top-notch in every respect:

faithful production design in a post–World War II New York City setting; clever scripts very much in the vein of the Frederic Dannay/Manfred Bennington Lee novels and short stories; and note-perfect performances from Jim Hutton (Ellery) and David Wayne (Ellery's police inspector father, Richard Queen). The mysteries are "fair": Key clues are presented along the way, and Hutton breaks the fourth wall at the end of the third act, challenging viewers to solve the case before he reveals the answer after the commercial break.

The show also boasts a sleek title credits sequence, anchored by Elmer Bernstein's bluesy, period-appropriate big band jazz theme. The cheerful swing number opens with walking bass, piano filigrees and cymbal brushes, which introduce a languid 1-1-4-5-5 motif played by soft unison horns; occasional blasts of brass and keyboard "stings" suggest light-hearted suspense. The theme plays over the slow pan of a chessboard laden with "clues"—a torn photo, ephemera from the Stork Club, broken spectacles, a telephone ripped from the wall—before a climactic *bam*-bump that focuses on a typewriter and a broken chess piece (the queen, of course).

Bernstein handled underscores for 17 of the single season's 23 episodes: mostly orchestral flourishes, along with soft jazz variations of the title theme. The post–World War II setting also grants ample opportunities for big band jazz heard as diegetic music from radios or performed by live orchestras at restaurants and nightclubs.

None of Bernstein's music survived beyond the series, which is tragic; worse yet, Ellery hasn't been seen since, on a screen of *any* size. That said, Hutton's actor son Timothy honored his father's work here in an episode of his larcenous 2008–12 series, *Leverage* (about which, more later).

The Big Screen

Gene Hackman and jazz composer Don Ellis reunited for *French Connection II*, which takes Jimmy "Popeye" Doyle out of his New York comfort zone and puts him in the dangerously unfamiliar territory of Marseille. He makes the trip ostensibly to help French authorities hunt for Charnier (Fernando Rey), since Popeye is the only person who knows what the elusive drug smuggler looks like. Unfortunately, the local cops—led by Lt. Barthélémy (Bernard Fresson)—resent the presence of this uncouth, loose-cannon American interloper, who can't speak a word of French. Worse yet, nobody tells Popeye that he has been set up as bait, in the hopes of luring Charnier and his minions out of hiding. That plan works *too* well, when Popeye is snatched from under police surveillance, tortured quite horribly, and then left to die. Ah, but he's a strong son of a bitch; Popeye recovers and, having made amends with Barthélémy, is on hand for a thoroughly satisfying final encounter with Charnier.

As director William Friedkin had done on the first film, John Frankenheimer elected not to use portions of Ellis' score, instead repeating cues written for other scenes. The title theme is far more conventionally melodic than what Ellis wrote back in 1971, with ferocious horns powering through stark credits. This brief cue immediately segues to a quieter, flute- and string-driven slow waltz that introduces the Marseille setting. Popeye's eventual kidnapping is heralded by drum rolls and an aggressive, cacophonous blast of horns. Ellis then shifts to dissonant synth effects for the subsequent montage, to amplify Popeye's mounting delirium when he's deliberately hooked on heroin, then given an overdose intended to kill him. When Popeye and Barthélémy subsequently track down Charnier, he flees during the ensuing confusion, the American doggedly on his heels. This foot chase gives Ellis an excuse for a cue written in one of his wonky time signatures—5/8—that echoes the film's main theme with mounting intensity and excitement. The pursuit runs long, concluding when Frankenheimer delivers one of the sharpest, most staccato final scenes in cinema history. Ellis caps the moment with a disconcerting synth echo that segues into a melancholy reprise of the main theme.

No soundtrack album appeared until 2001, when it was paired on a disc with Ellis' score for the first film. Unused sequel cues include "Popeye's Montage" and "Rehabilitation," funky jazz/fusion melodies probably too cheerful for the relentlessly dour and downbeat tone Frankenheimer desired.

Popeye wasn't the only American cop in unfamiliar territory. *Brannigan*, the second of John Wayne's clumsy, late-career police thrillers, exploits the veteran actor's awkward genre fit by making his character a true fish out of water: a Chicago cop unwillingly transplanted to London. Tough-talking Jim Brannigan is sent across the pond for the (supposedly) simple extradition of smarmy American gangster Ben Larkin (John Vernon), but the assignment becomes anything but routine. Obligatory action sequences blend with Brannigan's annoyance over the more restrained British approach to police work, and his new colleagues' patient efforts to tolerate *him*. The brew gains some pizzazz from Dominic Frontiere's energetic score, which mixes solid action jazz with droll cues for the lighter moments.

"[Wayne] used to call me 'composer,'" Frontiere laughed, "because he couldn't pronounce my last name. [He] was one of the only characters I ever saw on screen that no matter what you wrote for him, his character would come through."[7]

The credits hit the screen over a slow pan of police weaponry; Frontiere's vibrant title theme opens with a drum roll that segues to a trumpet-driven melody, backed by funk-laden percussion. Unison horns dominate the bridge, after which the theme concludes with an orchestral fusillade as the action begins. Once in Merry Olde, percussive bursts add tension when Larkin is kidnapped by a pair of thugs, who demand a sizeable ransom from the mobster's shady lawyer, Fields (Mel Ferrer). The ransom drop is surveilled, the money collected by a motorcycle courier who roars off to an unknown destination, and the chase is on; Frontiere responds with a vigorous blast of percussion, low-end strings and trumpet pops, as Brannigan closes in. This is mere preamble to the film's centerpiece chase sequence, when Brannigan later hijacks a civilian's yellow Ford Capri coupé to pursue a baddie through Central London, ultimately jumping across the half-raised Tower Bridge: a swinging, sax-driven action cue exquisitely timed to editor Malcolm Cooke's suspenseful cuts.

The soundtrack remained unreleased until 2003. The 2014 Blu-ray includes an isolated score track.

On the private eye front, Paul Newman finally took a second (and final) shot at the gumshoe he introduced in 1966's *Harper*, this time in an updated adaptation of Ross Macdonald's second Lew Archer novel, 1950's *The Drowning Pool*. The narrative shifts from California to Louisiana's bayou country, which affords composer Michael Small the perfect excuse for a lazy, bluesy score that emphasizes Cajun and Dixieland touches.

Harper is brought to the Pelican State by an old flame, Iris Devereaux (Joanne Woodward), who is being blackmailed by—she believes—a recently dismissed chauffeur. The case soon involves local oil tycoon Jay Hue Kilbourne (Murray Hamilton), who'll stop at nothing to purchase the Devereaux estate, to get at the black gold that lies beneath. While trying not to get smacked around by Kilbourne's goons, Harper also runs afoul of local Police Chief Broussard (Tony Franciosa) and his arrogant deputy (Richard Jaeckel). Sidebar distractions are provided by Kilbourne's abused and fearful wife, Mavis (Gail Strickland); a woebegone prostitute, Gretchen (Linda Haynes); and Iris' unmanageable teenage daughter, Schuyler (Melanie Griffith).

Much of Small's score is atmospheric shading, with scenes often bridged by brief Cajun/Dixieland bumpers. Gentle jazz touches include a languid guitar/horn theme that accompanies Schuyler's clumsy attempt to seduce Harper; and a sassy swinger that backstops the airboat swamp ride that brings the detective to his first meeting with Kilbourne. Small also contributes several mellow solo piano cues; most are brief, although he displays cool keyboard chops when the film concludes and cuts to the end credits. The most frequently heard theme, however, is an instrumental arrangement of Roberta Flack's 1973 No. 1 hit, "Killing Me Softly with His Song." Charles Fox—who wrote the song with lyricist Norman Gimbel—is credited with scoring and conducting this and other jazz covers, which director Stuart Rosenberg employs as the wistful, what-might-have-been backdrop to Harper's scenes with Iris.

No soundtrack album was released.

In a similar old-school vein, *Night Moves* is a beguiling crime thriller that evokes pleasant memories of Raymond Chandler. Los Angeles–based investigator Harry Moseby (Gene Hackman) is hired by fading actress Arlene Iverson (Janet Ward) to find her runaway 16-year-old daughter, Delly (Melanie Griffith, again playing a jail-bait tart). Harry quickly realizes that Delly has begun an angry campaign of seducing her mother's former lovers; he therefore flies to the Florida Keys, where her stepfather Tom Iverson (John Crawford) lives with a sorta-kinda girlfriend, Paula (Jennifer Warren). Delly is indeed present, but she refuses to return to California; it also becomes clear that something much more sinister is going on.

Michael Small's score is one of his best: gently swinging jazz, smooth as silk, which perfectly evokes the story's milieu. Most cues are variations on Small's primary theme—actually Harry's theme—which debuts over the opening credits. Strong bass licks and funk-laden percussion introduce a melody that emerges on electric keyboard. Woodwinds and trumpets rise in the background, lending the cheerful impression that Harry is a man wholly at peace with himself, and with his work. Once in Florida, he manages to get the oddly evasive Paula into bed. A gentle solo guitar is joined by bass and reeds during this intimate encounter; while the surface impression is erotic, there's an underlying sense of sorrow and resignation, as if both Harry and Paula know they're coupling for the wrong reasons.

Harry ultimately solves the case, but at great cost. Penn slowly pulls the camera back on the final scene, while Small reprises the main theme one final time; the by-now familiar bass, percussion and electric keyboard are heightened by rising sax and trumpet fanfares. This theme continues for a full 45 seconds after the end credits conclude, and the screen has gone black.

No soundtrack album appeared, which isn't likely to change; the score's master tapes are known to be lost.[8]

Speaking of Chandler…

The image is iconic: Robert Mitchum's Philip Marlowe stands, framed by the window of a flea-bag hotel, cigarette smoke swirling in front of his chiseled features, a glass of whiskey in one hand, while he stares thoughtfully at the late-night streets of early 1940s Los Angeles. Add David Shire's sinuous theme—powered by dreamy solos from Dick Nash (trombone) and Ronnie Lang (alto sax)—and we're swept into a time, place and mood that perfectly evoke

Chandler's world-weary private detective. Many have tried to replicate the rich, atmospheric blend of story, image and music that characterized classic post–World War II *film noir*; few have succeeded as well as director Dick Richards, with his lavishly mounted adaptation of *Farewell, My Lovely*.

Marlowe is hired by ex-con Moose Malloy (Jack O'Halloran) to find Velma, the girlfriend he hasn't seen during his seven years in prison. While pursuing this case, Marlowe is asked to accompany Lindsay Marriott (John O'Leary) on a ransom drop, to recover a valuable jade necklace that was stolen from "a friend." The drop goes badly; Marlowe is knocked unconscious and recovers to find Marriott dead. Further

"I thought about the score for *Farewell, My Lovely* as homage to *film noir*," Shire acknowledged during a 1999 interview, "an opportunity to pay a tribute to this sort of music." He succeeded, and then some; this score deservedly stands alongside genre classics such as Jerry Goldsmith's work on *Chinatown* and *L.A. Confidential* (courtesy Film Score Monthly).

investigation leads him to the necklace's likely owner, Helen Grayle (Charlotte Rampling), the promiscuous trophy wife of the elderly but still powerfully connected Judge Baxter Wilson Grayle (Jim Thompson). Marlowe becomes convinced that Marriott's murder and Velma's disappearance are related, and that they somehow involve Helen and her association with high-rolling hoodlum Laird Brunette (Anthony Zerbe); he runs a casino on the Lido, a gambling ship anchored just outside the three-mile limit.

"That came very easily" Shire acknowledged, years later. "It was the kind of theme and score that I'd been aching to write for a long time."[9]

His affinity for this *noir* atmosphere is obvious. The aforementioned title theme opens with a gentle piano filigree; subsequent trombone and sax solos expand the melody orchestrally, with sweeping strings lending an atmosphere of disenchantment and regret. A shrill, unsettling soprano sax sets the stage when Malloy aggressively asks Marlowe to "find my Velma," after which Shire's score cues remain orchestral and mostly atmospheric for a time; jazz is limited to diegetic cues such as the solo pianist in the bar where Marlowe seeks a lead; and the combo jazz later heard on a radio belonging to Jessie Florian (Sylvia Miles). When Marlowe finally connects all the dots, he and Malloy head out to Brunette's gambling ship; Shire backs them with propulsive action jazz driven by a bank of horns, twitchy reeds and intense piano. Once aboard the Lido, an on-board band performs some spritely 2/2 swing; the melody is introduced by Justin Gordon's clarinet, and then handed off to solos on muted trumpet and piano, with trombone, guitar, bass and drums keeping things lively in the background. The denouement is swift and vicious; back on land, Marlowe wanders alone down the city's dark streets, while the end credits scroll up the screen to a final reprise of the melancholy title theme.

The soundtrack album includes the bulk of Shire's music, along with the lively combo source cues.

On the blaxploitation front, Tamara Dobson's Cleopatra Jones went international for her follow-up assignment. *Cleopatra Jones and the Casino of Gold* takes the bad-ass special agent to Hong Kong and Macao, where she matches wits with another Caucasian drug queen, dubbed the Dragon Lady (Stella Stevens). This sophomore outing more aggressively taps into the kung fu craze, with Dobson often overshadowed by the martial arts moves of her petite sidekick (Ni Tien).

The story begins in Hong Kong, as Cleo's two friends—Matthew and Melvin (Albert Popwell and Caro Kenyatta)—attempt to penetrate a drug-running operation overseen by Soo Da Chen (Shen Chan). They land in the middle of a turf squabble between Chen and the Dragon Lady, and wind up as the latter's "honored guests" (prisoners). Cleo jets in, determined to rescue the boys; she's helped by Hong Kong detective Mi Ling Fong (Tien), who—with her three biker associates—proves quite useful when the going gets rough. Everything climaxes in a sensational melee that wrecks the Dragon Lady's opulent casino.

Dominic Frontiere's vibrant score is an exciting, orchestrally lush blend of jazz and funk, with an exotic Asian undertone occasionally reminiscent of Lalo Schifrin's work on *Enter the Dragon*. Most of the score's action cues are adapted from Frontiere's main theme, which opens the title credits with an explosion of brass, before settling into a sultry R&B anthem—"Playing with Fire"—performed by a breathy female chorus. The theme immediately reprises as a tense instrumental; unison trumpets and strings belt out the melody when Matthew and Melvin head for their ill-fated meeting with Chen. When Mi Ling later gets ambushed in her apartment by a squad of Dragon Lady thugs, the resulting martial arts skirmish is choreographed to jagged trumpet fanfares and furious pentatonic runs. On the other hand, Frontiere's spotting decisions for two chase sequences are downright bizarre: silly, fiddle- and washboard-hued "hoedown" cues that belong to a chaotic cowboy bar fight in a Hollywood Western.

The Dragon Lady's opulent Macao casino gives Frontiere an excuse for several diegetic cues. The first—a droll, bluesy duet on piano and bass—is heard in the background, when we first glimpse this gambling palace. A quieter lounge ballad, by the same duo, serves as ironic counterpoint while the Johnson brothers make the most of their captivity. The final casino melee detonates as Frontiere powers the entire orchestra into an exciting blast of action jazz, replete with vigorous percussion, slashing strings and taut brass fanfares. Rarely has a lavish set been destroyed with such pizzazz.

The soundtrack album didn't appear until 2010, when it was paired with the J.J. Johnson/Joe Simon score for 1973's *Cleopatra Jones*.

Paranoia abounds in director Sydney Pollack's masterfully suspenseful *Three Days of the Condor*, a clever blend of conspiracy anxiety and nasty spy craft. The script is adapted faithfully from the provocative premise in James Grady's debut novel, and the film gets considerable tension from Dave Grusin's slick blend of engaging R&B and twitchy, nervous-making atmospheric cues.

Joseph Turner, code-named Condor (Robert Redford), is one of half a dozen low-level CIA agents working for the "American Literary Historical Society," in Manhattan's Upper East Side. He returns from a lunch run one day and finds that everybody else in the building has been assassinated. Subsequent developments make his superiors worry that perhaps Turner is a rogue agent turned killer. Unable to trust anybody on his side, and with unknown bad guys also after him, Turner randomly "kidnaps" Kathy Hale (Faye Dunaway), to have a safe—if temporary—haven at her apartment. Sensing Turner's innocence and vulnerability, Kathy overcomes her initial terror and proves quite useful, when he employs years of resourceful book-smarts to work out a plan that might extricate himself from this dangerous mess.

Grusin's score is dominated by two primary themes, the first of which is a six-note motif initially heard on trumpets, while the title credits overlay the story's prologue. The second theme is a more complex melody played on cimbalom, backed by synthesizer comping and playful percussion. The larkish jazz is as light and frothy as the banter between Turner and his colleagues.

Following their collaboration on *The Yakuza*, Dave Grusin became director Sidney Pollack's go-to composer for the rest of the latter's career, and the score for *Three Days of the Condor* is a terrific precursor of even greater things to come. Future projects would include *Absence of Malice* and *The Firm*, discussed in subsequent chapters (courtesy Film Score Monthly).

"The cimbalom melody is very straight, and it was shadowed by a synthesizer," Grusin recalled. "I always took every chance to work with Emil Richards, because he had the most amazing collection of ethnic and esoteric percussion instruments. He had *warehouses* full of this stuff."[10]

The film previewed several times, prior to its release. "I got a call from [director] Sydney [Pollack]," Grusin laughed. "He said, 'Tell me if I should be worried about this. People are *tapping their feet* during the main title.' I said, is that a problem? And he said, 'Well, I don't want them to feel too *comfortable*.' And I said, Well, maybe they *should* feel comfortable, because everything that comes after is gonna shock them!'"[11]

Once Turner is on the run, having drafted Kathy to his cause, she generously allows him to take her to bed: an improbable seduction backed by an achingly sexy love theme built from the primary six-note motif, with Tom Scott's lazy sax leading the melody against soft synth. The next day, Turner is armed with a strategy of sorts; Grusin supplies a series of unsettling atmospheric cues—muted horn, uneasy percussion, jarring synth and nervous bass, accompanied by sinister strings—as this plan is put into action. Although Turner ultimately gets answers, his life remains in jeopardy ... or maybe not. Grusin's signature piano noodlings segue to a bright, optimistic reprise of the love theme when Turner uncorks a final surprise. But the piano riffs hesitate and trail off, as the camera freezes on a close-up of Turner's face; we're left to wonder if this Hail Mary play will be successful.

The initial soundtrack LP is quite unsatisfying, dominated by the longer cues that feature both the "Condor Theme" and "Goodbye for Kathy" (the love theme), with less attention paid to Grusin's suspense cues. The 2012 digital release resurrects Grusin's full score, paired with his work on 1973's *The Friends of Eddie Coyle*.

In the realm of spoof *noir*, director Blake Edwards and star Peter Sellers revived their beloved franchise with *The Return of the Pink Panther*, in many ways the series' most satisfying entry. It's also the only other film—after the first one—that is an actual caper comedy. The story opens with a slick heist sequence, as a masked intruder breaks into a museum in the fictional country of Lugash, evading high-tech security to steal the Pink Panther diamond; a white glove with a monogrammed "P" is left in its place. This points to Inspector Clouseau's old nemesis: Sir Charles Lytton (Christopher Plummer), notoriously known as The Phantom. The language-mangling inspector heads to Nice, where Lytton lives with his wife, Claudine (Catherine Schell). As it happens, Lytton had nothing to do with the theft; he therefore evades Clouseau and the Lugash secret police to clear his name. To make matters worse, an unknown assassin keeps trying to kill Clouseau. Everything builds to a droll climax with a satisfying twist.

Henry Mancini once again delivers a delectable string of character and "setting" cues, most of which are fully realized melodies in a variety of styles. Famed *Panther* saxman Plas Johnson wasn't available, but Tony Coe's tenor sax work is equally choice. The whimsical title credits, again designed by animator Richard Williams, run a leisurely four minutes; Mancini expands his rhythmic "Pink Panther Theme" with sleek solos on flute and muted trumpet, against cool keyboard comping. The late-night heist sequence follows immediately, set to a slower version of the "Panther" theme against suspenseful bongos and expectant sax licks, while the masked intruder evades various security measures. Later, when Lytton is forced to flee, he heads to Lugash and a dangerous meeting with a notorious criminal known as the Fat Man; this encounter takes place against a swirl of belly dancers, giving Mancini an excuse for a couple of sexy diegetic cues dominated by distinctive Middle Eastern instruments.

Claudine, meanwhile, has decoyed Clouseau to Gstaad, Switzerland; sleek walking bass and cheerful trumpets spot the inspector's effort to be suave. Mancini himself supplies the keyboard chores on a briefly heard, cocktail-style diegetic cue when Clouseau endures a clothes fitting by the hotel tailor. He ultimately solves the case—sort of—during a climax that leaves everybody happy except his long-suffering boss, Chief Inspector Charles Dreyfus (Herbert Lom); the end credits roll against a sprightly reprise of the title theme.

The soundtrack album includes all the major themes, many reorchestrated and expanded to showcase various soloists. Unfortunately, the truncated arrangement of the title credits theme omits Adrian Brett's peppy flute solo.

Subsequent entries in this series—*The Pink Panther Strikes Again* (1976), *Revenge of the Pink Panther* (1978), *Trail of the Pink Panther* (1982), and *Curse of the Pink Panther* (1983)—continued to feature Mancini scores, but his style shifted as the films became increasingly overblown. Full-length swing and jazz cues gave way to pop tunes and conventional orchestral spotting; the only exception is the evergreen title theme. *Son of the Pink Panther* failed to revive the series in 1993, and Mancini's score drifted even further from its jazz roots. Things finally improved musically when star Steve Martin and director Shawn Levy rebooted the series in 2006 (about which, more later).

Even the weakest *Pink Panther* effort is better than *The Black Bird*, a failed attempt to spoof 1941's big-screen adaptation of Dashiell Hammett's *The Maltese Falcon*. Time has made the ill-conceived *Black Bird* even worse, particularly with respect to the racist humor milked from gumshoe Sam Spade's name. The idiotic storyline finds Sam Jr. (George Segal) suddenly besieged by various individuals—the urbane DuQuai (John Abbott), Russian *femme fatale* Anna Kemidov (Stéphane Audran), and a bald Nazi dwarf named Litvak (Felix Silla)—who seek the Maltese Falcon stored somewhere in his office. Sam Jr., can't understand the fuss, because he *knows* this particular statuette is a fake ... then again, what if it isn't? The height of humor (?) comes from Sam Jr.'s inability to park his car on San Francisco's hilly streets; everything else—the maladroit dialogue, and the half-hearted efforts at physical humor—succumbs to lack of interest.

This torpor also affected Jerry Fielding, who delivered one of his weakest scores; it barely contains enough jazz to warrant mention. The best examples are diegetic cues performed by the resident jazz band at The Rythm Room—the misspelling apparently intended as a joke—where Sam Jr., first encounters Anna. Both cues are medleys of up-tempo "jump jazz" numbers that would have been common during the era of the 1941 Bogart classic; one of this film's weak running gags is that Spade and his various clients dress and frequent locations typical of that time period, despite the story being set in 1975. Other sorta-kinda jazz touches include the sultry clarinet cue against which Anna reveals some of her past; and a drum-fueled arrangement of the "Hawaiian War Chant," with brass taking the melody, heard when Sam Jr., tries to escape from the four huge Hawaiian thugs in Litvak's employ.

The soundtrack album didn't appear until 2010.

Meanwhile, Across the Pond...

ITV's *New Scotland Yard* opened the door for serious dramas that examine conflicted police officers willing to bend the rules in pursuit of justice; *The Sweeney* blew that door off its hinges. This grimly violent series is driven by John Thaw's starring performance as Det. Inspector Jack Regan: a walking rage machine who works for the Metropolitan Police's Flying Squad, which focuses on violent crime. (The show's title is shortened from *Sweeney Todd*, which via Cockney rhyming slang conveys "Flying Squad.") Regan is partnered with the younger Det. Sgt. George Carter (Dennis Waterman), who usually plays "good cop" to his impetuous, temper-prone companion. The characters were introduced on June 4, 1974, in an episode of the anthology series *Armchair Cinema*. Response was positive, and *The Sweeney* began its four-series run the following January 2. (Thaw and Waterman also starred in a pair of big-screen adaptations, *Sweeney* and *Sweeney 2*, made between the third and fourth series.)

The show's hard-charging title theme is by veteran jazz pianist and big band leader Harry South, who slid into TV and film work after two busy decades as a leader, sideman and composer/arranger for luminaries such as Annie Ross, Jimmy Witherspoon, Buddy Rich and Sarah Vaughan. South's theme opens with five sustained notes that descend the scale against a pounding 4/4 rhythm section; unison horns then blast the 3-3-9 motif that British TV fans recognize to this day. The theme plays against blue-hued still shots that grant considerable attention to Regan's car, while introducing the stars; the tempo slows as South concludes the theme against a final credit that reveals the episode title. The end credits melody is entirely different: a softer, slower ballad arrangement, with an atmosphere of regret.

South's title theme is the only music composed specifically for the show. Episode underscores are tracked with cues from UK "production music" libraries such as Bruton, Chappell, De Wolfe and KPM (Keith Prowse Music). That said, the uncredited music supervisor(s) who assembled these underscores frequently focused on jazz; many episodes are laden with swing, funk, big band and R&B from a veritable Who's Who of British talent. Source cues tend to be softer, with ballads from famed jazz pianist Marian McPartland a frequent go-to choice.

South expanded both his title and end credits themes for an EMI single. The former was covered by the Alan Tew Orchestra, on a single released by Epic.

Interest in the show's music increased with time, finally resulting in a 2001 digital compilation: *Shut It! The Music of The Sweeney*. Die-hard fans wanting more must have been delighted by the dogged efforts of an enthusiast who painstakingly assembled a collection of 335 library tracks, available via the Internet gray market.

The characters were revived for a 2012 big-screen film that starred Ray Winstone as Regan, but Lorne Balfe's dreary synth score doesn't come close to jazz.

Session composers who wrote and performed cues for music libraries rarely got an opportunity for name-brand recognition; pianist/arranger Alan Tew is among the lucky exceptions. He scored the eight-episode ITV miniseries *The Hanged Man*, which aired February 15 through April 5, 1975. The gritty crime drama stars Colin Blakely as construction company entrepreneur Lew Burnett, who finds himself the target of multiple murder attempts. After narrowly surviving the third try, he decides to "stay dead," to clandestinely figure out who is determined to kill him. The search sends him to numerous countries to confirm or discard friends and business rivals who might hate, love or envy him enough to want him out of the way.

Tew gathered a tight combo of fellow session players—provocatively dubbed Bullet—whose identities have been lost to the mists of time, although best guesses include Alan Hawkshaw (keyboards), Alan Parker (guitar), Les Hurdle (bass) and Barry Morgan (drums). The resulting score became a cult favorite and (decades later) a much-sampled collection of funk-laden jazz/rock cues.

The title theme opens with a suspenseful 3-6-3 rhythmic ostinato, while Burnett drives a small skip-loader down a rickety bridge, unaware that he's being observed from afar. The cue crescendos when the vehicle malfunctions, plunging him into the water below; a synth melody rises as the distant watcher smiles with satisfaction, when Burnett fails to reappear. Bongos add to the rhythmic intensity as the saboteur strolls away. But he leaves too quickly; Burnett breaks the surface, sputtering, as the synth melody reprises. The eight episodes make frequent use of synth-heavy jazz and funk cues: slow, tense swingers characterized by heavy two-beats; fast-paced action jazz; bluesy flute and vibes ballads; tense, twist-the-knife suspense cues; and numerous arrangements of the title theme.

It's uncertain how many cues Tew composed specifically for the miniseries, as opposed to those he may have written and recorded for earlier production libraries. A soundtrack LP was issued—highly unusual, for a show with such a short run—and quickly became a cult collector's item. Tew's expanded title theme arrangement is even more aggressive, with a growling electric guitar bridge; the other 13 tracks are pulsating street jazz at its torrid best. Four bonus tracks were added for a 2011 digital release, as part of an Alan Tew compilation that includes dozens of additional tracks from KPM's Themes International music library.

5. So Smooth: 1975

* * *

A decade after the very American George Segal was badly miscast as the title character in 1966's *The Quiller Memorandum*, novelist Elleston Trevor's mysterious British spy starred in a BBC-TV production simply titled *Quiller*. The 13-episode series aired in late 1975 and then promptly vanished: one of the many shows destroyed during BBC's "great tape purge." Star Michael Jayston is a far more satisfying Quiller, a top agent working for a clandestine British spy organization known only as The Bureau. He's sent around the world on various spycraft assignments: preventing assassinations, investigating bizarre murders, rescuing kidnap victims, assisting defectors, and so forth.

All episodes are scored collaboratively by Richard Denton and Martin Cook, both guitarists, keyboardists and orchestra leaders now best known for their themes and underscores for several 1970s BBC programs and documentaries. Their title theme for *Quiller* is a terrific blast of funk-laden action jazz that opens with drums, bongos, throbbing bass and a killer rhythm ostinato; random synth and piano riffs eventually coalesce into a melody of sorts, as unison brass helps the orchestra build to a breathtaking climax. The theme is remembered today thanks to an extended arrangement featured on a 45 single released when the show debuted. The B-side features "General Direction," an expanded, rock 'n' roll arrangement of an underscore cue that includes a cool jazz bridge dominated by brass and keyboards. It's impossible to know what the rest of the underscore cues sounded like.

Denton and Cook included both *Quiller* tracks on their 1980 compilation album, *Hong Kong Beat & Other BBC TV Themes*.

On the big screen, *Diamonds* gave composer Roy Budd an opportunity for a rare musical mash-up: a score that blends mainstream jazz and blaxploitation funk with Israeli klezmer and folk traditions. The modest crime drama is as much a travelogue as "impossible heist" puzzler, with considerable footage devoted to culturally significant sites and locales in and around Tel Aviv and Jerusalem.

The story begins in London, when wealthy diamond merchant Charles Hodgson (Robert Shaw) "arranges" a relationship with ex-con safecracker and jewelry forger Archie (Richard Roundtree) and his grifter girlfriend, Sally (Barbara Hershey). Charles outlines an audacious plan to empty the vault of Tel Aviv's fabled Diamond Exchange, reputed to be impregnable due to state-of-the-art security measures. They fly to Israel, spending several weeks in preparation; they cleverly throw suspicious police detectives off the scent by concocting a parallel—but entirely bogus—plot to steal a priceless religious artifact. The film's lengthy third act is devoted to the actual heist, which climaxes with an unexpected twist.

Budd assembled an eclectic orchestra that blends electronic keyboards, saxophones, harpsichords, *wah-wah* guitars and drums, with unusual elements such as cimbalom, tablas and all manner of exotic Israeli percussion instruments. Many of the resulting cues—including the main title—open with a sparkling "shimmer" of chimes, intend to convey the glitter of diamonds. The title theme is fueled by deep, 2/2 blasts of percussion; the melody emerges as a 4-4-1-2-8 motif on electric piano, with Duncan Lamont's soulful sax adding a wistful quality at the bridge. The film's most frequent cue is a repetitive, funk-laden seven-note suspense motif at the extreme bass end of the keyboard, propelled by Chris Karan's rapid-fire drumming. This cue's most extensive use comes during the third act, at several different tempos, while Charles and Archie navigate each security obstacle en route to the Exchange's vault.

Budd also wrote a trio of mainstream jazz swingers, probably intended to be inserted as diegetic music, but none wound up being used in the film.

The soundtrack album includes those unused diegetic cues, along with three versions of the title song by Three Degrees. Several of Budd's other cues have proved popular with rap and hip-hop artists, and have been sampled by Snoop Dogg, Wu-Tang Clan, LTJ Bukem, AraabMuzik and others.

6

God's Lonely Man: 1976

Lalo Schifrin gave an enlightening response, when asked to describe the difference between scoring a feature film versus a television episode.

"If you write a letter to some relative, about a trip to Hawaii, you can write many things, all the details. [But] if you have to send a cable, you have to make it concise: reduce it to a minimum, and say as much as you can. Television [scoring] is like a telegram."[1]

As had been true for the past decade, Schifrin once again worked both ends of that spectrum this year.

The Small Screen

Depression-era private detectives may have worked on the big screen, but television was a cruel client. The Academy Award success of *Chinatown* likely influenced the arrival of NBC's *City of Angels*, and the atmosphere feels right; tough-talking, rule-bending gumshoe Jake Axminster works from an office in L.A.'s famous Bradbury Building, drives a 1934 convertible Studebaker, and constantly is at odds with the shamelessly corrupt police department. Jake's cases are lifted from actual Depression-era scandals: the T&M Studio, with its stable of movie starlet look-alike prostitutes; the 1933 "Business Plot" conspiracy attempt against President Franklin D. Roosevelt; and other sordid events that involve Nazism and the Ku Klux Klan. Alas, boyish Wayne Rogers is badly miscast as Jake, and the show never found an audience.

Nelson Riddle contributed a jazzy, brass-heavy title theme and at least one underscore during the 13-episode run that began February 3, but his style is much too "modern" for the 1930s setting. Unison horns launch the 6-5-4 motif against a sepia-hued montage of vintage clips, interspersed with snippets of Rogers doing investigative peeping, spying and photographing. The melody reprises against a pulsating 1-2-2 rhythm ostinato, followed by a countermelody during a brief bridge; the initial motif reprises again and climaxes with an orchestral flourish. Riddle's underscore maintains the jazz ambiance, but the cues are too "cheerful" for the show's attempt at Chandler-esque, *noir* moodiness. Worse yet, many action jazz cues sound like what Riddle wrote for *Batman*: definitely *not* the right touch.

None of Riddle's music enjoyed any sort of afterlife.

Depression-era Los Angeles wasn't the only "Angel" on the season's TV schedule.

John Forsythe's off-camera narration opens each episode of ABC's *Charlie's Angels*, and—even allowing for context and historical perspective—the first sentence is teeth-grindingly patronizing: "Once upon a time, there were three little girls who went to the Police Academy." Despite being "talented operatives" at a private detective agency run by the unseen Charlie Townsend (Forsythe), Kate Jackson, Farrah Fawcett-Majors and Jaclyn Smith spend an impressive amount of time going undercover as bikini models, beauty pageant contestants, student nurses, belly dancers, cheerleaders, housemaids and anything else that allows their assets to bounce as much as possible (hence the demeaning descriptor "jiggle TV").

The memorable Jack Elliott/Allyn Ferguson main theme is a masterpiece of disco sensibilities over rhythmic jazz, and a dire indication of things to come. The heavily orchestrated (4)-3-3-3 motif—against a heavy, *thump-thump* disco beat—repeats endlessly during an inane credits sequence, which features clips of the three stars doing dangerous stuff like roller skating, driving fast, running who knows where, and drawing a gun on an unseen adversary.

Elliott and Ferguson were credited for all underscores during a five-season run that began September 22, but assignments actually were divided among numerous composers. "Inevitably, there would be the car chase, or one of the Angels was in trouble and she'd have to get away," explained Scott Smalley, son of orchestrator Jack Smalley. "So we'd crank up the rhythm section and have a big band screaming through it. With the big band, we could give it an element of fun, even though they were being chased by some serial killer or drug lord that they were going to arrest."[2]

Smalley *fils* was being kind. Very few of the underscore cues could be considered jazz, big band or otherwise, but the title theme was a bona fide phenomenon. Covers came from The Ventures (UA) and Netherlands chanteuse Donna Lynton (EMI Holland). Henry Mancini's uptempo arrangement, with its cool Randy Waldman organ solo, is the version most folks heard; it entered *Billboard's* Hot 100 chart on March 19, 1977, and peaked at No. 45—on April 30—during a nine-week run.

The series begat two big-screen features as the new century dawned: *Charlie's Angels* and *Charlie's Angels: Full Throttle*. ABC commissioned a reboot in 2011, which ran a paltry eight episodes before being deservedly canned. None of these Angels-come-lately jiggled to jazz.

Fortunately, other efforts treated TV cops with more respect.

In the real world, John P. St. John was a phenomenal Los Angeles Police detective, spending 43 of his 51 years of service as a dogged homicide investigator whose career began with the notorious 1947 Black Dahlia murder; when he retired in 1993, it was as LAPD Detective Badge No. 1. His fame prompted *Los Angeles Times* journalist Al Martinez to write a 1975 biography titled *Jigsaw John*, a nickname initially given the detective after one of his early cases was a dismemberment murder; it lingered because of the attention to detail that enabled St. John to "piece together" clues.[3]

He was ripe for pop-culture exploitation, and a well-cast Jack Warden introduced St. John to American viewers in a pilot telefilm, *They Only Come Out at Night*, which aired April 29, 1975. The response was positive, and an eponymous NBC series debuted the following February 2. Unfortunately, very few of the scripts exploit St. John's patient analysis of cold cases; most are routine murder investigations, and the show was canceled after only 15 episodes.

Pete Rugolo's terrific jazz theme plays against an inventive credits sequence. Dynamic rhythm and urgent unison horns back a flurry of action clips; a sudden shift to swing tempo highlights a sleek electronic keyboard solo, as further clips are superimposed on large, three-dimensional jigsaw puzzle pieces that slowly "build" St. John's Badge No. 1. The melody reprises on unison strings and horns, alongside additional keyboard comping, as the camera pulls back to reveal Warden staring down at the assembled badge. A climactic orchestral salvo is followed by a final brass fanfare, and the sequence fades to black. Sen-*sa*-tional.

Alas, none of Rugolo's music survived beyond its broadcast run.

John P. St. John was a phenomenal cop; so was Frank Serpico. But poor David Birney couldn't begin to fill Al Pacino's big-screen shoes, when ill-advised NBC execs brought *Serpico* to television, following a modestly successful pilot film—*Serpico: The Deadly Game*—that aired April 24, 1976. The resulting series debuted five months later but ran only 14 episodes, the character having become just another cookie-cutter loner.

The show was humdrum, but you'd never suspect as much from its title theme. Elmer Bernstein hearkened back to his *Staccato* days, with an electrifying, drum- and rhythm-heavy big band jazz cue that screams for attention. It opens with two quartets of slow, thundering beats, then launches into a suspenseful 2-3-5 rhythmic ostinato that supports a blazing unison brass melody; this plays against an action-filled montage intercut with newspaper clippings and blistering Internal Affairs letters. The melody yields to a brief but scorching sax solo at the bridge, then returns to the ostinato before shuddering to an abrupt climax.

Bernstein's involvement concluded with the pilot film and title theme; his successors didn't deliver anywhere near the same intensity. The show—and its music—are all but forgotten.

ABC's *Most Wanted* gave Robert Stack another starring role in a law enforcement series, this time as Capt. Linc Evers, head of an elite LAPD task force charged with nailing criminals on the city's "Most Wanted" list. He's assisted by Sgt. Charlie Benson (Shelly Novack) and Officer Kate Manners (Jo Ann Harris). The series began as a pilot film telecast on March 21, 1976; it featured Tom Selleck as a fourth member of the team, but he opted not to return when *Most Wanted* was okayed for a full season in October. (He'd soon be otherwise occupied.)

The resulting series is undistinguished, but it does features another of Lalo Schifrin's energetic title themes (taking over from Patrick Williams, who scored the pilot film). Schifrin opens with a 3-3-7 rhythmic ostinato, against which a vibrant 6-6 synth melody plays as a laughably grim-faced Stack is shown in numerous action clips. The theme builds to a pair of 3-5 brass fanfares as Stack and the other cast members are identified, then Schifrin repeats the original melody via strings, before concluding with an orchestral flourish. Schifrin also scored the debut episode, providing crackling cues for a plot that involves an airplane hijacker. Richard Markowitz scored the second, but most of the rest were tracked from library cues. After a few episodes, the credits sequence was "adjusted" slightly, to include some clips of Stack *smiling*. The title theme also changed a touch, perhaps reflecting an alternate take. This suggestion of a "kinder, gentler" Stack didn't help; the series perished after a single season.

Schifrin's title theme and first episode underscore finally were digitized in 2019, as part of *The Quinn Martin Collection, Volume 1: Cop and Detective Series*.

Schifrin included the title theme on his 1977 album, *Towering Toccata*; the expanded, heavily disco-fied arrangement features sleek bass work by Will Lee, and a cool electric violin solo by John Blair. "He uses a five-string violin which goes to a low C, like a viola," Schifrin explained. "He plays very soulful, like Jean-Luc Ponty, only more funky."[4]

The Big Screen

Despite the passage of time, *Taxi Driver* remains a powerful, deeply disturbing portrait of barely repressed rage, and a grim reminder of just how mean New York City's streets were, back in the 1970s. This modern *noir* is graced with a taut, psychologically dense script; Michael Chapman's sublime cinematography; an utterly unforgettable performance by star Robert De Niro, who somehow makes the unhinged Travis Bickle both dangerously unstable and oddly endearing; and a vividly moody, jazz-hued score.

"[Bernard Herrmann] was my first and only choice," director Martin Scorsese insisted. "Travis Bickle was the kind of person who didn't listen to anything besides the voices in his own head, and I was convinced that the only person who could capture this state of mind was Bernard Herrmann."[5]

The composer who delivered so many of Alfred Hitchcock's iconic scores sets precisely the right mood during the title credits montage. The sinister, string-laden opening is what Herrmann's fans expected; the jolt comes when Chapman's camera cuts to a close-up of De Niro's eyes, at which point we hear the smoky, sultry jazz theme—its melody line delivered primarily on alto sax (Ronnie Lang), with an occasionally assist on trumpet (Malcolm McNab)—that becomes a musical signature for Travis' lonelier moments.

"When that first cue came up, it surprised *me*," Scorsese recalled, years later.[6]

Herrmann called this mournful tune "Betsy's Theme," for the young presidential campaign worker (Cybill Shepherd) who catches Travis' fancy, and who he ineptly attempts to date. Scorsese employs this cue as the film's dominant melody; it most tellingly accompanies Travis' first meeting with Iris (Jodie Foster), the teenage prostitute he'll soon attempt to "save." It even reprises as phonograph source music when Iris' creepy pimp (Harvey Keitel) "cajoles" her into accepting her street-walking lot in life.

Herrmann's music was rearranged and reorchestrated for the initial soundtrack LP, apparently to make the album more "commercial"; the overwrought result is completely unfaithful to the film's bleak atmosphere. Arranger/conductor Dave Blume transformed the primary cue—now called "Theme from *Taxi Driver*"—into a radio-ready love song, with the sax melody given a pop-oriented "lift" echoed by disco-esque percussion. Herrmann never would have okayed such artistic gutting, but he wasn't around to object; the great composer died in his sleep on Christmas Eve 1975, mere hours after completing the studio recording of *his* score.[7]

"The so-called 'original soundtrack album' was actually a re-recording," noted orchestrator Christopher Palmer, "made a day or two later, and following Herrmann's death, for which [Ronnie Lang] was no longer available, and that Tom Scott subbed."[8]

The initial 1985 digital reissue repeated this artistic offense. Fortunately, Arista made up for earlier transgressions with 1998's expanded edition. Fans finally could hear Herrmann's music as he wrote it, and as it was used in the film: everything from the appropriately mournful "Betsy's Theme" to the orchestral leitmotifs, dominated by unsettling harp, percussion and string passages, that characterize Travis' deteriorating state of mind.

Given cinema's proliferation of raging, self-styled social avengers, Clint Eastwood's Harry Callahan began to look mild by comparison.

The perfunctory elements of feminism inserted within Callahan's third thriller may have seemed progressive at the time, but the results haven't worn well. *The Enforcer* too frequently suffers from lazy scripting; the primary bad guy—DeVeren Bookwalter—is a ludicrously exaggerated, kill-crazy psycho with all the credibility of a cartoon character.

More troubling—for our purposes—is the suspicion that director James Fargo had little use for music. Much of the film goes unscored, giving composer Jerry Fielding—standing in for Lalo Schifrin—little opportunity to deliver the jazz vigor for which he had become known.

In a nod to the then-notorious Symbionese Liberation Army, Harry's opponents are a gaggle of violent militants who curry media "respect" by calling themselves the People's Revolutionary Strike Force, when in fact they're merely vicious, greedy thugs. The film gets most of its dramatic heft from the initially prickly relationship between Harry (Clint Eastwood) and new partner Kate Moore (Tyne Daly), foisted upon him by "enlightened" politicians. Kate gives as good as she gets, and the growing bond she shares with Harry is far more interesting than the militants' contrived antics.

Fielding salted his massive studio orchestra with a ringer: saxman Art Pepper, who delivers a prominent solo during the swinging jazz waltz—boasting plenty of percussion, piano and blasts of brass—employed as a title theme. The score's highlight, however, comes midway through the film: a suspenseful, swinging minisymphony in multiple jazz movements, which follows Harry and Kate as they doggedly chase a suspect along and above the streets of San Francisco. Fargo presents the sequence as a lengthy, six-minute montage without dialogue; Fielding's cue supplies the excitement. The first movement is dominated by snare drums, *wah-wah* guitar, brass fanfares and a wicked flute solo; this segues abruptly to double-time swing powered by walking bass, electronic keyboard, plenty of brass fanfares and Pepper's screaming sax solo. Furious flute riffs are joined by staccato 2-2-2 blasts from the horn section; then the tempo shifts again, the third movement fueled by funky, midtempo bass and percussion. Backing horns climb the scale as they build to a climax, and then the tempo slows again; Fielding pulls back on everything except twitchy bass and edgy cymbals, when Harry *finally* gets his man. At which point, viewers are as breathless as Kate, who has been running just as stubbornly.

Alas, the rest of the film lacks the sizzle of such musical steak. Fielding manages a few brief swing cues elsewhere: a variation of the title theme—absent Pepper's sax solo—when Harry and Kate depart after watching a demonstration of a portable M72 LAW anti-tank weapon; and some sleepy, funkified percussion and bass, heard when some innocent black militants are arrested by Harry's reflexively racist superior.

Fielding's score finally was released in 2007, at which point fans had vivid proof of the shameful way Fargo had treated the music. The album's 13 tracks are sensational: definitely one of Fielding's best-ever jazz scores.

Schifrin, meanwhile, was busy with *Special Delivery*: a peculiar beast that can't decide what it wants to be. The film begins as a serious heist thriller, when gun-toting Jack Murdock (Bo Svenson) and three buddies steal $500,000 from a metropolitan bank. Their getaway goes seriously awry; one of Jack's comrades is killed, and the other two are arrested. Jack escapes, but only after stuffing a briefcase—containing his share of the loot—into a street-corner mailbox: an act observed by both Graff (Michael C. Gwynne), a drug-dealing bartender; and Mary Jane (Cybill Shepherd), a free-spirited bohemian artist. The film's tone changes completely at this point, becoming a light-hearted romance complete with flirty one-liners and a fuzzy little dog, while Jack and Mary Jane try to figure out how to retrieve the briefcase before the mailbox is emptied, just before midnight. Graff, in turn, has his own scheme for snatching the loot.

Schifrin's funk-laden score is all business: a solid action jazz experience very much in the mold of his work on *Bullitt* and *Dirty Harry*. The title theme opens with growling bass, horns and rhythmic kick drums; the propulsive melody is introduced via strings and unison brass, while cinematographer Harry Stradling, Jr., follows the gang via a distant tracking shot, as they travel along a freeway and eventually arrive at the bank. The robbery gains its nervous energy from plenty of bass, percussion and twitchy, low-end piano; drums and bongos enhance the anxiety when Jack and his cohorts begin their ill-fated departure.

The underscore then retreats for a bit, aside from a couple of diegetic cues. The first comes from a solo jazz pianist, performing at the restaurant where Mary Jane briefly meets her ex-husband; the second is soft combo jazz highlighted by electronic keyboard, heard in the background when Jack visits a massage parlor to give a packet of cash to the wife of his dead comrade. Funk-laden bass and kick drums resume when the opportunistic Graff puts his plan into motion; Schifrin injects more twitchy piano filigrees and a sleek rhythmic ostinato when everything builds to an action jazz-laden car chase.

Special Delivery did almost no business when it was dumped into theaters in the early summer of 1976: no surprise, then, that it failed to generate a soundtrack album.

Schifrin didn't have time to worry about it, since he jumped immediately into *St. Ives*. This tricky crime thriller is one of Charles Bronson's softer starring vehicles, but there's nothing soft about Schifrin's energetic jazz score, highlighted by a kick-ass title theme with a cool swinging groove. The film is drawn from thriller author Ross Thomas' *The Procane Chronicle*, but the adaptation is a mess, with far more double-crosses and duplicitous side-bar characters than this economical 94-minute film can endure.

Bronson is uncharacteristically smirky as Raymond St. Ives, a retired newspaper crime reporter turned would-be novelist who—needing the money—acts as a go-between when the wealthy and reclusive Abner Procane (John Houseman) agrees to pay a $100,000 ransom to recover five stolen journals. Every potential ransom exchange gets derailed by another dead body, which puts St. Ives in the crosshairs of two investigating police detectives (Harry Guardino and Harris Yulin). Procane eventually reveals himself to be a master strategist of complicated heists, with the assistance of live-in companion Janet Whistler (Jacqueline Bisset); they include St. Ives in their latest caper, which promises a $4 million score. Things … go awry.

Schifrin's propulsive score generates more tension than the film deserves. The title theme opens with a driving 4/4 beat that introduces the melody's rapid-4/slow-3 motif on sax (Bud Shank), backed by pulsating bass; the cue develops with strings and Dennis Budimir's *wah-wah* guitar, as Bronson's well-dressed figure fills the frame. Shank repeats the seven-note motif as the cue softens; gentler bass and guitar riffs fade out as the credits conclude. Janet gets a quieter sax cue, when St. Ives meets her, but the bulk of the score is classic Schifrin action jazz: plenty of horns, synth effects, percussion and, at times, a throbbing electric bass. The score's showpiece is a lengthy cue that anticipates the heist: a montage that opens with energetic vibes and bongos, slides to soft percussion and the eerie sound of brushed piano strings and builds to a fast-paced beat and tense piano riffs. Cue the final "surprise" twist, followed by a satisfying resolution and a welcome, uptempo reprise of the main theme, as the end credits roll.

Schifrin's score screamed for release, but no album ever appeared. Even so, sports fans grew quite familiar with the title theme, which was used by CBS Television for its golf broadcasts in the 1970s and early '80s.

* * *

As a distressing example of the way film studios sometimes operate, Keith Laumer's 1971 novel *Deadfall*—a clever Sam Spade/Philip Marlowe pastiche—was turned by W.D.

Richter into an equally droll, *noir*-hued screenplay titled *Fat Chance*. But 20th Century–Fox lost interest and kept the film shelved for a year; when finally released in 1976, it was chopped to an unsatisfying 87 minutes and retitled *Peeper*.[9] Despite bombing at the box office, the film isn't nearly as bad as its reputation suggests, and one wishes for an opportunity to see the original cut. Albert Brenner's production design is vintage post–World War II Los Angeles, and Richter has a lot of fun with the narrative voice-overs spoken by transplanted British gumshoe Leslie C. Tucker (Michael Caine). Busy television composer Richard Clements, on his sole big-screen assignment, honors the genre with a bluesy jazz score that emphasizes sultry sax.

Tucker is hired to find the long-lost daughter of gangster Anglich (Michael Constantine), who left her at an orphanage decades earlier. Clues lead to the wealthy Prendergast family, specifically to daughters Ellen (Natalie Wood) and Mianne (Kitty Winn), one of whom is certain to be the girl in question. Tucker's efforts to solve this mystery are hampered by their eccentric mother (Dorothy Adams) and uncle (Thayer David), along with two bungling assassins (Timothy Agoglia Carey and Don Calfa) who keep popping up at inopportune moments.

The clever title credits are presented by a Sam Spade lookalike who ambles up a darkened alley and *speaks* them in a Bogart drawl; Clements contributes a haunting solo piano source melody, presumably from a nearby bar. A melancholy sax cue heralds our first glimpse of Tucker, as he introduces himself via a mildly self-deprecating voiceover. From that point forward, most of Clements' score is a succession of suspenseful action cues during Tucker's various encounters with the clumsy (but determined) assassins. The narrative builds to a comic climax aboard a luxury liner; once Tucker solves the case, the end credits crawl up the screen to a reprise of the moody sax main theme.

No soundtrack album was produced.

Meanwhile, Across the Pond…

British disciples of the audaciously weird and wacky retain fond memories of *Gangsters*, a surreal crime drama from the cheekily demented minds of writer Philip Martin and producer David Rose. The 12-part series was unexpectedly outré and even shocking by mid–1970s standards: the sort of deliberately bizarre "storytelling" that David Lynch and Mark Frost would unleash 15 years later, in the States, with *Twin Peaks*.

Tough-as-nails former SAS officer John Kline (Maurice Colbourne) is recruited by law enforcement to become an undercover agent, assigned to suss out warring criminal factions in savagely multi-ethnic Birmingham. Violence and racial prejudice are pervasive; Kline's efforts to blend with—and contain—the city's lawless elements take place in a heightened reality that evokes the American Wild West. Smash-cut inserts reference old movie posters, *film noir* clips, Bollywood hits, kung fu B-flicks and graphic text elements; supporting characters included neo-*femme fatale* CIA agent Sarah Gant (Alibe Parsons), human trafficker Aslam Rafiq (Saeed Jaffrey), Chinese Triad gang leader Shen Tang (Robert Lee) and an unapologetically racist night club comedian (Rolf Day, playing himself).

Prog rock keyboardist/composer David Greenslade's memorable main theme is a hypnotic swinger with a deliberately unsettling melody against an infectious rhythm section. It kicks off against a montage of Kline running along a motorway that leads into an underground tunnel; the show's credits are overlaid in white text against this action. Briefs inserts arbitrarily highlight a belly dancer and random movie preview clips that promise "high voltage drama" and "a most colourful drama of hate and love." Kline emerges from the tunnel and races up to an elevated walkway, now running in slow motion (!). Like, *crazy*, man.

Greenslade beefed up the instrumentation and keyboard elements for the second set of six episodes, bringing in R&B singer Chris Farlowe to croon a newly added vocal element. Greenslade also recorded a fresh arrangement of his instrumental theme for a 45 single in early 1976.

John Kline wasn't the only television character thrust into bizarre situations.

When last seen in the spring of 1969, Patrick Macnee's John Steed and Linda Thorson's Tara King had accidentally blasted themselves into space, during the tag scene of *The Avengers'* final episode. "They'll be back," insisted their portly boss, Mother (Patrick Newell). "You can depend on it."

He was only half right. After numerous hiccups, false starts and near misses, Macnee's Steed did indeed return to British television on October 22, 1976, as the star of *The New Avengers*. He's accompanied this time by expert marksman/martial artist Mike Gambit (Gareth Hunt) and former Royal Ballet trainee Purdey (Joanna Lumley). This new team energetically tackles another collection of delightfully bizarre adventures that frequently stray into science-fiction territory. Laurie Johnson gave this reboot an updated title theme and supplied original underscores for every episode during the two-season run. Each adventure features the same blend of sly, suspenseful cues and big band action jazz that were Johnson's hallmark during the latter years of *The Avengers*.

"One day, leaving my office at Pinewood [Studios], heading downstairs to the restaurant, I 'heard' the theme almost complete," Johnson recalled. "I instantly returned to my office, wrote it down at my desk, and arrived at the restaurant 15 minutes later. As I've said, 'themes' are the easy bit. The series required two minutes of theme and eventually about 13 hours of scored, synchronized music made up of about 650 pieces of recorded music."[10]

The reworked title theme opens with the familiar 1-4-1-4 rising brass fanfare, then segues to a martial-esque drumbeat augmented by sleek bass work; this accompanies Macnee's on-screen credit. Two drawn-out crescendos of unison horns, followed by staccato, five-note fanfares, introduce Hunt and Lumley. A brief bridge—a descending 3-3-5-3 motif—concludes with a dynamic five-note flourish.

Johnson's underscores vary wildly, depending on a given episode's theme and tone. The tense cues for the straight espionage of "To Catch a Rat" have an Eastern bloc flavor, for a story that concerns the hunt for a long-buried double agent within the British security service. "The Tale of the Big Why" prompts a road trip propelled by a sassy, midtempo swinger, when Steed & Co. embark on an odd treasure hunt. Lighter episodes—"Sleeper," "Forward Base" and "Emily"—find Johnson in a whimsical mood; the latter opens with a sizzling chase cue, but the episode is dominated by a cute tuba/banjo *oom-pah* melody written for the title character (a vintage automobile).

Johnson recorded an expanded arrangement of the title theme for a 45 single, backed by a stitched-together "track" of dialogue and music clips dubbed "A Flavour of *The New Avengers*"; he later included both on digital anthology albums such as *The Professional: The Best of Laurie Johnson* and *Cult TV Themes*. The show finally got its own full-length soundtrack disc in 2009, as part of the box set *The Music of Laurie Johnson, Volume 3: The New Avengers*.

This, finally, was the last we'd see of John Steed and *The Avengers*... until 1998's ghastly big-screen adaptation, about which the less said, the better.

Thrilling espionage is at the heart of *The XYY Man*, which boasts a premise familiar to American viewers. Cat burglar William "Spider" Scott (Stephen Yardley) began life in Kenneth Royce's 1970 novel of the same title. (The title refers to an "extra" Y chromosome that Scott possesses, which supposedly makes him prone to larcenous activities.) After three stretches in prison, Scott resolves to go straight, but the British Secret Service decides that his B&E skills could be quite useful. Worse yet, Scott remains in the radar of former underworld associates who *also* desire his talents. Although MI5 liaison Fairfax (Mark Dignam) can protect him to a degree, it's not enough to keep tenacious police Det. Sgt. George Bulman (Don Henderson) from dogging Scott's every move, hoping to throw him right back into the pokey.

Scott's adventures were perfect for television, and ITV delivered a three-part adaptation of Royce's first book in July 1976; it proved popular enough to generate a 10-episode season of original stories.

Mike Moran's captivating title theme is a finger-snapping slice of jazz funk; it plays behind a title sequence that shows Scott's silhouette against a montage of clips that suggest his escape from prison, his wall-hugging second-story activities, and his efforts to elude police capture. Moran opens with a smooth rhythmic ostinato, then introduces a brief melody (of sorts) via solo sax. That instrument's touch is more prominent during the longer end credits arrangement, backed by lively unison brass and impudent keyboard comping. Episode underscores are limited mostly to diegetic music emanating from radios, record players and the like: everything from contemporary pop/rock to classical and, yes, occasional jazz.

None of Moran's music enjoyed any sort of afterlife. Scott's television adventures concluded in the summer of 1977, after which Henderson's Bulman and his associate, DC Derek Willis (Dennis Blanch), were spun off into their own series, *Strangers* (about which, more later).

* * *

On the big screen, filmmaking increasingly was becoming a multinational affair, often with lamentable results; *Killer Force*—released in the States as *The Diamond Mercenaries*—is a classic example. Telly Savalas made this Irish/Swiss/U.S. stinker in between seasons of TV's *Kojak*; co-stars Peter Fonda and Hugh O'Brian probably hoped to prop up their lackluster acting careers. The low-rent result is hack pulp, replete with clumsy edits, poor scene matching, and aerial cinematography marred by an obvious smudge on the lens. It warrants mention here solely because of composer Georges Garvarentz's slick title theme and a few interior jazz cues.

Harry Webb (Savalas), security chief for the South Africa–based Syndicated Diamond Corp., kills suspected smugglers first, and asks questions second. Security officer Mike Bradley (Fonda) tolerates this harsh environment while enjoying occasional visits from magazine cover girl Clare Chambers (Maud Adams), daughter of the diamond mine administrator. Webb's concern proves genuine: Several mercenaries led by John Lewis (O'Brian) *are* planning to steal a sizeable stash of diamonds, evading the compound's extensive security measures with help from an inside informant dubbed "Father Christmas."

The title credits burst onto the screen while Mike and a colleague roar over sand dunes in a Land Rover, scouting the horizon for nefarious activity; Garvarentz's main theme opens with dynamic percussion, walking bass and a fast-paced melody delivered by a wall of brass and aggressive Hammond B3 comping. This action cue recurs several times, most notably during the third act's action-oriented shoot-outs. Garvarentz also channels his inner

Schifrin for some of the lengthy heist cue's diverse movements, with suspense supplied by *wah-wah* funk and unison horns. Garvarentz slides with equal aplomb into a romantic theme for Mike and Clare: a lyrical ballad introduced on solo piano, expanding with strings as they pleasure each other in the shower.

The soundtrack album blends Garvarentz's action cues with three versions of the love theme, along with a diegetic vocal (lyrics co-written by Charles Aznavour).

Elsewhere in the World

Mention must be made of the Australian action series *Chopper Squad*, in part because of producer/keyboardist Mike Perjanik's sizzling title theme, and also because the show likely deserves the credit (or blame) for inspiring the beach-based American show *Baywatch*, roughly a decade later. *Chopper Squad* began as a pilot film that debuted November 5, 1976, in Melbourne; other parts of Australia weren't able to view it until a year or more later. The subsequent 26-episode series finally began June 10, 1978. The action follows the exploits of a helicopter surf rescue team based along Sydney's northern beaches; Jebbie Best (Dennis Grosvenor), Phil Hardy (Eric Oldfield) and Barry Drummond (Robert Coleby) handle plenty of their own stunts during infantile stories that feature an equal measure of baddies and bikini babes.

Funk-laden *wah-wah* guitar and breathless brass fanfares kick off Perjanik's title theme, which plays against staccato footage of the team's rescue boat and VH-FHF (Bell 206B) Jet Ranger helicopter, as it darts and swoops along picturesque portions of Australia's beaches and rugged coastline. The double-time 5-5-3-5 motif introduces the stars via grinning close-ups; sun-bathing cuties wave at the passing copter while Perjanik reprises the melody and then builds to a final blast of unison brass.

Perjanik expanded the title theme for the soundtrack album, adding a mildly threatening sax and synth solo at the bridge. The other tracks feature funk-laden brass and guitar melodies ("Making It," "Man Alive"), suspenseful skulking cues ("Tequila Surprise"), droll synth themes ("Blue Zone") and even an occasional romantic ballad ("After Hours").

7

Bleak, Bad, Big City Dawn: 1977–78

John Williams' one-two punch, with *Close Encounters of the Third Kind* and the debut of the *Star Wars* franchise, enhanced the allure of sweeping orchestral scores for the next several years. *Saturday Night Fever, Grease, American Hot Wax, Convoy, FM, Thank God It's Friday* and *Smoky and the Bandit*, in turn, accelerated studio interest in both song scores and disco tunes.

The writing was on the wall … and they weren't jazz lyrics.

The Small Screen

Charlie's Angels—and its music—may have hastened crime TV's slide into popcorn nonsense, but NBC's *CHiPs* accelerated the descent from the moment of its debut on September 15, 1977. Larry Wilcox and Erik Estrada star as (respectively) motorcycle cops Jonathan "Jon" Andrew Baker and Francis Llewellyn "Ponch" Poncherello. Most episodes involve multiple breezy encounters representing a typical day on the job, accompanied by glimpses into the guys' personal lives. Jon is cautious and conservative; the impetuous Ponch is a wild child.

The show's tone was at least half-serious during the initial 1977/78 season; this is reflected by conventional action-oriented underscores from (among others) Billy May, Nelson Riddle, J.J. Johnson, Mike Post and Pete Carpenter, and John Carl Parker. The latter also delivered the jovial, quasi-jazz title theme, which opens with a rising four-note fanfare by unison brass; Parker then establishes a pounding, *bam-bam* disco beat with drums, synth (sounding siren-like) and strings. As the show's title is superimposed over footage of Jon and Ponch roaring down a Los Angeles freeway, Parker repeats the fanfare trumpet "call" and adds a 5-3 "response." This becomes the theme's primary motif, along with a bouncy countermelody during the bridge. Synth trills build the tune to a climactic flourish.

The tone changed with the second season, because new executive producer Cy Chermak wanted the show to be more youth-oriented and "hip." Fledgling soundtrack musician Alan Silvestri—who had begun his career as a jazz guitarist—was brought in as a full-time composer, with orders to ramp up the disco content. He obliged by reorchestrating Parker's title theme, eradicating any semblance of jazz; Silvestri also maintained this frothier ambiance with fresh disco cues for each episode. He remained the primary composer until the show was canceled after six successful seasons, contributing fresh scores for more than 100 episodes. He then began the high-profile, big-screen projects—*Romancing the Stone, Back to the Future*, etc.—that quickly made him an in-demand, Oscar-nominated Hollywood composer.

The disco group Corniche covered Parker's title theme for a single on the Windsong label; jazz/fusion musician and anime composer Yuki Ohno went one better, with an entire *CHiPs* tribute album released in 1981 by RCA Japan. Three full discs of Silvestri's themes and cues were produced, starting in 2006. Jazz lovers need not bother.

Wilcox and Estrada returned for 1998's made-for-TV reunion movie, *CHiPs '99*; composer Stacy Widelitz reinserted a bit of jazz into his updated arrangement of Parker's title theme. Dax Shepard and Michael Peña brought Jon and Ponch to the big screen in 2017's relentlessly crude *CHIPS*; composer Fil Eisler also acknowledged Parker's original theme.

On an even sillier note, creators Michael Gleason and Glen A. Larson mixed equal parts of *The Saint*, *It Takes a Thief*, *Zorro* and Dumas' *The Count of Monte Cristo*, and wound up with NBC's *Sword of Justice*, a hilariously overwrought adventure series that stars Dack Rambo as wealthy playboy Jack Martin Cole. Framed for embezzlement by white-collar rivals who subsequently stole and depleted the Cole family fortune, Jack learned the tools of the criminal trade while behind bars; he emerges to resume a superficial "career" as a playboy by day, while seeking revenge against his enemies by night. His calling cards—literally—are the three-spots from a deck of cards, representing the three years he unjustly spent in prison.

Larson, Stu Phillips and John Andrew Tartaglia collaborated on the show's music, with Larson credited for a superficial title theme with a 1-4-5 motif that repeats relentlessly against a double-time rhythm section: equal parts jazz and disco, satisfying as neither. The redundancy isn't immediately obvious, because the theme's lengthy middle portion is muted beneath a bombastic narrator who gives a lengthy summation of the circumstances that brought Jack to his current double life. Episode underscores are long on orchestral atmosphere and short on melody.

Following a two-hour pilot film that aired September 10, 1978, the series lasted only nine episodes before deservedly perishing. The music suffered the same fate.

Thankfully, attempts were made to counterprogram such foolishness. Actor Ron Leibman and writer Don Carlos Dunaway went old-school when they co-created CBS' *Kaz*, a contemplative, impeccably crafted drama series that also debuted September 10, 1978; Leibman also had a strong hand in shaping the show's pilot film and many of the single season's 22 episodes. He plays Martin "Kaz" Kazinsky, a convicted car thief who earned a law degree while serving his prison sentence; he reenters the world and lands a job as a criminal defense attorney and junior partner at a prestigious Los Angeles law firm run by Samuel Bennett (Patrick O'Neal). Kaz's background gives him a soft spot for lost causes and disenfranchised suspects. He lives in a tiny apartment over the Starting Gate, a jazz nightclub run by good friend Mary Parnell (Gloria Le Roy), where Kaz spends his down time, sometimes sitting in as the house band's drummer.

This jazz ambiance extends to the nifty title theme written by former big band jazz composer/arranger Fred Karlin, during one of his rare ventures into television work. It's an uptempo swinger with a 4-3 solo brass motif against a vibrant rhythm section powered by ferocious drumming and augmented by an equally sparkling countermelody during a tasty bridge. The theme builds to a sizzling blend of drums and unison brass and concludes with a punchy two-note fanfare.

Unfortunately, nothing is known about the show's underscores, although we can assume plenty of diegetic combo jazz during Kaz's visits to the Starting Gate. The series has vanished: no home video release, no Internet presence, and no indication of Karlin's title theme ever being covered or included in crime/action anthology albums.

The Big Screen

The Gauntlet (1977) may be one of Clint Eastwood's silliest movies, but it also features one of Jerry Fielding's best, swinging-est scores, dominated by trumpet screamer Jon Faddis and alto sax icon Art Pepper. The simple plot finds alcoholic Phoenix cop Ben Shockley (Eastwood) sent to Las Vegas to collect witness Gus Mally (Sondra Locke), and bring her back for a "nothing" courtroom trial. In truth, Shockley has been set up by a police commissioner in league with the Vegas mob, all of whom want Gus and her escort executed long before they return to Phoenix. The beleaguered pair bond while eluding numerous assassination attempts, leading to a bonkers climax when they slowly drive an armored bus down the final three blocks to the Phoenix courthouse, while hundreds of apparently subhuman cops blast thousands of rounds at the vehicle (nobody being smart enough to shoot the wheels out).

Fielding mischievously misleads us by opening the title credits montage—which follows Shockley early one morning, barely recovered from the previous night's bender—with a lazy, bluesy version of the traditional gospel tune, "Just a Closer Walk with Thee." After some sparkling piano riffs, Faddis' sweet horn takes the melody, backed by gentle drumming. As the depth of Shockley's inebriation becomes more apparent, Faddis' trumpet gets louder, as if scolding; the piano comping turns equally aggressive. Later, when Shockley meets Gus in a Vegas police cell, his response to her unwillingness to leave—knowing full well that a contract has been put on her head—is to wheel her out to an ambulance, strapped to a stretcher. Playfully uptempo percussion and piano spot this whimsical scene, with Pepper's meandering sax backed by cheerful blasts from a bank of horns.

Little music subsequently is heard until, after surviving several attacks, Shockley and Gus steal a motorcycle and attempt to outrun a pursuing helicopter. This chase is accompanied by a ferocious cue that opens with suspenseful bongos and other percussion effects, then roars into life with all horns blazing, led by Pepper's frenzied sax. The cue diminishes when Shockley and Gus pause for breath in a short mountain tunnel; when they burst back into view, the entire ensemble similarly explodes into life, this time with Faddis' shattering horn leading the charge. (Play this track at full volume, if you ever need to clear a room.) This is just a foreshadowing of the climactic cue, which accompanies the jury-rigged bus' freeway descent into downtown Phoenix, and its subsequent slow progress to the courthouse. The army of waiting Phoenix cops mobilizes to a military drum roll, Faddis' shrieking trumpet lending urgency against tasty walking bass. As the bus gets ever closer to this "gauntlet," the entire ensemble breaks into an explosive blast of suspenseful swing and horn fanfares: Will our heroes survive?

The terrific soundtrack album includes one cue—"The Black Sedan"—that went unused in the film. It's a cool improvisational number, with the full ensemble initially backing Fadis' way-out trumpet, after which Farmer delivers an equally spontaneous solo. Jazz fans also will recognize that the fourth track—named for the film—is lifted from the final movement ("Solea") on Miles Davis' iconic 1961 album, *Sketches of Spain*.

One would expect similar aural excitement from Don Ellis, but the electrifying intensity that he brought to his *French Connection* scores is totally absent in *Assault in Paradise* (aka *Maniac!* and *The Ransom*), a tawdry bit of exploitative rubbish that didn't deserve theatrical release. The incomprehensible story concerns a deranged nutcase who dons faux Native American garb and kills scores of innocents with a high-powered crossbow, while attempting to extort millions from the wealthy bastards who control a small Arizona town ironically named Paradise. Rich landowner Stuart Whitman hires international assassin Oliver Reed to "take care of the problem"; instead, the latter embarks on one of cinema's most hilariously unlikely love affairs, with numb-nuts TV news gal Deborah Raffin.

This turkey obviously was nothing more than a paycheck for all concerned, and Ellis was no exception. His title credits theme sags beneath the weight of heavy drums, dissonant brass fanfares, *wah-wah* guitars—which sound laughably out of place—and irritating whistle effects apparently intended to convey a Native American vibe. The underscore displays a bit of life only once, when Ellis supplies agitated percussion and low piano riffs while the killer takes out two cops in their own police station. From this point onward, Ellis delivers nothing more than rising and descending orchestral couplets, atmospheric *bleeps* and *bloops*, and a lot of the insufferable whistling.

No soundtrack album emerged, for which we should be grateful. Given the stylish promise with which Ellis began his film and TV scoring assignments, it's tragic that he ended his career with trash such as this and the even more repugnant *Ruby* (also 1977) and *Natural Enemies* (1979), the latter released shortly after his untimely death.

* * *

The Silent Partner (1978) is an ingeniously twisty crime thriller: a rare case where Curtis Hanson's script is vastly superior to *Think of a Number*, the 1968 Anders Bodelsen novel on which the film is based. It's also the only feature film scored by famed jazz pianist Oscar Peterson ... except that he *didn't* score it, contrary to the on-screen credits and every reference source from IMDB downward. He wrote several key themes, but the actual score was composed by Ken Wannberg, misleadingly credited as conductor and music arranger.

"Producer Joel Michaels asked me to write the music," Peterson recalled, years later. "I was heading for Japan, and I had a time limit and an upcoming tour, and unfortunately their film was running a little late. So instead of scoring the whole film, [producer] Joel [B. Michaels] asked if I could lay out the melodic end, and he brought out Ken to score it."[1]

Peterson clearly was disappointed by the results. "Ken didn't use a large orchestra, and the themes were written for a large orchestra. First of all, you really have to understand the film—to get into the film—and if you don't, then you're open for these kinds of results where you're just writing for empty spaces, and that's not the way to do it."[2]

The story focuses on Miles Cullen (Elliott Gould), a disenchanted teller at a branch bank in a Toronto shopping mall, who accidentally learns that the place soon will be robbed by an individual dressed as a bell-ringing Santa Claus. Miles clandestinely hides most of his cash transactions in a lunch box; when the ersatz Santa shows up and demands the drawer's contents at gunpoint, he walks away with far less than subsequently is disclosed during TV news reports. Miles nets a cool $48,300, and nobody suspects him. Nobody, that is, except the former Santa: Harry Reikle (Christopher Plummer), a vengeful sociopath who wants his due. Romantic entanglements are supplied by Julie Carver (Susannah York), a bank colleague whose interest is piqued by Miles' composure during the initial hold-up; and Elaine (Celine Lomez), the flirtatious nurse who has been caring for his father.

Wannberg built his gentle jazz score from the seductive cue—"Theme for Celine"—that Peterson wrote for Lomez. It's heard in numerous arrangements: a slow reading, when

Miles hatches his lunch box plan; a languidly sultry sax/piano variation, when Julie asks Miles about the stolen money; a more aggressively sexy version, when Elaine enters the story; and a lengthy rendition with trumpet taking the melody, over the end credits. Two more Peterson cues—"The Happy Hour" and "Elliott"—are intertwined as diegetic music by an unseen combo, when Miles and Elaine enjoy a restaurant dinner together. Wannberg's numerous suspense/terror cues—generally involving Harry—are typical low-end piano riffs, plucked bass and disorienting strings.

Peterson may not have been involved with the scoring process, but he made up for it with the subsequent soundtrack LP. It features three choice arrangements of "Theme for Celine," along with the misleadingly titled "Happy Hour"—actually a melancholy sax and piano ballad—and "Party Time USA," a 4/4 burner that swings like crazy. "Elliott's Theme" is expanded into a sweet piano, vibes and sax anthem that suits Gould's contemplative performance; "Theme for Susannah" is more playful, as befits her character, and opens with a lengthy solo piano passage. Despite Peterson's popularity, the album never has been digitized.

Happily, that's not the case with Jerry Fielding's score for *The Big Sleep*.

Robert Mitchum was ideal as Raymond Chandler's world-weary Philip Marlowe in *Farewell, My Lovely*, so his return to the role was inevitable. Unfortunately, he isn't as well served by this glossy remake of *The Big Sleep*. Director Michael Winner—at this point best known for lurid exploitation flicks such as *The Sentinel* and the *Death Wish* series—also wrote the tawdry script, dragging Marlowe into the 1970s and shifting the action to London. The one solid element is Fielding's luxuriously smoky score, which evokes Marlowe's *noir* roots, even if nothing else does.

The famously convoluted plot begins when Marlowe is hired by the elderly Gen. Sternwood (James Stewart) to identify the blackmailer behind a series of threatening letters. Marlowe's presence piques the curiosity of Sternwood's elder daughter Charlotte (Sarah Miles) and her wildly uncontrolled, emotionally

Sharp-eared listeners will realize that Jerry Fielding recycled the title theme for *The Big Sleep* from his earlier assignments on 1970's *Hunters Are for Killing* and television's *Matt Helm* pilot movie, albeit with more grandiose orchestration.

disturbed younger sister, Camilla (Candy Clark). The case leads to bookseller/pornographer Arthur Geiger (John Justin) and his sinister employee, Agnes Lozelle (Joan Collins); the latter is allied with the equally unsavory Joe Brody (Edward Fox). Geiger is shot dead by an unknown party during one of his photo sessions; a nude and drugged-out Camilla is left as a giggling but useless witness. Marlowe's subsequent efforts to protect the Sternwood family name run afoul of gambling crime lord Eddie Mars (Oliver Reed) and his brutal hit man, Lash Canino (Richard Boone); everything ultimately revolves around the recent disappearance of Charlotte's husband, Rusty Regan.

Fielding's mesmerizing main theme opens with hypnotic bass and percussion, as we experience the drive to Sternwood's mansion from an unseen Marlowe's point of view. When the film's title splashes onto the screen, Fielding expands his theme into glorious big band swing, with a wall of trumpets and electric guitars handling the melody. Brass fanfares lend additional dazzle when Marlowe nears the estate; when he parks, Fielding dials the orchestra back, retreating to the quieter "traveling beat" that opened the cue.

Fielding supplies a funk-laden cue, heavy with bass and inquisitive bursts from the reeds, when Marlowe later follows a van laden with suspicious material from Geiger's bookstore. As if matters aren't already complicated enough, Marlowe picks up a tail—a little guy (Colin Blakely) in a gray car—whose pursuit is spotted with a whimsical blend of bass, ticking percussion and guitar flourishes. Another name keeps popping up: Mars' missing wife, Mona. Marlowe's discovery of her whereabouts leads to a dangerous confrontation at an isolated house; Fielding supplies fast-paced action jazz, pregnant with low-end piano riffs, when Marlowe cleverly outwits her captor. After a final reunion with Camilla and Charlotte—and the solution to the Sternwood mystery—Marlowe drives off the estate for the last time; the point-of-view camera shot resumes as Fielding reprises the pulsating main theme, concluding with a thunderous orchestral blast.

No soundtrack album coincided with the film's release, although a 19-minute suite of cues was included in 1990's double-CD anthology, *Jerry Fielding: Film Music*. A complete digital score finally appeared in 2009.

Director William Friedkin's jovial handling of *The Brink's Job* depicts the infamous armed robbery of Boston's Brink's Building on January 17, 1950, which netted the gang $1.2 million in cash, along with $1.58 million in checks, money orders and other securities. Scripter Walon Green takes serious liberties with details and people, mostly to transform the crooks into sympathetic mopes who are much more fun to watch than their real-life counterparts likely were. The first hour focuses on small-potatoes Boston crook Tony Pino (Peter Falk), as he and a gaggle of associates plot how best to take advantage of the fact that Brink's North End headquarters is anything but the "impregnable fortress" that the company wishes the world to believe. The heist goes off without a hitch, but the brotherly bond frays while the gang sits on the cash for six years, intending to wait out the statute of limitations.

Veteran British jazz pianist and screen composer Richard Rodney Bennett did little to earn his paycheck. The title credits are superimposed over a Boston street scene, as a sax-playing busker blows a lazy, Dixieland-style tune. A few brief, bluesy sax solos are heard elsewhere, but most of Bennett's remaining cues are light-hearted orchestral numbers suited to the film's comedic tone. He does include two vintage swing tunes: "Accentuate the Positive," performed by Bing Crosby and The Andrews Sisters; and the Glenn Miller Orchestra's iconic performance of "In the Mood."

No soundtrack album appeared.

Meanwhile, Across the Pond…

As production on *The New Avengers* wrapped up, creator Brian Clemens was approached by London Weekend Television to concoct a gritty new show that could compete with *The Sweeney*. The result, *The Professionals*, focuses on operatives assigned to CI5 (Criminal Intelligence 5), an extra-legal British law enforcement department encouraged by founder/head Maj. George Cowley (Gordon Jackson) to use any means necessary to out-maneuver, capture or kill exceptional criminals such as terrorists, assassins, espionage suspects or homegrown social agitators. Cowley's two most experienced men are the hot-tempered Raymond Doyle (Martin Shaw), quick to rush in where angels fear to tread; and former paratrooper and Special Air Service veteran William Andrew Philip Bodie (Lewis Collins), whose more relaxed appearance belies his hardened physical skills. The show was an immediate hit, ultimately running five seasons after its debut on December 30, 1977.

Laurie Johnson assumed full command of the musical tapestry, composing both a riveting title theme and (mostly) fresh underscores for all 57 episodes. He relished the challenge of not repeating cues, from one episode to the next. "The music is supposed to tell the story, when the dialogue doesn't. It was more difficult with *The Professionals*, than it was with *The Avengers*, because they [*Avengers* episodes] were like mini-features; each one had a particular character, which is more interesting. But in an action/adventure [show] like *The Professionals*, you're covering similar ground [in each episode]. So you try to ring the changes, but it's not as easy as when you have a completely different 'color,' as you do in *The Avengers*."[3]

The title credits sequence is a crackling 50 seconds of music and action. A car roars up to a military-style training course against a sustained low note, *wah-wah* guitar and 2/2 percussion, followed by a thundering 3-2-2-6-4 motif on bowed bass. This repeats, backed by brass, when everybody charges out of the vehicle. Cowley times his operatives—most prominently Doyle and Bodie—as they run, climb, jump, fight, swing and ultimately burst through the faux windows of an obstacle course, against a thumping swing bridge fueled by four rising brass triplets. The initial bass motif repeats, when Cowley waves his men back into the car, and they race off as Johnson concludes with a booming, three-note orchestral flourish. Like, *wow*.

Johnson's underscores include numerous arrangements of this theme, in various tempos and instrumentations. These are supplemented with all manner of big band compositions: buoyant, scene-establishing fanfares; agitated suspense cues, often driven by piano and horns; ominous drum rolls and twitchy strings during confrontations with baddies; midtempo "traveling music," usually heard during clandestine vehicular pursuits; gentle cocktail or dance combo melodies—highlighted by tasty woodwind or keyboard solos—for quieter, more intimate moments; and plenty of taut, hard-charging action jazz for brawls, chase scenes and all other manner of mayhem.

Johnson wrote expanded big band jazz arrangements of the title theme and six underscore cues for a soundtrack album; two tracks were extracted for a 45 single. An expanded digital score arrived in 2008, as part of the box set *The Music of Laurie Johnson, Volume 2: The Professionals*. By then, the title theme had become an obligatory part of crime/action jazz anthology albums.

In 1999, Clemens revived the concept as *CI5: The New Professionals*, which features a new team headed by Harry Malone (Edward Woodward), all working for Civilian

Intelligence Department 5. The program was commissioned for the satellite service Sky One, the UK's first non-terrestrial TV channel. Johnson supplied an updated arrangement of his ferocious title theme; episode underscores, by Hywel Maggs and Chris Winter, favor bland atmospheric synth and percussion. The reboot failed to excite audiences and was canceled after a single 13-episode season.

Back in 1977, *Target* didn't fare much better. It was the BBC's thinly veiled effort to mimic *The Sweeney*, but the new series duplicated little more than public outrage over a similarly lurid level of violence. *Target* focuses on a Southampton Regional Crime Squad led by Patrick Mower's DS Steve Hackett; the team tackles drug runners, hijackings, jewel and fine art thefts, police corruption and all manner of other criminal endeavors.

Transplanted Australian pianist/composer Dudley Simpson delivered a title theme and underscores for all 17 episodes during the course of two seasons. Alas, *Target* isn't one of his better efforts, perhaps because there isn't much with which to be inspired. The fast-paced, brass- and electric guitar-fueled title theme is a lackluster affair that repeats the same 4-5 motif—over and *over* again—against a dreadful credits sequence constructed from blue silhouettes. The longer end credits arrangement benefits slightly from a slow guitar counter-melody during an extended bridge. Rather surprisingly, Simpson isn't acknowledged anywhere. (He may not have minded.) His music had no afterlife, nor did the series.

* * *

Leslie Charteris' popular *Saint* books often concluded with a page bearing the iconic stick figure, along with this assurance: "Watch for the sign of The Saint—He will be back!" That promise proved equally true on television; Ian Ogilvy inherited Simon Templar's halo when ITV debuted *Return of the Saint* on September 10, 1978. While blessed with the same debonair charm that Roger Moore radiated—along with an eager bevy of young lovelies, many now shown hopping into bed with Simon—Ogilvy also is a rugged, much more athletic Saint, as befit the changing times. This revival didn't have the legs of its predecessor, lasting only a single 24-episode season, but it nonetheless kept Charteris' famed character relevant for a new generation of TV viewers.

Jazz pianist Brian Dee and composer/producer Irving Martin concocted a cool main theme for the clever title sequence. As had been the case with Moore's series, each episode teaser concludes with a halo appearing over Ogilvy's head, accompanied by a synth reprise of the famous eight-note Saint anthem. A rapid rhythmic ostinato on keyboard and drums then introduces the theme, while a Saint stick figure indulges in all manner of activity: racing a car along a picturesque European highway, stealthily breaking into a mansion, and wooing a beautiful socialite. A deliciously dirty sax introduces a 4-3 motif at this point; unison horns further develop the melody when the stick-figure Saint gets the drop on a gun-toting goon. The initial motif resumes through a quick series of clips until the stick figure pauses on a beach, and its shadow falls on a smiling, sunbathing babe. Cut to a final damsel, who tosses the halo away as she kisses the stick-figure Saint, at which point Dee and Martin conclude with a brass crescendo: a job well done, and applause from all.

(As it happened, European TV viewers heard an entirely different title theme: an atrocious pop vocal titled "Taking It Easy," *very* loosely derived from the Dee/Martin cue, and credited to "Oliver Onions," actually Italian brothers Guido de Angelis and Maurizio de Angelis.)

Dee and Martin delivered only the title theme; all episode underscores are by veteran jazz flutist, saxophonist, clarinetist and composer John Scott (who, among his many other accomplishments, played sax on John Barry's *Goldfinger* score and flute on The Beatles' "You've Got to Hide Your Love Away"). Scott's richly diverse scores have a little bit of everything: stealthy suspense cues, jolting stingers, culturally appropriate themes (for varied European settings), gentle bossa nova swingers (for Simon's romantic entanglements) and plenty of sax-fueled action jazz. Many of the latter reference the title theme in a wealth of instrumentations and tempos.

"The Saint has moved with the times," Scott explained, during production. "He's a much stronger character than in the earlier series. Equally, the stories are stronger. The music is therefore pretty forceful and driving. As the stories vary considerably, the scores stretch well beyond the musical sound one has come to associate with such a series; it is something more in line with the character of the new Saint. He seems to have acquired a harder sound, a sense of strength. The music, I hope, reflects this."[4]

Dee and Martin—leading a combo billed as The Saint Orchestra—added a softer horn/synth bridge for an expanded arrangement of their title theme, released as a 45 single. (The B-side features "Funko," one of the many library tunes used in *The Sweeney*.) It remained the sole mainstream release until Network's 2009 double-disc anthology set, *The Music of ITC*; it includes the original Dee/Martin title theme and end title, along with five of Scott's underscore cues and the vocal "Taking It Easy."

Television wasn't yet finished with Simon Templar. Australian actor Andrew Clarke donned the halo for *The Saint in Manhattan*, a failed American pilot dumped in the summer of 1987, as an episode of *CBS Summer Playhouse*. Clarke's lamentable handling of Templar notwithstanding, the hour-length adventure isn't helped by composer Mark Snow's slushy orchestral score, even if it does reference the original Roger Moore series theme. Two years later, the UK's London Weekend Television revived the character yet again (about which, more later).

Back in 1978, DS George Bulman (Don Henderson) and DC Derek Willis (Dennis Blanch) earned their own television series, following their debuts as supporting characters in *The XYY Man*. *Strangers* is a solid police procedural that finds Bulman heading a team of Manchester officers hand-picked from different parts of the country to form "Unit 23," with the goal of working cases too sophisticated for local coppers. The popular ITV series enjoyed a healthy five-season run. Later seasons found Bulman's team placed under the command of Jack Lambie (Mark McManus), as part of a new "Inner City Squad" covering the entire country.

Bulman and Willis aren't the only carryovers from *The XYY Man*; that show's title theme composer, Mike Moran, provides the same service for *Strangers*. Following an introductory bass ostinato, this unison horn melody bears a striking resemblance to Joe Zawinul's jazz classic "Birdland," which had debuted just a year earlier. Moran's cheerful tune plays against a montage of the primary cast members engaged in fairly routine duties. The longer end credits arrangement gives more space to the bass guitar and features a screaming sax solo during a brief bridge.

Because the first season was shot primarily on videotape, episodes are essentially bereft of underscores, with the exception of fleeting nods to the title theme during the "bumpers" that precede and follow each chapter. Subsequent seasons, increasingly replacing videotape with film, gave Moran the opportunity for additional underscore shading. He also delivered a fresh end credits arrangement from season three onward: a shorter 30-second cue that's primarily a suspenseful rhythmic ostinato, with a fleeting bit of melody from a solo sax.

None of the music for *Strangers* achieved commercial release.

Although gadget-laden, 1960s-style secret agents had largely vanished, this granted space for their more serious descendants. A few years before he became firmly identified as P.D. James' celebrated DCI Adam Dalgliesh, Roy Marsden starred in *The Sandbaggers*, one of the finest espionage dramas ever produced for British television. The bleak, gritty and at times callously realistic Cold War-themed series features Marsden as Neil D. Burnside, the ruthless Director of Operations for Britain's Secret Intelligence Service (SIS), in charge of an elite group of operatives nicknamed "sandbaggers," due to their occasional need to assassinate ("sandbag") enemy agents. Burnside sends his people on politically sensitive or highly dangerous assignments involving moles, potential defectors, security risks, rescue operations behind the Iron Curtain, and collaborative operations with the CIA.

The show's unsettling title theme came from Roy Budd, who employed a cimbalom to establish an ominous mood. That instrument opens the theme, with an eight-note ostinato that backs a mournful 1-7-8-9-8 melody heard against clips of spy craft: footsteps descending a staircase; a desk laden with telephones, passports and top-secret files; photographs and other ephemera. The theme concludes with an unresolved two-note brass fanfare, which fades as the episode begins. The end credits arrangement adds a melancholy sax that comps against the same melody. Most episodes have little or no underscore cues; dramatic events are left to stand on their own.

Budd never recorded this theme, and nobody appears to have covered it.

Elsewhere in the World

French crime thrillers were getting grittier.

Jazz sax and clarinet icon Gerry Mulligan performed sideman duties on several of the films discussed earlier in these pages, but he composed a full score for only one—1977's *La Menace (The Threat)*—with disappointing results. Although executive producer Denise Petitdidier specifically sought Mulligan, and director/co-writer Alain Corneau loved the result, eleventh-hour mishandling by distributors compromised this collaboration. Aside from the title and end credits, music is heard only half a dozen times—fleetingly—as the story progresses.

The story begins as Henri Savin (Yves Montand), working at a trucking firm owned by the wealthy Dominique Montlaur (Marie Dubois), attempts to extricate himself from a long-running affair with her. He has begun another relationship with the younger Julie Manet (Carole Laure), already a few months pregnant by him. The possessive Dominique refuses to let Henri go; when all else fails, she commits suicide in a manner guaranteed to imply that she was murdered by Julie, who is arrested for the "crime" by police Inspector Waldeck (Jean-François Balmer). Although it appears that Henri abandons Julie to her fate, he actually has something much more cunning in mind; the lengthy second act remains ambiguous until Henri's clever plan is revealed. Unfortunately, the film concludes with a nasty—and wholly unjustified—twist that is guaranteed to infuriate viewers.

"They sent me an English translation of a shortened version of the script," Mulligan recalled. "Then Alain Corneau came to talk to me, to flesh out the outline. He talked the movie through."

"Gerry was taking notes, but they were not written notes, they were musical notes," added Mulligan's wife, Franca. "He had already written the whole score on the spot. Alain said, 'I knew you were a genius, but that's incredible.'"

"[But] when they started playing [the film] for U.S. and Canadian distributors," Mulligan lamented, "they suggested cuts—everybody's a film critic. Well, they made a mishmash of it."[5]

Dave Grusin happened to visit the Mulligans at their Connecticut home at the time; he assisted in the scoring and played keyboards during the subsequent recording session. Filmgoers mostly hear only the two of them; the full jazz combo is far better showcased on the subsequent soundtrack album.

The title credits unfold against a cue that begins quietly, with Mulligan's sax sounding tentative and mournful against Grusin's unsettling keyboard chops, until the tempo accelerates slightly; on screen, a visibly angry Henri works out his frustrations by driving a truck in circles through a barren stretch of dirt. Grusin's lovely piano work later serves as a lyrical backdrop to the film's secondary theme ("Watching and Waiting"), when Mulligan's sad melody plays over Waldeck's discovery of Dominique's body. Elsewhere, Henri pensively stares at the sleeping Julie, after they've made love in her apartment. Mulligan takes the lead on another melancholy cue, backed by quiet synth single notes, when—Julie now having been arrested—Henri moodily walks through a vineyard and contemplates his options.

As the film nears its disturbing climax, we finally hear a full combo cue. It opens with Grusin's twitchy keyboard work: very much in the suspenseful, anticipatory mode of what he recently had written for *Three Days of the Condor*. Quiet cymbals and drums accelerate as Henri realizes that he's in unexpected trouble; Mulligan's sax enters after a minute, amplifying our realization that we're witnessing a slowly approaching crisis. Mulligan retreats as the rest of the combo roars into life, while the impending danger becomes more obvious; the sax returns with a roar when—we simply cannot believe it!—Henri meets a cruelly ironic fate. The scene shifts to Julie, waiting to catch a flight to Melbourne, having no idea that Henri won't be joining her; the end credits unspool against a reprise of the melancholy vineyard cue.

The soundtrack LP, initially released solely in France, offers a lovely 35 minutes of music; unused cues include several with titles—notably "Introspect" and "The House They'll Never Live In"—that indicate their intended placement in the film. The latter, a sweetly poignant bossa nova, opens with a delicate Grusin keyboard line backed by bass and synth; gentle percussion adds color when Mulligan's soft sax brings it to a close. The 1999 digital edition inexplicably is retitled *Watching & Waiting*.

Mulligan wasn't the only American jazz star working in France in 1977. Director Georges Lautner granted Stan Getz an honor rarely accorded a jazz musician in the world of mainstream cinema. *Mort d'un pourri*—released in the States as *Death of a Corrupt Man*—opens on a silhouette of the famed saxman, while he delivers an elegant solo version of the film's haunting main theme. This fleeting prologue segues to a montage of Paris at dawn, the title credits appearing when Getz's sax is joined by composer Philippe Sarde's orchestral strings and contemplative woodwinds.

Lautner's film is based on the 1973 political crime novel of the same title by French journalist Jean Laborde. The disturbingly cynical story begins when Philippe Dubaye (Maurice Ronet) wakens his assistant Xavier Maréchal (Alain Delon) early one morning, to confess that he has just killed Serrano, a colleague at Paris' Palais Bourbon government offices. We gradually learn that this entire branch of politicians is corrupt, controlled by wealthy racketeers who wield behind-the-scenes power in unions, infrastructure contracts and even the constabulary. Philippe has stolen Serrano's journal, which details these crooked dealings by named government officials; he gives it to Xavier before being killed by an unknown assassin. Xavier ponders how best to use this damning information, knowing he likely won't live long enough for such satisfaction; he can't trust anybody, except perhaps Valérie (Ornella Muti), Philippe's young mistress.

The film is dominated by its main theme, often as a solo tenor sax line orchestrated into a nostalgic dirge that reflects society's loss of a moral center, and Xavier's scant chances of success or survival. The one exception occurs when he first meets Valérie; Getz's reading this time is buoyant and cheerful, as befits her innocence and honesty. When she finds her apartment invaded, she panics and runs, with Getz's agitated sax hastening her terrified flight. Additional bodies pile up, most notably Philippe's frequently drunk and belligerent wife, Christiane (Stéphane Audran); Marcel Azzola's mournful bandonéon solo backs a slow pan over her shattered body.

The tone shifts dramatically via diegetic cues performed by an unseen jazz combo at a lavish nightclub, where Xavier encounters the corrupt Judge Lansac (François Chaumette) and the mysterious Nicolas Tomski (Klaus Kinski). The first cue is a larkish bossa nova duet between Getz and Andrew Laverne (electric keyboard), backed by Billy Hart's drumming and Efrain Toro's percussion. The second opens with Laverne's thoughtful solo on piano, and then expands to a contemplative reading of the main theme.

Getz delivers an even bleaker arrangement of that melody as the film concludes, with Xavier wondering aloud—while his lover Françoise (Mireille Darc) listens—whether he has done any good. They stare at their city, deceptively peaceful in these early morning hours; the orchestra swells as the end credits appear, Getz's sax delivering a final, ambiguous riff that sounds like both a question mark and a eulogy.

Getz earned a well-deserved photo on the jacket of the French soundtrack album. It features a combo track ("Getz o Mania") not heard in the film: a vibrant, uptempo swinger dominated by Getz and Laverne, against lively drumming and bongos. The digital edition (2002) offers much longer arrangements, and is unusual for another reason: The LP and CD share only seven tracks in common, each disc also offering five unique tracks. The CD's nicest treat is a cheerful orchestral jazz variation of the main theme, offered as a tribute to the film's star: "Dans le regard d'Alain Delon."

Moving farther east, Hong Kong's multinational studio endeavors were becoming more common, sometimes with lamentable results. Roy Budd must've owed a favor to co-director Terence Young, because nothing else could explain the composer's involvement with a spy flick as inept as 1977's *Foxbat*. It's close to unwatchable, thanks to an incomprehensible script, dreadful acting and a tone that veers from gadget-laden espionage to slapstick farce. Budd obviously wasn't inspired; aside from a solid main theme, the rest of his score is built from unremarkable action jazz cues, many spotted sloppily by primary director Po-Chih Leong.

The story begins reasonably well, when a Soviet military pilot defects and flies a top-secret MIG-15 "Foxbat" jet to Japan's northernmost island of Hokkaido. Intelligence operatives throughout the world are eager to get their hands on the aircraft data, so a cloak-and-dagger U.S. "Agency" sends Michael Saxon (Henry Silva) to infiltrate a top-secret briefing. He photographs various plans with a miniature "eyeball camera," and then conceals the microfilm in one of the candies he routinely carries in a little tin. The story then goes off the rails, when the confection accidentally is swallowed by Mr. Cheung (James Yi Lui), a mugging, accident-prone celebrity chef who spends the rest of the film fleeing assassins who work for unspecified baddies.

Budd opens the film with explosive brass and suspenseful percussion, while the title

7. Bleak, Bad, Big City Dawn: 1977–78

credits unspool over an aerial sequence that concludes when the stolen jet lands on a Hokkaido airfield. Budd's primary theme debuts when Saxon is briefed by his boss; the engaging 6-6-5-5-6 melody is presented in a full orchestral jazz arrangement. Numerous reprises, most often during action sequences, offer this tune on either electric guitar or cimbalom.

Budd also contributes some diegetic cues: soft piano jazz heard during a lavish party that gathers all the key cast members; and a couple of sassy big band disco/swing numbers played during a runway fashion sequence. The oddest spotting choice emanates from a bath house PA system, where Saxon is stalked by a menacing sumo wrestler determined to kill him; this skirmish takes place against some leisurely swing, with the tasty melody carried by vibes.

The soundtrack LP, released on Hong Kong's Bang Bang label (no relation, I assure you), features 10 tracks with titles that don't translate well: "Night Sky Rippling," "Colorful Fashion Will" and so forth. The supposed digital edition from 1999—which includes Budd's scores for *The Internecine Project* and *Something to Hide*—treats *Foxbat* quite poorly. Its nine tracks include lesser arrangements of the main theme, along with several cues—notably one that sounds like a love theme (no idea where *that* might have been used!)—which aren't heard in the film. The track titles are mere spotting designations: "FB M1," "FM M14" and so forth.

8

That Old Feeling: 1979–81

As most frequently employed, the descriptor "instant classic" is a ridiculous oxymoron. And yet it applies perfectly to John Barry's score for 1981's *Body Heat*.

"I try and look for a musical theme that captures the whole essence of the picture," Barry explained, years later. "It's to do with the personalities, the story, the physicality of the movie. [The title theme for *Body Heat*] is a very strange, angular kind of weaving piece of music. That's very much [about Kathleen Turner's] character, a manipulative sexual operator."

"It's hard to tell now which came first," Turner added, "the heat and the pace that [director Lawrence] Kasdan created, or the music. They're inseparable to me."[1]

Jazz *noir* fans still go into rapture upon hearing the initial 4-4 motif of Barry's title theme, and no wonder; it's the gateway to one of the genre's finest-ever scores.

The Small Screen

Shortly after achieving cult immortality as the voice of Darth Vader in *Star Wars*, James Earl Jones made his series television starring debut in CBS' *Paris*. Jones slides smoothly into the role of LAPD Capt. Woody Paris, who schools the quartet of young cops under his wing: Charlie Bogart (Jake Mitchell), Stacy Erickson (Cecilia Hart), Willie Miller (Michael Warren) and Ernesto Villas (Frank Ramirez). Episodes divide their attention between investigative street work, interpersonal tensions within the precinct, and Paris' off-duty home life with wife Barbara (Lee Chamberlin).

The series is enhanced by a lyrical jazz theme from Fred Karlin, who also contributes similarly tasty, jazz-inflected underscores. The title theme opens with a gentle, midtempo rhythm section; a solo muted trumpet introduces the melody against softly comping vibes, while Paris strolls into the station house on a typical morning. The visuals switch to still shots as the theme develops into a charming jazz ballad; the orchestra swells and repeats the melody via unison horns, as the supporting players are introduced. A final crescendo accompanies a camera freeze on Jones.

Many underscore cues are in a similar vein, particularly those that back Paris' home life. Karlin is equally adept at dramatic tension; he garnered an Emmy Award nomination for the eighth episode, "Decisions," which focuses on Paris' anguish after an innocent bystander is killed during an undercover assignment. (It was a good year for jazz TV scores; John Cacavas also was nominated, for *Eischied*, but both he and Karlin lost to Patrick Williams, for *Lou Grant*.)

Sadly, *Paris* disappeared 13 episodes after its debut on September 29, 1979. Karlin's music similarly enjoyed no afterlife.

8. That Old Feeling: 1979–81

Speaking of *Eischied*, Joe Don Baker parlayed a busy big-screen career—most frequently playing heavies, villains and tough guys—into a similarly short-lived NBC series that cast him as southern-born NYPD Chief of Detectives Earl Eischied. Although blessed with a talented squad of younger detectives, Eischied spends plenty of time on the streets himself, where suspects have a tendency to mistake his southern drawl for limited intelligence (always to their regret). He lives alone, his sole companion a pet cat dubbed PC (for "police commissioner"). This show similarly ran only 13 episodes after its September 21 debut.

Cacavas earned the Emmy nomination for his jazz-inflected score to the two-part series opener, "Only the Pretty Girls Die," a grim serial killer tale strongly suggested by David Berkowitz's then-recent "Son of Sam" murders. The show's title theme is an uptempo swinger with a melancholy melody anchored by a 1-5 motif; it's delivered first by a solo sax, then echoed on brass, against a series of clips of Baker shown within fat letters that slowly spell out the show's title: E-I-S-C-H-I-E-D.

Paris and Eischied could have been drinking buddies, but they'd have kicked Tom Sloane out of the bar. Network television secret agent shows didn't come much sillier than NBC's *A Man Called Sloane*, which debuted September 22 and felt like a mid–1960s flop. Robert Conrad (s)mugs his way through the starring role as Thomas Remington Sloane III, top agent for a high-tech American spy network dubbed UNIT, which devotes its resources to battling the criminal organization KARTEL. Sloane is assisted by 6-foot-5 Torque (Ji-Tu Cumbuka), a powerful partner whose steel hand can be equipped with all manner of lethal attachments. Missions are monitored and updated by "Effie," an EFI Series 3000 computer that delivers intel via Michele Carey's sexy voice. The episode scripts are appalling.

The show's wink-wink-nudge-nudge tone clashes with Conrad's overly earnest performance: a weird dichotomy further exacerbated by Patrick Williams' silly jazz title theme. It opens like a bossa nova tune on steroids, against a clip of Conrad grimly racing toward the camera; unison brass introduces the 1-4-3-2 synth motif, backed by comping flutes, while Conrad and Cumbuka do their action-oriented spy stuff in various clips. The melody repeats as the cast members are identified, then builds to a unison brass fanfare against cute, ray gun-like sound effects. It's not a bad theme, but it's ill-served by so much cartoonish orchestration. Episode underscores—by Don Bagley, Billy Byers and Les Hooper—feature considerable action jazz, but (again) the orchestrations and arrangements are hilariously overwrought.

Nobody was surprised when Sloane and UNIT quickly were defeated by an enemy even more powerful than KARTEL: bad ratings.

Sloane had b.a.d. company. Hollywood has produced no shortage of dreadful TV shows, but ABC's *B.A.D. Cats* nonetheless deserved some sort of award when it debuted January 4, 1980. It's an insipid, live-action cartoon for viewers who found *Charlie's Angels* too intellectually stimulating. The premise finds former race car drivers Nick Donovan (Asher Brauner) and Ocee James (Steve Hanks) joining the LAPD as members of a squad dubbed Burglary Auto Detail/Commercial Auto Thefts (ergo, B.A.D. Cats). They ostensibly answer to the usual long-suffering commander (Vic Morrow); the show goes into chauvinistic overdrive that was offensive even for its time, when around perky Officer Samantha Jensen (Michelle Pfeiffer).

Barry De Vorzon's revved-up 4/4 title theme gets plenty of play during each episode, because Nick and Ocee tend to run their suspects off the road after lengthy car chases that involve the destruction of strategically placed public property. The theme is built from a melody that holds a note for six beats, then follows with a 4-2 motif: not very complicated, but undeniably catchy. The credits sequence alternates clips of vehicular mayhem and highway road sign graphics, and (naturally) concludes with a shot of Pfeiffer in a bikini.

Even undiscriminating viewers quickly tired of this program's juvenile antics; it left the schedule after only six episodes. De Vorzon's theme perished with it.

Viewers wondering whether Hollywood had lost its magic touch, must've been relieved when CBS struck gold.

Hawaii Five-O saw its final sunset in April 1980, but the island state wasn't absent from weekly TV for long; just in time for Christmas that year, Tom Selleck shot to fame in *Magnum, P.I.* The new detective series caught on immediately, thanks to Selleck's laid-back charm, a solid mix of supporting characters backed by engaging scripts, and—yes—the captivating Hawaiian setting.

Thomas Magnum's background as a Vietnam Naval Intelligence veteran serves him well as a newly minted private detective, under circumstances that his gumshoe peers could only covet from afar. In exchange for safeguarding the lavish beachfront Oahu estate of wealthy writer Robin Masters—never seen, but occasionally voiced by Orson Welles—Magnum is granted gratis living quarters and access to many of his employer's toys: most notably a $50,000 firecracker red Ferrari. This vexes Masters' pompous British manservant, Jonathan Quayle Higgins III (John Hillerman), who takes a dim view of Magnum's free-wheeling lifestyle. The arrangement leaves Magnum plenty of time to handle outside cases, with assistance from wartime buddies Theodore "T.C." Calvin (Roger E. Mosely) and Orville "Rick" Wright (Larry Manetti).

Although the Mike Post/Pete Carpenter title theme is as beloved as Selleck's come-hither grin, this piece of music wasn't initially attached to the series. The show debuted with an entirely different theme from composer/conductor/arranger Ian Freebairn-Smith, who dabbled only occasionally in film and TV scoring. His old-school jazz anthem accompanies the show's initial credits sequence, which displays action clips behind a shifting Cross of Lorraine motif (referencing the rings worn by Magnum, T.C. and Rick). The cue doesn't feel like jazz at first blush, opening with *wah-wah* bass guitar and rising strings that evoke Barry White's "Love's Theme." But this quickly segues to the primary 1-1-1-5 motif in unison brass, the melody expanding as Selleck's co-stars are introduced; Freebairn-Smith then adds a wicked piano solo during a hip-swaying swing bridge (heard in its full-length glory only during the two-part pilot episode's opening credits). The core motif reprises and builds to an orchestral flourish, which climaxes when Selleck smiles and raises his eyebrows in a swoon-worthy close-up.

Jazz chops notwithstanding, the melody isn't particularly hummable. The producers turned to Post and Carpenter, who concocted the sassier, snappier and far more exciting theme that *immediately* catches a viewer's attention; Larry Carlton handles the dynamic guitar work. "[That one was] very easy to do, because I knew the character so well," Post recalled. "I'd gone to grammar school, junior high and high school with Tom Selleck, been friends with him my whole life. It was easy to capture him; he was just *right there*."[2]

This Post/Carpenter composition popped up as a portion of their underscore for episode eight—"The Ugliest Dog in Hawaii"—and replaced Freebairn-Smith's title theme beginning with the 12th episode, "Thicker than Blood." This new theme plays against a more dynamic credit sequence: faster-paced action clips that perfectly suit the action-oriented, jazz/rock ambiance. The sequence opens with a literal roar, when a helicopter dives toward the ocean against an A-theme: a rising four-chord brass and synth fanfare, which develops into a 4-1-1-3 prelude against a powerful 4-4 rhythm section. This segues smoothly to the B-theme, built from a 4-4-5-5 synth and strings motif. The A-theme reprises as the clips come faster, in the staccato style reminiscent of *Hawaii Five-O*; a final burst of seven rising chords backs the shot of Selleck lifting his eyebrows.

Post and Carpenter also supplied original underscores for each episode: lazy, gentle synth noodling, to establish scenes or transition between them; brass and/or guitar variations of the title theme; "shimmering" riffs for underwater ocean activity; dynamic rhythmic cues and suspenseful action jazz for car chases, fist fights and other perilous encounters; and mocking little melodies for lighter moments, such as Magnum's often snarky encounters with Higgins. Two episodes feature noted jazz artists as guest performers: Chuck Mangione appears in the fourth season's "Paradise Blues," and David Sanborn can be seen playing sax in "L.A.," the two-part episode that opens season seven.

Post expanded the title theme for a sizzling 45 released in early 1982; the background drumming is heavier, the synth and guitar more impudent, and a lengthy bridge features a brazen alto sax solo against insistent keyboard comping. The single enjoyed a healthy 17-week run in *Billboard*'s Hot 100 Chart, peaking at No. 25 on May 8 and 15. Post included the track on his Elektra album *Television Theme Songs*, also released in early 1982; it sat in *Billboard*'s Top LPs and Tapes Chart for 17 weeks as well, peaking at No. 70 on the same two days. The Post/Carpenter *Magnum, P.I.* theme eventually became ubiquitous on crime/action TV anthology albums.

In what many fans decried as an act of sacrilege, CBS introduced a reboot of *Magnum, P.I.* on September 24, 2018, with Jay Hernandez in the lead role. Credit where due, the brief title credits sequence does include an abbreviated arrangement of the Post/Carpenter theme.

As it happened, the original *Magnum P.I.* was merely the opening salvo of a must-see-TV one-two punch.

NBC's *Hill Street Blues*, which debuted January 15, 1981, forever changed the medium. The tightly scripted, rat-a-tat police drama plays like stream-of-consciousness viewing: a quasi-documentary approach with production values that look and sound cinematic. Each episode feels like a minimovie populated by a few dozen recurring characters, all portrayed to perfection by a richly varied and highly talented ensemble cast. Everything revolves around Hill Street Station, a grievously overworked inner-city precinct in an unspecified Eastern metropolis; many episodes take place during a single hectic day, starting with roll call and concluding with late-night discussions or lamentations regarding fresh developments in ongoing, interwoven storylines. The chaos is overseen by the deceptively soft-spoken Capt. Frank Furillo (Daniel J. Travanti), who often maintains order solely through sheer force of will.

Hill Street Blues was one of the first serial shows to benefit from newly arrived VCR technology, which made it easier to catch every single episode.

Less enlightened executive producers would have sought a gritty, street-funk title theme that matched the show's rough edges and grimy, "lived in" atmosphere. Mike Post—on this rare occasion, working without frequent partner Pete Carpenter—had other ideas. "I went to CBS Studio Center, and saw the [pilot episode]. I'd never seen a TV show like that; I was just blown away. We went back to [co-creator Steve] Bochco's office, and we all sat down ... and Bochco finally goes, 'Hey, what do you think?' And I said, 'Well, you could go against it. You could write something really kinda poignant, but not sloppy-sentimental, just kind of like, you nod your head and go, Man, there's gonna be somebody born, there's gonna be somebody died, a whole lotta stuff is gonna go down in this 42 minutes, but the clock's gonna keep ticking.'"

Encouraged to pursue that approach, Post drove the half-mile to his house. "I sat down at the piano. I was immediately in E-flat; I don't know why. I messed around with it for 30 minutes. I called Bochco and said 'Hey, I got something.' He and [co-executive producer Gregory] Hoblit came over, walked in the door, and [I played it]. He went 'Do that again.' [I did.] He said 'Do that. *Exactly* that.' I said 'Okay. Bye.' That was it. You know when you've *connected*. I knew it would go really good with the film. It jumped off the screen. [The music] becomes a character; it becomes an integral part of the fabric of the drama. I know most everything technical about [music], and I don't know anything about it emotionally, except that it's magic."[3]

Post's "magic" is a soft, sweet jazz ballad that opens with a pair of three melancholy solo piano chords, while a police car charges out of the precinct garage to begin another day. The final chord echoes briefly, then the piano resumes, working into a melody supported by lingering synth, strings and a rhythm section. Now at midtempo, those initial piano chords develop into the 3-3-6-3 motif that listeners *immediately* associate with the series. The melody expands as the cast members are introduced, and finally resolves into a 1-2-2 fanfare when, on screen, a police car pulls back *into* the station garage.

Post added a bit more pizzazz for an expanded arrangement on a 45 single; it also features a solemn guitar solo by Larry Carlton during an extended bridge. The tune enjoyed a healthy 22-week run on *Billboard's* Hot 100 Chart, peaking at No. 10 on November 14 and 21. It also became a double Grammy Award winner, for Best Pop Instrumental Performance, and Best Instrumental Composition.

Only one other artist dared cover the tune: jazz pianist Rodney Franklin, whose hipper, trumpet-laden and more enthusiastically buoyant arrangement was released by CBS in December 1981.

Post wrote underscores for every one of the 140 episodes during the show's seven-season run. In 1985, the Daniel Caine Orchestra recorded extended arrangements of the best cues, for what became a *de facto* soundtrack album.

The Big Screen

Scripter Larry Gelbart's handling of 1980's *Rough Cut* focuses more on flirty banter than the heist with which the plot is concerned, and there's no doubt that Burt Reynolds, Lesley-Anne Down and David Niven had fun making the film. As befits this breezy approach, Nelson Riddle's score is dominated by big band covers of numerous Duke Ellington classics: most arranged sumptuously, aside from the occasional overkill of thumping, disco-style drums.

The narrative—based only loosely on Derek Lambert's 1975 novel, *Touch the Lion's Paw*—begins when transplanted American playboy Jack Rhodes (Reynolds) glimpses knockout Gillian Bromley (Down) at a high-society London party. This "chance" encounter isn't accidental; Gillian is being blackmailed by Scotland Yard Chief Inspector Cyril Willis (Niven), who has threatened to jail her for past larcenous indiscretions if she refuses to cooperate. Willis, weeks from retirement, wants to prove that Rhodes is a professional jewel thief who (thus far) never has been caught. The bait, which Gillian has been coached to dangle, is a $30 million shipment of diamonds heading from London to Antwerp. She confesses all to Rhodes after they fall in love, and he impishly plans the heist *anyway*, to further annoy the pesky detective.

Riddle salted his orchestra with some seasoned jazz pros—Bob Findley (trumpet), Bill Watrous (trombone), Plas Johnson (tenor sax) and Emil Richards (percussion)—each of whom gets several opportunities to shine.

"David Merrick, the producer, was insistent that the score consist primarily of Duke Ellington's melodies," Riddle recalled, "and it was up to me to arrange these tunes to fit the many situations occurring in the picture. 'Sophisticated Lady' made for an elegant main title, whereas 'Caravan' supplied the material for the chase sequence toward the end of the picture, with many other Ellington gems sprinkled throughout."[4]

The title credits actually unspool to a cha-cha arrangement of "Satin Doll," during the party montage where Jack first spots Gillian. She plays coy; when he's forced into a bit of upper-story skulking to learn why she slipped into an upstairs bedroom, his nimble moves take place against a mildly suspenseful cover of "Sophisticated Lady." Gillian later demonstrates her high-speed driving skills—in a stolen sports car—by eluding police pursuit with help from an uptempo reading of "C Jam Blues," highlighted by Findley's sleek trumpet line. Once Jack accepts the challenge, he assembles a crew that includes Nigel (Timothy West), Ernst (Patrick Magee) and Fergie (Al Matthews). The latter works as a keyboardist at a disco club; while Jack outlines the caper, Fergie noodles through a few solo bars of "Mean to Me," "Ain't Misbehavin'" and "On the Sunny Side of the Street."

Final preparations and the actual heist unfold during a prolonged montage fueled by a swinging mash-up of "C Jam Blues" and "Caravan": an arrangement that would have been a lot more fun without the pounding 2/2 disco drums. Even so, the lengthy cue helps build suspense, during some aerial acrobatics involving two identical planes, along with the subsequent ground-level chase between Jack and Gillian, and a bevy of pursuing police cars. A final unexpected twist signals the end credits, which unspool against a swinging arrangement of "Caravan" (absent distracting disco influences).

Sadly, the film didn't make much noise, but the soundtrack album was a welcome treat when it finally arrived in late 2019.

Riddle had something elegant to work with; Lalo Schifrin wasn't nearly as lucky. Irving Szathmary's catchy main theme isn't the only thing missing from 1980's *The Nude Bomb*—originally titled *The Return of Maxwell Smart*—which is an impressively incompetent effort to resurrect television's *Get Smart* on the big screen. Barbara Feldon's Agent 99 took one look at the awful script and bolted, as did the rest of the show's intelligence agency. Instead of working for CONTROL, Don Adams' Maxwell Smart has been reassigned to the Provisional Intelligence Tactical Service, as in the PITS ... which is precisely what this movie is. The numb-nuts plot finds KAOS threatening the world with a series of bombs that eradicate all fabric, leaving every man, woman and child desperate for clothing to be provided—at usurious prices—by the evil Nino Salvatori Sebastiani (Vittorio Gassman).

Schifrin must've been dismayed. The usually reliable composer didn't put much effort into this project, starting with an obnoxious disco title song—"You're Always There," delivered with shrieking overkill by gospel singer Merry Clayton—which accompanies spoof-Bondian credits. Schifrin gamely tries to invigorate various brawls, chases and shoot-outs, with fitful results. A Universal Studios tram chase gets mild pizzazz from propulsive percussion, guitar and horns; a similar action cue fuels an eyebrow-lifting sequence that finds Max pursuing his quarry while driving a motorized desk (?!?). A soft, slinky piano trio tries to add seductive sizzle to a bedroom encounter between Max and the flirty Agent 22 (Andrea Howard), but the cue is wasted on bad acting and zero chemistry.

This turkey missed it by a lot more than "that much," and—no surprise—didn't produce a soundtrack album. Not one to give up, original TV show executive producer Leonard Stern would gamely try again a decade later.

* * *

Body Heat, screenwriter Lawrence Kasdan's impressive 1981 directorial debut, is a magnificent modern neo-*noir*. It's also famous for John Barry's smoky jazz score: one of the composer's best, and as elegantly sensuous and torrid as the film's sweltering Florida setting. The haunting cues—particularly the main theme—are as much a dramatic presence as the superbly constructed characters, who swirl around a devious plot that borrows from *Double Indemnity* and *The Postman Always Rings Twice*, and is embellished further by sizzling sexuality.

Although Barry assembled a full orchestra, his score is dominated by familiar jazz sidemen: Ronnie Lang (alto sax), Dick Nash (trombone), Mike Lang (piano), Chuck Domanico (bass) and John Guerin (drums).

"[John Barry] loved Paul Desmond," Ronny Lang recalled, years later. "That's what he had in mind. He didn't want blatant, smeary, tons of vibrato. He wanted a more ethereal approach."[5]

The combo players are prominent in the subtly malevolent main theme, which drifts behind title credits superimposed over blurred flames and naked flesh; the cue opens with a dreamy 4-4 synth motif that expands with a flutter of bass and piano filigrees. Ronny Lang's

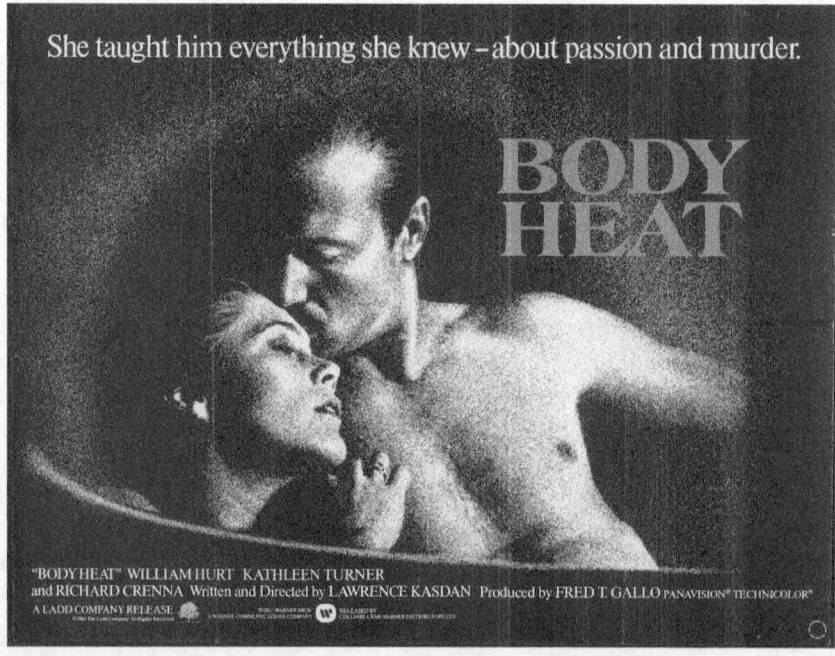

John Barry's music for *Body Heat* demands endless playback, likely having fueled many late-night bedroom antics; it remains one of the finest *noir* scores ever composed. The film's success ignited a mini-genre of similarly stylish—and sexy—crime thrillers during the subsequent decade.

8. That Old Feeling: 1979–81

wandering alto sax introduces the melody, backed by quiet piano comping. This theme belongs to Matty Walker (Kathleen Turner), the *femme* most *fatale* who'll soon wrap her little finger—and everything else—around Ned Racine (William Hurt), the "not too smart" attorney whose feeble hold on wisdom vanishes entirely, once lust is involved.

"The theme came very quickly," Barry explained. "I just thought back to all those Humphrey Bogart movies, and all those wonderful movies that were made in the '30s and early '40s. The main theme is a jazz ballad, plus the figure from the piano: the striding figure of the chords, and the low end is just the strings, so it had a fullness. It's very simple, but there's a great clarity to it."[6]

The cock-sure Ned believes that his initial encounter with the seductive Matty is pure chance: an assumption he'll live to regret. The lawyer's mounting desire is characterized by a secondary 3-3-3-3 sax motif of rising and repeating notes, which suggests the hapless urgency with which he craves her body. Her underlying intention emerges soon enough: Life would be so much simpler, she fantasizes aloud, if only her wealthy husband, Edmund (Richard Crenna), weren't around. Ned takes the hint, and he isn't entirely stupid; he concocts a clever murder scheme that'll make it look like Edmund died accidentally. But things go wrong almost immediately; a series of damning surprises arouses suspicion from Ned's two best friends: assistant deputy prosecutor Peter Lowenstein (Ted Danson) and police detective Oscar Grace (J.A. Preston). Ned finally realizes that he's being played; Barry's most ambitious cue—all the primary themes rising and falling—spots a lengthy sequence that cuts between Ned's final, late-night confrontation with Matty, and Oscar's reluctant decision to arrest his friend.

But all is not as it seems. Flash-forward to an incarcerated Ned, as an epiphany strikes and he realizes precisely what Matty did. But this revelation is too little, too late: His life and career are in shambles, and Barry's 4-4 synth motif signals a final, bitterly ironic alto sax reading of the main theme, backed by mocking touches on bass and piano.

Barry also supplies numerous diegetic cues, starting with a pair of numbers performed by the large jazz band at the outdoor amphitheater where Ned first spots Matty: a midtempo, brass-laden cover of the classic "That Old Feeling," followed by a gently swinging original ballad in the style of Harry James. Mike Lang contributes a pair of cocktail-jazz solos, as an unseen pianist in the bar where Ned next meets Matty; much later, a jazz quintet is heard playing a dreamy number at a Miami bar, where Ned bumps into a fellow attorney who supplies the first clue that Matty may have been less than candid about herself.

The film was quite successful, and everybody raved about Barry's music; even so, the score's journey to mainstream availability was unusually tortured. A limited-edition LP and (later) CD were remixed and released without Barry's approval; for nearly two decades, they were the only game in town. The London Symphony Orchestra delivered a digital rerecording in 1998, which served as a more readily available substitute. Finally, a definitive two-disc edition arrived in 2012, with *all* of Barry's music; the package includes the 10 demo recordings that persuaded Kasdan to hire him.

Jazz is similarly front and center in 1981's *Sharky's Machine*, an exhilarating, fast-paced adaptation of William Diehl's debut novel. This dynamic crime thriller gets its momentum from star Burt Reynolds' taut direction, crisp editing by William D. Gordean and Dennis Virkler, and a swinging big band score that boasts sizzling new arrangements of Great American Songbook classics. Music supervisor Snuff Garrett assembled an awesome roster of jazz talent, working alongside arrangers Al Capps, Bob Florence and Bill Holman.

Although frequently backing iconic singers such as Joe Williams, Sarah Vaughan and Peggy Lee, the group also powers through instrumental underscore cues.

The title credits unfold against a sweet sax solo backed by gentle electric keyboard; vocalist Randy Crawford then gives a breathy introduction to her hit, "Street Life," which roars into a fresh, brass-laden arrangement while the credits continue, and Reynolds' Tom Sharky—an Atlanta narcotics detective—struts confidently across the screen. He pursues a gun-toting perp against furious percussion and guitar licks; the bust goes south when a civilian is injured, and Sharky is demoted to the department's undesirable vice squad. Elsewhere, the villainous Victor (Vittorio Gassman) is introduced in his high-rise penthouse, while the band delivers a fast-paced swinger anchored by cool vibes and Buddy De Franco's clarinet solo, with support from a wall of brass. Victor's messier assignments are handled by his brother Billy (Henry Silva), a sociopath whose lethal activities are backed by unsettling strings and nervous bongos.

The chance discovery of Victor's prostitution ring prompts Sharky and his new "machine" (team)—Arch (Bernie Casey), Papa (Brian Keith) and Nosh (Richard Libertini)—to surveil the apartment belonging to Dominoe (Rachel Ward), a gorgeous escort. Sharky and Nosh bug her room while grooving to a fresh diegetic arrangement of the Manhattan Transfer's "Route 66"; Sharky later shadows her to a dance class, where dozens of nubile women gyrate to a groovy, uptempo exercise cue led by Doc Severinsen's vibrant trumpet. "My Funny Valentine" subsequently becomes Dominoe's theme and is heard several times as the narrative progresses: most ironically when Chet Baker's memorable reading is used as a diegetic cue, as the tearful Dominoe begs Victor to release her. Sharky and his comrades work the clues in a procedural montage powered by a terrific Severinsen swinger ("High Energy"), backed by the ensemble's wall of brass. The score's jazz elements then yield to muted atmospheric cues—twitchy percussion and synth—while the film builds to a violent climax within Victor's high-rise.

The soundtrack album predictably focuses on the vocals, leaving most of the instrumental cues behind. Two of Severinsen's underscore efforts made the cut—"High Energy" and "Sexercise"—but not his lovely handling of "My Funny Valentine." And although the album opens with Crawford's turbo-charged reading of "Street Life," this arrangement skips the haunting sax/keyboard prologue heard in the film. It's worth seeking the elusive 21-track bootleg, which gives a better sense of the complete score.

The year 1981 was a great one for jazz-enhanced crime and action dramas. Dave Grusin's fifth collaboration with director Sydney Pollack, *Absence of Malice*, is a thought-provoking thriller that touches on crime, politics, journalism and—most particularly—ethics. The moral center of Kurt Luedtke's Oscar-nominated screenplay has become even more significant with the passage of time, particularly during the pugnacious second decade of the 21st century, when it began to seem as if honor and integrity were no more than weaknesses to be scoffed at.

Events are put into motion by junior federal prosecutor Elliot Rosen (Bob Balaban), who—frustrated by his inability to tie Miami liquor wholesaler Michael Gallagher (Paul Newman) to the disappearance and presumed murder of a longshoremen's union official—"accidentally" leaks word of the investigation to ambitious *Miami Standard* reporter Megan Carter (Sally Field). She publishes the story with the best of intentions, not realizing that Gallagher is an honest and innocent man. The subsequent fallout destroys his reputation, ruins his business, and puts unexpected pressure on his longtime friend, Teresa Peron (Melinda Dillon). She's the one person who can provide him with an irrefutable alibi, but the circumstances are deeply personal. The situation goes from bad to worse, until Gallagher decides to beat everybody else at their own unscrupulous games.

Grusin's title theme has the bouncy excitement of a newsroom deadline: a staccato, highly percussive quasi-march that cheerfully hammers a core melody heard from trumpet and flute. This cue accompanies the pressroom assembly line process involved with plating, printing and ultimately delivering a daily paper. Variations of this theme reprise throughout the film: notably when Megan pursues an angry Gallagher, wanting to get his version of events; and later, in softer arrangements, as their relationship becomes ... complicated.

"I can't remember if it was intentional," Grusin admitted, "or just sort of happened by osmosis. I do think I tried to find something that would identify, not only the location, but the genre. I don't know what 'journalism music' is exactly, but I guess that was my attempt to try to make it sound like it had to do with that area."[7]

Quiet, heartstring-tugging solo piano melodies have long been one of Grusin's strengths, and he supplies several here. By far the film's most powerful scene belongs to Dillon, when Teresa—wanting to help Gallagher—reluctantly shares the all-important alibi with Megan, who splashes it on the front page of the next day's paper. Grusin supplies a soft, tragic flute cue as a terrified Teresa gets up early that morning and, not wanting anybody to read about this incident that shames her so deeply, frantically scoops up newspapers from all of her neighbors' driveways.

Grusin also contributes several diegetic cues appropriate to the Miami setting: a few lively Cuban melodies, heard in the bar where Megan often meets friends after work; a lovely jazz theme by an unseen solo pianist, in the restaurant where Megan and Gallagher have dinner; and a particularly touching calliope theme that suggests Teresa's vulnerability, when she finally meets Megan in a public park.

Although the score has much to do with the story's dramatic vigor, the film contains barely 15 minutes of music: less than half of what Grusin delivered, due to Pollack's careful, often minimal application of cues. No soundtrack album coincided with the film's release, although Grusin did expand one of the interior themes, invited Sally Stevens to write some lyrics, and published the resulting tune as "Who Comes This Night." It has become a Christmas carol, most famously "introduced" by James Taylor on his 2006 holiday album. In 2019, Grusin's full score finally was issued.

Meanwhile, Across the Pond...

The BBC's *Shoestring* has long maintained a devoted following wholly out of proportion to the modest, two-year run of 21 episodes that began with its debut on September 30, 1979. Fans have dubbed it Britain's answer to *The Rockford Files*: Both shows feature somewhat lighthearted, character-driven scripts; both focus on personable, laid-back detectives who aren't always successful in their efforts to avoid nasty encounters; both shows are populated by engaging supporting players. But Eddie Shoestring (Trevor Eve) slides into the detective gig quite unexpectedly; while between jobs, he sorts out a potential scandal involving a popular DJ at the local Radio West station. Eddie thereafter becomes the station's resident sleuth, soliciting call-in clients via a weekly radio show titled "The Private Ear of Eddie Shoestring."

The scoring assignment went to rising film and television composer George Fenton, and his title theme is a lazy, bluesy little ballad inspired by Eddie's ambling walk. Fenton worked with a septet: alto sax/clarinet, grand piano, synths, harmonica, electric guitar, bass guitar and drums. The credits sequence follows Eddie while he strolls through the streets and byways of an unspecified city in the west of England (possibly Bristol, where the show was filmed). The title theme opens with a bold fanfare, then segues to a leisurely melody dominated by keyboards, bass guitar and drums; harmonica and alto sax add color during a meditative bridge. The melody builds to an apparent conclusion, then rises again for a final flourish.

Fenton and his combo also delivered a varied collection of underscore cues, during a single eight-hour session at London's Lansdowne Studios, Holland Park.[8] Many of these cues are saucy little jazz numbers, often heard while Eddie is clandestinely following a suspect, or (illegally) breaking into a building, or engaged in some other form of skulking. Vibrant action jazz is rare, because *Shoestring* isn't that sort of show; even so, Fenton's engaging music has enough personality to make it a character in its own right.

The show's radio station setting also made the series a gold mine for fans of classic and contemporary pop tunes by everybody from the New Seekers and Blondie, to Dusty Springfield and Eric Clapton (which prevented home video release for decades, due to labyrinthine music rights issues).

Fenton expanded the title theme for a BBC single. The harmonica is front and center on this arrangement, and the alto sax and guitar get a lot more action during a lengthier bridge. The "radio dial" sound effect also is more pronounced at the beginning and conclusion.

Over at ITV, Mike Moran cleverly built horseracing excitement into his propulsive title theme for late 1979's *The Racing Game*, a six-episode series suggested by the *oeuvre* of famed thriller novelist Dick Francis. Mike Gwilym stars as jockey-turned-reluctant private investigator Sid Halley, whose new profession results from a riding accident that claims his left hand and lower arm. All episodes are set in the horseracing world, with Halley assisted by his rough-and-tumble best friend, Chico Barnes (Mick Ford).

Moran's title theme opens with a treble keyboard ostinato against a heavy rhythmic two-beat—almost disco, but not quite—while horses charge up a track toward the camera. Suspenseful unison brass triplets rise against throbbing drums, with stingers perfectly timed to clips of horses jumping over track obstacles; this sequence depicts the accident that ruins Halley's riding career. The camera then smash-cuts to his trench-coated detective garb, artificial hand in evidence; the keyboard filigree repeats, as do the rising brass triplets, climaxing in a final orchestral fanfare.

Moran's underscores blend the usual orchestral shading with dollops of funky urban jazz: a shrewd artistic choice, as it emphasizes the conflicts resulting from Halley's "lower class," street-level status, since he operates in a moneyed realm populated by British aristocrats who view him with snarky disapproval.

Nothing further became of Moran's music, once the miniseries concluded. Ian McShane starred in a trio of 1989 telefilms loosely adapted from other Francis novels—*Bloodsport*, *In the Frame* and *Twice Shy*—but their frivolous pop/rock orchestral scores aren't within shouting distance of jazz.

9

Gumshoe Piano: 1982–84

Just like that, television all but abandoned jazz.

Hit (and failed) action/adventure shows became known either by "jukebox scores" laden with pop/rock title songs (*Hardcastle & McCormick, Riptide, Legmen, Hawaiian Heat, Cover Up*) or disco-laden synth anthems (*Knight Rider, Blue Thunder, Airwolf*). Both styles became even more ubiquitous after *Miami Vice* arrived in September 1984. Jan Hammer's pulsating synth title theme spent 22 weeks on *Billboard's* Hot 100 chart, rising all the way to No. 1 on November 9, 1985; it won two Grammy Awards the following year. The show's first soundtrack album (of many) blended Hammer's underscore cues with equally popular pop/rock songs; it spent 34 weeks on *Billboard's* Top 200 Albums chart, hitting No. 1 for an astonishing 11 weeks: a TV soundtrack record that stands to this day.

With results like that, network execs wanted *every* new show to open with synth or pop/rock songs. Or, better yet, a catchy pop vocal *backed* by synth.

Mike Post had little use for jukebox scores. "Any producer can put a quarter in, and punch J6, K9," he scoffed. "That doesn't make a show *special*."[1]

The Small Screen

Henry Mancini wrote two title themes for NBC's *Remington Steele*, which represented one of his final assignments for a weekly TV series. The show's mildly complicated premise is recited via voiceover during the first season's opening credits, when newbie private investigator Laura Holt (Stephanie Zimbalist) is chagrined to discover that her name on the door doesn't attract potential clients. She fabricates a fictitious male agency head—"Remington Steele"—and becomes the belle of the private eye ball. The situation grows more captivating with the arrival of a suave British fellow (Pierce Brosnan) who agrees to *pretend* to be Steele, thereby satisfying clients who want to meet the "boss" in person. Neither Laura nor TV viewers ever learned about this mysterious fellow's background during five successful seasons that began October 1, 1982.

Zimbalist recites this back-story during an introductory montage presented against a slow, luxuriously smoky jazz ballad—the melody traded between solo horns and vibes—right out of Mancini's *Peter Gunn* playbook. Unfortunately, it's hard to enjoy the music, buried beneath the narration. A shorter arrangement of what came to be known as the "Laura Holt Theme" plays behind the end credits, absent voiceover, but brevity makes it less satisfying.

Beginning with the second season, a fresh credits sequence—sans narration—is accompanied by Mancini's actual "Remington Steele Theme": a slow, cheerful march with a strong two-beat backing a 4-1-5-2-4-3 motif in unison brass, which repeats in a couple of different keys, against a bit of synth comping. The droll melody perfectly suits the Mutt 'n' Jeff pairing of Zimbalist and Brosnan, well matched in frivolous adventures that borrow heavily from *The Thin Man* and other mixed-duo detective shows. As with Pete and Edie on *Peter Gunn*, Laura and "Remington" are more than mere professional colleagues; frequent smooches give underscore composer Richard Lewis Warren many opportunities for nods to Mancini's "Laura Holt Theme."

Warren had a lot of fun in general. The faux Remington is a rabid fan of old movies, so he often quotes lines or even acts out classic scenes, while he and Laura pursue leads. This allows Warren to insert appropriate musical references to said films, with underscore cues that run the gamut of styles from screwball comedies to atmospheric 1930s and '40s horror films, and from melodramatic *film noir* mysteries to 1960s secret agent thrillers. Indeed, Warren occasionally mimics John Barry's action jazz stylings for James Bond (rather ironic in hindsight, since Brosnan eventually wound up playing 007).

Although neither of Mancini's themes earned release on singles, he included an expanded arrangement of Remington's theme—with a swinging sax solo during an extended bridge—for his 1988 album, *Premier Pops*.

Brosnan's Remington was suave and *cool*. In great contrast, ABC's *T.J. Hooker* was an embarrassment in the post–*Hill Street Blues* landscape of TV police shows: an old-school, overwrought melodrama that probably shouldn't have been taken seriously (but absolutely was, in the eyes of star William Shatner). Today it's dismissed as a parody of older cop shows, but it was popular enough to run five seasons after its spring 1982 debut. Shatner's Sgt. Thomas Jefferson Hooker is a 15-year veteran of the (fictitious) LCPD Academy Precinct. He shepherds younger officers Vince Romano (Adrian Zmed), Jim Corrigan (James Darren) and—most notoriously—Stacy Sheridan (Heather Locklear); she's present mostly to be poured into bikinis and tiny dresses, then kidnapped or otherwise endangered. Car chases and gun battles are ubiquitous, the "horrors" of street patrol alleviated by plenty of macho humor.

A program with so much visual sizzle demanded an equally aggressive title theme, and composer Mark Snow obliged. He opens the credits sequence with slashing strings, fiery brass and rapidly thumping drums during a brisk action montage that crescendos when Shatner faces the camera, gun drawn; a 3-2-3-2 unison brass motif anchors the subsequent melody against another staccato montage of clips showing everybody in action. The furious tempo doesn't let up until a final, slower five-note fanfare follows a squad of jogging cadets into the police academy. Snow echoes this action jazz ambiance in many of the underscore cues he wrote for five early episodes; John E. Davis maintained this tone when he took over for the lion's share of subsequent original underscores … for the first two seasons.

Beginning with season three, Snow's title theme was heavily reorchestrated, the melody and fanfares now handled by pounding synth, rather than brass and strings; the rhythm section was kicked into a temple-throbbing, *bam-bam* two-beat. Any semblance of jazz evaporated, the cue having been transformed into overstated disco swill. Davis had little choice but to follow along; all subsequent underscores are dominated by monotonous thumping drums, angry synth and uptempo dance music often heard as source cues in (no surprise) discos. None of the show's music had any sort of afterlife.

Few television dramas experienced a pregnancy as difficult as that endured by CBS' cop series, *Cagney & Lacey*. The concept began as a pilot film broadcast on October 8, 1981, with Tyne Daly comfortably situated as the happily married Mary Beth Lacey, alongside

Loretta Swit as the single Christine Cagney. The film is anchored musically by "Ain't That the Way," a sassy blues anthem written by Michael Stull and sung with gusto by Marie Cain. The credits sequence plays behind the song, which also pops up midway through the film. Mark Snow contributes a mostly undistinguished underscore, which dabbles in orchestral klezmer and includes only one solid action jazz cue, during the story's suspenseful finale.

The film generated enough interest to be picked up as a six-episode series that debuted March 25, 1982, thus becoming the first American television "buddy drama" anchored by two women. But Swit was tied down by the television incarnation of *M.A.S.H.*, so the role of Christine Cagney was recast with Meg Foster. The blend of police action and personal drama is anchored by the two leads' ongoing struggle for respect from their male colleagues, while enduring all manner of chauvinistic behavior. Executive producer Barney Rosenzweig brought in Nelson Riddle to write a title theme and underscores, and his propulsive big band jazz theme is excellent. It opens with suspensefully rising strings, then ramps up with a series of rising 2-3 "call and response" brass motifs against a finger-snapping rhythm section, while Cagney and Lacey—in beat cop uniforms—race across town to make an important collar. A softer string and brass bridge follows, when they're rewarded with detective's shields; the music cleverly segues to "Ain't That the Way," while the cast members are introduced. The end credits play against a rousing instrumental version of the song.

Riddle's underscore cues are equally lively, with frequent arrangements of the title song—often punctuated by impertinent electric guitar licks—blended with combustible action jazz (some of it *still* sounding like stuff he wrote for *Batman*) and some deliciously sultry cues. Big band stingers bookend acts between commercials; even the softer suspense cues swing like crazy.

Unfortunately, CBS execs—worried that Foster appeared too "butch"—canceled the show. Behind-the-scenes negotiations resulted in a change of network heart, but when the program earned a full second season beginning October 25, Christine Cagney was recast yet again: this time with Sharon Gless. Producer Barney Rosenzweig, worried because his show would follow two popular CBS comedies—*M.A.S.H.* (ironically) and *Newhart*—shrewdly abandoned the action-oriented style of the initial credits sequence and replaced Riddle's title theme with a fresh composition from Bill Conti.

"Barney was figuring [the series] out," Conti recalled, "and he said, 'You know, with this main title, I don't want anyone to think that it's a cop show, [because] I follow a comedy. I have a cop show; it's as dramatic as whatever. There's nothing funny about it. [But] I'm gonna trick 'em; I want to hold that audience. I want them to stick around for a little bit longer.' [Conti hums the first few bars of his theme.] So that was the directive: I had the little saxophones, and it was kind of light and funny. It *could* be a comedy show."[2]

Conti's theme opens with larkish noodling on twin alto saxes—Ray Pizzi and Ernie Watts, playing in thirds—as an overhead camera zooms across a cityscape and descends to reveal Cagney and Lacey striding down a sidewalk; the melody accelerates into a cheerful 4-1-2-2 horn motif. This new credits montage is softer; although Cagney and Lacey are seen at work in the precinct, other clips show Cagney being pulled away from a dress shop, while Lacey gets a send-off smooch from her husband, Harvey (John Karlen). Not until the montage concludes do we finally get some quick action sequences, after which Conti concludes with more byplay from the alto saxes. The end credits arrangement is even livelier, with some vivacious sax comping behind the melody.

The series became a hit—despite another brief cancellation—and ultimately ran seven seasons. Most original underscores were traded between Dana Kaproff and Ron Ramin, with nearly a dozen other composers handling a few each. Given the nature of the show—Rosenzweig worked hard to ensure an atmosphere of realism, rather than contrived car chases or street pursuits—the underscore cues favor orchestral shading; action jazz is quite rare.

None of Riddle's music endured beyond broadcast, nor did Conti expand his title theme for a single.

As it happened, the year's best new jazz theme was attached to a show nobody watched. NBC's all but forgotten *Cassie & Co.* was Angie Dickinson's only post–*Police Woman* attempt to star in another weekly series, but the show flopped. Her Cassie Holland is essentially Pepper Anderson a few more years down the road: a former cop who decides to go solo, by taking over a one-person private detective agency previously run by the retiring Lyman "Shack" Shackelford (John Ireland). A mere four episodes after its January 29 debut, *Cassie & Co.* lost its PI license.

If only the series had been as smooth and sophisticated as its title credits. The clever sequence shows only Cassie's legs, as they transport her through an average day: from morning exercises through the hustle and bustle of work, then dinner at some swanky restaurant, and concluding as she kicks off heels and rests her weary feet on a desk. At this point, the camera finally pulls back to reveal Dickinson's face. The sleek, 80-second split-screen montage is synched to a gorgeous jazz ballad by famed saxophonist Grover Washington, Jr. The lyrical melody is set against a gentle, almost bossa nova rhythm section; it rises to a lingering soprano finale when the camera drifts away from Dickinson, and the show's title appears on the screen.

Washington had nothing to do with the underscores, which are as routine as the show itself. He expanded what became "Cassie's Theme" for his 1982 album, *The Best Is Yet to Come*, fronting a combo that features Billy Childs (piano and synth), Richard Tee (keyboards), Lee Ritenour (guitar), Abe Laboriel (bass), Harvey Mason (drums) and Victor Feldman and Kevin Johnson (percussion). This even more seductive midtempo arrangement boasts an extended sax interlude against Ritenour's deft comping. "Cassie's Theme" went on to become one of Washington's signature compositions, and today's fans undoubtedly have no idea that it began life as the theme of a failed TV series.

January 1983 heralded the arrival of another pop-culture sensation, and subtlety definitely wasn't on the table when Frank Lupo and Stephen J. Cannell created NBC's *The A-Team*. The same is true of the Mike Post/Pete Carpenter title theme that introduces the show each week. This cartoonish adventure series—the ultimate in mindless, guilty pleasure viewing, lasting five seasons—is built around wretched excess: from the explosive destruction of vehicles, commercial property and even entire landscapes; to equally exaggerated brawls that often level an entire bar or restaurant. Voice-over narration during the title sequence introduces the four characters—Lt. Col. John "Hannibal" Smith (George Peppard), Lt. Templeton "Face" Peck (Dirk Benedict), Capt. H.M. "Howling Mad" Murdock (Dwight Schultz) and Sgt. 1st Class Bosco "B.A." Baracus (Mr. T)—as a "crack Vietnam commando unit" sent to military prison for a crime they didn't commit. After escaping from a maximum security stockade, they "disappear" in Los Angeles, trying to clear their names while being available as soldiers of fortune who help folks unable to obtain justice via conventional means.

The mildly jazzy (at best) Post/Carpenter title theme opens with a low snare drum vamp beneath the introductory narration; this concludes when the show's title is "bulleted" onto the screen, at which point the iconic 4-3 horn fanfare signals a series of explosive action clips. This expands into a pulse-quickening power march that gets maximum voltage from a series of brief, similarly exciting brass statements. Then the theme takes an unexpected turn.

"[It came about] really easily," Post recalled. "I laughed till I cried, reading the script. We went and talked to [Stephen J.] Cannell and said well, look; it's gotta be military, 'cause [of how] these guys met. And let's rip off Cream's 'Sunshine of Your Love' for the middle section, because it'll be like Vietnam. So we did a big guitar thing in the middle. Easy little thing to do."[3]

The rock guitar interlude hits just as the sequence focuses on antics by Schultz's Murdock. This is followed by a brief string bridge that segues back to the brass fanfares, timed to Mr. T's door-pulverizing entrance. Post and Carpenter even get acknowledged during this breathtaking 90-second sequence, which concludes with a screaming flourish against additional on-screen destruction. The theme was reorchestrated during subsequent seasons, the music gaining more prominence once the voice-over narration was deemed unnecessary. By the fifth season, most of the brass had been replaced by synth, and the rhythm section was modified to make the theme sound more like disco.

Post expanded the first-season arrangement for a 1984 45 single, which was included on the eponymous LP—*Mike Post*—that he released simultaneously. This version forgoes the snare drum introduction, instead moving directly into a synth melody backed by thumping 2/2 disco bass; the Cream-style middle section runs longer, with an encore before returning to the principal theme. This version was nominated for a Grammy Award, for Best Instrumental Composition; Post lost to John Williams and Randy Newman (in a rare tie). Fans preferring the original brass arrangement—with voiceover—can find it on TVT Records' 1987 double-album set, *Television's Greatest Hits 70s & 80s*.

Post and Carpenter also handled the bombastic underscores; this wasn't a show for soft, subtle music. Although they never released an official soundtrack, the Daniel Caine Orchestra obliged with a 15-track cover LP—*The A-Team*—also released in 1984. Their big band handling of the title theme is superior to Post's synth-hued single, and the melody is referenced in several other tracks. Mild whimsy turns up in cues such as "Young Hannibal," with its larkish keyboard and guitar licks; "Showtime" and "The A-Team in New York City" include a bit of saucy swing. BMG digitized Post' album—under the new title *It's Post Time*—in 1998.

Hannibal Smith and his crew later jumped to the big screen in an equally preposterous 2010 adventure. Alan Silvestri's similarly extravagant, synth-based score—definitely not jazz—includes an awesome arrangement of the Post/Carpenter title theme, complete with rock guitar interlude.

* * *

Consider the irony: Raymond Chandler's old-school sensibilities helped change the television programming landscape for the first time since the medium's creation.

The lavish, meticulously crafted *Philip Marlowe, Private Eye*—a U.S./UK collaboration that became the first dramatic series produced for the fledgling pay-TV service HBO—is one of the finest Chandler adaptations ever developed for the small *or* large screen. All 11 episodes are authentic to the 1930s Los Angeles setting of the short stories on which they're based, and produced with the attention to period detail for which HBO soon would become famous. The cinematography is as lush as the sloe-eyed *femme fatales* who populate most stories, and Powers Boothe is the quintessential Marlowe: one of the few actors who looks *and* sounds the part, down to the sandpaper-dry, slightly sardonic voiceover that opens and periodically punctuates each case.

Viewers *knew* this show was something special, from the initial frames of Maurice Binder's sleek title credits sequence. It opens with explosive gunfire as car headlights race toward a silhouetted figure fleeing in the foreground; bullet ricochets, smoldering walking bass, keyboard filigrees and sudden blasts of brass herald a sensational big band swing theme by British jazz composer John Cameron. This musical prologue makes room for echoing sound effects—a cocktail shaker, Marlowe loading and flipping the barrel of his gun—and then shifts to a rising sax melody that smolders as much as the silhouetted babe who lights Marlowe's cigarette. Screaming brass and background piano provide an ostinato for a climactic wail of sax, while Marlowe's image is distorted when he fires into a pool of water, then … smash-cut to the episode's opening scene. Bold, brilliant and breathtaking.

Five short stories were adapted in a brief first season that ran weekly beginning April 16, 1983: "The Pencil," "The King in Yellow," "Finger Man," "Nevada Gas" and "Smart Aleck Kill." Cameron supplied original underscores for each; many scenes are punctuated by slow, mournful solo sax or trumpet. Lazy swing cues amplify Marlowe's insolent disrespect for criminals and cops; women of mystery are introduced by solo sax ballads dirty enough to leave a stain. Sizzling action jazz propels chases and climactic shoot-outs; big band dance tunes pop up as diegetic cues in restaurants and bars. The music is terrific throughout.

Several years passed before the series was renewed for a second season of six episodes, beginning April 27, 1986. In an astonishing example of artistic idiocy, Binder's title sequence was dropped in favor of the bland, credits-on-neutral-background style of 1974's *Chinatown*. Cameron's music also was absent, replaced by a slow, mournful Moe Koffman sax theme reminiscent of (hmmm) Jerry Goldsmith's main theme for *Chinatown*. This period-similar musical *homage* isn't bad *per se*, but it also isn't as strikingly original as its predecessor. Koffman's second season underscores aren't nearly as busy; they focus more on orchestral shading, and less on the era's swing influence.

Film noir fans would have killed for a soundtrack album—particularly from Cameron's initial season—but none was forthcoming.

Period jazz also set the stage for television's revival of another iconic literary gumshoe. In 1939, decades before he would become the famed composer of television title themes and underscores, Earle Hagen played trombone and wrote arrangements for Ray Noble's big band. Hagen composed "Harlem Nocturne" that year, as a bluesy homage to Duke Ellington and Johnny Hodges; the song quickly gained fame as an instrumental, eventually becoming an oft-covered jazz standard.[4] Jack Dumont handled the memorable alto sax solo when Noble's band introduced the tune, and sax thereafter became firmly identified with it. Flash-forward not quite half a century, and Hagen's classic melody became equally familiar as the title theme for Stacy Keach's rendition of Mike Hammer.

But Keach wasn't the first actor to play Mickey Spillane's tough-guy gumshoe in a made-for-television film. That honor fell to Kevin Dobson, who starred in 1981's lackluster *Margin for Murder*. It didn't capture the essential "Mike Hammer atmosphere," and even the usually reliable Nelson Riddle's mildly jazz-hued score—"borrowed" from his work on the earlier PI series, *City of Angels*—was disappointing.

Keach assumed the role in the telefilm *Murder Me, Murder You*, which aired April 9, 1983. "[The theme] was [supervising producer] Lew Gallo's idea," Hagen recalled. "He called me up, and said 'You know, the *quality* of this character is 1940s; he's a throwback, even though he's living in the present time. "Harlem Nocturne" would be a great theme for the show.' I sent him a Georgie Auld recording, and he cut it into the temp track. And Stacy, who's a jazz piano player, went nuts about the idea of using 'Harlem Nocturne,' [saying] 'That's the perfect theme for a guy who's a throwback.'" Hagen duly recorded a fresh arrangement of his iconic melody, with Bud Shank taking the sax solo.[5]

The tune doesn't debut until *after* the "typewritten" title credits, which are superimposed over a brief prologue during which two young women are murdered. The scene cuts to an overhead view of New York City; Shank delivers the memorable first six notes of the iconic theme, the bluesy melody continuing while the camera slowly pans down to the window of Hammer's office, and then inside. The music fades as Keach delivers a world-weary PI voice-over, while Velda (Tanya Roberts) circles her desk in a scarlet dress that barely conceals her assets. A similarly luxurious arrangement of "Harlem Nocturne" returns for the end credits, and Hagen also references it several times during his similarly swinging underscore. A particularly lovely big band variation boasts sleek solos on piano and vibes, when Hammer—driving slowly through the city—easily evades a rather clumsy tail. The film's mid–1980s setting notwithstanding, Keach and Hagen's music are resolutely post–World War II: both somehow appropriate despite the anachronistic mismatch.

CBS green-lit a series even before the film aired. *Mickey Spillane's Mike Hammer* debuted January 26, 1984, with a second two-hour telefilm—*More than Murder*, with Velda now played by Lindsay Bloom—that Hagen also scored. He wastes no time introducing the music; a smoky "Harlem Nocturne"—smoldering sax backed by melancholy strings—is heard behind similarly "typed" title credits. The film also boasts plenty of underscore swing cues and concludes with a philosophical ballad highlighted by jazz guitar, heard beneath Hammer's voice-over postmortem.

The series settled into its weekly timeslot two nights later, with "Harlem Nocturne" front and center behind the title credits. J.J. Johnson added similar big band sass to the remaining episodes of the short first season; jazz arrangements of Great American Songbook classics such as "Moonlight Serenade" often pop up as source music on the jukebox at the Lite N Easy bar, where Hammer hangs out. Johnson and Hagen collaborated on all 14 episodes of the second season. Jazz great Herbie Hancock pops up (as himself) in the episode "Firestorm," and jazz guitarist George Benson has a key role in "Deadly Reunion." Keach occasionally noodles some jazz piano on camera, when Hammer's in a contemplative mood.

The second season's brevity resulted from Keach having to spend six months in England's Reading Prison, after being caught with cocaine during a random body search at London's Heathrow Airport.[6] That would've ended most shows, given CBS' anxiety over whether the American public would forgive Keach, but executive producer Jay Bernstein was tenacious. A compromise was reached: yet another "pilot telefilm." *The Return of Mickey Spillane's Mike Hammer* reunited the entire cast—and Hagen—for a nasty kidnap saga that takes Hammer out of his Manhattan comfort zone and improbably sends him to Los Angeles. Hagen once again provides an appropriately jazzy backdrop; the film drew respectable ratings when it aired April 18, 1986, and CBS duly put the show back on the weekly roster that September.

A few things changed. *The New Mike Hammer* dumped the cleavage-baring bimbo brigade, to lure female viewers, and—most distressing—Hagen was absent. The title credits still unfold against "Harlem Nocturne," but arranger/conductor Bruce Miller transformed it into an obnoxious, rhythm-heavy, uptempo dance arrangement that owes more to disco. It's also telling that the melody is carried by solo and unison brass, rather than the sultry sax. Some underscores are positively dire: nothing but wall-to-wall synth swill. Fortunately, most episodes were handled by Ron Ramin, who *tries* to maintain a jazz ambiance. An episode (ironically) titled "Harlem Nocturne" is a standout, both for the returning presence of George Benson—this time in an acting role—and for a bluesy score laden with diegetic jazz emanating from strip clubs and The Three Deuces Bar, where Hot Mama Vibes (Isabel Sanford) holds forth.

Ratings weren't strong enough for more than one 22-episode season, but this wasn't the end of Keach's reign as Hammer. Subsequent reruns on the recently launched cable/satellite USA Network proved unexpectedly popular, which encouraged CBS and Bernstein to mount yet another telefilm.[7] *Mickey Spillane's Mike Hammer: Murder Takes All*—which aired May 21, 1989—is wholly disappointing, mostly due to the ill-advised decision to send Hammer to Las Vegas. On the positive side, Ramin gives the score a bit of jazz bounce, and it's nice to hear a more languid, sax-driven arrangement of "Harlem Nocturne" over the title credits.

That should have been the final nail in the Keach/Spillane coffin, but—remarkably—it *still* wasn't. Not quite a decade later, Bernstein and Keach reunited for a single season of *Mike Hammer, Private Eye*, which ran in syndication from September 1997 through June 1998. Almost everything about this revival looks cheap, recycled and tired. Keach—older, wiser but still authoritative—is the sole attraction, slipping once again into the role, as if it were a comfortable pair of shoes. Eric Allaman scored all 26 episodes, favoring laid-back mainstream jazz cues; softly contemplative riffs often back the precredits teaser, and the provocatively dressed Velda (Shannon Whirry) usually earns a few bars of something salacious. Keach still demonstrates tasty piano chops on occasion, usually when killing time at Lou's, the more trendy bar that replaces Lite N Easy as his favorite hangout, and which sometimes features small swing combos.

The two-part episode "Songbird" is a treat for jazz lovers; the story focuses on a sweet-voiced chanteuse (Moira Walley) foolish enough to fall in love with a mobster. Her live performances are backed by a quartet led by jazz trumpeter Jack Sheldon, alongside Ross Tompkins (piano), Bruce Lett (acoustic double bass) and Jake Hanna (drums).

The popularity of "Harlem Nocturne" notwithstanding, Hagen never issued his own arrangement of the song (although he performed on Ray Noble's 1939 recording). None of the various incarnations of this TV series produced a soundtrack album, nor did "Harlem Nocturne" ever get rebranded as the show's theme on a 45 ... at least, not in the States. The Netherlands' Edward Visser Band released a 1985 arrangement on CNR, with the paper jacket sporting a black-and-white photo of Keach's brooding Hammer, complete with faux bullet holes.

The Big Screen

Everybody remembers John Barry's *noir* score for *Body Heat*, but his similar approach to 1982's undersung *Hammett* has fallen off the radar. That's a shame: Barry's bluesy, brooding score is terrific, and the film is a clever homage that once again adopts the conceit of placing a mystery writer—in this case, Samuel Dashiell Hammett—into his own hard-boiled investigation. Sadly, the film was DOA, due to the bad publicity associated with an extremely troubled shoot; producer Francis Ford Coppola and director Wim Wenders had radically divergent views on how to shape the story and tone.

The story, set in 1928 in San Francisco, begins as Hammett (Frederic Forrest) finishes his newest Continental Op story. Jimmy Ryan (Peter Boyle), a colleague from Hammett's Pinkerton days, drags the author into a missing persons case: A young Chinese prostitute named Crystal Ling (Lydia Lei) has vanished, and numerous shady characters want to find her. Hammett's reluctant participation is motivated by his desire to retrieve the sole manuscript copy of that new story, which distressingly winds up in the hands of opium drug lord Fong Wei Tau (Michael Chow). Hammett soon is hip deep in bent cops, irritable gunsels, a loyal lady librarian (Marilu Henner) and sidebar characters played by *film noir* veterans such as Elisha Cook, Jr., Royal Dano and Hank Worden.

Barry sets the mood with an elegantly sultry title theme that opens with Mike Lang's languid piano solo, which yields to Ronnie Lang's bluesy clarinet on the core melody: lazy, melancholy and rich with late-flapper-era decadence. Short variations of this theme serve as bumpers between scenes; piano and clarinet later convey the dismal news that Crystal has been killed. Or has she? When the key blackmailer is revealed and the case wraps up, Hammett winds up with a better story than the one he fails to retrieve. Barry's bluesy main theme returns, piano comping behind clarinet, as Hammett attacks the typewriter and pounds out this new tale.

Barry also wrote numerous diegetic cues: all of them leisurely, Dixieland-style swingers, many of which never made it into the finished film.

"I loved doing *Hammett*," Barry noted, years later. "That was a terrific movie. I wasn't the director's first choice, but a friend said why don't you just go along and do something, so I went into a studio and I recorded a demo of it, with a clarinet, and sent it to [him]. I went to London and came back, and he called me at, like, 3 in the morning, very enthusiastic, and we just got on like a house on fire after that."[8]

The eventual 2000 soundtrack album includes Barry's full score and eight diegetic tunes: far more music than moviegoers heard.

Almost a year before Stacey Keach donned Mike Hammer's fedora, the character hit the big screen with all the berserker rage that made Mickey Spillane's 1947 literary debut so memorable. The updated remake of *I, the Jury* (1982) is lurid trash, but Spillane suffered that same accusation when the novel debuted. Armand Assante slides into Hammer's pavement-pounding shoes with the ferocity of a bulldog, his unrelenting recklessness as engaging as the modern *noir* atmosphere concocted by director Richard T. Heffron and cinematographer Andrew Laszlo. The icing on the cake is Bill Conti's exhilarating jazz score, which gets much of its intensity from Anthony Ortega's smoky sax and Mike Lang's electrifying piano work.

The film opens as Jack Williams is killed by an unseen assailant. Propelled in part by guilt over having failed to stay in touch with the guy who saved his life in Vietnam, Hammer follows clues that lead to gorgeous sex surrogates who "assist" male clients at a clinic run by Dr. Charlotte Bennett (Barbara Carrera). Although these public activities are legit, the clinic also is a front for a CIA brainwashing operation run by Romero (Barry Snider), who employs knife-wielding psychotic Charles Kendricks (Judson Scott) to dispose of anybody who gets in the way. Organized crime boss Charles Kalecki (Alan King) is a minor distraction, as is a misleading tip from Hammer's longtime cop buddy Pat Chambers (Paul Sorvino), but Mike isn't fooled for long. When Velda (Laurene Landon) is kidnapped by Kendricks, Hammer explodes into a righteous rage that climaxes with a suspenseful, one-man assault on Romero's heavily guarded compound.

Lang's awesome, hyper-staccato keyboard chops kick off the pulse-pounding credits sequence, with Conti's vibrant title theme delivered by a wall of brass and Ortega's occasional sax riffs. Somber sax and mournful woodwinds then accompany Hammer, when he views Williams' body. The first lead sends Hammer and Velda to the reclusive Joe Butler (Geoffrey Lewis); their chat is interrupted when gun-toting thugs prompt a pell-mell vehicular chase along twisty mountain roads. Conti spots this thrilling sequence with pounding percussion, *wah-wah* guitar and a screaming trumpet solo. The tempo shifts to rapid-fire 4/4 swing when Ortega's sax joins the fun.

Later, a captured Hammer escapes from Romero's men and races across the city to save Velma; Conti spots this trip with ferocious horns, twitchy bass licks and another of Lang's vigorous keyboard solos. The eventual assault on Romero's compound is backed by a symphony of swinging, trumpet-laden action jazz; the melee climaxes as Hammer finally confronts the baddie, set against a hypnotic, eight-note bass piano riff that evokes Henry Mancini's *Peter Gunn* theme. The subsequent epilogue faithfully replicates the book's notorious final scene, and the final line that Assante tosses off with icy contempt: "It was easy." The end credits signal a reprise of Lang's hard-driving keyboard work on the explosive main theme.

The soundtrack album finally arrived in 2013.

* * *

Lalo Schifrin enjoyed a high-profile double-header in 1983, although the end results were poles apart.

Clint Eastwood's Harry Callahan turns co-conspirator in *Sudden Impact*, while in pursuit of a mass murderer whose actions he eventually deems justifiable homicide. The core plot concerns a woman's vengeance against the people who, years earlier, gang-raped her and her teenage sister. Schifrin, returning to the series, addresses Harry's seismic morality shift in an edgier score with deeper psychological elements: less action jazz and more atmospheric suspense.

That said, his main theme—introduced as the title credits appear over a montage of late-night San Francisco—is as vibrant and arresting as ever, albeit with a nod to the decade's disco influence. The cue opens with furious drumming and Abe Laboriel's throbbing Fender bass; the melody enters via unison brass against jagged synth. The effect is both exciting and apprehensive, suggesting that Harry's world has become more

If it seemed as if Lalo Schifrin's name was ubiquitous in the early 1980s, that was no accident. He scored five big-screen films and a TV movie in 1981; five big-screen films and three TV movies in 1982; and four big-screen films—including *Sudden Impact*—in 1983, along with three TV movies. He also earned three of his six Academy Award nominations during this decade, but never won a competitive award; he finally received an honorary Oscar in 2019 (Photofest).

dangerous. And indeed it has: He spends the first act dodging murderous attacks by a series of syndicate assassins, the first which occurs late at night, giving Schifrin an opportunity for some percussion-heavy action jazz. Eager to get Harry out of harm's way, his supervisor sends him down to investigate a murder in San Paulo: a drive that Callahan makes against Schifrin's familiar "melancholy theme." A mournful solo trumpet opens this melody, and then boosts the tempo and orchestration: no longer a requiem, and now more a journey toward some new adventure.

From this point forward, the score is dominated by orchestral elements: nervous strings, dissonant chords, suspenseful percussion and—notably during flashbacks to the awful rapes—Schifrin's disturbing waterphone effects. The increasingly edgy tone is lightened only by a diegetic cue, performed by an unseen combo at the bar where Harry has his initial chat with artist Jennifer Spencer (Sondra Locke). Schifrin counterpoints the scene's tension with a gentle jazz ballad; the melody is handled by unison vibes and piano, against soft drumming and tasty bass licks. Later, after considerable dust has settled, the end credits roll against a triumphant reprise of Harry's melancholy theme, the melody taken by solo sax against the swelling orchestra.

Sudden Impact was the first Dirty Harry film to produce a concurrent soundtrack album, of sorts: a compilation LP titled *Sudden Impact and the Best of Dirty Harry!* The album includes Roberta Flack's lovely vocal version of the melancholy theme, now titled "This Side of Forever," with the benefit of Dewayne Blackwell's lyrics. The full score didn't arrive until 2008; a careful listen reveals that many of Schifrin's cues weren't used in the film.

Even so, the result was vastly superior to Schifrin's experience on *The Osterman Weekend*.

Scripters Ian Masters and Alan Sharp made absolute hash of Robert Ludlum's espionage thriller. The result is exploitatively sleazy and utterly incomprehensible: a sad epitaph for director Sam Peckinpah, who died a year later. Schifrin's bland, jazz-lite score does little to elevate this mess, although that accusation might be unfair; his cues are employed quite poorly, at times working against on-screen events. Case in point: The primary love theme debuts while a (gratuitously) naked young woman is killed by two masked intruders, who inject poison through her eye socket, and into her brain. That *couldn't* have been what Schifrin had in mind for this lyrical blend of synth, Hammond B3 and Ernie Watts' sweet sax.

CIA agent Laurence Fassett (John Hurt) persuades muckraking TV journalist John Tanner (Rutger Hauer) that his best friends—Bernard Osterman (Craig T. Nelson), Richard Tremayne (Dennis Hopper) and Joseph Cardone (Chris Sarandon)—actually are deep-cover agents affiliated with a Soviet spy network. Tanner and his wife, Ali (Meg Foster), annually host all three for a weekend reunion; one such event is coming up, and Fassett hopes to "turn" one of the men by applying psychological stress via a surveillance network added (just for the occasion) to Tanner's home. Tension and paranoia mount while everybody turns against each other, and then Tanner discovers that he has been duped by Fassett, who has a nasty agenda that involves getting back at his CIA boss (Burt Lancaster).

Most of the score is atmospheric and unmelodic. One exception is a second sultry sax cue, against gentle synth and what sounds like canned percussion, which backs Tanner's late-night spying on his friends. Schifrin also contributes two diegetic cues. The first is the attention-grabbing theme for Tanner's interview show, *Face to Face*: a striking blend of electric keyboard and synth that sounds *just* like a network news theme. The second is a larkish sax and B3 melody that backs a televised travelogue-type show about Switzerland.

The monotonous percussion and warbling sax are deliberately typical of the puerile smooth jazz that infected radio stations during the 1980s.

The soundtrack album concentrates on uninspired arrangements of the various sax cues, including two versions of the ill-used romantic theme. Two tracks aren't in the film; the best is a dynamic title theme—aggressive Hammond B3 against solid percussion work from Emil Richards and Paulinho Da Costa—that Schifrin obviously intended for the opening credits. It's the only trace of "true Schifrin" on an album that otherwise sounds like elevator jazz.

* * *

Although 1984's *The Pope of Greenwich Village* died when United Artists foolishly released it amid high-profile summer competition, the crime film has since achieved cult status. Credit belongs to its cheeky blend of drama and dark comedy, and the mesmerizing performances by Mickey Rourke and Eric Roberts, as (respectively) Charlie and Paulie, a pair of fast-talking mopes whose dreams forever outstrip their aptitude. They're low-life denizens of a Greenwich Village neighborhood ruled by the Italian mob: cousins forever bonded, despite the many times that the reckless Paulie gets them into trouble.

Dave Grusin's urban-hued score cleverly straddles a melodic line between the story's many polar opposites: the Italian mobsters and the equally crooked Irish cops; the moments of burlesque humor that unnervingly segue, in the blink of an eye, to bursts of violence and deadly danger; and the contrast between the prudent Charlie, always "just an inch away" from becoming a better version of himself, and the childish, foolishly cocky Paulie. Grusin handles the film's grimmer moments with sinister strings, synth and percussion, with an occasional sax added for unsettling emphasis. These atmospheric cues contrast with the jovial big band arrangements of jazz standards—"Blue Moon," "You Stepped Out of a Dream," "New York, New York" and others—heard in the bars and restaurants frequented by these colorful characters.

"It was during the time of electronics being used as score, and we all wanted to be as hip as possible," Grusin later admitted. "I had dabbled a little bit in that approach, while never becoming totally enamored of it. But though I went back to preferring acoustic piano and orchestral stuff as opposed to synthesizers, there seemed to be a use for some of that in terms of the contemporary aspect of this story, to integrate traditional scoring techniques with modern jazz for these two characters."[9]

The title credits—choreographed against a montage of Charlie dressing to the nines, while he gets ready for his evening shift as a restaurant maître d'—unspool against Frank Sinatra's iconic rendition of "Summer Wind." (Grusin's melancholy, synth-and-trumpet title theme went unused.) This job doesn't last long, thanks to Paulie's habit—in his capacity as a waiter—of shorting the table checks. Charlie vents his frustration with girlfriend Diane (Daryl Hannah), and their conversation unfolds against Grusin's love theme: a sweet mélange of piano, strings and soft percussion. Charlie and Diane share a dream of one day running a country inn; a day trip to the venue they hope to purchase allows Grusin to insert a cheerful flute and trumpet ballad that mirrors their happiness.

Things turn dire when a safe-cracking job—"the nicest, easiest score you've ever heard of," Paulie promises—actually involves ripping off the neighborhood's most dangerous gangster. The subsequent whiplash shifts of tone leave no space for Grusin's effervescent jazz/funk/fusion, although an earlier example stands out: a montage of Charlie and Paulie strutting the streets, choreographed to a groovy blend of synth, droll trumpet and electric guitar. Grusin also contributes a pulsating synth/sax diegetic cue for the aerobics class that Diane teaches.

The eventual 2012 soundtrack album includes the big band source cues and several versions of the unused title theme; Grusin's solo piano arrangement is particularly haunting.

The Cotton Club proved a splashy addition to the 1984 holiday season. Director Francis Ford Coppola's crime saga is more vaudeville extravaganza than conventional drama: a blend of fact and fiction that serves as a stylized valentine to the famed Harlem nightclub. The late 1920s and early '30s setting grants composer/music supervisor John Barry ample opportunity for dozens of period jazz classics, with an appropriately heavy focus on Duke Ellington's songbook. Barry's melancholy and foreboding underscore cues—laden with sultry horns and smoky, low-end piano—run a distant second to the vibrant jump jazz numbers that spill off the Cotton Club stage.

Parallel storylines follow two star-crossed couples on different sides of the racial barrier. Pretty-boy jazz cornetist Dixie Dwyer (Richard Gere) is hopelessly in love with Vera Cicero (Diane Lane), otherwise "taken" as the girlfriend of sociopathic mobster Dutch Schultz (James Remar). Talented tap dancer Sandman Williams (Gregory Hines) is similarly smitten by chanteuse Lila Rose Oliver (Lonette McKee), who hopes to further her career by passing for white. These and a multiplicity of sidebar characters are little more than one-dimensional archetypes, all of whom play superficial roles in a crime saga that focuses on the power struggle between rival Irish, Italian, Jewish and black gangsters. But no matter how dire the increasingly violent confrontations, the Cotton Club continues to be a carefree oasis of high-steppin' entertainment. (If the credits are to be believed, Gere handled his own cornet solos.)

The Art Deco title credits are juxtaposed against a jam session at the Bamville Club, where—unlike the Cotton Club—black patrons are allowed to enjoy performances by their own musicians; the cross-cutting is backed by a bluesy cover of Ellington's "The Mooche," which sets the tone for what follows. Dixie's slide into the hazardous underworld kicks off during a party when he performs "(Back Home Again In) Indiana" and "Oh, You Beautiful Doll," while barely able to take his eyes off Vera; elsewhere, Sandman is equally enraptured by Lila Rose's sinuous dance moves during a sensuous reading of "Creole Love Call." Schultz and Dixie's upstart younger brother, Vincent (Nicolas Cage), later provoke a gang war during a montage that gets ironic intensity from Lila Rose's mournful delivery of Ted Koehler and Harold Arlen's "Ill Wind." Fateful conversations and confrontations take place during Cotton Club stage shows, the most vibrant performed against jump jazz cues dubbed "Cotton Club Stomp #1" and "Cotton Club Stomp #2."

Coppola's final sequence is a masterpiece of effervescent, break-the-wall filmmaking, as various characters head off to unexpectedly happy (and highly unlikely) outcomes, while Cotton Club singers and dancers leap off the stage to pop up in train and subway stations. The audacious sequence is set to Barry's sparkling arrangement of a "Daybreak Express Medley" that incorporates Ellington's "Wall Street Wail," "Slippery Horn," "High Life" and "Daybreak Express." As the screen slowly fades to black, Dixie and Vera board the 20th Century Limited for a new (safer) life in Hollywood, where he has become famous as the starring actor in the gangster flick *Mob Boss*.

Only a couple of Barry's instrumental cues appear on the soundtrack album, which is dominated by dance and vocal stage numbers. At just 15 tracks, that barely scratches the surface of the film's extraordinarily sumptuous musical palette, which easily could fill another couple of albums. Sadly, that never happened—likely because *Cotton Club* was a financial flop—nor did Barry's full underscore ever gain its own release.

Meanwhile, Across the Pond...

Mention must be made of *The Bill*, and not merely because when it finally went off the air on August 31, 2010, its 27-year reign made it the UK's longest-running police procedural. The series delivered a staggering 2,425 episodes, at its peak broadcasting three times per week, 52 weeks a year.

The show technically debuted on August 16, 1983, as an isolated episode of the anthology series *Storyboard*. There's no opening credits sequence; the episode title—"Woodentop"—merely flashes briefly on the screen, against silence. When *The Bill* became its own show on October 16, 1984, viewers were introduced to the theme that would become an integral part of the pop-culture scene for the next several decades. Drummer/composer Charlie Morgan and bass guitarist/composer Andy Pask's bouncy little instrumental ("Overkill") accompanies a droll montage that opens on the slowly walking feet of two coppers—one male, one female—while they casually stroll their beat, moving toward the camera. This ramble is intercut with images of the precinct neighborhood; the camera ultimately rises and focuses on the badges affixed to the officers' headgear, their eyes just visible at the bottom of the frame. The entire sequence is cut smartly against a mildly saucy, infectiously rhythmic tune that defies expectations, given its 7/4 time signature. A final quick drum roll is synched to the show's title, and the music and credits cut off as the episode begins.

The end credits offer an expanded arrangement of the theme—with synth elements stronger during an improvisational keyboard bridge—against the same two pairs of feet, this time slowly walking *away* from the camera. This cue remained constant for many years, even as Morgan and Pask modified the title arrangement, adding brass and synth, and more vigorously enhancing the delightful 7/4 meter. A big change came in 1998; the title theme was shortened to a quick 15 seconds, the core melody handled by vibrant sax against a rhythmic beat that was less noticeably 7/4. The tempo slowed and the theme lengthened again a few years later; subsequent revisions drifted further away from the core melody, thanks to new arranger Lawrence Oakley.

All these revisions notwithstanding, the version most readily recognized by listeners is the expanded arrangement released by Columbia UK as a 45 single. It features a couple of wild keyboard and guitar bridges in standard time, which makes each shift back to the septuple meter even more enchantingly disorienting.

* * *

Moving to the big screen, director Desmond Davis' 1984 adaptation of Agatha Christie's *Ordeal by Innocence* is world-class deplorable, although the same cannot be said of its sumptuous jazz score.

The film gets minor points for maintaining the late 1950s setting of Christie's novel, but little else can be said about a dreary, colorless murder mystery that wastes a top-flight ensemble cast. The plot has a classic Christie hook: Paleontologist Arthur Calgary (Donald Sutherland) returns from an extended Arctic expedition, to discover that he could have provided an alibi for an innocent man who died in prison, having been convicted of murdering his adoptive mother (Faye Dunaway). Calgary travels to the isolated Dartmouth estate of the Argyle family, assuming they'll draw some comfort from learning that their adoptive son Jacko was innocent; surprisingly, everybody—starting with patriarch Leo Argyle (Christopher Plummer)—seems content to let the matter rest. Calgary belatedly realizes that he has stirred up a hornet's nest, particularly since the *actual* murderer won't obligingly wait to be revealed.

The film initially was scored by Pino Donaggio, who provided a series of eerie and suspenseful orchestral cues that were well suited to the material (however ineptly handled). But the film fared poorly during test screenings—no surprise—and Donaggio was otherwise occupied when uncredited replacement director Alan Birkinshaw shot new sequences and restructured the existing material. Somebody had the bewildering notion to hire Dave Brubeck as a replacement composer; he balked at the producers' request for an all-new score within a tight time frame but agreed to deliver fresh versions of his existing material. During studio sessions alongside son Chris (electric bass, bass trombone), Bill Smith (clarinet, sax, recorder) and Randy Jones (drums), the elder Brubeck did ultimately write one original tune: "Kristen's Theme (One Misty Morning)," which is heard toward the end of the film.

Although it's always a pleasure to hear Brubeck's material—and his fresh arrangements of roughly a dozen tunes are truly lovely—the music couldn't be more disconcertingly out of place, and wholly wrong for the film. The title credits sequence—a lengthy montage, as Calgary arrives at the Argyle estate by boat—gets an atmospheric lift via Brubeck's thoughtful blend of "Truth" and "Symphony," but all subsequent cues are bizarrely inappropriate. The mismatch reaches a ludicrous zenith when "Blue Rondo a la Turk" is heard when Calgary discovers that an alcoholic suspect's husband has been killed. The inept spotting does the impossible: It makes an appalling film even *worse*.

Brubeck never released his "score" on an album, which is a shame; detached from the film, it would have been a marvelous listening experience.

10

Tequila Dreams: 1985–89

Things had become grim for session jazz musicians.
Irritating enough that rock 'n' roll song scores were replacing instrumental title themes and underscores. Matters were made even worse by the expanding versatility of synthesizer keyboard technology, which network bean-counters regarded as an economical step forward. Never mind that 95 percent of the resulting synth scores sounded identical, like so much somber electronica mush; the significant advantage was that only one musician required a paycheck, as opposed to all the combo or orchestra members traditionally hired to breathe life into a composer's work.

To add disrespectful insult to injury, in some cases commissioned instrumental underscores were shunted aside when it came time to assemble a soundtrack album. The song score elements were emphasized as a means of securing radio play, thereby helping to promote the film (the marketing ploy that hadn't worked in the 1960s). When the contributions of heavyweights such as Herbie Hancock and Dave Grusin are all but ignored on the resulting album, clearly the situation has become dire.

"One of my favorite recent soundtracks is *Rushmore*," noted director Jay Roach, a decade later. "It has all of your favorite pop or vintage tunes from the film, and several of the great score cues are interwoven, and it completely evokes all of the great moments in the film. That's the downside of the trend to use soundtracks primarily as a promotional tool: They don't give you the feeling that you're taking a little bit of the film with you, in your car or on your boom box."[1]

This would become even more prevalent, as the new century approached.

The Small Screen

Steve Bochco and co-creator Terry Louise Fisher hit another home run with NBC's *L.A. Law*, which drew viewer and critical praise during an eight-year run that began September 15, 1986. Following the *Hill Street Blues* template, this new show blends parallel storylines—often lifted from real-world headlines—with interpersonal drama, gallows humor and a huge ensemble cast initially headed by Harry Hamlin, Susan Dey, Corbin Bernsen, Jimmy Smits and Richard Dysart. The scoring assignment went to Mike Post, but Bochco and pilot episode director Gregory Hoblit proved hard to please. After numerous potential title themes had been rejected, Post had had enough.

"After the fourth one, I said okay, you two guys, over to my office," Post recalled. "They sat on a couch. I said, I'm gonna start playing; I'm gonna start talking. When I do something you like, tell me. So I said, Look, it's the law; it has majesty. So, French horns: I messed around and finally came up with *bum ... bum ... bum-bum-bum*. [They liked that.] I said, Great; we're saving it. I said, It's California, so we're gonna put this great big 'Born in the USA' snare drum in there. It'll feel like the Beach Boys meet the law: *Boom ... boom ... boom ... boom*. Then I said, What else is this show about? *Sex!* That's what you're doing in this office. [So], alto saxophone. [They said] 'Great.' Done. Finished."[2]

Post supplied two distinct versions of the title theme, depending on the tone of the precredits teaser: Solemn storylines demanded the melody be delivered via melodramatic synth, while more amusing plots called for a playful sax riff from David Sanborn. Post also provided original underscores for all 171 episodes, along the way establishing numerous character and situational cues that became almost as familiar as the title theme (which pops up, in various arrangements and instrumentations, during every episode). As he predicted, the lascivious alto sax gets plenty of exercise, given the intimate encounters frequently taking place in the Los Angeles–based offices of McKenzie, Brackman, Chaney and Kuzak. The overall musical palette leans more toward pop/rock than jazz—particularly when synth and that wicked snare drum dominate a given cue—but it's impossible to ignore that sax, along with some lovely jazz flute touches.

Post expanded the title theme and some underscore cues for a 1988 soundtrack album. It earned a Grammy Award nomination for Best Pop Instrumental Performance (Orchestra, Group or Soloist), and Post's title theme won the Grammy for Best Instrumental Composition.

Most cast members reunited eight years after the show concluded, but Post wasn't among them; the unremarkable music for *L.A. Law: The Movie* was handled by David Williams.

ABC's lackluster *Fortune Dane* was pro football player-turned-actor Carl Weathers' first attempt to parlay a TV series from his supporting roles in four *Rocky* films. He stars as the title character: a former football star (there's a stretch) turned police detective in the fictitious city of Twin Rivers, where he routinely goes nuclear on all manner of perps. The unpleasantly vicious pilot film—it aired February 15, 1986—ends tragically, when Dane fails to catch the maniacal killer who has slaughtered numerous people. The disillusioned detective surrenders his badge and moves to the West Coast's equally fictitious Bay City, where the feisty mayor (Penny Fuller) decides she likes his style. She must've been the only one, since the show was axed after only four episodes.

That said, there's no denying the pilot film's energetic jazz title theme, composed by Douglas Fraser and given impish pizzazz by Gary Herbig's exuberant alto sax touches. The credits sequence opens with a mildly melancholy solo sax riff, while the camera pans over Weathers' perfectly toned body during a workout session; pounding rhythm kicks in while the exercise routine continues. Herbig's sax riffs turn feisty, backed by unison horns, as Weathers steps into a shower, water slowly pouring down his muscled frame. (Can we be surprised that he also was credited as "supervising producer"?)

The bluesy swing ambiance and Herbig's cheeky sax riffs continue throughout the film—with some tasty jazz piano briefly popping up as diegetic music in an illegal gambling club—although this underscore is a collaborative effort by David Kurtz, Stewart Levin and Ron Ramin. Subsequent episodes are divided between yet more hands; none of the music endured beyond broadcast.

Weathers may have fumbled his first television play, but William Conrad always scored touchdowns. He also inspired a certain style, for composers tasked with writing title themes for his shows. John Carl Parker's jazz tuba melody perfectly suited the actor's outsized frame and lumbering gait in *Cannon,* and Dick DeBenedictis took a similar approach with his theme for CBS' equally popular *Jake and the Fatman*. He opens with a heavy two-beat ostinato that suggests the portly actor's heavy tread; the subsequent 2-2-1-2-2 horn motif sounds vaguely soldierly, like a call to arms. Dan Higgins' sax riffs add sarcastic bounce, which perfectly matches Conrad's gruff and grumpy character. The overall result is an aggressive, boldly impudent swinger that signals the show's blend of PI melodrama and light humor.

As introduced on September 26, 1987, Conrad's Jason Lochinvar "Fatman" McCabe is an ex-cop turned blunt, tough-as-nails district attorney in an unspecified Southern California metropolis. Investigative work is handled by his flashy young assistant, Jake Styles (Joe Penny); comic relief is supplied by McCabe's elderly pet bulldog, Max. An abrupt second-season shift to Hawaii was prompted by CBS' desire to maintain a show set in the islands, following the cancelation of *Magnum, P.I.* McCabe was rebooted as an investigator assigned to the Honolulu prosecutor's office; Jake and Max came along for the ride. But McCabe apparently missed grilling suspects in the witness box, and soon resumed his efforts as a prosecuting attorney. This arrangement continued through the show's fourth season, after which everybody suddenly returned to Southern California—and their former occupations—for the fifth and final season.

Such geographical hopscotching forced DeBenedictis to modify his title theme over time. The first-season arrangement is muted beneath some narrative banter between McCabe and Jake, while they introduce each other to viewers; the volume rises as the show's title is superimposed over Conrad's grim stride through the courthouse, perfectly timed to the rhythm section, while Higgins chugs along on sax. The core motif slowly climbs the scale against a clip montage, concluding with a six-note horn fanfare when Conrad and Penny scowl at each other, then burst into laughter. The narration was dropped when the second season began; DeBenedictis' fresh arrangement is given peppier bounce by a rolling rhythm section and an understated presentation of the 2-2-1-2-2 motif; the sassy sax riffs are correspondingly more prominent. A new clips montage reflects the Hawaiian setting; the core melody takes over midway through the arrangement, climbing the scale as before, with the sax dialed back a bit. DeBenedictis shifts to quasi-swing for the final scene, as Conrad and Penny once again josh each other against a slightly longer horn fanfare.

Once back in SoCal, season five's theme again opens with a "weighty" 2-2-2 statement; this segues to a suspenseful, midtempo rhythmic ostinato against vibrant treble couplets. Action clips herald feisty sax riffs, as DeBenedictis teases with deconstructed portions of the core motif; it finally emerges—in brilliant, unison brass glory—midway through this 60-second arrangement. Brass and sax battle for dominance when the melody again climbs the scale; this time the sax triumphs, with an impudent downward spiral ... until a final, unresolved six-note brass statement.

DeBenedictis maintained this jazz ambiance in early first-season episode underscores. Subsequent assignments were divided between Artie Kane, Morton Stevens and Joel Rosenbaum, the latter ultimately sharing most of the work with Peter T. Myers. Although the overall tone became unremarkable—the usual suspenseful strings and orchestral shading—each composer included jazz variations of the title theme, in various tempos and instrumentations. Sax-laden cues also are common, particularly when Jake drives somewhere in his gray 1950s Porsche 356 speedster. (He traded it for a white 1988 Mustang Cobra GT 5.0 convertible when the show moved to Hawaii.)

None of the music enjoyed any sort of afterlife.

Had NBC's *Private Eye* been cast and crafted with the pizzazz that went into its music and production design, it could have run for years. Unfortunately, star Michael Woods lacks anything remotely resembling screen presence, and the scripts are strictly from hunger. Creator Anthony Yerkovich apparently believed his new show needed nothing beyond the glossy sleekness obviously copied from *Miami Vice* and *Crime Story*. Those hit shows were set in the 1980s and '60s, respectively; *Private Eye* is a creature of the *noir*-drenched 1950s. But this isn't Peter Gunn's jazz-hued neck of the woods; these stories unfold against the hipster vibe of Los Angeles' rebellious rock 'n' roll influence. That said, Joe Jackson's title theme is pure bluesy swing, and many of the episode underscores—particularly those by Shorty Rogers and Lalo Schifrin—deliver an intriguing battle between non-diegetic jazz cues and the prototypical rockabilly tunes frequently inserted as source cues.

Woods stars as former cop Jack Cleary, unfairly bounced from the LAPD on a bribery charge (a total bum rap). His older brother Nick—who runs a successful private detective agency—winds up dead, supposedly by accident; Jack vows to prove that his brother was killed, and by whom. Jack "inherits" his brother's bad-ass sidekick, hep cat Johnny Betts (Josh Brolin), whose juvie insolence is matched by a flair for helpful acts of larceny. After solving this initial case—during the September 13, 1987, premiere—Jack makes a serious go of the private eye biz, with Johnny at his side. Alas, the duo worked only 11 more cases before the network pulled the plug.

The title credits sequence is as sleek and sassy as Jackson's theme, which opens with a blast of brass over a toe-tapping, *boom-chuck* rhythm section. A flurry of acoustic piano complements the horns, when a passing car "drags" the show's title across the screen. It's difficult to extract a melody from what follows: mostly a series of pulsating jazz riffs set against an equally vibrant montage of 1950s late-night clubs, restaurants, bars and music joints. All slide across the background as Jack slowly motors along the city's mean streets, a cigarette dangling contemptuously from his smirking lips; Johnny, also enjoying an evening cruise, approaches from the other direction. The two cars stop alongside each other; Jack and Johnny exchange half-smiles, as the theme concludes with a final rising crescendo of horns. This is a show with *attitude*.

Well, yes ... but nothing else. None of the show's music endured beyond its brief television run.

Over at CBS, New Age string maestro George Doering and rapidly rising TV soundtrack composer Dennis McCarthy made an odd collaborative pair; that said, there's no denying the down-and-dirty atmosphere they evoke with their title theme for *Houston Knights*. The oil-and-vinegar premise finds Chicago cop Joey LaFiamma (Michael Paré) shuttled off to Houston, to evade a Mafia contract on his head; he winds up partnered with laid-back Levon Lundy (Michael Beck), grandson of a Texas Ranger. Naturally, the two don't get along initially; naturally, they overcome that antipathy to become best buds. The show ran a season and a half after its debut on March 11, 1987.

The title theme plays over a montage that reminds viewers how Joey winds up in Houston, after which the supporting cast is introduced; the style is Texas blues-rock, but do take note of the cool sax that opens the tune. It's soon joined by a feisty slide guitar that carries the melody against a finger-snapping rhythm section highlighted by sassy bass. McCarthy also handles the episode underscores; the Texas setting demands plenty of solo guitar and harmonica, along with country/western tunes frequently popping up as diegetic cues.

The title theme eventually found afterlife on crime/action jazz anthology albums.

* * *

More than two decades passed before somebody had the inspired notion to develop a television series from 1967's *In the Heat of the Night*. Howard Rollins and Carroll O'Connor were excellent choices as, respectively, Det. Virgil Tibbs and Police Chief William Gillespie; the popular show ran seven seasons—first on NBC, then on CBS—after its debut on March 6, 1988. The series functions as a long-running sequel to the film's storyline, allowing for the need to be contemporaneous with the late 1980s and early '90s. Philadelphia-based police detective Tibbs, accompanied by his wife, Althea (Anne-Marie Johnson), returns to his (fictional) home town of Sparta, Mississippi, to attend his mother's funeral. Local police chief Gillespie persuades Tibbs to become the department's head detective, to address the squad's racial imbalance, and also as a means of demonstrating sensitivity to the local black community.

Writer/producer James Lee Barrett recognized the importance of the iconic title song, but allowed arranger Chris Page to update it; veteran jazz/rock musician Bill Champlin gives the tune a bluesy growl during a 60-second title sequence that identifies the ensemble cast via blue-tinged silhouettes against a montage of police cars prowling Sparta's late-night streets. The end credits version is a softer instrumental, with the melody taken by a sassy blues harmonica.

Most original underscores are handled by composer/arranger Nan Schwartz, the first female composer to earn an Emmy Award nomination for dramatic underscore (for an episode of *The Devlin Connection*). Six more nominations followed, including one for "Family Reunion," a fifth-season episode of *In the Heat of the Night*. Her scores favor swinging tack piano, harmonica and lazy guitar riffs; this cocktail contributes to the series' nervous, sweaty atmosphere, where characters and situations often seem poised at the edge of spontaneous combustion. Schwartz also inherited—and makes generous use of—numerous cues that Dick DeBenedictis wrote for the two-part pilot episode, which is dominated by Mac Dougherty's guitar licks and unhurried, contemplative scat singing. These became one of the show's many musical signatures, often heard as bumpers before and after commercial breaks. Following the first season, Schwartz traded episodes with David Bell; the two of them handled 127 original scores until the series concluded with a quartet of telefilms, the last of which aired May 16, 1995.

All that music notwithstanding, the series never generated a soundtrack album or single, although Champlin included an extended arrangement of the title song on his 1994 album, *Through It All*.

As the decade came to a close, ABC revisited the rotating "wheel" format. The network's timing was good. Burt Reynolds' big-screen status had begun to wane, so he made a calculated return to television on February 13, 1989, as the title character in the light-hearted *B.L. Stryker*: one of three *ABC Mystery Movie* "spokes" alongside *Gideon Oliver* and Peter Falk's revived *Columbo*. Reynolds slipped easily into the role of Buddy Lee Stryker, a Vietnam War veteran and former New Orleans police officer who has "retired" to life as a good ol' boy gumshoe in Palm Beach, Florida. He's a gentler take on John D. MacDonald's Travis McGee: Buddy Lee lives on a houseboat, drives an old Cadillac, and frequently shoots the breeze with best friend/former boxer Oz Jackson (Ossie Davis).

The indefatigable Mike Post pulled double duty on this particular assignment, composing title themes for both the *ABC Mystery Movie* "wheel" credits sequence, and the *B.L. Stryker* titles. The former is a bouncy little melody with a catchy 4-4-2 hook anchored by a mildly spooky rhythm section, which includes whispered *ka-chik-ka-ka-ka* vocalese. Unfortunately—during the first season—it plays against a dreadful credits sequence laden with clips of "mysterious" things such as a fluttering bird, a swinging lamp, a dangling phone, a smashed photo and quite a bit more: the sort of a montage one would expect in front of a cheesy horror flick. Wiser heads prevailed during the second season; Post's theme is put to far better use against a more conventional sequence that focuses on the stars of an amended lineup: *B.L. Stryker* and *Columbo* returned, but *Gideon Oliver* was dropped in favor of Jaclyn Smith's *Christine Cromwell* and Telly Savalas' return as lollipop-loving *Kojak*.

Post's *B.L. Stryker* theme is another of his ear worms: a "striking" improvisational keyboard melody against a catchy rhythm section, augmented by a mischievous sax solo at the bridge. The tune plays against a handsome montage of clips within huge letters that spell out the show's title, as they slowly slide right to left across the screen. The melody concludes with a five-note keyboard statement against a lingering shot of Reynolds silhouetted against a Florida sunset. Post also supplied original underscores for the first three episodes, although the cues rarely hover anywhere near jazz.

Rather oddly, Post's *Stryker* theme was discarded when the second season began; it was replaced by a softer, sax-and-strings ballad by Snuff Garrett, Clarke Rigsby and Kevin Stoller. This combination lasted only one episode; their theme and any semblance of a credits montage were dumped in favor of running credits over the opening act, with no consistent title theme. Steve Dorff contributed most of the second season underscores, which favor conventional orchestral shading.

Post collaborated with Stephen James Taylor on the title theme for *Gideon Oliver*, a surprisingly bland orchestral cue for a series about an Indiana Jones wannabe. Lee Holdridge's theme for *Christine Cromwell* is similarly unremarkable orchestral pop, and the music for the revived *Kojak* also isn't worth discussing. *Columbo* never had a title theme, and the same is true of this revival.

Over in Robert Parker's neck of the woods, the best-selling novelist's popular private detective had enjoyed a healthy three-year run on ABC's *Spenser: For Hire*, which concluded in the spring of 1988. As in the novels, Robert Urich's Spenser shared the action with Avery Brooks' richly enigmatic portrayal of the lean and mean assassin, Hawk. The latter was born for a series of his own, and ABC debuted *A Man Called Hawk* on January 28, 1989. Whereas Spenser had conducted his sleuthing to synth-style rock 'n' roll, *Hawk* is backed by a sensational jazz palette that smartly complements the ultra-cool audacity with which the character confronts every problem. The show's failure to run more than 13 episodes is bewildering. *A Man Called Hawk* must've been ahead of its time, just as celebrated jazz bassist/composer Stanley Clarke's electrifying, fusion-based contributions—further sweetened by avant-garde cornetist and jazz composer Butch Morris, as music director—defied conventional television scoring methodology.

Jazz trumpeter/composer Steven Bernstein recalled a meeting between Morris and ABC heads, early on during the series' production. "Butch was the charmer of all times. He shows up in the meeting and the president says, 'Mr. Morris, you're such a fantastic artist, your music is so visionary, we're so proud to have you involved with this project, we can't tell you how much this means. But I need to tell you that [despite the] incredible amount of respect we have for your ability to create brand new music, for TV it's just not commercial enough, you know?' Butch looks at him and says, 'Well, you're the president of this TV network, right? Well, make a decision: *You* call it commercial.'"[3]

The show's determination to be unique is evident from the credits sequence, which opens with a hawk soaring above Washington, D.C., while synth "whistles" what sounds like a Native American chant. The hawk swoops toward the camera while a propulsive rhythm section kicks in; the "whistle" becomes a hypnotic ostinato when a close-up of the raptor's face morphs into Brooks' equally stern gaze. Action clips take over as the cue kicks into an aggressively unmelodic high gear; Clarke, Morris and Brooks (who share credit for this title theme) add brass statements, rolling rhythm, ferocious drumming and exhilarating bass licks. The result is breathtaking, but viewers would be hard-pressed to hum that theme.

Every episode is rich with music; Clarke and Morris rarely leave scenes unscored. The show's premise finds Hawk forsaking Spenser's Boston to return to his own "hometown" of D.C., where he rights wrongs with plenty of 'tude ... and his massive .357 Magnum. Brooks' way-cool manner and deportment—tailored black suits, dark sunglasses and a predatory smile—are complemented perfectly by Clarke's assertive underscore cues. Each episode also is laden with plenty of conventional mainstream diegetic cues, most often provided by the combos in residence at Mr. Henry's, the jazz club that serves as Hawk's second home. (We never see his *actual* home.) Brooks also supplies some of the jazz flavor, whether noodling tasty riffs on a piano, or allowing Hawk to exorcise some demons via an angry session on vibes. ABC could have tried a catchy slogan: "Come for the drama; stay for the music."

No soundtrack album emerged—more's the pity!—but an expanded arrangement of the title theme can be found on *TV Faves*, an obscure 2009 anthology release. Clarke, meanwhile, went on to a highly successful secondary career as a film composer.

Eclectic studio composer/arranger and session keyboardist Doug Katsaros wasn't nearly as lucky.

Author Steve Sohmer turned his novel of Washington's movers and shakers—*Favorite Son*—into an equally successful television miniseries in the fall of 1988. As sometimes happens, one of the supporting characters became popular in his own right: cynical, world-weary FBI agent Nick Mancuso, forever threatening retirement, and memorably played by Robert Loggia. He jumped at the chance to continue in the role, and NBC's *Mancuso, FBI* debuted on October 13, 1989. Still based in D.C., Mancuso became another maverick investigator who cheerfully ignores policy and procedure, in pursuit of genuine justice.

Katsaros' résumé spans film, television and theater work, alongside collaborations with all manner of pop/rock performers. His swooningly bluesy main theme for *Mancuso*—a saucy duel between acoustic piano and sax—is just right for Loggia's grizzled performance. The credits sequence slowly pans across the items on a desk in a darkened room—typewriter, telephone, clock, newspaper, autographed baseball and so forth—until a hand dips down to snatch an investigator's shield, gun, keys and ID badge. A vaguely defined figure heads out the door, pausing to admire the nearby White House dome, rising above the early morning mist. The rumpled, fedora-clad figure turns, briefly revealing Loggia's profile, as the show's title appears. This montage opens and closes with inquisitive piano chords that bookend a mournful, repeating 4-3 sax motif; this slowly climbs the scale against a melancholy rhythm section. It's the ideal theme for an old-school investigator rendered all but obsolete by the passage of time.

Katsaros also wrote original music for the initial eight episodes, developing a library from which the remaining 12 episodes were tracked; alas, very few cues share the title theme's smoky jazz ambiance. Mancuso got his wish when NBC put him into forced retirement after only half a year; Katsaros' title theme lives on solely via a cover version on the 1994 anthology album, *Jazz in Prime Time*.

Over at ABC, writer/director Blake Edwards took one more shot at reviving his iconic private eye. The TV movie *Peter Gunn* aired April 23, 1989, and was designed as a series pilot. The telefilm opens appropriately with the smooth walking bass of Henry Mancini's "Fallout!" theme, in a fresh arrangement that emphasizes piano riffs and a cool woodwind solo; the volume builds as the cue reaches its climax, concluding with a burst of brass when a crime boss is electrocuted in his swimming pool. An immediate cut to the iconic "Peter Gunn" theme plays over rather bland credits; this slightly faster arrangement has pep but lacks the "depth" of Mancini's original recording.

The film's subsequent jazz elements are more satisfying, starting when Pete (Peter Strauss) wanders into the laid-back club run by Mother (Pearl Bailey), just as Edie (Barbara Williams) launches into a soulful rendition of Ellington's "I Got It Bad (and That Ain't Good)." She's backed by a gently swinging combo that features vibes, piano, a muted trumpet, bass and drums; suddenly we're right back where Edwards wants us, particularly when Pete 'n' Edie pop outside for some flirty banter. The faintly heard combo backs them with a soft, vibes-driven cover of "Blues for Mother's," but the coy sparring doesn't last long; Pete is "escorted" from the club by two goons, just as the combo switches to a sparkling, vibes-fueled reading of "A Quiet Gass."

Pete gets caught between rival gangsters Tony Amatti (Charles Cioffi), who wants to know who arranged his deceased adversary's shocking swim; and Gus Spiros (Richard Portnow), who hires Pete *not* to find out. Comic interludes are supplied by Maggie (Jennifer Edwards), Pete's completely useless secretary; and Amatti's girlfriend Sheila (Debra Stipe), who reprises Sherry Jackson's entrance from the 1967 big-screen film, by popping up unexpectedly—and nearly naked—in Pete's bedroom. Gunn's back-story has been updated; he's now an ex-cop and former partner of his good friend Lt. Jacoby (Peter Jurasik), who gets grumpier as the body count mounts.

Much of the film's music is diegetic, occasionally reviving other familiar themes from the original series. A bluesy cover of "Joanna" is performed by an unseen solo pianist when Pete meets Amatti and Sheila in a fancy restaurant; when the hot-tempered Spiros later hosts a party, another unseen solo pianist entertains the crowd with a leisurely cover of "The Brothers Go to Mother's."

Mancini also contributes plenty of fresh material, such as the walking bass, muted trumpet and nervous piano that backstops Pete when he's "taken for a ride" by some of Spiros' gunsels. Later, seeking leads, Pete visits the pool hall frequented by one of his favorites stoolies, the diminutive Speck (David Rappaport); Mancini supplies a slow, swinging cue performed by a piano/trumpet quartet, as diegetic music probably emanating from a jukebox. Agitated horns and piano riffs climb the scale during Pete's furious fight with one of the baddies: a lengthy skirmish partly played for laughs, as both men gradually become exhausted. Matters resolve soon thereafter, allowing Pete to wander back to Mother's, just as Edie and the combo launch into a reading of "Dreamsville."

No soundtrack album was produced, and the proposed series never materialized.

Pete wasn't the only iconic TV character resurrected this year. Mindful that 1980's *The Nude Bomb* made the catastrophic blunder of separating Maxwell Smart (Don Adams) from his loyal Scooby gang, original series producer Leonard B. Stern corrected that mistake with *Get Smart, Again!*, an ABC telefilm that aired February 26, 1989. Max once again is reunited with former CONTROL comrades Hymie the robot (Dick Gautier), Larrabee (Robert Karvelas), Agent 13 (Dave Ketchum) and his beloved and far more resourceful spouse, Agent 99 (Barbara Feldon). Irving Szathmary's memorable title theme also returns, although only second-hand; the rest of composer Peter Rodgers Melnick's underscore is unmemorable, with only a few cues barely qualifying as jazz.

The story finds KAOS—once again led by Conrad Siegfried (Bernie Kopell)—threatening the world with a weather machine, unless the United States forks over $250 billion. Max fumbles and bumbles his way into saving the day, although the film isn't helped by what looks like the world's worst spray tan blotching Adams' face.

Melnick delivers a quick burst of action jazz during a filing cabinet fight between Max and a KAOS thug; mild excitement also is generated by cues that accompany a parking lot skirmish and car chase (with Max forced to drive backwards). The pratfalls and dumb one-liners are faithful to the original series' tone, but quickly wear out their welcome. Maxwell Smart's antics always worked better in a half-hour format … which Adams, Feldon and yet *another* team of overly optimistic producers revived one final time, with a short-lived FOX reboot that debuted January 8, 1995. James J. Covell's synth- and surf guitar-hued update of Szathmary's theme is horrible, as are the bland synth cues posing as underscore. This ill-advised disaster deservedly perished after only seven episodes.

The Big Screen

The Protector (1985) was rising martial arts star Jackie Chan's second early effort to crack the American film market. His disillusionment is understandable; hack writer/director James Glickenhaus blends Chan's signature stunt work with the sleaze typical of the era's exploitative trash—gratuitous profanity and female nudity—and the uneven result is quite dismal. (Chan was so annoyed that he personally reedited the film for its Hong Kong release.) That said, the producers were wise enough to seek a jazz/funk score similar to what Lalo Schifrin had delivered for *Enter the Dragon*. If composer Ken Thorne's efforts aren't up to that standard, he isn't entirely to blame; Glickenhaus compounded his many other felonies by hacking and slashing the action cues, with frequently tone-deaf results.

The threadbare narrative finds New York City cops Billy Wong (Chan) and Danny Garoni (Danny Aiello) sent to Hong Kong, to eradicate a heroin pipeline orchestrated by crime lord Harold Ko (Roy Chiao) and Manhattan-based gangster Martin Shapiro (Ron Dandrea). Numerous violent skirmishes ensue.

Thorne's aggressive main theme opens with a dynamic drums and bass ostinato, augmented by growling low brass; the melody's oft-repeated 1-3-3-4 motif promises hard-charging action, which Chan delivers on numerous occasions. Unfortunately, we don't hear this cool theme until well into the film; Glickenhaus instead runs the title credits against dull synth. A disco-ized variation of the main theme spots Billy and his first partner (Patrick James Clarke, as Michael), while they attempt to enjoy an after-hours drink, and wind up trading gunfire with a gang of toughs. When events shift to Hong Kong, Thorne delivers plenty of propulsive action jazz; one of the best highlights is a dynamic brass cue employed when assassins ambush Billy and Danny in their hotel room. Thorne also ramps up the intensity for a massage parlor scuffle, but—and this is typical of Glickenhaus' ineptness—the director interrupts the lengthy action cue with a Chinese female pop vocal: completely, utterly wrong for the on-screen mayhem. Fortunately, Thorne's suspenseful swing/synth cue for the climactic brawl atop a harbor cargo lifter, high above the water below, is left mostly untouched.

The soundtrack album, finally released in 2018, includes several unused cues.

Speaking of Schifrin, he succumbed to the dark side with 1986's *Black Moon Rising*, a thoroughly preposterous action thriller that nonetheless entertains as a guilty pleasure. The composer departed from his signature jazz stylings in favor of a score dominated by the repetitive, deep bass synth cues that John Carpenter made (in)famous with 1978's *Halloween*: undoubtedly no accident, since *Black Moon Rising* is co-scripted by Carpenter. Much of Schifrin's score is disappointing. The main theme is little more than a slow 1-4 motif, repeated endlessly over an eight-bar, heavy-bass ostinato synth line backed by drum pads. Fortunately, he compensates for this electronic drivel with a smoky, sax-driven love theme, some lyrical solo piano cues, and a tantalizing suspense cue played at the upper end of the keyboard.

The story begins as former professional thief Sam Quint (Tommy Lee Jones), now working for the FBI, breaks into the Las Vegas offices of the Lucky Dollar Corp., to steal a computer disk with damning financial evidence. He gets the disk but triggers alarms, forcing him to hide the prize in the back bumper of a prototype race car dubbed the Black Moon; inventor Earl Windom (Richard Jaeckel) and two colleagues are in Vegas to attract investors. Unfortunately, the Black Moon is one of numerous vehicles snatched that night by Nina (Linda Hamilton) and a crew of professional car thieves, all of whom work for Ed Nyland (Robert Vaughn), head of a huge stolen car syndicate. Quint charms his way into Nina's confidence, and—with the assistance of Windom's team—they concoct a plan to retrieve the Black Moon and its concealed computer disk.

Schifrin doesn't honor his jazz roots until Quint and Nina fall into bed; their lovemaking takes place against a smoky jazz anthem, with the melody traded between sinuous sax and electronic keyboard. The climactic heist gets a series of tasty action cues, starting with the throbbing bass, percussion and *Mission: Impossible*-style piano chops that highlight Quint's precarious entry through the Nyland Towers roof. Orchestral action jazz boosts the suspense when Quint rescues Nina, who has fallen out of favor with Nyland; they reach the car ... at which point the score shifts back to monotonous synth. Once the dust has settled, and Quint and Nina wind up back in bed, Schifrin concludes with a reprise of the sexy sax love theme.

No soundtrack album appeared.

Having won a well-deserved Academy Award for his original screenplay for *Chinatown*, Robert Towne returned to crime-laden territory with 1988's *Tequila Sunrise*, which he also directed. Sadly, the terrific premise and delectable romantic triangle—involving dedicated cop Nick (Kurt Russell), longtime drug smuggler Mac (Mel Gibson) and upscale restaurateur Jo Ann (Michelle Pfeiffer)—are sabotaged by an increasingly ludicrous third act.

The playfully erotic banter between Jo Ann and Nick—and, later, between Jo Ann and Mac—is as smolderingly sexy as the theme that Dave Grusin wrote for the leading lady. David Sanborn's sax dominates this cue, with an assist from Alan Kaplan's trombone and some keyboard comping; the track debuts when Nick manages a rain-drenched clinch with Jo Ann in her restaurant. The theme later returns—more forcefully—during a steamy hot tub encounter between Jo Ann and Mac. Lee Ritenour's contemplative guitar is heard elsewhere, notably when Nick and Mac are silhouetted late one afternoon, the sun having just set, while they try to discuss their way clear of an increasingly uncomfortable situation. Grusin also supplies plenty of diegetic music—a tight jazz ensemble plays softly in Jo Ann's restaurant—and some energetic percussive action cues, particularly during the film's crazed climax.

Unfortunately, Grusin's fine work is poorly represented on the soundtrack album. Only two short cues—"Tequila Dreams," featuring Ritenour's guitar lament; and "Jo Ann's Theme," starring Sanborn—are present on a disc dominated by pop songs. (Far too many movies feature Bobby Darin's cover of "Beyond the Sea.")

Further on the subject of disappointments, Clint Eastwood's farewell to Dirty Harry—1988's *The Dead Pool*—is an awkward beast. The tone is deliberately arch, and the script is laden with movie-making winks and nods; Callahan has become a parody of himself. Socio-political commentary is abandoned in favor of the typical pursuit of a serial killer, whose identity isn't concealed beyond the second act. The plot focuses on the production crew and stars of a low-rent slasher film being shot in San Francisco. As a tasteless gag intended to bond his crew, director Peter Swan (Liam Neeson) invents "the dead pool," wherein each participant attempts to predict eight upcoming celebrity deaths in the Bay Area, whether by accident, violence or natural causes. Things turn serious when the individuals on Swan's list are murdered sequentially; Callahan is vexed to discover that *his* name is on the list.

Dave Grusin had amassed four of his (eventually) eight Academy Award nominations when *Tequila Sunrise* came along; he won his sole Oscar for *The Milagro Beanfield War*, released earlier in 1989. He earned the second of his two Emmy Award nominations—shared with Alan and Marilyn Bergman—for co-writing "Just Getting Started," the theme song to 2017's charming documentary *If You're Not in the Obit, Eat Breakfast* (Photofest).

Lalo Schifrin returned for his final collaboration with Callahan, but the synth-heavy score offers little of the action jazz that enhanced previous entries. The main theme opens like a blast of bad disco, while title credits appear over a montage of late-night San Francisco; erratic brass and recurring keyboard riffs don't even suggest a melody. Most subsequent cues are undercurrents of dissonance that convey the killer's derangement: eerie strings, twitchy percussion, repetitive keyboard filigrees and waterphone effects. The few action jazz elements are confined to a subplot involving repeated ambushes by gun-toting thugs in the employ of criminal kingpin Lou Janero (Anthony Chamota). A good example comes early, when a routine drive home turns deadly as Harry is boxed by two cars; Schifrin introduces slow, suspenseful percussion and rising strings as the pursuing vehicles grow ever closer, the tempo increasing when Harry realizes that he's trapped. No matter: Triumphant brass bursts forth as Harry coolly blasts the baddies with his signature .44 handgun, after which Schifrin slyly includes the bowed bass and descending four-note motif that fans will recognize from *Dirty Harry*.

A romantic subplot is supplied by dogged TV news reporter Samantha Walker (Patricia Clarkson). Schifrin delivers a lovely diegetic quartet cue for her first drink with Calahan: a sweet sax ballad backed by lyrical piano comping. After the film builds to its predictable finale, Harry and Samantha depart, arm in arm; the end credits scroll up against a lovely, big band jazz arrangement of the familiar melancholy theme. Schifrin introduces the melody on trumpet; the theme expands via electronic keyboard and additional brass elements, until holding on a final note that fades into silence.

The eventual 2009 soundtrack album includes every second of the spare, 36-minute score.

The year 1988 also saw the release of *Action Jackson*, a tawdry, mean-spirited cop/crime thriller that thoroughly debases co-stars Sharon Stone and Vanity and did nothing to help Carl Weathers' solo starring career. This sleazy, dim-bulb production wouldn't be worth mentioning, were it not for the presence of jazz icon Herbie Hancock, who shares scoring duties with Michael Kamen: an uneven collaboration at best.

Detroit police detective Jericho "Action" Jackson (Weathers) is two years into a demotion that resulted from his vicious handling of the psycho son of celebrated businessman Peter Dellaplane (Craig T. Nelson). Behind the scenes, Dellaplane has hired professional assassins to kill uncooperative automobile union officials, to install a corrupt figurehead leader. Gruesome murders, extravagant explosions and the gratuitous destruction of property trail in Dellaplane's wake; Jackson, meanwhile, gains the trust of the businessman's sexpot wife, Patrice (Stone), and mistress, Sydney (Vanity). He eventually brings Dellaplane's larcenous career to a gory conclusion.

The soundtrack is dominated by radio-friendly pop and R&B songs; occasional bits of instrumental underscore feel like an afterthought. Anxious, funkified bass is heard early on, when precinct Capt. Armbruster (Bill Duke) gives Jackson the obligatory "shape up" speech. A seductive, bluesy cue accompanies Patrice's sexy shower; a libidinous sax lingers on every exposed curve. Hard-charging jazz highlights Jackson's rather novel method of "catching" a cab; the cue develops modest excitement with uptempo drumming and groovy bass licks. After that, the remaining "music" is little more than repetitive bursts of techno synth and reverbed bass. The one exception is a sweet little jazz cue that serves as a love theme for Jackson and Sydney.

The soundtrack album is dominated by songs from Vanity, the Pointer Sisters and others. Hancock gets one track out of 10, and it's audio drivel: a weird mélange of random synth keyboard, sound effects and reverbed bass. Definitely not his finest hour.

Tom Scott's wicked sax work is far more integral to the risqué tension in 1989's erotic thriller, *Sea of Love*. Burned-out New York City homicide detective Frank Keller (Al Pacino) pursues a serial killer who targets men who place poetic ads in the lonely hearts section of a local newspaper. Clues at each scene include unknown fingerprints and a 45 single of "Sea of Love" by Phil Philips and the Twilights, left on each victim's phonograph player. Keller concocts an unorthodox scheme, placing a similar ad in the same newspaper, and arranging to meet the responding women in a series of "speed dates"; each potential suspect's fingerprints are captured on a wine glass, in the hopes of finding a match. Alas, Frank falls for one of the respondents, a feisty divorcée named Helen Cruger (Ellen Barkin). Their relationship blossoms despite numerous clues that heighten Frank's mounting suspicion that he's sleeping with a cunning psychopath.

Trevor Jones' score veers between two extremes: seductively charged themes, powered by Scott's sax and Malcolm McNab's trumpet, which accompany Frank's lustful encounters with Helen; and string-laden suspense cues—Scott's sax licks hesitant and wary, against jittery percussion—that mirror Frank's anxiety each time he uncovers another "coincidence" that ties her to the murders. The main theme debuts over a credits montage that tracks Frank's slow, late-night drive through the Big Apple's mean streets; it opens with tense, forceful percussion and nervous bass licks, followed by Scott's smokin' sax introduction of the 4-6 motif that anchors the melody. Subsequent titillating cues sometimes slide unexpectedly into disturbing dissonance, with occasional bass panpipes heightening Frank's mounting suspicions. Jones ultimately uncorks an explosive blast of action jazz during the satisfying climax, when answers are revealed during a crafty plot twist.

The soundtrack album isn't nearly as satisfying, with numerous—and quite similar—versions of the main theme, along with two vocal versions of "Sea of Love." The underscore tracks display a certain sameness, and even the sexier cues have been reorchestrated in a way that diminishes their impact.

Redundancy aside, Jones' score suits *Sea of Love* quite nicely. The same cannot be said of jazz pianist-turned-Broadway composer Cy Coleman's score for 1989's *Family Business*: a clumsy mess of a movie with disparate elements constantly at war with each other, starting with the absurd notion that Sean Connery, Dustin Hoffman and Matthew Broderick are age-appropriate or otherwise credible as a grandfather/father/son trio. The film can't decide whether to be a heist thriller or angst-y family drama and succeeds at neither. And although Coleman delivers plenty of effervescent big band jazz, such upbeat music is wholly at odds with the story's darker, often tragic elements.

Jessie McMullen (Connery), an incorrigible career criminal, has long been estranged from son Vito (Hoffman), who went straight years earlier and now runs a successful meat-packing business. Vito's son Adam (Broderick), in awe of his grandfather for all the wrong reasons, becomes tantalized by the "easy money" of criminal endeavors. Adam's science-focused college studies lead him to a "foolproof" plan to steal valuable research and sell it to a competitor for a cool $1 million: a caper that immediately intrigues Jessie. Vito reluctantly tags along to keep an eye on his son, but the scheme goes horribly wrong; the story's unsatisfying second half focuses on the splintering family dynamics that result from this catastrophe.

The title credits unfold to a blast of rollicking, big band jazz that evokes Duke Ellington, Woody Herman and Benny Goodman; the cue shifts to bluesy 4/4 swing as the sequence concludes. It's an odd choice for a movie that opens on a solemn Passover Seder and establishes the prickly relationship between Vito and Adam. Frivolous jazz band cues continue when Adam shares the caper details with Jessie and Vito; the music segues to slower swing when the trio cases the lab they'll soon invade. It subsequently feels like Coleman believed he was scoring one of his 1960s Broadway shows—an impression supported by the insertion of diegetic tunes such as "Red Roses for a Blue Lady," "Almost Like Being in Love" and an overblown "Tenement Symphony"—because the music absolutely *never* matches the on-screen action.

The aural tapestry improves, if only briefly, after the scheme collapses. A melancholy sax cue plays when Vito confesses what has happened to his wife (Rosana DeSoto); muted trumpet and piano cues accompany subsequent, equally dismal plot developments. But things turn weird again when Vito and Adam reconcile, while spreading Jessie's ashes.

Director Sidney Lumet gets one final shot at incompetent spotting, by undercutting this moment's solemnity with another cheerful blast of big band jazz, as the end credits roll.

No soundtrack album was produced.

Disappointing as it is, *Family Business* is a classic compared to 1989's *Cat Chaser*. It's impossible to know whether this bomb could have been a decent film, but the atrocious version in circulation is incomprehensible. It didn't begin that way; the film is based on Elmore Leonard's 1982 novel, and rising director Abel Ferrara had helmed a few inventive episodes of TV's *Miami Vice*. But the shoot was notoriously difficult; the finished footage was snatched from Ferrara and hacked down to 90 minutes by the producers. One of the novel's two major plots was lost along the way—the one that explains the title—and the surviving storyline makes no sense.[4] On top of which, jazz legend Chick Corea—his sole feature film assignment—does the project no favors. His mostly cacophonous score isn't merely terrible; it's actually harsh and off-putting.

Former American paratrooper George Moran (Peter Weller), now the owner/manager of a small Miami beachfront hotel, is visited by fellow veteran Nolen Tyner (Frederic Forrest). Back in the day, George had participated in the 1965 Dominican Civil War, earning the name "Cat Chaser" from a 16-year-old rebel girl, Luci Palma, who saved his life. George returns to Santo Domingo, to determine if she's still alive; meanwhile—at some previous point not made clear—he had an affair with Mary DeBoya (Kelly McGillis), the unhappy wife of former Dominican Gen. Andres DeBoya (Tomas Milian). She reenters George's life when he arrives in Santo Domingo. Back in Miami, Nolen has hooked up with former New York cop Jiggs Scully (Charles Durning); they scheme to steal $2 million from DeBoya and try to persuade George and/or Mary to help them. There's no reason why any of these characters would trust or even know each other, and George's search for Luci becomes little more than an afterthought; everybody wanders from one choppy scene to the next, in a state of apparent confusion.

Corea's so-called music doesn't help. The film's title credits, appearing against one of George's memory flashbacks, are heralded by a harsh blast of percussion, horns and random, shrieking vocal inflections. The rest of the score, regardless of a given scene's dramatic content, relies on standard-issue synth shading, with random timpani and percussive elements. Corea's supposedly seductive cue for the film's love scene is equally lazy; he simply didn't put any effort into the assignment.

With one notable exception.

The lengthy cue that accompanies the end credits is a salsa-hued melody highlighted by gentle trumpet, slick keyboard noodling and hot bass licks: a lovely showcase for an ensemble composed of Ramon Flores, Mark Isham and Harry Kim (trumpets); Steve Kujala (flute); Corea (keyboards); Scott Henderson and Peter Sprague (guitars); John Patitucci (acoustic double bass); Vinnie Colaiuta (drums); and Efrain Toro (percussion).

The film didn't generate a soundtrack album, and nobody should suffer through a viewing, just to hear that one cue.

Meanwhile, Across the Pond…

Two years after *The Saint in Manhattan* flopped, producer Donald L. Taffner went international with his next attempt to revive Leslie Charteris' iconic character, which resulted in a "series" of six telefilms shot by crews in various parts of the world. Two each were made in England and France, followed by one in Germany, and the last in Australia. The very British Simon Dutton stars as Simon Templar, and the varied locales certainly fit the globe-trotting qualities of The Saint's post–World War II literary adventures. Had the scripts been better, the series might have enjoyed a healthy run … but they weren't, and it didn't. The six films were syndicated at odd times in the States, between September 1989 and August 1990: no way to build viewership.

French composer Serge Franklin handled the British and French episodes, and also wrote the 45-second title theme that anchors all six films. It's an uptempo, heavily rhythmic sax swinger punctuated by occasional *rat-a-tat* blasts of brass, apparently intended to mimic gunfire; the tune plays against an animated credits sequence that blends the iconic Saint stick figure with gold silhouettes of Templar's passport—granting an excuse for Dutton's photo—along with blue outlines of skylines and famous buildings from the countries where these adventures take place. In a nice nod to tradition, Franklin concludes his theme with a treble keyboard version of Charteris' memorable little "Saint whistle."

Although most of Franklin's rhythm-heavy underscore cues are limited to orchestral shading, he frequently references the title theme, along with bits of action jazz and other incidental swing cues. His work on "The Brazilian Connection" includes a particularly lovely bossa nova arrangement of the title theme, the melody carried by jazz guitar. Jazz pianist, bandleader and composer Günther Fischer also does nice work on the Germany-based episode, "Wrong Number"; that telefilm opens with a lovely combo ballad traded between piano and sax.

Franklin's title theme, bumpers and three of his complete underscores finally were issued in 2016's three-disc box set, *The Saint*. (Tapes for the fourth apparently are lost.)

Roughly a quarter-century after Dutton dropped the halo, The Saint rose once again: the eternal phoenix. Adam Rayner assumed the role in 2013, for another television pilot that failed to sell; the 91-minute adventure respectfully includes supporting appearances by Roger Moore and Ian Ogilvy. The film was released commercially in 2017, as a tribute to the recently departed Moore. For the most part, Neal Acree's synth score is relentlessly monotonous, but he does give frequent winks and nods to both Edwin Astley's 1960s theme, and Charteris' "Saint whistle."

* * *

A few years prior to Dutton's brief reign as The Saint, John Barry bid farewell to James Bond on 1987's *The Living Daylights*. The score delivers only modest examples of the action jazz that dominated his earlier efforts, and more frequently evokes the sweeping orchestral cues that brought him an Academy Award for 1985's *Out of Africa*. That aside, Barry's 007 swan song is notable for two reasons, starting with his use of synthesized rhythm tracks. "We've used them on about eight pieces," he explained, at the time, "and when we got them mixed in with the orchestra, it sounded really terrific, with a lot of energy and impact: a slight freshness and a more up-to-date sound."[5] Barry also was creative in the song department; he co-wrote the title theme with the Norwegian pop trio a-ha, and also co-wrote two interior tunes with Chrissie Hynde, of the rock band The Pretenders. Melodically, the underscore is one of Barry's best, as he smoothly works instrumental arrangements of all three songs into numerous cues; the result simply doesn't have the raw excitement of his previous Bond assignments.

Bond (series newcomer Timothy Dalton) is hired to help Soviet intelligence officer Georgi Koskov (Jeroen Krabbé) defect to the West; the escape nearly fails due to the intervention of a sniper (Maryam d'Abo, as Kara Milovy), whose attempt is stymied when an observant Bond shoots the rifle from her hands. But his efforts are in vain; Koskov subsequently is kidnapped from an MI6 safe house by the ruthless Necros (Andreas Wisniewski), and bundled back to the KGB. Or *is* he? Koskov's supposed defection turns out to be fake, and Kara a duped innocent whose sniper rifle held only blanks; Koskov actually is in league with warmongering American arms dealer Brad Whitaker (Joe Don Baker), who hopes to inflame British/Russian tensions to make a fortune by selling weapons to the latter.

The precredits teaser involves an MI6 training exercise on Gibraltar, which goes awry when an enemy agent hijacks an explosives-laden Jeep; Dalton's face is revealed against a few soft measures of the iconic "James Bond Theme," and then Bond leaps atop the Jeep when it roars down Gibraltar's hillside roads. The synthesized rhythm elements add a tough edge while the iconic melody cranks into high gear ... but Vic Flick's throbbing guitar is missed nonetheless. This newly synthesized "James Bond Theme" reappears during a later action sequence, when Bond and Kara—evading Soviet pursuit in a newly tricked-out Aston Martin V8 Vantage Volante—roar along snow-covered roads and atop an ice-covered lake. Similarly propulsive instrumental arrangements of the title theme—again enhanced by synthesizer rhythm tracks—accompany a rooftop foot chase in Tangiers, and the climactic battle at a Russian military base in Afghanistan.

Necros' lethal activities are foreshadowed by vocal and instrumental arrangements of "Where Has Everybody Gone," one of the Barry/Hynde collaborations. The second one, "If There Was a Man," supplies emotional weight while Bond and Kara slowly fall in love; it debuts as a sweet alto flute solo, when they first meet. The remaining cue of note is a brief bit of saucy sax, when Bond is "abducted" by two gorgeous women who turn out to be CIA agents working alongside his longtime American colleague, Felix Leiter (John Terry).

In a nice touch that acknowledges Barry's series departure, he's shown—at the end of the film—conducting the orchestra that features Kara as a soloist on Tchaikovsky's *Rococo Variations*.

The soundtrack album was the first Bond score released simultaneously as a traditional LP and digital CD. As usual, given the limitations of LP technology, much of Barry's music was left behind. A "deluxe edition" followed in 1998; its nine additional tracks include an alternate version of the film's end title.

Barry, alas, had had enough. "It lost its natural energy," he lamented, of the Bond scoring process. "It started to be just formula, and once that happens, the work gets really hard. The spontaneity and excitement of the original scores is gone, so you move on."[6]

The "excitement" was indeed gone; moving forward, so was any trace of jazz. Following unsatisfying one-offs by Michael Kamen (*Licence to Kill*) and Eric Serra (*Goldeneye*), David Arnold became the keeper of the flame for the next five entries, from 1997's *Tomorrow Never Dies* through 2008's *Quantum of Solace*. Although his initial efforts are quite effective and can be viewed as synth-oriented Barry pastiches, Arnold soon segued completely into techno-pop, with soulless cues that all sound the same. Thomas Newman took over with 2012's *Skyfall* and continued with 2015's *Spectre*; his more agreeable blend of orchestra and synth brought emotion back to the franchise. But aside from every film's obligatory use of "The James Bond Theme," the series closed—and locked—the jazz door in 1987.

* * *

British filmmaker Mike Figgis made a stylish feature debut with 1988's *Stormy Monday*, a slow-burn crime thriller laden with attitude, malevolence and cheeky irony; the film gets additional bite from a diverse score that wanders from raucous free jazz and B.B. King classics to Figgis' own combo underscore cues. The story's setting in Newcastle-Upon-Tyne evokes fond memories of 1971's *Get Carter*, while Figgis guides a solid cast through his nasty little story.

Corrupt American businessman Cosmo (Tommy Lee Jones) hopes to make a fortune by developing entire blocks of a depressed neighborhood; he unwisely tries to intimidate Finney (Sting), the apparently mild-mannered owner of the Key Club, a nightspot that caters to new and old jazz. Drifter Brendan (Sean Bean), having just taken a menial job at the club, meets cute with high-class call girl Kate (Melanie Griffith), not realizing that she's "owned" by Cosmo. The Irish stranger repeatedly winds up in the right place at the wrong time, while Finney proves more than able to handle Cosmo; Kate, against her better judgment, falls genuinely in love with Brendan. Everything builds to an explosive climax.

Figgis' small combo cues favor Clark Tracey's heartbeat percussion and Alex Dankworth's ominous bass licks, occasionally augmented by nervous strings. The film opens on just such a cue, while Roger Deakins' camera cuts between Kate's early morning reluctance to rise from bed, and a pair of thugs hired to make Finney an offer he'd better not refuse. Cosmo's wooing of Newcastle movers and shakers occurs amid a welcoming "America Week" celebration, with most events staged in the ballroom of the Royal Station Hotel; many of these scenes take place against a corny electric keyboard combo tune appropriately dubbed "Muzak for Lovers." Elsewhere, Kate and Brendan eventually consummate their growing bond against a sweet jazz ballad highlighted by Ray Warleigh's sensual alto sax.

Dissonant free jazz touches are inserted as diegetic sidebars courtesy of the ironically dubbed Krakow Jazz Ensemble, initially booked as a feature attraction at the Key Club, but also detoured into Cosmo's ballroom extravaganza. This sextet stumbles its way through a hilariously dreadful cover of "The Star-Spangled Banner," and later delivers a similarly atrocious number that draws enthusiastic applause from Key Club patrons. The Don Weller Quartet—Weller (tenor sax), Mick Pyne (piano), Andrew Cleyndert (acoustic double bass) and Mark Taylor (drums)—has a fleeting on-camera appearance at Weegee, a retro jazz club named for the famed New York City photojournalist, where Kate has her "legitimate" job as a waitress.

B.B. King warbles "The Thrill Is Gone" from a jukebox when, early on, Kate and Brendan share their first drink; King returns as the end credits roll up the screen against his iconic reading of "Stormy Monday."

The soundtrack album blends the aforementioned cues and tunes, along with an energetic, New Orleans–style cover of the gospel classic "Just a Closer Walk with Thee"—with Figgis on trumpet—which propels an enthusiastic Newcastle street parade in honor of America Week. That scene's intended across-the-pond sincerity is as false as Cosmo's smile.

11

Freshly Squeezed: 1990–94

Call it accident, serendipity, deliberate planning or merely ironic.

Just as Hollywood was losing interest in traditional instrumental film and television music, a new business model began to "rescue" and breathe new life into older, often neglected scores. Intrada, founded in 1985 and based in Oakland, California, became the first in a small wave of special-interest labels devoted to resurrecting, remastering and often expanding vintage film scores, many of which hadn't yet been issued digitally. Longtime soundtrack collectors, increasingly tired of being ignored by major labels, enthusiastically embraced this development. Intrada tested the waters carefully; early releases—in modest, limited-edition runs of 1,000 or 1,500 units—focused on much-desired scores by fan-fave Jerry Goldsmith: *Poltergeist II: The Other Side, Islands in the Stream, First Blood* and others. Once it became clear that there were enough worldwide collectors to make this a viable endeavor, Intrada broadened the composer roster and rapidly increased the number of titles issued each year. Over time, the label also began to debut titles that hadn't previously seen release of *any* kind.

Intrada was followed by Film Score Magazine/Monthly (FSM), which released 250 richly varied titles between 1996 and 2013, when the label ceased production. Much of this book's contents wouldn't have been possible without the efforts of Intrada, FSM and—in their wake—Screen Archives Entertainment, La-La Land, Kritzerland, Quartet (in Spain) and numerous other small tiffany labels, all of which continue to produce impeccably remastered scores generally accompanied by meticulously researched and detailed liner notes. One need only examine this book's discography to appreciate the welcome impact these companies have made.

Although *new* jazz scores were increasingly scarce, it became much easier to obtain beloved vintage film and television music.

The Small Screen

Angelo Badalamenti's music for ABC's *Twin Peaks* has enjoyed an *amazing* afterlife. Considering the series produced only 30 episodes during slightly more than a single season that began April 8, 1990, it had a wildly outsized influence on the American pop culture scene. The aggressively surreal David Lynch/Mark Frost creation is introduced as a small-town murder mystery that draws the attention of FBI agent Dale Cooper (Kyle MacLachlan), but that's a McGuffin; the show's *raison d'être* is its population of peculiar characters, and their increasingly *outré* relationships and conflicts. The opulent production values—luxurious cinematography, inventive direction and cinema-style editing—made it must-see TV; even when the scripts make no sense, it looks great and is atmospheric as hell.

The music is just as unique; Badalamenti gives the series an aural identity just as rich and eccentric as the setting and townsfolk. His otherworldly title theme—a mildly portentous counterpoint to a montage of Pacific Northwest forests, waterfalls and lumber mills—features little more than dreamy synth and slowly throbbing electric guitar. That theme and similar atmospheric cues aside, the show also has a jazz component that Badalamenti emphasizes with bluesy, smoldering compositions dominated by drum brushes, finger-snaps, throbbing bass licks and unsettling bursts from an electric piano. Additional color comes from sax, flute and clarinet riffs. The saucier cues back the sultry behavior of Audrey (Sherilyn Fenn), whose off-camera antics *clearly* are a lot naughtier than what network television was allowed to reveal.

Twin Peaks left all manner of hanging chads when the show ceased after its final episode. An aggressively bizarre big-screen prequel—*Twin Peaks: Fire Walk with Me*—hit movie theaters during the summer of 1992, prompting only snorts of derision from fans and critics. The original show nonetheless achieved cult status during the next quarter-century; Lynch and Frost finally unveiled a fresh 18-episode season on the Showtime network in 2017. It reunited the key original cast members—along with Badalamenti—and proved a rousing success.

Interest in Badalamenti's music turned the initial soundtrack album into a hot seller that received *very* heavy play on college campuses. Over time, additional albums became something of a cottage industry. Badalamenti's score for *Fire Walk with Me* debuted in 1992; he and Lynch subsequently collaborated on 2007's *Twin Peaks: Season Two and More*, on the latter's own private label. Starting in 2011, Lynch began issuing more than 200 cues—collectively known as *The Twin Peaks Archive*—as digital downloads from his own website. The 2017 revival generated yet another Badalamenti album, *Twin Peaks (Limited Event Series Soundtrack)*. When it comes to this show's music, apparently there's no such thing as too much.

* * *

Celebrated indie filmmaker John Sayles embraced a network TV series only once thus far in his distinguished career, and *Shannon's Deal* is a quiet masterpiece. The disillusioned title character is a former corporate lawyer whose self-destructive tendencies prompt a soul-searching change of life. Jack Shannon (Jamey Sheridan) begins to represent the disenfranchised and downtrodden; he works from a dilapidated inner-city office and does his best to *avoid* bringing his clients into a courtroom, where he knows they'll lose. Instead, he craftily negotiates settlements, pushes for reduced (or even dropped) charges, and—as the show's title suggest—cannily cuts deals. No surprise, he's also a poker player.

Shannon was introduced in a popular and critically praised telefilm of the same title, which aired June 4, 1989. It feels like a scruffy legal drama filtered through Raymond Chandler's sensibilities, with an initially "simple" case that morphs into something far more sinister; cinematographer Andrew Dintenfass' *film noir* touches are no accident. In a stroke of both genius and good fortune, the production team secured 27-year-old Wynton Marsalis to provide the music: the rapidly rising trumpet impresario's first film scoring assignment. He roughed out several themes and then spent two studio days with an octet of sidemen, improvising the score as the film unspooled on a screen.

"This was just when Wynton was starting to get well known, and it was unusual to

11. Freshly Squeezed: 1990–94   167

be using jazz for a TV show," Sayles recalled. "I went to that first session, where they were recording the music for the first episode. I saw this learning curve where he was just watching the scene, and by the second cue, he understands that he's playing with the cast on the screen. This wasn't about making a song that everyone's going to be humming the next day. Part of the song has already been written up there on the screen."[1]

Marsalis' ambitious score complements the film's opening sequence—which takes place beneath the title credits—of a plane approaching a small airport. Dissonant percussion, piano and brass riffs suggest an unsettling mood that's justified by the obviously dodgy men in the cockpit. Marsalis' trumpet gradually resolves into a melody of sorts, with a repetitious, descending five-note phrase; backing horns add to the air of unease. The music fades when the plane makes an unscheduled late-night stop at a small airport, where U.S. Customs officials discover a huge shipment of drugs. "Hope you got a good lawyer," the now-handcuffed pilot is told, whereupon we smash-cut to Shannon dealing himself poker hands onto a desk in a small office still stacked with unopened boxes; Marsalis' title cue—Shannon's theme—abruptly debuts. The melody's oft-repeated single trumpet note, against a swinging rhythm section, gives the scene a gently mocking and slightly wistful tone.

Marsalis delivers an Ellington-esque symphony as the film continues, highlighted by separate movements and distinct character themes that weave in and out of the whole.

"We have maybe six themes," he noted, at the time. "I tried to introduce all of the thematic material at the beginning of the movie. As the plot develops, the themes develop too; they're played different ways, and different things are added to them. All the themes are related in some way. You might not hear it, but they have a harmonic relationship."[2]

The well-received film prompted a weekly NBC series that debuted not quite a year later, on April 16, 1990. A 65-second version of Marsalis' theme for Shannon became the title credits cue: initially submerged beneath Sheridan's introductory voice-over, as he explains—against a montage of clips—how his previous life was "built on garbage." The narration concludes when the show's title is revealed, and the final 25 seconds of music—lovely trumpet and piano counterpoint—proceed without interruption, while the cast members are introduced. Marsalis even gets acknowledged, for "Shannon's Theme," just prior to Sayles' credit.

Marsalis and his combo also provided enough material for the early first-season episodes; supplementary underscore cues came from Tom Scott, who maintained the jazz ambiance. Viewer response was positive, so NBC okayed a second season … and then dithered for almost a year, before returning *Shannon's Deal* to the schedule in March 1991. But the momentum had been lost; despite high-quality scripts and an ongoing devotion to jazz—individual episodes were scored by Scott, guitarist Lee Ritenour and pianist David Benoit, among others—the show was canceled after just two months. It has yet to be released in any home viewing format, leaving a major portion of Marsalis' early jazz career—along with all those other great underscores—unavailable.

Marsalis never recorded any of the show's music, although he did expand one character theme into a tune he called "The Seductress"; it's included on his 2008 album, *Standards & Ballads*.

Not to be outdone by his older brother, trombonist Delfeayo Marsalis put a similar stamp on ABC's *Moon Over Miami*, a short-lived detective series that debuted September 15, 1993, and feels like a slightly more serious riff on *Moonlighting*. Runaway bride Gwen Cross (Ally Walker), wanting to escape the aristocratic life preordained by her wealthy parents, winds up working as a secretary/assistant for the private investigator—Bill Campbell, as Walter Tatum—initially hired to find her. Their playful adventures are set within Miami's music community, thanks to Walter's father and grandfather being well-known jazzmen.

Marsalis' title theme is a jovial, mildly smoky brass anthem set against a midtempo rhythm section, while the credits unfold over a romantic montage of clips showing the stars romping on deserted beaches, dressed to the nines for a social engagement, or simply staring thoughtfully at each other. The cue concludes with four descending inquisitive notes that convey the amorous, will-they-won't-they tension between these two characters. The end credits theme is entirely different: a jolly, midtempo brass swinger with a catchy 1-1-1-3-1-2 melodic refrain.

Each episode is steeped in jazz, whether non-diegetic underscore or as source music emanating from radios, home entertainment systems or live combos in nightclubs, restaurants or lavish parties. (It feels like incidental characters listen to jazz *all the time*.) The flirty banter between Walter and Gwen often is heard against blithely inquisitive solo brass or piano riffs. Not all underscore cues came from Marsalis; "additional music" is credited to composer/arranger Jim Latham, who "shadows" Marsalis' efforts quite skillfully. It's difficult to determine who wrote which cues.

Alas, *Moon Over Miami* failed to find an audience, and was canceled after only 10 episodes. It has yet to be revived for home viewing, although one fragment of Marsalis' work can be enjoyed. He expanded his end title theme into a tune titled "Brer Rabbit," included on his 2006 Troubadour Jass album *Minions Dominion*.

* * *

Early signs of what would become a huge shift in television viewing options arrived in the early 1990s, when more cable/satellite channels—until then content to survive by stripping old shows—began investing in new material. Lifetime's first evening of original series programming—Tuesday, July 23, 1991—concluded with *Veronica Clare*, another of the small screen's occasional efforts to recreate the *film noir* 1940s as a stylish private eye drama. The twist: Since Lifetime billed itself as "the women's channel," the dick is a dame ... or, to be more precise, a "private eyeful" who wields the Walther PPK so beloved by James Bond. Sultry Canadian actress Laura Robinson stars in the title role, as both a PI and part owner of a swanky, Art Deco restaurant/jazz club in Los Angeles' Chinatown district, which she shares with partner Duke Rado (Robert Beltran).

Robinson evokes the Lauren Bacall/Veronica Lake *femme fatale*, although the "enlightened" Veronica favors cases involving women in distress: a female boxer, a battered amnesia victim, a kidnapped singer, and so forth. The show's cinematographers excel at the arty camera angles and darkened shadows characteristic of classic *noir*; first-person narration, smoke-filled rooms, period cars and skin-tight dresses further sweeten the atmosphere. The show's jazz ambiance is supplied by Gil Mellé, who contributes both the beguiling title theme and original underscores. Veronica's jazz club hangout—where she meets clients and suspects—also allows for plenty of diegetic jazz, sometimes with unusual combos (piano, bass and accordion?).

Unfortunately, the show was doomed by weak scripts, inadequate publicity and too much competition from the established networks. *Veronica Clare* was canceled after only nine episodes, which are nowhere to be found in today's market. The same is true of Mellé's music.

HBO's *Philip Marlowe, Private Eye* had set a high standard for faithfully replicating the tone, style and feisty writing of such *noir* material; Showtime's *Fallen Angels* topped it. This anthology series delivered six episodes in the summer of 1993, followed by another nine in the autumn of 1995. Each playlet is adapted from a story by a famed *noir* author and is blessed with a phenomenal attention to detail appropriate to post–World War II Los Angeles: a heavily stylized depiction of the city, populated by all manner of dangerous dames, no-account gunsels, bent cops and hapless innocents. The lush, shadow- and blood-drenched cinematography honors the genre's roots without succumbing to parody, and top-flight stars persuasively chew into hard-bitten dialogue tough enough to break teeth. Very few of these stories conclude happily, and evil occasionally emerges triumphant: par for the course, when surfing the hard-boiled waters originally penned by Raymond Chandler, Jim Thompson, Evan Hunter, Cornell Woolrich, Dashiell Hammett and Mickey Spillane, with one by modern *noir* impresario James Ellroy thrown in for good measure.

First-season episodes are introduced by a slinky *femme fatale* dubbed Fay Friendly (a smoldering Lynette Walden), who sets up each premise while slithering—in *noir*-drenched black-and-white cinematography—to a sensuous title theme by Elmer and Peter Bernstein. It opens with haunting strings and inquisitive piano notes, followed by Teddy Edwards' salacious tenor sax; he introduces a melody dominated by a 3-7-3-5 motif, while Ms. Friendly slithers across the screen. The theme continues against a leisurely montage of *noir* leitmotifs—swirling cigarette smoke, a sparkling cocktail, a gun slipped into a woman's purse—until the camera slides back to Fay, whereupon she archly sets the stage for the playlet to follow. She's greatly missed during the second season prologues, which offer similar smoke-laden montages but are introduced instead by an off-camera Miguel Ferrer.

All episodes are filmed in color, although they have the grainy, chiaroscuro ambiance of 1940s cinematography; the result feels just otherworldly enough to turn each story into a *very* bad nightmare penned from a quill dipped in arsenic-drenched ink.

Peter Bernstein handles the similarly sultry underscores, which also rely heavily on macabre piano filigrees and sax melodies that wander from lonesome to tragic. Most episodes also are filled with stylish—and often ironic—period jazz and torch classics, usually emanating from well-placed radios. The unflinching adaptation of William Campbell Gault's "Dead End for Delia" is punctuated by a couple of Stan Getz covers—"All the Things You Are" and "The Folks Who Live on the Hill"—while Evan Hunter's "Love and Blood" gets additional dramatic heft from Sarah Vaughan's "Smoke Gets in Your Eyes" and Buddy De Franco's "Star Sapphire." Woolrich's "A Dime a Dance"—focusing on the exhausted young women who spend their evenings cutting a rug with all comers—is a veritable cornucopia of torch songs by Vaughan, Tony Martin, Jill Stafford and Dinah Washington, along with jazz standards such as "Poor Butterfly," "Make Believe," "The Way You Look Tonight" and many others, all performed by a dance hall quintet (actually Joey Altruda, Doug Webb, Willie McNeil, Red Young and James Intveld).

The series concluded with an adaptation of Chandler's "Red Wind," which takes the provocative step of casting Danny Glover as Philip Marlowe; his investigation into a series of murders is set against a smoky playlist that includes Red Young's "Piano Boogie Tribute" and Clifford Brown's "Can't Help Lovin' Dat Man."

The Bernsteins' title and end themes are the only underscore cues on the soundtrack album, which is filled with a delectable collection of classics by Charlie Parker, Billie Holiday, Benny Carter, Nat King Cole and J.J. Johnson.

We'll not soon see another anthology series that can match this one's faithful attention to mood and detail ... if, indeed, we *ever* do.

The Big Screen

Late-period *noir* doesn't get much nastier than 1990's tough-as-nails handling of hard-boiled crime author Jim Thompson's 1963 genre classic. *The Grifters* pulses with underlying menace from the first frame, its three main characters mesmerizing in the manner of coiled rattlesnakes. Elmer Bernstein's darkly humorous, soft jazz score cleverly plays against this malevolent tone, starting with the quirky bounce of his playful main theme: an electronic-esque melody against gentle, tick-tock percussion—with slow, ragtime-style bass piano chords supplying the rhythm—and mordant sax comping.

"The film felt like a fable of some sort," Bernstein recalled, years later. "That's why I scored it with what, to me, sounded like a street band: a *Three Penny Opera* kind of sound. I think it worked very well in the film; I was very pleased with it."[3]

Roy Dillon (John Cusack), a twentysomething "short con" grifter, is caught between the two women in his life: girlfriend Myra Langtry (Annette Bening), a larcenous tart who cheerfully trades her body for favors and rent bills; and his estranged mother, Lilly (Anjelica Huston), a veteran con artist steadily employed by bookmaker Bobo Justus (Pat Hingle). Roy is no match for either woman; both will do anything—betray anybody—to serve their own amoral ends. Donald E. Westlake's taut, rigorously faithful script smoothly blends the narrative with flashbacks and one brilliant plot twist, en route to a finale that confirms that there's room for only one lion in this particular jungle.

"[Director Stephen Frears] loved the score, but he did something that nobody's ever done," Bernstein continued. "There were about 33 pieces of music—cues—in the film. When he got through with it, only three of the pieces remained in the spots for which they were originally written. The reason the score survives anyway, is that basically it was a monochromatic score. It wasn't a score with themes for people, or anything like that; it was an atmospheric score for the general atmosphere of the film."[4]

Bernstein's primary theme is used most frequently for Myra, particularly when she's about to hustle another victim. But Frears' intriguing use of the rest of Bernstein's music begins with the title credits, which unfold against a tense blend of bouncing bass piano, anxious horns and a plaintive clarinet. The clarinet and some echo effects open the main title, which accompanies a split-screen montage that introduces Lilly, Roy and Myra individually at work with their respective cons. (This cue, titled "The City" on the soundtrack album, became a popular staple of Bernstein's subsequent live performances.) Insouciant banjo and piano add sparkle when Roy later fleeces a group of sailors at dice. Things turn unpleasant when the story progresses to its third act, which exposes Myra's black soul: a revelation accompanied by a nastier, tick-tock arrangement of the main theme. After the final shocking surprise, Frears repeats the jauntier version, when the end credits roll.

The soundtrack album includes an uptempo disco number, "Do Ya, Do Ya Love Me," heard briefly during a flashback to Myra's earlier days.

Lilly and Myra notwithstanding, *femmes fatales* don't come much more conniving than the lascivious bitch played by Virginia Madsen in 1990's wickedly erotic *The Hot Spot*. The sizzle on this already salacious steak is a bawdy jazz/blues score that unites Miles Davis and John Lee Hooker. The story's *noir* sensibilities are no accident; the film is based on crime author Charles Williams' 1952 novel, *Hell Hath No Fury*. Indeed not.

The story begins during the heat of summer, when drifter Harry Madox (Don Johnson) motors his 1957 Studebaker Golden Hawk into the tiny community of Landers, Texas, where he takes a job as a salesman at a used-car lot run by George Harshaw (Jerry Hardin).

Harry immediately catches the eye of Harshaw's slutty wife, Dolly (Madsen), although he's more interested in the firm's younger, gentler bookkeeper, Gloria Harper (Jennifer Connelly). Carnal delights are set aside briefly, when he pulls off an easy heist at the local bank, hiding the money in the nearby woods; he's immediately suspected, as a newcomer, but "saved" when Dolly provides an alibi. Everybody is manipulating somebody else, and events build to a deadly climax.

Composer Jack Nitzsche backed Davis and Hooker with a terrific band that includes Taj Mahal (acoustic guitar), Roy Rogers (slide guitar) and Earl Palmer (drums). The instrumentation is intriguing, with Davis' trumpet replacing the harmonica that blues fans might expect. The combo delivers an earthy score that suggests the baking Texas swelter with the same intensity that John Barry's work on *Body Heat* embellishes that film's Florida humidity. Some cues have a sultry sameness: the slow, funk-laden drawl of Hooker's guitar, with the veteran bluesman humming a gentle melody and adding occasional phrases—"Sad, sad, sad," "Used to be," "It ain't right," and so forth—against lazy licks by Rogers and bassist Tim Drummond, while Davis' horn carefully comps and echoes Hooker's vocal shading. But the cues *aren't* identical; Davis' trumpet elements are as distinct and precise as would be expected when a scripter employs a specific word.

The title credits introduce Harry as he gazes at empty, scorching desert, while taking a break from his drive from somewhere; Drummond and Palmer lay down some swinging, uptempo gut-bucket, with Davis' trumpet supplying a warning edge. The implication is clear: The Devil is about to drive into Landers, which already *has* a resident fiend. This title cue later expands into a full-tilt boogie when an adrenaline-charged Harry makes his audacious daylight bank robbery. The mood shifts when he persuades Gloria to confess why a local creep has such a powerful hold over her. Her shaky explanation plays out in flashback, as keyboardist Bradford Ellis delivers a dirge-like piano line supported solely by Davis' doleful trumpet. Harry's subsequent plan to frame the guy for the bank robbery veers dangerously awry; Hooker moans cautionary syllables against troubled bass and synth, while Davis' sweet horn adds more anxiety. In the eventual aftermath, Harry drives out of town with a woman at his side; the uptempo title cue repeats, Hooker and Davis trading malicious licks that match these two amoral schemers.

The soundtrack album is a phenomenal collaboration that deserves far better exposure than its current afterthought status as a mere "movie score."

On the international front, Branford Marsalis' silky-smooth soprano sax anchors Jerry Goldsmith's melancholy score for 1990s adaptation of John Le Carré's *The Russia House*. The spycraft is handled by bickering British and American colleagues, who neither trust nor get out of each other's way; the only ethical character is Bartholomew "Barley" Scott-Blair (Sean Connery), the alcoholic head of a tiny British publishing firm. Goldsmith's score—and Marsalis' sax work—exquisitely complement the grim and unapologetically duplicitous world of betrayal in which Barley finds himself.

He comes to the attention of shadowy British Intelligence officers Ned (James Fox) and Clive (Michael Kitchen) when they learn that a young Soviet woman, Katya Orlova (Michelle Pfeiffer) has—quite unexpectedly—sent Barley a manuscript containing detailed information about the Soviet Union's ability to wage nuclear war. Ned and Clive collaborate with their American CIA counterparts (Roy Scheider and John Mahoney) on a plan to send Barley into Moscow as a spy. His goal: to coax additional information from Katya and Dante (Klaus Maria Brandauer), a man he once met at a Moscow writers' retreat, who actually is renowned Soviet physicist Yakov Saveleyev. A renewed liaison reveals that Saveleyev has entrusted Barley to publish these Soviet military secrets as a means of forcing *glasnost* with the West. Tensions mount further when Katya learns, during one of her regular phone calls from Saveleyev, that he has been compromised by the KGB.

Goldsmith built his score on a primary theme for Katya, with supplementary cues for Barley and Saveleyev. Barley is defined, in part, by his love of jazz; he's a reasonably accomplished amateur on sax, and Marsalis ghosts Connery during a few diegetic performances of Cole Porter's "What Is This Thing Called Love."

The film's title credits open with a lyrical reading of Katya's theme; pianist Mike Lang comps softly behind Marsalis' wistful soprano sax. Barley's recollection of his first chat with Dante/Saveleyev, at the writers' conference, is shaded by a blend of his theme—a soprano sax variation of Katya's theme—and the somber cue designed for the Russian; the melody is given a graceful Slavic touch by an Armenian duduk (a double-reed flute). Once in Moscow, lyrical piano filigrees are joined by inquisitive sax, when Barley contacts Katya. The tone shifts once they meet and awkwardly inspect each other; her theme emerges via sax and balalaika (a Russian stringed instrument with an opulent, triangular-shaped body). Piano, sax and balalaika supply a lovely version of her theme when Barley takes a brief side trip to Leningrad. After they're both compromised, Barley embarks on an impulsive plan; his actions are backed by wary sax, piano and percussion. When the story concludes, the swell of Katya's theme—and Marsalis' triumphant reading of the melody—tell us what we need to know, before the final freeze-frame. The end credits roll as Goldsmith shifts into swing tempo, with Marsalis and Lang trading licks enthusiastically.

The initial soundtrack album featured much of Goldsmith's score, along with one of Barley's diegetic performances of the Cole Porter tune.

"*The Russia House* is now my favorite score," Goldsmith admitted, during a 1992 interview, "[but] I put too much music on the CD. I'd love to pull 10 minutes out of it, so the score wouldn't sound so redundant."[5] He likely would be even less pleased with the expanded 2017 digital release, which features his entire score. That followed a 2016 Blu-ray, which includes an isolated score track.

Back in 1986, *F/X* had become an unexpected hit, with its tricky saga of a film special effects maestro—Bryan Brown's Rollie Tyler—who employs his technical wizardry to defeat Mafia thugs and a corrupt Justice Department official. The B-film's delights aside, Bill Conti's symphonic score was an odd choice, as it often deadened the story's momentum. Director Richard Franklin didn't repeat that mistake with 1991's *F/X2*; he turned to Lalo Schifrin, who responded with an appropriately suspenseful and energetic score. Unfortunately, this sequel vacillates wildly between grim drama and clumsy slapstick humor, and not even Schifrin can bridge that divide; worse yet, his music was mishandled.

Mike (Kevin J. O'Connor), the cop ex-husband of Rollie's girlfriend Kim (Rachel Ticotin), asks him to stage a special-effects scenario to help arrest a serial killer. The situation goes awry when a second baddie (John Walsh, as Rado) kills Mike: a "twist" arranged by bent cop Ray Silak (Philip Bosco), whose malfeasance was about to be exposed by Mike's interest in a cold case. Rado quickly comes after Rollie, Kim and her young son (Dominic Zamprogna), because they all know too much; the story expands to involve the Mafia and stolen gold medallions crafted by Michelangelo (!).

The film was caught in the downward spiral of Orion Pictures, soon to declare bankruptcy. Postproduction was rushed; although Schifrin turned in a finished score, a European concert tour prevented his further participation, when the film was savagely reedited.

Session composer/keyboardist Michael Boddicker was hired to "sweeten" and rewrite some of Schifrin's cues. The result is lamentable; Boddicker's soulless synth and percussion "enhancements" work against Schifrin's thematic continuity, making portions of the film sound like dozens of other interchangeable action movie scores.

But the news isn't all bad. A sassy, bluesy sax emerges from an orchestral "shimmer" effect while the title credits unfold against throbbing percussion; the sax launches the call-and-response melody, with a rising/falling 3-4-4 motif. Bouncing synth dominates the bridge, followed by an explosion of brass when the credits conclude. Rollie's flirty behavior with Kim is accompanied by a droll, midtempo shuffle that opens on synth and segues to sax; he and Kim dance to a seductive diegetic ballad that plays on their home stereo system. Action cues spot Rado's later attack on Kim and Chris; this leads to a frantic melee in an empty supermarket, where they're saved by Rollie's improvised skill with "found" weapons. Events build to a surprise assault on a palatial Mafioso estate, undercut by a series of Boddicker's redundant, jacked-up percussion and synth cues; in the aftermath, the end credits roll to his heavy-handed reprise of the main theme.

Happily, a few of Schifrin's other diegetic cues were left intact: some wicked, guitar- and sax-fueled funk, which emanates from a shop during a street scene; a nifty bit of piano- and sax-driven boogie-woogie, which Rollie pulls up on a jukebox; and a dreamy piano trio heard in the apartment belonging to Assistant DA Liz Kennedy (Joanna Gleason).

The long-delayed 2013 soundtrack includes the diegetic tunes, along with several Schifrin cues that were discarded in favor of Boddicker's weaker efforts.

The *F/X* franchise would return on the small screen (about which, more later).

Rollie Tyler's antics involve misdirection and surprise: qualities also present in 1992's *Sneakers*. This low-key heist adventure is an underappreciated gem; its breezy tone and character banter are complemented perfectly by James Horner's whimsical jazz score, fueled throughout by Branford Marsalis' effervescent tenor sax.

Martin Bishop (Robert Redford) heads a San Francisco–based team of security specialists that includes ex-CIA operative Donald Crease (Sidney Poitier), electronics technician and conspiracy theorist Darren "Mother" Roscow (Dan Aykroyd), blind audio wizard Irwin "Whistler" Emery (David Strathairn), and apprentice hacker Carl Arbogast (River Phoenix). After reluctantly agreeing to steal a cryptographer's "black box" on behalf of some pushy NSA agents, Martin and his buddies discover that they've been conned; the two guys aren't with the NSA at all, and the stolen whatzit proves to be a powerful "skeleton key" capable of breaching even ultra-secure encryption systems. Possession of this hot potato proves increasingly dangerous, and possible salvation requires stealing the black box *again*, this time from a much more secured environment: a complicated mission that involves the *slowest* heist ever masterminded on the big screen.

Horner (keyboards) and Marsalis worked with a small combo on most of the cues. The tone is light and frothy, dominated by a primary melody—the rhythmic "Sneakers Theme"—built from rapidly changing pairs of single piano notes that sound like exploratory computer keystrokes. The quirky result, both peaceful and enigmatic, debuts after the title credits—the two-note motif carried by both keyboard and sax—while the team completes a routine assignment. After getting hired by the (supposed) NSA agents, the "Sneakers Theme" repeats when the black box is snatched, a success celebrated during a party at the gang's warehouse operations center. Rumbling percussion and low-end piano signal Martin's mounting unease, which blossoms into full-blown paranoia when the subsequent hand-off goes awry; he's kidnapped by Cosmo (Ben Kingsley), a former college buddy turned criminal. He has masterminded the entire charade and has his own designs on the whatzit.

A sad solo piano theme follows Martin when he's dumped onto a San Francisco street, his former illegal hacker activities fully revealed by Cosmo's "adjustment" of a government law enforcement database. Realizing that his only salvation lies in getting the black box into *actual* NSA hands, Martin and his team suss out Cosmo's headquarters. Horner and his musicians shine during the lengthy cue that shadows the planning and subsequent invasion of this facility, which reaches its tense climax—against march-style percussion, low-register piano runs, horn pops and quizzical sax—when Martin reaches Cosmo's office. Various surprises lead to a witty finale, which signals a final reprise of the "Sneakers Theme," while the end credits roll.

Jazz fans will appreciate Horner's insertion of some classic tracks as occasional diegetic cues: Miles Davis' "Flamenco Sketches" and Charlie Byrd's covers of "The Girl from Ipanema" and "Corcovado."

The official soundtrack album is enjoyable, but an expanded bootleg disc is much more satisfying.

* * *

The *noir*-drenched *The Public Eye* (1992) is inspired by the career of New York City–based press photojournalist Arthur Fellig—better known by the nickname "Weegee"—who was famed for his stark, black-and-white depictions of metropolitan crime, poverty, injury and death. The film spins a provocative, coulda-happened yarn that pulls Weegie surrogate Leon "Bernzie" Bernstein (Joe Pesci) into a web of feuding crime families, World War II-era corruption, and his ill-advised sympathy for the owner of a posh nightclub.

The indefatigable Bernzie has earned a spooky reputation for beating cops to the scene of often horrific crimes or accidents. He knows everybody in the city, good and bad, and is tolerated because he never takes sides; his expertise and insight come to the attention of Kay Levitz (Barbara Hershey), who has assumed control of the Café Society nightclub, following her husband's death. Unfortunately, she's targeted by a mob enforcer demanding a partnership; Bernzie likes her and agrees to investigate. At first, it seems that Kay is "merely" caught between rival crime bosses Farinelli (Richard Fotonjy) and Spoleto (Dominic Chianese), but Bernzie discovers that the situation is much worse; a nasty conspiracy involves the illegal distribution of black-market gasoline ration coupons. Blinded by his growing attachment to Kay, Bernzie recklessly takes a side.

Trumpeter/electronic keyboardist/composer Mark Isham had been building a steadily expanding Hollywood career when this assignment came along. He complements the story's larcenous activity with a primarily symphonic score, which adds melancholia via mournful strings, wary woodwinds, gently expectant percussion and suspenseful, treble-register piano filigrees. Jazz elements are present as lively diegetic combo cues performed by the house band at Café Society; these numbers are produced and arranged by West Coast trumpeter/jazz icon Shorty Rogers. Two of them—covers of the war-era hits "Flying Home" and "Undecided"—are uptempo jump jazz swingers, both boasting sassy vocals by Oren Waters. At another point, trumpeter Roy Eldridge highlights a smooth cover of Gershwin's "Embraceable You," while saxman Plas Johnson and pianist Gerald Wiggins lend sparkle to a midtempo big band arrangement of "Topsy." Johnson and Wiggins also are front and center for "Café Society Blues," a Rogers original that makes ample use of vibrant brass.

Isham's atmospheric cues dominate the soundtrack album, although it does include four of the diegetic combo tunes. Perhaps of equal (if not greater) interest is the score that *wasn't* released: Jerry Goldsmith was the first composer hired, but for unknown reasons his work was deemed unacceptable. Evidence strongly suggests that Goldsmith completed a full score of 23 cues, which were orchestrated by Alexander Courage, but the majority of this music remains unheard; only one brief cue is available online.[6]

Moving back to the modern era, 1993's *The Firm* was the first of criminal defense attorney-turned-author John Grisham's popular novels to hit the big screen: a prestige production anchored by director Sydney Pollack and star Tom Cruise. The film marks the eighth of Pollack's collaborations with Dave Grusin, who—inspired by the plot, characters and (most particularly) the Memphis setting—turned in a truly unique score. Although Pollack exploits the locale with well over a dozen sassy jazz and blues diegetic cues—several performed on camera—Grusin's non-diegetic underscore is entirely solo piano. This decision was almost unprecedented in modern Hollywood, which regarded solo keyboard as a relic of the silent era. Even Grusin was wary.

"I got a call from Sydney," Grusin recalled, "and he said, 'I've been going to B.B. King's club every night. What do you think about a piano blues score?'"[7]

"I was sure we were going to have to go back and sweeten things with an orchestra," he admitted, years later. "[But] we chipped away at each cue, and Sydney was like a bulldog with the idea of not using anything but piano for this thing."[8]

The score earned Grusin the last of his eight Academy Award nominations: the only time, in cinematic history, that a solo piano score had garnered such an honor. (He lost to John Williams, that year's sure thing, for *Schindler's List*.)

The story begins as cocky, overachieving Harvard Law School grad Mitch McDeere (Cruise), scrambling to make ends meet while subsisting in a tiny apartment with his wife, Abby (Jeanne Tripplehorn), signs with the boutique Memphis firm of Bandini, Lambert and Locke. Life changes overnight for Mitch and Abby, now rolling in money and perks, but something isn't quite right; his joy evaporates after clandestine contact with FBI agents, who explain that his new employers actually are a front for a Chicago-based crime family. Mitch is cornered both by the FBI, which demands that he act as an informant—which would violate his ethical code as a lawyer—and by his own rash behavior during a trip to the Cayman Islands, which gives the firm blackmail leverage. How can he even *survive* such dangerous company, let alone figure out a way to play his firm and the FBI against each other?

The film opens with a title credits montage of the not-quite-graduated Mitch's daily routine: a blur of interviews, class work, part-time jobs and stress-relieving pick-up basketball games. Grusin scores this sequence with the bounciest of his four primary themes: a rich, foot-pounding R&B cue quite appropriately titled "Memphis Stomp," with a driving two-beat bass line and sparkling treble elements that never quite coalesce into an actual melody. Grusin shifts to a much gentler tone when Mitch and Abby drive their meager belongings to Memphis; this sweet keyboard cue is the love theme, which deftly complements the couple's mutual devotion. A reworking of this theme is heard during the Caymans trip, when the naïve Mitch allows himself to be seduced by a young woman, unaware their lovemaking is being photographed. Grusin's improv work for this sequence is quite clever: simultaneously sexy, as the woman overcomes Mitch's wavering unwillingness; and tragic, as the cue's mournful echoes of the love theme hint at his marital betrayal. Later, on the run from mob assassins, Mitch's panicked flight is spotted by Grusin's heartbeat rhythm, twitchy bass keyboard riffs, brushed piano strings and agitated treble chords, all of which build tension to a screaming point.

The expansive diegetic cues are a rich, atmospheric blend of Memphis blues, straight-ahead jazz and Cajun-influenced pop tunes. Local talent includes the Lannie McMillan Jazz Quartet, Teenie Hodges and T-Bone Walker.

The initial soundtrack album is divided between Grusin's primary character themes and numerous diegetic songs, but the instrumental tracks represent barely a quarter of the composer's 65 minutes' worth of music. The subsequent 2015 release offers the entire instrumental score, along with numerous alternate takes.

Bad behavior also abounds in 1994's *The Last Seduction*. It's a terrific jolt of modern neo-*noir*, thanks to a provocatively nasty original script, all-stops-out performances by Linda Fiorentino and Bill Pullman, and Joseph Vitarelli's cleverly understated jazz score: primarily a keyboard/bass/percussion configuration with silky highlights on trumpet, sax and clarinet.

The story begins in New York City, where Bridget (Fiorentino) works as an aggressive telemarketing manager; her husband Clay, (Pullman), is training to become a doctor while selling stolen pharmaceuticals on the side. A $700,000 score proves too tempting for Bridget, who steals the money and flees to the small upstate town of Beston. Fully aware than her enraged husband won't quit looking for her, she changes her name to Wendy Kroy, establishes roots and begins a boy-toy relationship with local guy Mike Swale (Peter Berg). Clay, meanwhile, hires a private detective to locate his wife. Not one to play defense, Bridget/Wendy escalates her calculated hold over the gullible Mike, viewing him as a permanent solution to her increasingly troublesome hubbie.

The title credits appear against an uptempo jazz waltz that kicks off with a catchy bass/brushed drumbeat that backs Vitarelli's flirty piano work. The melody is handed off to sax and trumpet as the credits segue to a montage that cuts between Bridget at work, rapaciously belittling her call center staff; and Clay standing beneath a bridge, about to make the dangerous drug deal. The cool, unhurried melody reflects Bridget's Machiavellian calmness. The shading for Clay is quite different: a flurry of faster, more random and almost comic runs from the keyboard and horns, mirroring his pathetic inability to control any situation. By the time Bridget finds a rental home in Benson, it has become obvious that Vitarelli's purposeful, meditative approach to his gentle improvisational cues is as rigorously controlled as Bridget/Wendy herself.

The film's atmosphere shifts quite dramatically, once she has Mike firmly under her control. The cues become slower; a sinister trumpet theme obliterates the teasing keyboard runs we've heard up to this point. Vibrating cymbals build the tension further, when all three confront each other back in New York. Although Bridget appears to be in mortal danger, there's no doubt that her wily instincts will triumph; we know this, because Vitarelli reprises her cool, calmly controlled character theme.

The soundtrack album includes three of the earthy blues/rock vocals heard as diegetic cues.

Thanks to his smoldering score for *Body Heat*, John Barry was the go-to choice for another Florida-based erotic thriller. *The Specialist* is only vaguely based on John Cutter's book series, and director Luis Llosa's approach is exploitative, to say the least. All that said, the slowly developing *pas de deux* between stars Sylvester Stallone and Sharon Stone is suspensefully effective, and Barry's languorous, luxuriously carnal score is the perfect backdrop for this cat-and-mouse pursuit; the humidity is palpable both on the screen and in his jazz cues.

"I particularly liked the fact that the Stallone character and the Sharon Stone character don't meet until about a third of the way through the movie," Barry acknowledged, at the time. "The fact that he stalks her, they have telephone contact, and he starts to fall in love with her just through this type of contact, I found really interesting. So the music has a major part to play, I felt, in getting that relationship going, because as they weren't actually physically together from the start, it helped set the mood between the two of them."[9]

A brief prologue establishes the uneasy relationship between CIA explosives experts Ray Quick (Stallone) and Ned Trent (James Woods): a partnership that dissolves when the latter callously dismisses the death of a child as "collateral damage." Years later, Ray has established himself in Miami, living off the grid and working as a freelance assassin, taking morally justified cases from unseen clients who get in touch via an Internet bulletin board. His services are requested by May Munro (Stone), who as a little girl watched her parents murdered by thugs in the employ of Tomas Leon (Eric Roberts), son of crime lord Joe Leon (Rod Steiger). The situation becomes stickier when Ray discovers that Ned now works for Joe and Tomas. Although Ray's initial executions proceed like clockwork, some clever narrative twists change the game, leading to a truly explosive (if laughably improbable) climax.

Barry's *noir* score is ubiquitous. He supplies a measured, pulsating action cue for the title credits; the bulk of the subsequent score is dominated by a love theme dubbed "Did You Call Me?" It's built from the sexy 10-note motif that accompanies the numerous phone conversations between Ray and May, as he guardedly considers her appeal. This sensuous theme, with alto sax and/or piano carrying the melody, is a sublime counterpoint to their relaxed banter. When Ray's precisely designed "shape" explosives begin to eliminate the targets, one by one, Barry's restrained, disciplined approach to the score cleverly mutes some of Llosa's gratuitous tendencies—such as a decapitated head that winds up in a fish tank—and gives the film a more refined tone than it deserves.

Unexpected circumstances finally throw Ray and May together, at which point Barry's love theme builds to a throbbing climax during a steamy scene in a hotel shower. Alas, Ned has put the pieces together; a furious fight scene in the hotel kitchen takes place against an action cue that sounds very much like Barry's later James Bond efforts. Ned, May and Ray ultimately face off in the latter's workshop/home, which is booby-trapped with all manner of explosives. Barry supplied a cheerful reading of the love theme for the happy conclusion and end credits; alas, Llosa didn't use it, instead running the credits against one of the film's many uptempo diegetic salsa tunes (a decision that greatly annoyed Barry, when he found out).[10]

Two soundtrack albums appeared. The Latin/funk/pop song score is dominated by Gloria Estefan, Cheito, Miami Sound Machine and numerous other vocalists; Barry's instrumental score is represented by only two tracks. Happily, his efforts are the sole focus of a second instrumental CD, although several of the action cues are left behind, in favor of numerous arrangements of the love theme.

12

Chili Hot: 1995–99

As the new century approached, a rapidly rising number of American television programs abandoned a formal title credits sequence, in favor of credits superimposed over first-act events. The reason: artistic self-preservation. Between 1980 and 2000, the number of commercial minutes per hour jumped radically, from roughly 8.5 to 12. That left only 48 minutes for the actual show: a quantity shortened further by obligatory end credits and—if used—a title credits sequence.

(This expanding glut of advertising would get even grimmer. By 2009, broadcast networks granted commercials 13.5 minute per hour; cable networks were worse, at 14.5. As of 2013, this increased to 14.25 and 15.5, respectively.)

Since it was becoming increasingly difficult to tell a solid story in an ever-diminishing time frame, show-runners no longer could justify the 30 to 60 seconds lost to a title credits sequence, no matter how much it might have helped a program's name-brand visibility. No opening credits sequence also meant no title theme. A tradition that had delivered memorable pieces of music to two generations of television viewers—and, starting in the mid-80s, spawned a cottage industry of TV theme compilation albums—began to vanish. Rapidly.

Viewers who relished music-and-credits sequences for their own sake—as familiar "minimovies" that anchored a favorite show each week—must've felt a chill.

Needless to say, this had a deleterious effect on studio/session musicians and orchestras; it also came close to finishing jazz TV themes.

The Small Screen

The oddly titled *Pointman* (1995) is an amiable update on the Simon Templar/Travis McGee archetype, with Jack Scalia's Constantine "Connie" Harper an independently wealthy adventurer who helps those in need. Once a successful Wall Street investment banker railroaded by rivals, Connie served slightly more than two years before being released; he received a huge settlement for false imprisonment, which enabled him to purchase—and ostensibly manage—a Florida coast beach club. Thanks to dodgy "skills" learned while in prison, Connie is drawn to folks in trouble through no fault of their own; he's also on a clandestine "list" shared with victims in dire need of last-resort help. The engaging series debuted January 26 and was an original programming effort by the short-lived Prime Time Entertainment Network.

The quiet synth of Dale Menten's title theme hovers beneath Scalia's voice-over recitation of the events that led to his current "occupation." This segues to a sassy sax, augmented by additional synth and female vocalese—against a montage of bikini babes and Scalia's handsome features—while Connie explains his new-found dedication to helping others in trouble. This signals the show's title, as the narration stops and the sax takes over against a growling rhythm section. Menten's original underscores also favor sultry sax themes—for Connie's various romantic dalliances—along with impish salsa and bossa nova cues that back his frequent efforts to *avoid* violent encounters. Action sequences are limited mostly to percussion and synth.

Menten's title theme and Scalia's narration were dropped midway through the first season, the former replaced by a fresh composition from Mike Post: a faster, sassier blend of sax, synth, guitar and percussion against a montage of Connie at his action-oriented best. This didn't enhance viewership, and the show's second season ended prematurely. None of the music has resurfaced.

The New Orleans setting of the USA Network's *The Big Easy* demanded a lively and varied jazz palette, and local boy David Torkanowsky accepted the challenge. (The quirky Crescent City piano player resists being called a "pianist," insisting that term be reserved for those whose taste runs to Chopin and Liszt.)[1] He delivered all manner of regional sounds as resident musician on (thus far) his only TV series assignment. The laid-back, music-laden crime show, based on the 1986 Dennis Quaid/Ellen Barkin film of the same title, produced a respectable 35 episodes during a two-season run that began August 11, 1996. Hunky Tony Crane took over the role of New Orleans police detective Lt. Remy McSwain, with seductive Susan Walters at his side as state district attorney Anne Osborne. Each episode divides its time between intriguing cases and their flirtatious banter.

Torkanowsky, who regards himself as equal parts composer and "audio janitor,"[2] was heavily involved in all aspects of the series' music, starting with his bouncy main theme. The colorful title credits montage kicks off as somebody shouts "Big *Eeeeaaaa* ... *zee*," after which Torkanowsky opens with a heavily percussive New Orleans strut; lively unison brass takes over against a montage of jazz musicians, raucous nightclub action, brightly illuminated neon signs, and come-hither close-ups of the two stars. The horns shift to one- and two-note fanfares when an enthusiastic piano player takes over; male and female vocalists add some lyrics until the brass climbs the scale during a climactic final blast that fades as a smoldering chanteuse seductively coos, "Big Easy, baby."

Music is ubiquitous throughout every episode: drifting out from bars and restaurants, *thump-thumping* from passing Dixieland bands, emerging faintly from tiny radio speakers. This pulsating aural tapestry is as much a character as Remy, Anne and the supporting players, and each episode showcases (if only briefly) as many live performances as possible. Several scripts focus on musicians, as when Remy and Anne investigate the supposedly supernatural death of a jazz cat, in the first-season episode "Hotshots." Familiar guest artists—popping up either as themselves, or in small parts—include Jimmy Witherspoon, Coco Robicheaux, Willie Lockett, Kermit Ruffins and many others.

"I'm really lucky to be working for [the show's producers]," Torkanowsky noted, during production, "because they really understand the music of the region. As opposed to most people in the business, who just see New Orleans as nothing more than a cool set." Given his reputation with the city's wealth of jazz talent, he'd often find a way to work around budget limitations. If—for example—the show lacked the money to "rent" a particular Earl King tune, "I'd bring Earl into the session to play along."[3]

The Big Easy deserved better than its bad time slots and/or neglect by USA. None of Torkanowsky's myriad themes endured beyond broadcast.

Few spoof secret agent shows rise to the high level of *Get Smart*, and 1997's short-lived

Spy Game is no exception, although it does boast a droll premise. Old-school agent Lorne Cash (Linden Ashby) reluctantly abandons retirement and joins the Emergency Counter-Hostilities Organization (ECHO), to capture unemployed domestic and international agents who—annoyed at not being able to ply their tradecraft for legitimate causes—are wreaking havoc as unpredictable rogues. Cash is partnered with the sexy, gadget-happy Max London (Allison Smith); the two bicker endlessly while (more or less) completing each assignment.

The title credits sequence, fueled by Christophe Beck's deliberate riff on 1960s action jazz, is by far the best part of each episode. Ashby and Smith cavort against giant plastic letters that spell out the show's title, their antics intercut with fleeting clips of stunts, car chases, karate chops and London's mocking smile. The sequence plays like an amped-up version of the iconic John Steed/Emma Peel season five *Avengers* title credits, against Beck's aggressively rhythmic, guitar-heavy theme. He also handles the underscores, which often reference this theme while supplying equally dynamic action jazz cues for the bonkers stunt sequences.

Imitating the embarrassing third season of *The Man from U.N.C.L.E.* did little to help sell this send-up, despite amusing cameos by iconic spy guys such as Robert Culp, Patrick Macnee and Peter Lupus. ABC put *Spy Game* on hiatus only three episodes after its March 3 debut; it returned for a six-week run that summer, and then was axed for good ... leaving Cash and London just as much a security risk as the rogue agents they'd been tasked to secure.

On a much more positive note, CBS' *Buddy Faro* is one of the most entertaining failed detective shows TV ever produced, in great part because of the enthusiasm with which Chicago cop-turned-character actor Dennis Farina inhabits the title role. The premise is captivating: Methodically competent—but hopelessly unhip—private detective Bob Jones (Frank Whaley) is hired by the mysterious Julie Barber (Allison Smith) to find Faro, who has been missing for 20 years. During his heyday, he was the "quickest-thinking, hardest-hitting, wildest-loving investigator of them all." Then he vanished, without warning, on September 9, 1978. Bob tracks Faro to a small Mexican town, where he has become a disheveled wreck; once dragged back to Los Angeles, Bob's preppy enthusiasm encourages Faro to clean up. Trouble is, in his mind it's as if no time has passed, and his version of 1978 looks and sounds far more like *1958*. The once-again-suave Buddy swans around Los Angeles expecting to hear Frank and Dino on the radio; expecting to drive a fin-laden, gas-guzzling convertible Cadillac or Packard; and expecting to encounter cocktail-swilling ladies eager to swoon at his slightest come-hither glance. Needless to say, the music, cars and women of 1998 continue to disappoint.

The title sequence is a *noir* swirl of hyper-edited clips that efficiently supply back-story and introduce the main characters. Joel McNeely's retro big band main theme evokes fond memories of Mancini (*Peter Gunn*), Basie (*M Squad*) and Bernstein (*Staccato*). McNeely opens with a roaring rhythm section, blasts of brass and a rising six-note fanfare that introduces a suspenseful melody delivered by all manner of unison horns, while Farina's credit slides across the screen. Whaley debuts against a wailing muted trumpet; Smith is granted a crescendo of big band brass. The entire ensemble delivers an even more emphatic reprise of the core 1-3-6 motif, concluding with a final three-note blast of brass. Coo-coo, Charley!

McNeely maintains this feisty swing ambiance in the episode underscores, lacing the lighthearted adventures with plenty of action jazz. Bob gets his fondest wish when Buddy suggests they become partners; Los Angeles crooks have no idea what's about to hit them. The ongoing gag is that Buddy somehow finds pockets of the 1950s vibe, where lavish nightclubs remain laden with beautiful women who can cut a rug to swinging rhythms. McNeely and music editor Mary Parker further spice the underscores with plenty of Rat Pack–era jazz vocalists, both as source and non-diegetic cues; the show is simply *fun*.

Alas, most viewers didn't get the gag. Buddy's retro antics ceased only eight episodes after the show's debut on September 25, 1998; five more episodes never saw the light of day. McNeely's music had no afterlife.

The Big Screen

Walter Mosely's Ezekiel "Easy" Porterhouse Rawlins, featured in more than a dozen books, debuted in 1990's *Devil in a Blue Dress*. Their gumshoe trappings aside, the novels also are impeccably researched historical fiction, with a focus on post–World War II race relations—and injustice—in Southern California. Rawlins made a stylish leap to the big screen in 1995, with director/scripter Carl Franklin's sumptuous adaptation of *Devil in a Blue Dress*. Denzel Washington's Easy projects just the right blend of wariness, righteous indignation and—when things get unpleasant—carefully controlled fury. He's assisted by longtime best friend Raymond "Mouse" Alexander, played to sociopathic perfection by Don Cheadle. The case begins simply enough, when Easy is hired to find a woman named Daphne Monet (Jennifer Beals), who has gone into hiding; as bodies stack up, the "simple" case soon involves the Los Angeles mayoral race, blackmail and some heinous behavior by one of the candidates.

The film is awash in jazz, with source music drawn from classics by Memphis Slim, T-Bone Walker, Duke Ellington, Jimmy Witherspoon and numerous others. They're complemented by Elmer Bernstein's smoky, melancholy score, which hearkens back to his *noir* roots. In classic genre fashion, Easy narrates much of his story: often against Bernstein's mournful, four-note solo piano theme. That cue recurs throughout the film, particularly when Easy recognizes that he's about to do something foolish (or in the aftermath of same). Bernstein augments this "Easy Theme" with a sultry sax melody when our hero first meets Daphne, who—true to the story's title—is wearing a blue dress. She evades Easy more than once; the subsequent cat-and-mouse pursuit takes him to a few after-hours clubs of questionable legality, where onstage combos deliver either smokin' jump jazz, or the song score supplies just enough of Thelonious Monk's "'Round Midnight" to be recognized. Bernstein's quiet keyboard lament never is far away, returning for the final time when Easy and Mouse drive up Route 9 to the isolated cabin where matters will conclude, one way or another.

The soundtrack album is devoted primarily to the diegetic music; Bernstein gets only three tracks. That said, bootlegs of his complete score aren't hard to find, with 29 instrumental tracks filling just shy of a delectable hour. The 2015 Blu-ray includes an isolated score track.

The equally engaging adaptation of *Get Shorty* (1995) is scrumptiously faithful to the tone of Elmore Leonard's mischievous saga of bi-coastal wise guys: those in the Mob, and those in Hollywood. Leonard's arch point is that they're more or less indistinguishable, with betrayal coming naturally to both. John Travolta is the epitome of cool as Miami-based enforcer Chili Palmer; he's sent to Las Vegas to find a chump who has taken advantage of his supposed death, to ignore a debt to trigger-happy mob boss Ray "Bones" Barboni (Dennis

Farina). Vegas associates send Chili to Southern California, to collect an even bigger debt from grade-Z filmmaker Harry Zimm (Gene Hackman), who unwisely courted investment funds from larcenous limo company owner Bo Catlett (Delroy Lindo). Catlett, in turn, is in bed with vicious Colombian drug dealers. Once in Hollywood, Chili decides that the movie biz is far more appealing than shaking down losers, so he craftily rights wrongs, orchestrates nasty outcomes for genuine bad guys, and gets his own parking space on a major studio lot.

The scoring assignment went to saxophonist John Lurie, who with his brother Evan is best known for having co-founded the eclectic rock-hued jazz ensemble The Lounge Lizards. *Get Shorty* is Lurie's first mainstream, high-profile film; his droll, funk-laden music is as much a thematic signature as the cheeky script and Travolta's smirky grin. The capriciously retro, uptempo score is anchored by a quartet—jazz organ, electric guitar, bass and drums—and frequently augmented by trumpet, vibes and Lurie's alto sax.

Interesting, then, that director Barry Sonnenfeld failed to use some of what Lurie wrote. Interesting, as well, that the film's two most prevalent themes come from other parties! The cheeky title track—"Chili Hot," heard over the opening credits—is by the London-based jazz-rap group Us3, founded by Geoff Wilkinson and Jim Hawkins; the cue boasts Gerard Presencer's killer trumpet/flugelhorn work, along with Jim Mullen's equally vibrant electric guitar solo. Sonnenfeld also gets well-placed *oomph* from Booker T.'s iconic "Green Onions," notably when Chili scopes out an airport locker that he knows is being surveilled by DEA agents.

None of this minimizes Lurie's contributions. The film opens with a contemplative, slow-burning cue while Chili chats with a longtime pal; this first glimpse of our star is given additional punch by a smoldering quartet featuring John Medeski (organ), Danny Blume (guitar), Tony Garnier (electric and acoustic bass) and Dougie Bowns (drums). Zimm is introduced with a quirky theme that augments his puffed-up insincerity; Bo enters the story with a lively strut that calls attention to his immaculately dressed *savoir faire* and an underlying aura of menace. Lurie's sax dominates the reprise of Chili's theme, over the end credit crawl; this version expands on the earlier cue with additional touches on piano, baritone and tenor sax, trumpet and percussion.

A careful comparison of the film and its soundtrack album reveals significant differences. Numerous cues employed in the film don't appear on the CD; several of Lurie's CD tracks aren't found in the film. It's clear where certain cues were *intended* to be used; the most obvious example is "Chili and Karen at Sunset," a scene found quite easily within the film … where it's spotted instead to "Tana's Theme," a cue from Henry Mancini's score for 1958's *Touch of Evil* (!). It's a logical choice, since *Touch of Evil* is one of Chili's favorite movies—and because this narrative playfully riffs that *noir* classic's plot—but it obviously wasn't *Lurie's* choice.

The 2017 Epix TV series of the same title is (at best) merely suggested by Leonard's novel; Antonio Sanchez's relentlessly redundant drum and synth score is painful as an isolated listening experience.

There's also plenty of bad behavior in 1995's aptly titled *Bad Company*, a sexually charged modern *noir* scripted by crime/thriller novelist Ross Thomas. Although Carter Burwell's score favors string-laden orchestral cues, traces of jazz creep in around the edges, along with several mainstream jazz vocals and instrumentals heard as diegetic music.

The thoroughly sordid story begins when disgraced ex-CIA agent Nelson Crowe (Laurence Fishburne) is hired to join The Toolshed, a private company that specializes in blackmail, extortion, espionage and other black-ops dirty tricks on behalf of private clients. The company is run by Vic Grimes (Frank Langella) and his second-in-command, Margaret Wells (Ellen Barkin). Crowe is scarcely through the door before beginning a torrid affair with Wells, who suggests they kill Grimes and take over the company. Ah, but neither she nor Grimes knows that Crowe has been planted by the CIA, which wants to take over The Toolshed for the agency's own black-ops purposes. All this duplicity, manipulation, greed and amorality is combustible; of course, it ignites, leaving only a (proportional) innocent to profit from the resulting debris.

Burwell's title theme opens with ominous atmospheric touches and gloomy strings, yielding to driving percussion punctuated by Erik Sanko's sleek bass licks and Charlie Davis' muted trumpet. As the cue gains intensity, Burwell adds an unsettling piano melody. This combination—heavy percussion, muted trumpet, almost subliminal bass and occasional keyboard riffs—reprises during most of the film's tense conversations and encounters. Burwell also employs solo piano cues, most notably during a scorching sexual encounter between Crowe and Wells.

Diegetic cues include Morphine's smokin' hot "You Look Like Rain," anchored by Dana Colley's sensuous sax and Mark Sandman's come-hither vocal; and Noel McCoy's bluesy R&B ballad, "Five Good Reasons." Music supervisor Frank Fitzpatrick contributes several soft jazz ballads, as the solo pianist at a restaurant where Crowe and a Toolshed colleague (Michael Beach) have a productive meeting.

No soundtrack album appeared.

Scheming duplicity also fuels director Phil Joanou's sumptuous 1996 adaptation of James Lee Burke's *Heaven's Prisoners*, second in the author's ongoing series of crime thrillers featuring former New Orleans cop-turned-investigator Dave Robicheaux. Alec Baldwin is precisely cast as Robicheaux, and the film captures the setting's sultry, sweaty humidity in a way that evokes *Body Heat*. As befits New Orleans and its surroundings, the score and many diegetic cues are a tasty aural gumbo: part jazz, part blues and part orchestral shading.

As the story begins, Robicheaux and his wife, Annie (Kelly Lynch), are living quietly in the Louisiana swamplands, renting boats and fishing equipment to locals and tourists. A smuggler's plane crashes in the water; Robicheaux dives after the sinking wreck and saves a little Salvadoran girl, whom they adopt and name Alafair. The sudden arrival of a DEA agent (Vondie Curtis Hall) raises questions, leading Robicheaux to former childhood friend Bubba Rocque (Eric Roberts), now the area's top drug kingpin. Although Bubba seems unconcerned, Robicheaux's interest clearly irritates *somebody*; an assault by a pair of thugs is mere warm-up to tragedy. The aftermath sends the three-years-sober Robicheaux into an alcoholic tailspin, from which he emerges only with the help of former girlfriend Robin (Mary Stuart Masterson). Once he regains equilibrium and sobriety, Robicheaux mounts an investigation, propelled now by naked rage.

Many of British stage and film composer George Fenton's underscore cues are melancholy, string- and woodwind-based laments, as befits the emotional punishment Robicheaux endures, but the two-movement main theme qualifies as jazz. It opens with a pensive solo piano melody, then blossoms into a vibrant, midtempo blend of thumping percussion, bass and guitar, with electric keyboard adding a sinister touch. The film's most ambitious action sequence is a later ferocious rooftop and street chase/fight, which Fenton spots with pulsating drums, angry electric guitar and equally furious reeds. Following a final confrontation with Bubba, the end credits crawl up the screen to a reprise of the main theme; the doleful piano melody offers a suggestion of hope with the rise of strong, confident percussion and jubilant electric keyboard. Robicheaux's future may be uncertain, but at least he *has* one.

The soundtrack album is devoted solely to the blues vocals heard as diegetic cues in the various bars and strip clubs Robicheaux visits. Fortunately, almost all of Fenton's score is available on a 12-track bootleg disc.

Late-period *noir* doesn't get much better than 1996's *Mulholland Falls*, crafted with similar genre love by director Lee Tamahori, scripter Pete Dexter, and cinematographer Haskell Wexler. The smoky Chandler/Hammett vibe derives from a plot set in the 1950s, based loosely on the actual "Hat Squad," a quartet of tough LAPD robbery division detectives who operated in the '50s and early '60s, pretty much calling their own shots. Although easily able to handle the occasional imported Chicago gangster, this film's Hat Squad is challenged by a case that starts with blackmail and pornographic films, and expands to include tight-lipped military officials, the Atomic Energy Commission and the barren, radiation-laden Nevada Test Site. It all starts with Allison Pond (Jennifer Connelly, a 1940s *femme fatale* to the hilt), a promiscuous young woman whose oddly crushed body is found flattened into the dirt of a housing construction site.

The quietly threatening mood is enhanced by an intoxicating, seductively *noir* score from Dave Grusin, who supplements a powerful action theme with an equally memorable "love lost" title theme, along with dozens of foreboding atmospheric cues. Much of the score is quite delicate, limited to quietly haunting piano work. The melancholy primary theme, which debuts over the opening credits, is dominated by a repeating seven-note motif, initially backed by dreamlike strings and soft, mournful horns.

The quick segue to an action cue is startling, when the squad—Max Hoover (Nick Nolte), Elleroy Coolidge (Chazz Palminteri), Eddie Hall (Michael Madsen) and Arthur Relyea (Chris Penn)—deals with some imported mob riff-raff; the catchy, heavily percussive melody bounces between time signatures while delivering an electric jolt of tension. This cue repeats every time Max and his comrades pile into their car, en route to a crime scene or a confrontation with an uncooperative witness. Randy Kerber's sensitive keyboard work is equally striking during the story's quieter interludes, particularly when a falling-down-drunk Max stumbles home, rocked to the core by the state of Allison's body. The inquisitive piano, shaded only by quiet strings, mirrors the curiosity in his wife Katy's (Melanie Griffith) eyes; the flicker of doubt in her gaze is augmented by the cue's unresolved chord.

A taut suspense cue rises as the story nears its conclusion, when Max and Elleroy arrange for a final meeting with the Nevada Test Site's civilian commander, Gen. Thomas Timms (John Malkovich). Grusin inserts military drum rolls, horn fanfares and ominous percussion effects, as Max suddenly realizes precisely how Allison died. Following a melancholy epilogue, the end credits appear against a sad reprise of the main theme, this time with a somber sax taking the melody line against lyrical piano comping.

The score shares space with a couple of swinging diegetic cues: Aaron Neville's bluesy reading of "Harbor Lights," heard in a nightclub; and Count Basie's "Who Me," playing as some outdoor party music.

The initial soundtrack album was eclipsed by an expanded 2011 release that features Grusin's entire score.

Director Robert Altman eschews his signature overlapping dialogue for overlapping *music* in 1996's *Kansas City*, a gorgeously mounted crime drama set in 1934, on the eve of an important political election. The narrative is rather threadbare, and the cast is wildly uneven—Jennifer Jason Leigh overacts atrociously—but the jazz is sublime, and the music is ubiquitous. Altman interrupts the plot each time the house band at the Hey-Hey Club, enjoying an all-night jam session, launches into a new tune. After anywhere from a few seconds to several minutes, each of these diegetic cues becomes the nondiegetic backdrop for the next chunk of story arc. This ensemble is salted with all manner of established and rising jazz heavyweights, including Joshua Redman and James Carter (tenor sax); Cyrus Chestnut and Geri Allen (piano); Ron Carter and Christian McBride (bass); and Russell Malone (guitar).

"People say if you use jazz, the movie has to be about a jazz subject," Altman explained, when his film premiered at the Cannes Film Festival. "That doesn't work for me, because I don't want to make a film about [jazz] players. Then it occurred to me that if I'm going to deal with jazz, that should be the structure of the whole movie."[4]

The improbable plot begins when petty thief Johnny O'Hara (Dermot Mulroney) unwisely robs a guest of ruthless gangster Seldom Seen (Harry Belafonte), who runs the Hey-Hey Club. Johnny's desperate wife, Blondie (Leigh), knowing that he's certain to be murdered as an object lesson, kidnaps the wife of a local politician, believing that he has the connections to intervene. The abducted woman, Carolyn (Miranda Richardson), proves an almost useless handful, thanks to her addiction to laudanum. The frequent cutaways to the Hey-Hey musicians prove far more captivating than the tediously talky script's slow build to its inescapable conclusion.

"I decided to make a song out of the story of the two women," Altman continued. "As it developed, the whole movie is jazz. Harry Belafonte is like a brass instrument—when it's his turn to solo, he does long monologues and riffs—and the discussions of the two women are like reed instruments, maybe saxophones, having duets."[5]

The music is sensational, with the ensemble covering a wealth of period classics. The plot and primary characters are introduced to Lester Young's "Tickle Toe," Bernie and Buster Moten's "Moten Swing" and the MacDonald/Hanley classic, "(Back Home Again in) Indiana." "I Surrender Dear" is an ironic counterpoint to Blondie's futile attempt to plead her case before Seldom Seen; Count Basie's "I Left My Baby" proves equally sardonic, once we learn more about Blondie's background. A subplot involving voting fraud climaxes against "Piano Boogie," a frisky keyboard duet between Chestnut and Allen.

Two musical sequences are stunners, starting with "Yeah, Man," dominated by a lengthy sax duel between Redman and Craig Handy; Altman holds on this scorching tune for several minutes, cutting away only briefly as Seldom's men viciously deal with a traitor in their ranks. After the story reaches its unhappy climax, the end credits roll up the screen while Carter and McBride trade bass licks on a solemn reading of Ellington's "Solitude," while Don Byron lends a plaintive touch on clarinet.

The film was a critical and box office flop, but its music was too good to ignore; the initial soundtrack album—*Kansas City: Original Motion Picture Soundtrack*—was followed quickly by *KC After Dark: More Music from Kansas City*.

Bad gals carve out a slice of the action in *Bound*, a 1996 neo-*noir* that offers just enough jazz to warrant acknowledgment. Although most of Don Davis' music is atmospheric—dissonant brass and strings, aggressive drum loops and Gloria Cheng's nervous, lower-end piano chords—the opening act showcases a few slinky cues dominated by Chuck Berghofer's acoustic double bass. It's a shame, given the story's erotic content, that Davis didn't deliver more in that vein.

Ex-con Corky (Gina Gershon), newly hired as an apartment maintenance employee, becomes intrigued by the couple living in the unit adjoining the one she's renovating. Caesar (Joe Pantoliano) is a midlevel Mafioso; his girlfriend Violet (Jennifer Tilly) flirts with Corky when he isn't around. The two women begin an ill-advised affair that becomes even more dangerous when Violet proposes they steal the $2 million that Caesar is holding until a Mafia boss collects it. Although not entirely trusting her new lover, Corky concocts a clever plan that relies on psychology and Caesar's hair-trigger temper. But he doesn't react as anticipated, and the situation quickly spirals out of control when Corky's involvement is exposed.

She initially encounters the couple in the building's elevator; her eyes lock on Violet while Berghofer delivers a brief but unmistakably carnal solo bass cue. A bit later, as Corky struggles with a messy plumbing chore, Violet pops in for a formal hello. This visit takes place against a smoky mambo cue heard as diegetic music from Corky's portable radio, which mirrors the flirtatious verbal dance between the two women. Berghofer's sly, sensual bass dominates their next meeting, which blossoms into a smoking-hot sexual encounter. This entire sequence is backed by a cool, languid jazz cue: bass, drums and piano, against enticing strings.

Alas, that's it; the rest—the bulk—of Davis' music doesn't go anywhere near jazz. His score is available only on a promotional CD that wasn't released commercially.

For authentic, hard-edged *noir*, it's difficult to beat 1997's handling of *L.A. Confidential*, set in 1953 Los Angeles and adapted from James Ellroy's novel. The film earned an impressive nine Oscar nominations, including one for Jerry Goldsmith's richly atmospheric score, but—sadly—took home only two (due to being up against *Titanic*.)

The complex plot follows a trio of LAPD officers: plainclothes cop Wendell "Bud" White (Russell Crowe), with a pronounced distaste for men who beat up on women; narcotics detective Jack Vincennes (Kevin Spacey), a "Hollywood cop" who moonlights as a technical advisor on the hit TV series *Badge of Honor*; and the young but highly ambitious Edmund "Ed" Exley (Guy Pearce). They report to Capt. Dudley Smith (James Cromwell), who manages a squad that ranges from earnest do-gooders to racist, sadistic thugs. The story initially focuses on a multiple homicide at a coffee shop dubbed The Nite Owl; the victims include a young woman Bud briefly glimpsed in the company of smarmy Pierce Morehouse Patchett (David Strathairn). Over time, Ed deduces that Patchett and his stable of escorts—high-class prostitutes surgically altered to resemble film starlets—are connected to lingering details concerning the Nite Owl slaughter. Ed piques Jack's curiosity, and the two poke around the edges of what emerges as a scheme—orchestrated from *within* the police department—to take over gangster Mickey Cohen's heroin trade.

The soundtrack is a blend of Goldsmith's compositions and carefully selected period tunes; the non-diegetic score isn't even heard for the first 15 minutes. Goldsmith's first cue—unsettling percussion and crashing drums, building to sustained horn blasts—erupts when Ed tries to stop a gaggle of drunk and enraged cops from beating up half a dozen Mexican men. The film's primary theme—which gets its emotional impact from a mournful trumpet solo—will be familiar to longtime movie fans: The opening six-note motif is "lifted" from the lonely French horn that plays the same notes at the beginning of Leonard Bernstein's score for *On the Waterfront*. Following the Nite Owl massacre, Goldsmith supplies action jazz when clues lead to a drug den and shoot-out. The violence having ceased for the moment, the next several sequences are spotted by diegetic tunes: notably lively instrumentals by Chet Baker and the Gerry Mulligan Quartet.

The suspenseful climax, an ambush at a dilapidated motel, finds Ed and Bud confronted by overwhelming odds; the subsequent shootout is spotted with angry drums, throbbing percussion and fidgety, low-end piano. In the aftermath, the orchestra delivers an uptempo reprise of the main theme, the trumpet now sounding relieved and triumphant.

Two soundtrack albums were produced. The first is dominated by period vocals and instrumentals, along with two of Goldsmith's score cues: the primary theme and his terrific swinger for the *Badge of Honor* TV show (lamentably brief, at only 22 seconds). The second album, devoted to Goldsmith's score, is nonetheless disappointing. The reorchestrated tracks represent barely half of his 56 minutes of music; they're also seriously out of order, and in some cases are quite different from what's heard in the film. Fortunately, Goldsmith's full score is isolated on the film's 2008 Blu-ray release.

Book-to-film crime dramas definitely were on a roll. The thoroughly engaging adaptation of John Grisham's *The Rainmaker* (1997) is highlighted further by Elmer Bernstein's gently swinging score. The story follows fresh-faced Memphis attorney Rudy Baylor (Matt Damon) as he battles a corporate law firm hired to defend an insurance company—led by legal shark Leo F. Drummond (Jon Voight)—that refused to honor a legitimate claim that would have saved a low-income Tennessee couple's ailing son. Along the way, Rudy also becomes aware of a battered young wife (Claire Danes) who won't press charges against the husband who, if the pattern isn't broken, almost certainly will kill her. Although we never forget the seriousness of these events, the film's tone remains light, even occasionally amusing; the same is true of Bernstein's score. The film opens with a rich, Deep-Southern-fried main theme—Bernstein titled it "Sharks," for obvious reasons—that evokes his iconic theme from 1962's *Walk on the Wild Side*. The waltz-time "melody" is powered by sassy percussion and gut-busting Hammond B3 solos.

"I have to credit [director Francis Ford Coppola] with the bluesy 6/8 idea in a roundabout way," Bernstein recalled, a few years later. "When I first got on *The Rainmaker*, Francis wasn't going to have a score as we know a score to be. At first, he was going to go the B.B. King route—in other words, real Memphis stuff with some very minor connective things in scoring. But as he began to develop the film, he began to feel that he needed to depend more on score. So it was my decision to use the Hammond B3 organ, but it came out of his idea of Memphis ambiance. Out of that ambiance, I retained the three instruments you hear a great deal of: the Hammond B3, the muted trumpet, and the guitar."[6]

Sweet guitar dominates "Kelly," a cue devoted to Danes' character: a lovely lament that touches our heart each time we see her. Muted trumpet is equally poignant during a cue heard when Rudy tells his primary client about Drummond's insultingly lowball, pretrial "go away" offer.

The title theme and character cues aside, much of Bernstein's score is orchestral mood music, employed as short bumpers that bridge key events from one scene to the next. As a result, most of the cuts on the soundtrack album are minisuites built from several such cues strung together: sometimes smoothly, sometimes a bit clumsily. The album concludes with the swinging, impudent arrangement of "Sharks" heard during the end credits.

* * *

Secret agent spoofs had been absent from the big screen for more than a generation, when 1997's cheeky *Austin Powers: International Man of Mystery* burst onto the scene. Mike Myers' script cleverly lampoons all sorts of genre clichés, from the nuclear finale in *Dr. No*, to the distinctive sound made by the hot line phone in *Our Man Flint*. In keeping with this game plan, George S. Clinton's energetic score begs, borrows and steals melodic riffs from

John Barry's jazziest Bond themes, along with nods toward Burt Bacharach, Henry Mancini and Lalo Schifrin. That said, Clinton wasn't responsible for the title theme that plays over the flamboyantly colorful opening credits—the moddest of all possible street dances, set in 1967 London—which is choreographed to Quincy Jones' "Soul Bossa Nova," taken from his 1962 album, *Big Band Bossa Nova*. The tune's original title has almost been lost; in our post–Myers world, it's now known as the "Austin Powers Theme."

"I wrote that in 1962, in 20 minutes, for a big band bossa nova album right after we left Brazil with Dizzy Gillespie, when bossa nova first started," Jones recalled, years later. "And it won't go away. Mike Myers used it for the themes of the Austin Powers films. It's still here."[7]

The film's madcap premise takes off when the villainous Dr. Evil (also played by Myers), constantly thwarted by Austin Powers in the 1960s, puts himself into cryogenic suspended animation and wakens 30 years later, prepared to resume his nefarious deeds in 1997. Ah, but Austin does the same thing; teamed with the delectable Vanessa Kensington (Elizabeth Hurley), the dentally challenged hero scrambles to prevent Dr. Evil from detonating a nuclear warhead miles beneath the Earth's surface.

Clinton delivers plenty of jazzy cues, many employed as bumpers and stingers to bridge action scenes. "What I try to do is come up with the score that I think the character imagines for himself," Clinton explained. "Even though to us the characters are silly and funny, they don't know that. They think they're really hip or evil, in the case of Dr. Evil."[8]

Sultry bass, vibes and trumpet are heard when Austin works his erotic mojo on the pulchritudinous Alotta Fagina (Fabiana Udenio); a variation of this theme follows Austin's hazardous exploration of a Las Vegas casino men's room. Dr. Evil's nasty nuclear weapon is readied to a percussive cue that blends sinister horns with guitar licks that echo Vic Flick's work on "The James Bond Theme"; the seductively dangerous "fembots"—with bullet-shooting bras stolen shamelessly from Ursula Andress' similarly lethal bikini top, in 1965's *The 10th Victim*—are unveiled to their own horn- and organ-powered swinger.

Clinton's entire score is a lot of fun, for the way it evokes the 1960s spy vibe while losing none of its own jazzy, pop-oriented sizzle. Sadly, he's limited to a meager five-minute "Shagadelic Austin Powers Score Medley" on the soundtrack album; the other 14 tracks feature the many pop songs sprinkled throughout the film. Three years passed before RCA issued an album that includes highlights from both this film and its 1999 follow-up, *The Spy Who Shagged Me*. (Meanwhile, enterprising Internet sleuths could find copies of the promo CD that features Clinton's entire score for the first film.)

The Cincinnati Kid established the mold for all future poker films, with its solid blend of card action and character drama; most successors couldn't come close to that winning hand, but 1998's *Rounders* is an exception. Matt Damon stars as Mike McDermott, a "reformed" young gambler who tries to make a go of law school, until getting sucked back into poker action by manipulative childhood friend Lester "Worm" Murphy (Edward Norton). The film opens and closes with high-stakes Texas hold 'em matches between Mike and "Teddy KGB" (John Malkovich), a Russian mobster who runs an illegal underground poker room.

Jazz drummer-turned-film composer Christopher Young's rich swing score opens with a smoky main theme—percussion and bass licks laying a slow 4/4 beat for some bluesy keyboard riffs—while Mike assembles a massive cash stake to fund an all-in challenge against Teddy KGB. The match begins against a soft, disarmingly upbeat swinger that reflects Mike's cheeky optimism: a buoyant musical mood shattered all too quickly when he loses everything. Flash-forward nine months, at which point Mike is making ends meet by driving a delivery truck, while attending law school. Temptation returns with the arrival of Worm, a conniving hustler who never hesitates to cheat; he's introduced against a saucy, midtempo blast of naughty sax and backing trumpet pops. Mike's subsequent downward spiral is signaled by a softly ominous six-note piano motif: a doleful cue that accompanies every fresh setback. Even sadder is the quiet piano melody heard each time Mike's regression disappoints longtime girlfriend and fellow law student Jo (Gretchen Mol).

But the mood isn't relentlessly dour. Young contributes numerous buoyant cues during some of Mike's more successful sessions, such as the groovy 4/4 burst of percussion, sax and electronic keyboard when he and Worm fleece a group of wealthy college guys. A similarly uptempo funk cue—with a mean sax solo—backs an Atlantic City montage; jaunty percussion, sax and horns accompany another montage, when Mike rushes from one game to another, without sleep, while trying to raise $15,000 in five days.

The soundtrack album resequenced the music to alternate melancholy "atmosphere" cues with the faster-paced swingers.

The sleek 1998 adaptation of Elmore Leonard's *Out of Sight* was a slow starter, but it now enjoys a well-deserved reputation as a solid (albeit impish) crime thriller. The screenplay's twisty, nonlinear structure is laden with snarky one-liners, and the erotic chemistry shared by George Clooney and Jennifer Lopez is incandescent. He's career bank robber Jack Foley, recently broken out of prison; she's Miami-based U.S. Deputy Marshal Karen Sisco, determined to capture the guy, but also grudgingly captivated by his *savoir-faire*. The cherry on top is the sassy, jazz/funk score by Belfast-born DJ-turned-composer/musician David Holmes. The often throbbing underscore sounds like a throwback to 1970s-style action flick riffs, and with good reason; that was director Steven Soderbergh's mandate.

"I wanted a combination of Lalo Schifrin's *Dirty Harry* and the first year of *The Rockford Files*," Soderbergh explained, "and David just totally got it."[9]

Holmes' soundtrack blends carefully chosen jazz and pop tunes—Dean Martin, the Isley Brothers, Willie Bobo, Mongo Santamaria and Walter Wanderly's delectable cover of "One Note Samba"—with his own percussion-heavy electronica jazz riffs. They invariably make a listener smile: both as they're employed within the film, and also as an isolated listening experience. Some tracks are incredibly sexy, such as a steamy melody dubbed "Tub Scene," which accompanies a particularly close encounter between Clooney and Lopez. The score's get-down highlight, however, is the impertinent, beat-heavy "Rip Rip," which signals the story's explosive, violence-laden climax.

"I was drawing on influences of things that I was listening to when I was 15," Holmes admitted, "as a young mod who was just obsessed with rhythm & blues, and soul."[10]

The soundtrack album would be a wonderful make-out backdrop, if its 15 tracks weren't laden with so many intrusive dialogue clips. Determined fans are advised to seek Holmes' dialogue-free promo score, which floats around the Internet (although it lacks the pop/jazz vocals).

Out of Sight may have disappointed at the box office, but the next Holmes and Soderbergh pairing would suffer no such fate (about which, more later).

Jackie Chan's star also was on the rise. After his first attempts to make American action films failed in the mid–1980s, he got another chance when 1995's *Hung fan kui* (*Rumble in the Bronx*) became a surprise hit in the States. Interest ignited in his older Hong Kong films; this soon led to 1998's *Rush Hour*, which made him a bona fide American movie star. The light-hearted cop thriller teamed him with rapidly rising comic actor Chris Tucker; the resulting chemistry—Chan's cherubic, jaw-dropping athletic grace, and Tucker's motor-mouthed impudence—proved irresistible. The icing on the cake was director Brett Ratner's determination to enhance the action with the sort of film music that excited his younger self. "When I was a little kid, I saw *Enter the Dragon*," he recalled. "I would play it over and over, and the music would just amaze me. [Now it's] my favorite score of all time."[11]

Seeing no reason to accept a substitute, Ratner secured Lalo Schifrin.

The story finds Hong Kong police detective Lee (Chan) waging an ongoing war against a ruthless, never-seen crime lord known only as Juntao; several clashes have successfully retrieved priceless Chinese cultural treasures, but Juntao and his lieutenant, Sang (Ken Leung), always manage to escape. When Lee's good friend Solon Han (Tzi Ma) accepts a diplomatic post in Los Angeles, Juntao follows and—by way of revenge—kidnaps Han's adolescent daughter, demanding $50 million for her return. Han summons Lee to assist in the subsequent investigation; the FBI agents in charge, not wanting a "foreigner" to gum up their case, foist him off on disgraced, self-centered and hot-headed LAPD detective James Carter (Tucker). It's an insulting baby-sitting assignment designed to keep both men out of the way, but Lee and Carter—after overcoming mutual antipathy—stumble their way into saving the day.

Schifrin's title theme is a strong echo of the jazzy, hard-charging Western and Eastern sounds he blended so well for *Enter the Dragon*. It opens with a pulsating 4/4 drum ostinato—classic American urban funk—that expands with guitar, brass, Asian percussion and vibrant tam-tam explosions. "It sounds Chinese, but that's a mirage," Schifrin pointed out. "It's in the notes."[12]

The hypnotic melody is carried by horns and xylophone, with exotic touches supplied not by kotos and/or wooden flutes, but by cimbalom, Hawaiian Dobro guitars, banjos (!) and pitch-skewing strings. It's a terrific action cue in the classic Schifrin mold, and it entered his head in, well, a rush: "I went to the cutting room and [Brett] showed me a little bit, because they had a first assemblage. And that was when it came."[13] This theme reprises in numerous arrangements, most notably as a dynamic action cue when Lee and Carter face numerous thugs in Juntao's deceptively ordinary Chinese restaurant headquarters.

The film is laden with additional action cues: unison brass that climbs the scale against pounding rhythm, during an early failed bust that typifies Carter's reckless behavior; frantic, fast-paced brass pops, sizzling strings and pounding percussion, when Lee chases Sang into a darkened alley and up the side of a deserted building; and the sinister strings, woodwinds and brass that build to screaming horns against a drum-fueled ostinato, during the chaotic climax at a Chinese art exhibition.

Schifrin's score shares screen time with rap, R&B and gangsta vocals. As a result, the film generated two albums: *Def Jam's Rush Hour Soundtrack* and a 23-track instrumental album—*Rush Hour Film Score*—on Schifrin's Aleph label.

The popular film generated two sequels, but—in terms of jazz—*Rush Hour 2* (2001) and *Rush Hour 3* (2007) represent diminishing returns. Aside from a few big band swing covers of American songbook melodies heard as diegetic music during the former's Las Vegas sequence, Schifrin's scores are undistinguished synth and symphonic shading. Even the carryover title theme loses it zip by the final entry.

Speaking of sequels, 1999's *Austin Powers: The Spy Who Shagged Me* is even crazier—and more vulgar—than its predecessor, and composer George S. Clinton once again cheekily embezzles John Barry's bombastic Bond touches, alongside equally liberal nods toward other spy jazz stalwarts. This time out, the despicable Dr. Evil travels *back* in time, to 1969—two years into Austin's cryogenic suspended animation—to steal the agent's beloved sexual mojo. This dire theft is orchestrated by a repulsively obese Scottish villain dubbed Fat Bastard (also Mike Myers), leaving Dr. Evil to menace this three-decades-back Earth with a Moon-based super-laser. The now mojo-less Austin returns to 1969 as well, hooks up with promiscuous CIA agent Felicity Shagwell (Heather Graham), and does his best to terminate this plot before Dr. Evil destroys Washington, D.C.

Quincy Jones' "Soul Bossa Nova" once again fuels a hilarious title credits sequence. This time, though, Clinton had to write a fresh arrangement, so the orchestration would match the chaotic onscreen action: most prominently with rhythmic thumps perfectly timed to the climactic, Esther Williams–style swimming pool dance.

"I re-recorded 'Soul Bossa Nova' because there was no real ending on it, and [the filmmakers] wanted certain things to happen with the choreography," Clinton explained. "So the challenge was to take that beat and record it in a retro way, and have it sound as if Quincy had done a version of it with strings at the end, so it gets real big. I guess the highest praise was that when one of Quincy's people heard it, he said, 'Gee, I didn't know Quincy had done a different arrangement.'"[14]

The plot's space-oriented elements and frequent nods to *You Only Live Twice* also encouraged Clinton to reference Barry's score from that fifth Bond outing, most notably the title theme and ominous, march-oriented "Capsule in Space." Romantic wisps of the former are heard when a white-bikinied Felicity emerges from the ocean, *à la* Ursula Andress, and steps majestically onto the beach of Dr. Evil's volcanic lair; strong echoes of the latter add menace to various space activities, particularly during a precredits riff on that very sequence from *You Only Live Twice*.

Other musical highlights include a saucy swinger dominated by cheeky sax, when Austin's missing mojo results in a failed shag with Ivana Humpalot (Kristen Johnston); a swooningly sexy bossa nova ballad, the melody traded between sax, soft horns and electric keyboard, which backs Felicity's similarly frustrated effort to get Austin into bed; a mischievously rhythmic, *Pink Panther*-esque flute and muted trumpet anthem heard when Dr. Evil attempts to demonstrate a model of his lethal laser; and a hilarious take on the seductive orchestral cue Michel Legrand wrote for the infamous chess game in *The Thomas Crown Affair*. Clinton also supplies all manner of Barry-esque brass stingers and orchestral fanfares, which serve as rim shots for the film's endless stream of bad jokes and groaning puns.

Clinton's score was completely ignored on the initial soundtrack album, which focuses solely on the film's many pop tunes. He fares only slightly better on the supplementary album, *Austin Powers: The Spy Who Shagged Me (More Music from the Motion Picture)*, which includes a single track of his underscore cues: "The Austin Powers Shagaphonic Medley." Happily, Clinton's instrumental cues are the sole focus of a 2000 album that includes highlights from both *Austin Powers: International Man of Mystery* (seven tracks) and this sequel (10 tracks).

Myers, Myers, Myers and Clinton would return one more time (about which, more later).

From the silly, to the sinister: Patricia Highsmith's crafty sociopath debuted in her 1955 thriller, *The Talented Mr. Ripley*, but its ground-breaking depiction of a "likable" serial killer made it much too controversial for an immediate Hollywood adaptation. That fell to French director René Clément, and 1960's *Plein soleil* (*Purple Noon*) made a star of Alain Delon. Four decades passed before British writer/director Anthony Minghella delivered an updated version, with 1999's *The Talented Mr. Ripley*.

The provocatively perverse story begins when Tom (Matt Damon), struggling to make ends meet in 1950s New York City, trades on a chance misunderstanding to befriend wealthy shipbuilder Herbert Greenleaf (James Rebhorn). Led to believe that Tom attended Princeton with his son, Greenleaf hires him to travel to the Italian coastal village of Mongibello, where Dickie (Jude Law) and his fiancée Marge (Gwyneth Paltrow) are enjoying a life of hedonistic leisure. The goal: to persuade Dickie to return home, to assume his place in the family business. But after breezily insinuating himself into Dickie's circle, Tom grows too fond of this luxurious lifestyle. When his leech-like clinging and chameleon-like affectations prompt Dickie to end this "friendship," Tom kills him and—to every degree possible—assumes his life. He remains "sympathetic Tom" to the increasingly distraught Marge, but—elsewhere in Rome—he establishes an identity as Dickie, living well off the Greenleaf bank drafts he easily forges. This web of deceit grows ever more complicated as Ripley juggles these two identities in the presence of Marge's suspicious friend Freddie (Philip Seymour Hoffman), who knows him as Tom; and American socialite Meredith (Cate Blanchett), who knows him as Dickie.

Gabriel Yared's moody, Academy Award-nominated score is entirely orchestral and classical, although a few cues—sinister bass, vibes and solo clarinet—wander in the direction of jazz, because Dickie is introduced as a rabid jazz fan. Before his journey, Tom therefore gives himself a crash course; diegetic tunes—played on a phonograph—include Charlie Parker's "Ko-Ko," Chet Baker's "My Funny Valentine" and Sonny Rollins' "Tenor Madness." Once in Italy, jazz becomes ubiquitous. Dickie takes Tom to a Naples club, where the "Hot Jazz Vesuvio" performed by the Guy Barker International Quintet includes high-octane performances of Miles Davis' "Four" and the Salerno/Carosone anthem "Tu Vuo Fa L'Americano." This swinging combo surfaces again, when Dickie and Tom later travel to San Remo for its jazz festival; the performances include a reprise of "Four" and snatches of Rollins' "Pent-Up House" and Bobby Timmons' "Moanin.'" Once Dickie is dispatched, the jazz touches perish with him; Tom's actual taste is confined to solo classical piano.

The soundtrack album blends Yared's underscore cues with a dozen of the diegetic jazz tracks.

Tom Ripley would have been right at home with Donald E. Westlake's Parker, and few theatrical features have navigated a path as tortured as that endured by director/scripter Brian Helgeland's 1999 handling of *Payback*, a remake of 1967's *Point Blank*. He delivered a film as bleak, grimly amoral and *noir*-drenched as Westlake's novel: much to the displeasure of Paramount, which worried that this approach might damage the heroic image that was serving star Mel Gibson so well, at that point in his career. Helgeland was asked to "soften" the tone; he refused and was fired. Some sources claim that control of the final cut landed in the hands of production designer John Myhre (a questionable assertion, since Richard Hoover is the credited production designer on *Payback*). Regardless of who wielded the hatchet, Helgeland's film suffered the indignity of considerable reshot footage—including an entirely different third act—along with a new villain (the hastily cast Kris Kristofferson), a softer tone, an inappropriately upbeat ending, and superfluous voice-over narration by Gibson.[15]

We know all this because Helgeland got lucky: Several years later, Gibson and Paramount gave their blessing to a home-video release of the director's original cut. 2007's *Payback: Straight Up* represents Helgeland's best effort to preserve his vision: a restoration that included the hiring of an entirely new soundtrack composer. Chris Boardman's score for the theatrical release suits that version's action-oriented tone, whereas Scott Stambler's replacement score is as edgy and mordant as Helgeland's interpretation of Gibson's relentless killer.

Career criminal Porter (Gibson) pulls off a successful heist, but is double-crossed by his accomplice, Val Resnick (Gregg Henry). Worse yet, Porter is shot and left for dead by his own wife, Lynn (Deborah Kara Unger), who has fallen under Val's influence. He uses the stolen loot to reinstate himself with the Mafia-esque "Outfit" that controls organized crime throughout the United States; Lynn, unable to live with her betrayal, sinks into a heroin haze. Ah, but Porter survives, reappearing months later to confront Val and retrieve his share—$70,000—of the original haul. He works his way up the Outfit's chain of command, patiently bashing, shooting or killing each individual who refuses to authorize or fulfill this "reasonable request."

Boardman opens the theatrical release with an action-oriented title theme—propulsive percussion, John Goux's cool guitar licks and plenty of horns—which debuts over a montage that shows Porter scamming his way into a comfortable pile of walking-around cash. Boardman establishes a vicarious mood with subsequent cues: groovy organ, rhythm guitar and bluesy percussion, to highlight the audacious original heist (depicted during a flashback); and an impudent, trumpet- and organ-laden strut when it appears as though an Asian gang is about to get the best of Porter. Saucy, stripper-esque keyboards and *wah-wah* horns introduce Pearl (Lucy Liu), a fetish dominatrix who shares a bed with the equally sadomasochistic Val. Bits of Helgeland's darker moments survive in this cut, and Boardman responds in kind: most notably with the melancholy flute ballad that accompanies Porter's reunion with Lynn.

The mostly viewer-friendly tone is augmented by breezy lounge tunes such as "Ain't That a Kick in the Head," "You're Nobody 'Til Somebody Loves You" (both by Dean Martin), "If I Had My Life to Live Over" (Lou Rawls) and B.B. King's gut-bucket classic, "The Thrill Is Gone."

Helgeland's resurrected cut is meaner and leaner, running 10 fewer minutes. The entire Kristofferson third act is excised in favor of a grim finale that leaves Porter's fate ambiguous; other tucks and tweaks better emphasize his cold brutality. The eye-opening stunner is the viciousness of Porter's assault on Lynn, when he tracks her down. (Given the depth of her betrayal, his ferocity certainly isn't out of character.) Helgeland also dumped all but one of the vocals: Martin's "Ain't That a Kick in the Head," briefly heard on a radio.

Helgeland couldn't make Boardman's cues "fit" this fresh edit, so the director turned to music editor Scott Stambler, also known for creating work-print temp scores.

"This film required a lot of dark thinking, and that's where I went," Stambler recalled. "I had a five-minute main title to write, and I'd never written a main title before. It's a *huge* blank page, and I was terrified. I started writing speculative pieces, and [Brian] was liking what I played, but I could tell nothing was working for him. And he said, 'Why don't you stop writing '70s cues, and just write for the characters in the movie. And that's when everything started to click.'"[16]

Stambler's jazz/funk score offers plenty of cool bass; a bank of trumpets, trombones and saxes; and well-placed muted trumpet licks. The title credits montage is backed by a heavy 4/4 beat—purposeful, like Porter—along with a vibrant trumpet line and some shrill sax; the effect is quite unsettling. Action scenes unfold against hypnotic funk, insistent percussion and trumpet/sax fanfares that maintain this disorienting atmosphere. Suspenseful percussion and low-end piano riffs herald Porter's methodical elimination of the opposition during the blood-soaked climax; an implacable drumbeat signals impending doom when he's shredded by numerous bullets, and stumbles away, barely conscious. The title theme reprises during the subsequent end credits: cool piano runs backed by heavy percussion, strings and synth effects. The camera pulls back against foreboding trumpet bleats and jarring sax, and we're left to wonder: Do they herald Porter's departure from the moral realm?

Ironically, Stambler's softer cues are more poignant than Boardman's, most notably the sad solo guitar that accompanies Porter's distress over Lynn's heroin habit (*after* he beats her almost senseless).

The theatrical release's soundtrack album is dominated by the pop tunes, with only four cuts giving a sense of Boardman's instrumental score; he fares better on the 33-minute promo album devoted entirely to his contribution. Stambler's score for the resurrected version hasn't been released.

Elsewhere in the World…

The premise behind *F/X* and its sequel was too good to abandon, and Canada's *F/X: The Series* delivered similarly clever scripts for a respectable two-season run that aired on syndicated stations from late summer 1996 through the spring of 1998. Cameron Daddo and Kevin Dobson stepped smoothly into the roles of Rollie and NYPD Detective Leo McCarthy, replacing the big screen's Bryan Brown and Brian Dennehy.

The scoring assignment was offered to Christopher Beck, then an up-and-coming Canadian composer who accepted with grateful enthusiasm. "I'm pretty sure they needed to hire a Canadian composer," he recalled, "and that helped me get the gig. I learned *so* much. That was my first series gig, so you always remember your first one fondly."[17]

Beck's main theme, slickly synchronized to a stylish title credits sequence, opens with several bars of hip-swaying ostinato, until a sleek solo trumpet introduces the sassy melody against backing horns. The trumpet wanders cheekily through improvisational riffs that occasionally dip back to the core motif, against a montage of blue-hued clips that show Rollie and his team setting up some sort of elaborate special effects "gag," intercut against shots of a big-city skyline. Beck also favors solo trumpet in many of his episode underscores, again generally backed by a finger-snapping rhythm section, for mild action scenes such as surveillance work and clandestine car pursuits. The ambiance isn't solely jazz; Beck demonstrates an equal flair for orchestral and synth-laden suspense cues.

The show underwent a significant change when it returned for a second season; Dobson's Leo was replaced by Jacqueline Torres' Detective Mira Sanchez. The new credits sequence is more action-oriented, and Beck supplies an appropriately exhilarating arrangement of his main theme. Unfortunately, it's more dissonantly chaotic, with the trumpet melody all but buried beneath synth and obnoxious sound effects.

Although both big-screen films earned soundtrack albums, Beck wasn't as fortunate.

13

Heartbroken: 2000–03

As the new century dawned, jazz scores hadn't merely become an endangered species; context also shifted. Most now were reserved for period productions, or stories intended to evoke a sense of nostalgia for times gone by, or as a statement about characters who *live* in the past. Only rarely—as with 2000s update of *Shaft*, and 2003's *Out of Time*—did a jazz score propel a contemporary big-screen thriller.

The *process* also underwent an unfortunate shift.

"Motion picture scores are much more confined now," Elmer Bernstein reflected, looking back over his career. "They're confined by being full of popular songs. And they're confined by the fact that they put a temporary score in the film long before the composer ever gets there, to which the director becomes accustomed. So creativity, in today's world, is at a very low ebb; the composer doesn't have that blank canvas on which to paint. He's not allowed to. It's sad."[1]

Television networks, in turn, had all but abandoned title credits sequences and memorable title themes.

The Small Screen

Alongside HBO's *Philip Marlowe, Private Eye*, A&E's *A Nero Wolfe Mystery* is one of the most period-authentic adaptations of an established literary detective series ever presented on television. Everything is note-perfect to Wolfe's vaguely 1940s-'50s New York setting: the cars, clothes and clipped cadence with which the actors speak their slang-laden lines; the rigorously faithful screenplay adaptations; the opulent production design; and Michael Small's divine big band jazz score. The series pilot film, *The Golden Spiders*, aired March 5, 2000; it led to a 20-episode run through the summer of 2002.

Maury Chaykin is the pluperfect Wolfe—an irascible, short-tempered and shrewdly analytical armchair detective—and Timothy Hutton is equally fine as his wise-cracking leg man, Archie Goodwin. Their associates include Manhattan Homicide Bureau Inspector Cramer (Bill Smitrovich) and Sgt. Purley Stebbins (R.D. Reid); Wolfe's gourmet chef, Fritz Brenner (Colin Fox); and a trio of freelance investigators (Saul Panzer, Fred Durkin and Orrie Cather). One of the show's charming touches is the use of a dozen repertory players—including Ron Rifkin, Debra Monk, George Plimpton and Kari Matchett—in different non-recurring roles, from episode to episode.

The period authenticity extends to Small's score, beginning with a main theme—cheekily titled "Boss Boogie"—that opens with a mischievous clarinet line against a drum and cymbal ostinato, adds an impudent muted trumpet against staccato fanfares, and then introduces the 3-4-3-5 melody via sparkling unison brass. The percussion kicks into a mode that evokes the classic drum solo from "Swing Swing Swing," while various horns trade licks until the entire band brings the tune to a climax. Small's underscore cues maintain a similar swing ambiance, usually heard during Archie's surveillance or pursuit assignments "out in the world."

The title sequence always opens with an Art Deco rendering of the Queensboro Bridge, then shifts to a different style of images, depending on the nature of the episode. Small correspondingly delivers suitably appropriate opening themes: slow, dance-band swing ("Eeny Meeny Murder Moe"); a midtempo, tango-esque strut ("Door to Death"); a cheeky riff on spy jazz ("Death of a Doxy," the sole episode set in the mid–1960s); old-time "moldy fig" jazz ("Prisoner's Base"); and a cheeky flamenco swinger ("Murder Is Corny"). Small's jazz underscore cues jostle for space with diegetic classical pieces heard on radios and record players, since Wolfe's taste runs toward Shostakovich, Vivaldi, Mendelssohn and their brethren. Diegetic jazz cues also pop up: "In the Swing," "Zoot Suit Blues," "King Swing," "Clarinet Caprice" and many others.

Sadly, none of Small's work ever made it to a soundtrack album, although "Boss Boogie" is fairly easy to find via the Internet. The Wolfe Pack—the official Nero Wolfe Society—maintains an informative web site, which includes a section that lists and discusses each episode's diegetic music.

Composer Rob Cairns' saucy, synth-hued jazz tango sets a similarly perfect mood for ABC's *Thieves*, a woefully underappreciated blend of *It Takes a Thief* and *Moonlighting*, which lasted only briefly after its debut on September 28, 2001. Cairns' main theme backs a delightful title sequence that showcases a torrid dance between suave master thief Johnny (John Stamos) and the impetuous—but equally larcenous—Rita (Melissa George), as they lift each other's valuables while keeping time to the music.

The two meet by chance during the pilot episode, while trying to pull off the same heist. Cairns demonstrates his flair for droll underscore cues when Johnny and Rita—assessing each other over cocktails—briefly excuse themselves and use the break to search each other's hotel rooms. Cairns shifts to a slow, sensuous swinger when they later confront each other during a "feigned" bedroom encounter. They reluctantly join forces—arguing the entire time—but the caper turns out to be an FBI sting, at which point the penny drops: The Feds want them to steal ... as a team.

Johnny and Rita spend subsequent episodes bantering, flirting, arguing and getting in each other's way ... but never enough to prevent the successful completion of each fresh government assignment. These escapades are laden with music; Cairns alternates between sexy ballads, propulsive action jazz themes and plenty of suspenseful—but less musically interesting—synth. Stamos and George share terrific chemistry, and the show's playfully sexy tone should have made it a hit; alas, *Thieves* was canceled after only eight episodes. No home video release has appeared thus far, although a few episodes float around the Internet: enough to get a taste of Cairns' effervescent efforts.

The Big Screen

Updating a pop-culture classic such as *Shaft* was an audacious venture; assigning the music to British-born "white guy" David Arnold was even more daring. Both gambles paid off. Samuel L. Jackson possesses the strut, swagger and all-around cool that defines the character, and Arnold wisely sprinkles his score with references to 1971's iconic title theme, including an updated arrangement—"Shaft 2000"—that preserves Isaac Hayes' bad-ass vocal. Arnold painstakingly made his urban, funk-laden score as 1970s-accurate as possible.

"I wanted to use as many of Isaac's musicians, or musicians who were around at the time," Arnold recalled. "I wanted to use the instruments and all vintage stuff. I wanted it to be as authentic as possible, whilst still having a more contemporary sheen." First item on the list was a guitar with the appropriate *wah-wah* pedal, for the essential "funk echo" effect that was so pronounced in Hayes' original score; other key instruments include electric keyboards—a clavinet, Fender Rhodes and Wurlitzer EP 200—and a vintage "Big Muff" fuzzbox. Arnold also instructed his alto flutists to hit the "post–Detroit Motown sound ... the flutes just fall off the end of the notes. You get them to run down, and it'll be lazy and slightly sleazy, and a bit sexy."[2]

The thoroughly entertaining film is more thematic sequel than remake, with Jackson's John Shaft introduced as an NYPD detective. He and partner Carmen Vasquez (Vanessa L. Williams) come on the scene after racist, privileged white kid Walter Wade (Christian Bale) brutally murders a black college student; Wade subsequently makes bail thanks to his wealthy father, and the fact that the only witness—a barmaid named Diane (Toni Collette)—has been frightened into hiding. Wade jumps bail; two years pass, and Shaft finally catches him again ... and, again, Wade is freed on his own recognizance. Infuriated by the system's repeated failure, Shaft quits the force and goes private. The situation becomes more complicated when Wade gets involved with a Dominican drug baron with his own score to settle against the resourceful private dick; everything builds to a suspenseful climax that concludes on the courthouse steps.

The initial percussive riffs of Arnold's sleek update of Hayes' theme begin with the Paramount Studios logo; the *wah-wah* effects and iconic melody then play against a sexy title credits sequence worthy of the James Bond series. The lengthy cue continues as the film begins, shadowing Shaft when he drives to the club where the critically injured college student lies bleeding on the sidewalk. Arnold shifts to another cue with equally insistent, heartbeat percussion and a 3-3 flute motif, when Shaft confidently strides into the club and immediately zeroes in on Wade, who hasn't bothered to clean the victim's blood from his hand. A lengthy quote from Hayes' title theme fuels our hero's rage and subsequent smile, but that satisfaction proves short-lived.

Arnold is equally adept at his own action music, such as the fast 4/4 cue that backs a wall of energetic horns with ferocious drumming, when Shaft chases down a gun-toting thug. Other cues are simply cool: When Shaft attempts to get information from an uncooperative witness, he ambles up to the woman's front door against throbbing percussion, exploratory flutes and descending strings. Arnold anticipates the explosive finale quietly, with soft percussion and gentle trumpet riffs that follow Dominican thugs, while they sneak up the stairs toward the apartment where Shaft has hidden Diane; the cue accelerates with the first fired shot, the full orchestra roaring into life—the entire bank of horns backed by savage strings—when Shaft and his friends fight back. The subsequent car chase is even more exciting, spotted by full-throttle percussion, *wah-wah* guitar, keyboard runs and intense horns.

None of Arnold's score was included in the initial soundtrack album, which instead features Hayes' "Theme from Shaft" and the many R&B and hip-hop tunes sprinkled throughout the film. Arnold finally got his due with a 2014 release, which includes the "Shaft 2000" version of Hayes' title theme.

Cheeky attitude is similarly prominent in the 2001 remake of *Ocean's Eleven*. This equally star-laden update is far more satisfying than its 1960 predecessor; the twisty script is a bona fide "impossible heist" escapade—as opposed to a thin excuse for a bunch of songs—and the caper is *successful*. The plot finds recently released felon Danny Ocean (George Clooney) gathering a crew to orchestrate the simultaneous robbery of three Las Vegas casinos—the Bellagio, the Mirage and the MGM Grand—all of which are owned by the malevolent Terry Benedict (Andy Garcia). Ocean's motives aren't merely larcenous; he also hopes to regain the love and trust of his ex-wife, Tess (Julia Roberts), who has become Benedict's girlfriend.

David Holmes delivers a scrumptious, groove-laden score that's long on percussion, electronic keyboards, walking bass and plenty of rhythmic four- and eight-bar ostinatos. The funkified result swings like crazy; it's impossible to watch this film without grinning and nodding in time. Soderbergh is generous with the music, thanks to a narrative structure that includes numerous montages.

"[Steven] wasn't really after anything specific, except 'Let's just avoid the original *Ocean's Eleven*,' and update the whole thing," Holmes explained. "I had a pretty fair idea where he wanted to be. We were trying to have a little element of Vegas, without being obvious about it. I have a pretty deep record collection, when it comes to cinematic music. I just started compiling CDs with ideas, and the first CD I compiled had the Elvis track, 'A Little Less Conversation'—lyrically, it really spoke to the film, and it had a really heavy, compressed beat; it sounded really raw—and [Steven] already had chosen three tracks from my album, *Let's Get Killed*, that he wanted to appear in the film. Another track that I chose was 'Blues in the Night,' by Quincy Jones."[3]

Ocean and longtime friend Rusty Ryan (Brad Pitt) are introduced first, each to his own saucy, eight-beat groove. As they discuss who should join the team, Holmes contributes distinct cues while each candidate is shown "in the field." Explosives expert Basher Tarr (Don Cheadle) blows a vault to chaotic guitar, keyboards and aggressive drums; fast-handed pickpocket Linus Caldwell (Matt Damon) gets some smooth walking bass and sly synth effects. The elderly Saul Bloom (Carl Reiner) is recruited to Jones' impudent cover of "Blues in the Night," while the limber Yen (Shaobo Qin) demonstrates his body-folding skills to Arthur Lyman's cover of "Caravan." Tess also gets her own theme: a slow, achingly sexy strut first heard when she sashays down a set of casino stairs.

Once the caper gets underway, everything seems to go wrong ... but of course it all actually goes *right*; the members of Ocean's crew make their individual escapes to a jubilant, drum- and sax-fueled swinger, each man smiling at the thought of Benedict, left behind in an empty vault, trying to figure out what the hell happened.

The official soundtrack album is thoroughly obnoxious, because all of Holmes' groove-laden instrumentals are marred by dialogue and sound effects. It's far better to seek the instrumental-only promo score, which floats through gray regions of the Internet.

The Score (2001) is another sleek heist thriller, thanks to a solid cast and a clever premise with some nifty third-act twists. The film also boasts a terrific jazz score, although you'd never know that from the soundtrack album, devoted solely to Howard Shore's orchestral underscore; it completely omits the diegetic jazz cues sprinkled throughout the film.

The story takes place in Montreal, where veteran safe-cracker Nick Wells (Robert De Niro) considers retiring after a routine burglary nearly goes sour. He's talked into one final job by his longtime fence, Max (Marlon Brando), who has learned that a priceless French national treasure is being stored in the Montreal Customs House. The hitch: Max must take on a partner, the much younger Jack Teller (Edward Norton). He's impatient and impulsive, which Nick regards as bad news, but the lure of a $4 million payday—Max already has a buyer in place—is too tempting to resist. The "impossible heist" angle is suitably complex, as are Nick's ingenious methods of getting around each obstacle; the caper occupies the film's entire third act, during which Nick's concern regarding Jack proves prophetic.

Shore's percussive main theme debuts under the title credits: a pulsating cue with a descending six-note orchestral motif backed by bass, guitar and muted trumpet shading. This theme repeats frequently, serving as a tense action cue—notably when Nick and Teller establish the preliminary research—and, during the nail-biting climax, while the actual heist goes down. Shore also delivers a lighter blend of reeds and droll bass licks early on, when Jack outlines his extensive notes to an initially dubious, but ultimately impressed Nick and Max.

The film's best music emerges as a result of Nick's "day job," as the owner of a jazz nightclub. The numerous sequences taking place in this club—or within Nick's apartment—are accompanied by sleek diegetic cues performed by Tim Hagans (trumpet), Mike Lang (piano), Dave Samuels (vibes), David Torn (guitar), Charnett Moffett (bass) and Steve Schaeffer (drums). The offerings are even better during the club's business hours, with live performances by top talents. Cassandra Wilson croons a few lines of "You're About to Give In" early on; later, Jack shows up to go over a few details with Nick, while—in the background—Mose Allison growls his way through "City Home." The film's lengthy end credits are accompanied by Diana Krall's sultry, off-camera reading of "I'll Make It Up as I Go," a tune that deftly suits Nick's nimble triumph.

"Disappointing" is the operative term for 2002's *Austin Powers in Goldmember*. Although it boasts one of the best teasers and title credits sequences in cinema history, the film itself is a classic case of diminishing returns (with apologies to Verne Troyer's Mini Me). The script essentially abandons plot and secret agent spoofery, relying almost entirely on the slapstick, vulgarity and limp humor that has become quite stale. The bare-bones storyline finds Austin (Myers) trying to stop Dr. Evil (Myers) and the aptly named Goldmember (Myers again) from tractor-beaming a massive gold asteroid into the Earth's North Pole, thereby flooding the entire planet. Austin is assisted by Foxxy Cleopatra (Beyoncé), who is brought to the present from 1975.

Foxxy's point of departure gives returning composer George S. Clinton ample opportunity to riff the blaxploitation era, so her anthem—heard each time she sashays into action—is a rhythmic blast of *Shaft*-style fuzz guitar. But Clinton doesn't build that cue into anything approaching an actual melody, as also is the case with the fleeting sax and organ swinger assigned to Nigel Powers (Michael Caine), Austin's debonair secret agent father. The closest this film gets to action jazz is an exhilarating cue that backs a street chase between Goldmember's provocatively shaped getaway vehicle, and the adorable Mini Cooper in which Austin and Foxxy follow.

The rest of the film is spotted with the standard-issue synth cues that had become ubiquitous by these early years of the new century: quite a comedown, from the spy jazz that Clinton mimicked so well, in the first film. This one's soundtrack album is strictly a pop song affair, with none of Clinton's instrumental underscore. The latter is available solely as a promo album, and is fairly easy to find via the Internet.

* * *

John Williams acknowledged his jazz roots in 2002's *Catch Me if You Can*, a whimsical drama more or less based on the early life of Frank Abagnale, Jr., the notorious "paper hanger" (check forger), con artist and impostor who, between the ages of 15 and 21, became one of the youngest criminals ever placed on the FBI's Most Wanted list. Leonardo DiCaprio is spot-on as the giddily larcenous Abagnale; Tom Hanks stands in for the numerous FBI agents who relentless pursued the young man, often getting tantalizingly close before he vanished within another audacious identity (doctor, lawyer and airline pilot, among others).

Williams' title theme begins with hesitant, cheeky vibes and soft percussion snaps; the emerging "circular" melody—which never quite devolves into free jazz—takes impish flight with Dan Higgins' droll sax solo. The immediate impression is of impending suspense, the atmosphere very much in the mold of Leonard Bernstein's late 1950s sound. This theme recurs often, particularly when Abagnale is about to execute another con; between the melody's coquettish nature and DiCaprio's endearing performance, we can't help admiring the kid. The rest of Williams' underscore mostly eschews jazz for his more typical orchestral cues and shading, although he does deliver a warmly sentimental theme for the relationship Frank shares with his father (Christopher Walken). Higgins' solo sax turns mournful here, foreshadowing everything we can expect from a saga that—no matter how much fun along the way—obviously cannot end well.

The 1960s setting is given additional bounce by well-placed songs that include "Take the A Train"; Erroll Garner's cover of "Body and Soul"; Stan Getz's iconic collaboration with Joao Gilberto and Antonio Carlos Jobim, on "The Girl from Ipanema"; Frank Sinatra's effervescent "Come Fly with Me"; and even John Barry's familiar arrangement of "The James Bond Theme." The initial soundtrack album features a tasty blend of Williams' cues interspersed with five of the jukebox vocals. The composer's fans likely will be happier with a two-disc bootleg of his entire score; it's not difficult to find via the Internet.

The jazz is soft, smoky and similarly underrepresented in *The Good Thief*, because scripter/director Neil Jordan frequently ignores composer Elliot Goldenthal's cues in favor of more than a dozen French and English pop songs. That's unfortunate; Goldenthal's themes would have been a superior complement to the world-weary title character played by star Nick Nolte.

This 2002 drama is a remake of Jean-Pierre Melville's *Bob le flambeur* (see this book's 1950–1970 companion volume), with an updated narrative that adds a bit of 21st century grit. The core plot is identical: Bob Montagnet (Nolte), heroin-addicted but still suave, is a Hemingway-esque gambler who lives in Nice and is down on his luck. He comes out of "retirement" to mastermind one final great heist at a Monte Carlo casino: not for the money in its safe, but for the fabulous paintings displayed on its walls. Bob knows they're fakes, and that the actual paintings are stored elsewhere; to divert suspicion, he "carelessly" lets it be known that he is, indeed, after what's in the casino safe. Bob and his right-hand man Raoul (Gérard Darmon) assemble two crews: one for the actual heist, the second as the decoy. Alas, matters get complicated when Bob rescues teenage Anne (Nutsa Kukhianidze) from a nasty pimp and becomes her protector.

Goldenthal embraced the challenge of writing music for a character palette with so many diverse nationalities. "The music is very experimental," he explained. "It's inspired by North African rhythms and sounds, and American jazz, and it's up against the backdrop of Algerian rap. A lot of homemade instruments are used, created by Mark Stuart: plastic knives, spoons and forks put on a resonating board, and then pitched."[4]

The score's jazz elements center around Anne's immediate effect on Bob: initially due to protective paternal instincts, and later as her respect for him grows. He initially spots her in a noisy bar, while Goldenthal supplies a doleful sax and harmonica theme against tentative bass and quiet piano; the cue alerts us to the mutual attraction, but the music remains ambiguous enough to leave us wondering how the dynamic will play out. That question is answered shortly thereafter, when Bob takes Anne shopping for fancy clothes appropriate for their "distraction activities" at the casino. They'll spend the entire night gambling, giving him the perfect alibi while, elsewhere, his two heist teams do their thing. The shopping spree is accompanied by a delicate jazz waltz: a shy keyboard theme heard against soft bass and luxurious strings, with a forlorn echo on harmonica.

The rest of Goldenthal's cues are atmospheric: twitchy, bleak or startling bursts of synth, piano, bass and harmonica that either heighten suspense or signal danger. They work well within the context of on-screen action but are less satisfying as a listening experience on the soundtrack album, which alternates score cues with eight of the film's pop tunes. The jazz highlight is an extended rerecording of the poignant cue—"Waltz for Anne"—heard during the shopping excursion.

Momentum and Denzel Washington's charisma conceal a truckload of contrivances in 2003's *Out of Time*, a twisty thriller that also benefits from Graeme Revell's effervescent, samba- and bossa nova-hued score. The Florida setting evokes a sultry, laid-back atmosphere wholly at odds with the increasingly complicated—and dangerous—mess that envelops a small-town police chief, when he makes every possible wrong decision during a couple of chaotic days.

The story begins when Police Chief Matthias "Matt" Lee Whitlock (Washington) conducts a late-night patrol of his Banyan Key parish, his steps backed by smoky piano and sultry sax. Sleek brass and sassy bongos subsequently kick off the film's title credits, as Revell's title theme rises from the jubilant percussive cornucopia, the primary melody shared by trumpet and guitar. Matt's life goes awry when girlfriend Anne Harrison (Sanaa Lathan)—who's married to the abusive Chris (Dean Cain)—confesses that she's been diagnosed with terminal cancer ... although a "miracle cure" at a Swiss clinic might save her life. Matt believes this whopper (!) and foolishly loans her $450,000 in cash recently recovered from a high-profile drug bust (!!), reasoning that he'll (somehow?) be able to replace the money long before Drug Enforcement Administration agents arrive to collect it. But then a suspicious house fire kills Anne and Chris—leaving two charred bodies—and the money is gone. Circumstantial evidence makes Matt the prime suspect in a case led by his soon-to-be-ex-wife, Alex (Eva Mendes), and then DEA agents suddenly demand the cash, to arrest a drug lord further up the food chain. (What a mess!)

Revell relies on heavy percussion and anxious strings while the tension mounts, until a moment when—everything having gone to hell—Matt pauses at a crossroads; slow drums and a muted trumpet imply that he might give up and flee. Then an optimistic note: Alex wants to help. Lyrical piano, guitar and bass backs their heartfelt chat, suggesting that perhaps she still loves him as much as he always has loved her. Everything subsequently builds to a suspenseful climax during a storm-drenched night, after which Revell supplies a final reprise of the main theme, this time including a longer and more vibrant trumpet solo, as the end credits roll up the screen.

The soundtrack album is somewhat redundant, with four full-length versions of the main theme. On the other hand, Revell expands some of his shorter cues into richly smoky, suspenseful tracks—notably "Banyan Quay" and "Buddies: Matt and Chae"—that evoke the story's sinister atmosphere.

The atmosphere is equally ominous in *The Cooler*, a 2003 charmer that deftly navigates all manner of moods and genres: poignant romance, dark comedy, savage drama, and—most particularly—the nostalgic dismay experienced when something beloved is about to disappear. The "something" in this case is the classic, Rat Pack–era Las Vegas. The story takes place within the (fictitious) Shangri-La, the strip's sole remaining old-style casino; it's run by Mob-connected Shelly Kaplow (Alec Baldwin), who loathes "new Vegas" and settles problems with a baseball bat. Shelly maintains a tidy profit—despite dwindling attendance—thanks to his secret weapon: doleful, hard-luck Bernie Lootz (William H. Macy), whose mere presence at a table can turn winners into losers (hence his reputation as a "cooler"). But then Bernie falls in love with casino cocktail waitress Natalie Belisario (Maria Bello)—and she with him—and becomes deliriously *happy* for the first time in his life. Like Samson losing his strength after his hair is cut, joy disrupts Bernie's mutant power ... and Shelly can't have *that*.

Mark Isham returned to his jazz roots for a score that recalls the late 1950s/early 1960s Sinatra/Peggy Lee vibe; themes and cues evoke a romantic image of "classic Vegas," while also hinting at its sordid underbelly. Gentle piano chords back a melancholy solo sax, as it delivers the 6-3-3 motif—Bernie's theme—which becomes the score's backbone; this slow swinger plays behind title credits that appear against cinematographer Jim Whitaker's gorgeous, late-night montage of Vegas casinos. The camera descends and slides inside the Shangri-La; unison brass rises when as Bernie steps from an elevator, to "cool" one of the craps tables. He then retreats to a nearby bar for a cup of coffee; Adam Peppers' mournful baritone sax—backed by just a touch of vibes and gently brushed drums—takes over when the camera rises to reveal Bernie's hangdog face. It's a terrific theme: richly evocative and full of passion, pain and loss.

"I assigned the baritone saxophone to Bernie, which is slightly 'frumpy,'" Isham explained. "It's muffled, not as clear as the higher-sounding instruments. I felt that sound was right for him. I used a soprano sax for Shelly and the 'old school' Vegas. It spoke well for that, because it's the closest jazz instrument to sound like a violin. The alto sax is the instrument for Bernie's relationship with Natalie, which shows how beautiful it is. And as the film goes on, there's less and less baritone, and more and more alto. That beckons their relationship on."[5]

The Vegas setting also encourages the use of jazz-laden songs, including Diana Krall's "I'll String Along with You," Tierney Sutton's "My Funny Valentine" and Nick D'Egidilo's "Almost Like Being in Love."

The soundtrack album is divided evenly between those jazz covers and seven underscore tracks. Isham's fans are encouraged to seek a full instrumental bootleg score, which isn't terribly difficult to find via the Internet.

Meanwhile, Across the Pond...

Plenty of neo-*noir* dramas have focused on the unsavory link between boxing and organized crime, but most aren't packaged against a jazz backdrop. *Shiner* (2000) is an exception, with a cool, haunting score that complements the brutal title character's descent into hell.

Michael Caine channels the ferocity he displayed in *Get Carter* for his portrayal of Billy "Shiner" Simpson, a shady South London boxing promoter long banned from legitimate fights. The story opens with Billy's jubilant return to legitimacy, thanks to a title fight featuring his 20-year-old son, Eddie (Matthew Marsden). Billy has bet all his money on Eddie's "certain easy victory" over the visiting champion managed by loathed rival Frank Spedding (Martin Landau). The fight doesn't go as expected, which leaves Billy smelling a conspiratorial rat. Accompanied by his two gunsels—the loyal Stoney (Frank Harper) and recently hired Mel (Andy Serkis)—Billy vengefully confronts everybody who might have had reason to see him ruined. Unexpected tragedy adds an even grimmer note to this vendetta; it climaxes in true Shakespearean fashion, with bodies littered all over the stage.

Director John Irvin's approach is deceptive, with the first act just this side of dark farce. Billy's tawdry excess is played for laughs; Stoney and Mel squabble like an old married couple. This humor vanishes once the story's grimmer elements come into play.

Australian pianist and composer Paul Grabowsky cleverly addresses these atmospheric extremes, opening with a moody title theme powered by percussion and Mike Grabowsky's sleepy bass; Billy's character theme is introduced by Simon Grant's nonchalant solo whistle. This melody is built around a 10-note motif that repeats on both piano and vibes; the result sounds both mysterious and jaunty, as befits Billy's variable nature, and the giddiness he displays when the story begins.

"John [Irvin] was clearly concerned that the music should reflect a dry, laconic wit, at once a feature of the culture of Billy Simpson's world, and yet working as a foil to the spiraling violence and madness which characterizes his fall," Grabowsky explained. "We share a love of jazz, and the mordant bite of Miles Davis' recordings of the early '70s struck an immediate chord. I tried to evoke something of that spirit, in a kind of tribute to the great Miles, as well as finding a musical path that maps Billy's ironic, tragic collapse."[6]

Guy Barker delivers a sad, sweet trumpet solo when Billy chats with Eddie on the coliseum roof, shortly before the fight; the young man is terrified, the trumpet offering the first hint that events are about to take an unwelcome turn. Billy is undeterred; a bit later, he cheerfully taunts Spedding during a phone call given droll overtones by trumpet and bass clarinet, once again against an unhurried beat laid down with bass and percussion. When the saga later descends into its blood-soaked third act, the finale unfolds against unsettling bass and percussion: a hypnotic beat given further chilly edge by slashing strings and twitchy electric guitar. In the aftermath, Barker's solo trumpet introduces a somber reprise of Billy's 10-note motif, while the end credits roll.

The soundtrack album includes a couple of cues—"Backseat Drive" and "Golden Boy"—that aren't evident in the film, and likely were left on the cutting-room floor.

John Dankworth concluded his soundtrack career with a pair of British crime sagas, the first of which—2000's *Gangster Number One*—charts the violent rise of a casually ruthless mobster played by both Malcolm McDowell and Paul Bettany (as the former's younger self). The by-the-numbers script goes all the way back to 1931's *The Public Enemy*, but the cast is strong, and director Paul McGuigan's stylistic flourishes compensate for the familiarity.

Dankworth's underscore shares screen time with ironically placed pop tunes by Anthony Newley, Engelbert Humperdinck, Edmundo Ros and Neil Hannon, the latter crooning "The Good Life" behind a classy title credits sequence. Dankworth's jazz touches include the swinging trumpet combo cue that introduces Freddie Mays (David Thewlis), whose criminal empire is coveted by the story's vicious protagonist; and "Double Six Blues," a midtempo groover fueled by sassy horns and synth, named for the seedy club run by Freddie's loathed underworld rival, Lennie Taylor (Jamie Foreman). A bit of sassy acid jazz also stands out, when one of Freddie's gang members—mousey Eddie Miller (Eddie Marsan)—is spotted while unwisely chatting with Lennie.

The soundtrack album is divided between Dankworth's efforts, moody synth cues by Simon Fisher Turner, and the aforementioned pop vocals.

From the dour to the droll: Undeterred by the fact that it was quite late in the game, Rowan Atkinson upgraded his beloved Mr. Bean with a voice and an immaculately tailored tuxedo, and transformed him into a wannabe secret agent for 2003's *Johnny English*. This spy spoof doesn't have the retro atmosphere of Mike Myers' *Austin Powers* series, but Atkinson's shaken-*and*-stirred debut does boast a mildly Bondian score by Edward Shearmur, who enthusiastically evokes John Barry's 007 glory days. The gawky English may lay waste to all about him, but he does so with energetic jazz style.

"The comedy should rise out of the situation, out of the characters," Shearmur observed, "and the music should be the straight guy in the drama."[7]

English, lowest rung on the MI7 ladder, gets his shot at glamour when—through his own incompetence—virtually every other field agent is killed. He's therefore assigned to protect the British Crown Jewels from a rumored theft; the jewels are stolen nonetheless, but English and his assistant Bough (Ben Miller) connect the heist to avaricious French entrepreneur Pascal Sauvage (John Malkovich). English soon learns that the sinister Sauvage intends to exploit his *very* distant relation to Bonnie Prince Charlie, by making himself King of the British Empire after forcing Queen Elizabeth II to abdicate. With Bough and the mysterious Lorna Campbell (Natalie Imbruglia) at his side, can English foil this dastardly plot?

The Bondian template is mimicked all the way to an action-laden precredits teaser, when English resourcefully infiltrates a heavily guarded estate, accompanied by the heavy bass, throbbing guitar and shrill brass elements that highlighted many Barry 007 scores. This segues to Johnny's vibrant main theme, with a dynamic 5-3-3-2 motif; the cue softens to a sensuous, trumpet-fueled jazz waltz as English, now inside the mansion, disarms a gun-wielding *femme fatale* and moves in for a kiss … but it's all just the daydream of a guy parked behind an office desk.

Shearmur supplies pulsating instrumental arrangements of English's theme for most of the film's action sequences; a whimsical vibes/brass version is heard when a delighted Johnny takes possession of his sleek Aston Martin DB7 Vantage. This car soon plays an unusual role in the crazed vehicular pursuit of the getaway hearse carrying the Crown Jewels: a lengthy sequence spotted with pounding percussion, sizzling strings and furious brass. Later, when Johnny and Lorna meet during a formal dance in Sauvage's reception hall, an uptempo salsa arrangement of the main theme is performed as a live diegetic cue by the aptly named Bond String Quartet.

Numerous slapstick encounters later, everything climaxes during the ceremony where Sauvage is to be coronated. Exciting action jazz spots Lorna's battle with a sniper, while Johnny (literally) swings into the scene and snatches the Royal Crown, before it can be placed on the Frenchman's unroyal head. In the aftermath, Johnny and Lorna head off for a well-deserved romantic holiday on the French Riviera, which goes awry when he pushes the wrong button on the Aston Martin's control panel.

The soundtrack album includes songs by ABBA and Moloko.

Atkinson revived the character eight years later, but 2011's *Johnny English Reborn* was driven more by commercial desire than artistic merit. The sequel's music is particularly disappointing, the Barry-esque action jazz replaced by composer Ilan Eshkeri's bland, orchestral mickey-mousing. Aside from a main theme that displays minor bounce, the wall-to-wall cues are unremarkable. Demonstrating even more in the way of diminishing returns, 2018's *Johnny English Strikes Again* barely achieved release in the States; Howard Goodall's orchestral score is similarly unmemorable.

14

Sugar Plum Raid: 2004–2019

The baton has been passed.

Each new generation of young musicians matures with—and is inspired by—the efforts of those who came before. Although jazz scores were increasingly scarce as the 21st century continued, a small but dedicated group of film and television composers defiantly kept the genre alive by referencing the efforts of their idols. It's pretty cool when newcomers as diverse as Joseph LoDuca, Michael Giacchino, Christophe Beck, Guy Farley and Benjamin Wallfisch deliberately shape their original scores in the styles of John Barry, Quincy Jones, Lalo Schifrin and Dave Grusin.

At which point we can safely say that these artists—and this soundtrack genre—have made an historical impact.

The Small Screen

Most of the new century's first decade passed before the arrival of TNT's *Leverage*, a handsomely mounted heist series that enjoyed a respectable five-season run after its debut on December 7, 2008. The team is headed by Nathan "Nate" Ford (Timothy Hutton), a former insurance investigator now determined to assist clients persecuted by the rich and powerful. With assistance from his larcenous associates—sophisticated British grifter Sophie Devereaux (Gina Bellman), hacker/computer wizard Alec Hardison (Aldis Hodge), tough guy/weapons expert Eliot Spencer (Christian Kane) and cat burglar/safe-cracker Parker (Beth Riesgraf)—Nate orchestrates elaborate cons to fleece white-collar scoundrels. Matters often seem to go wrong in the third act, but inevitably are corrected during the fourth act … or were part of the plan to begin with.

The music assignment went to Joseph LoDuca. "*Leverage* is about high-tech capers, cons and heists with a group of flawed, funny and endearing specialists who reluctantly become a team of present-day Robin Hoods," he enthused. "In the collective unconscious of our TV imprinting, the templates [are] well set: It is the best-heard music of Quincy Jones and Lalo Schifrin, with all its funky beats and jazz inflections. I grew up on this stuff."[1]

He handled all scoring challenges during the show's entire run, providing a main theme, numerous character themes and all manner of action cues, frequently layering modern synth elements atop classic jazz stylings. Most scripts rigorously adhere to a story structure that includes one or more lengthy "setting up" montages, which grant LoDuca ample space for fully fleshed compositions. The show lacks a traditional title sequence, but fans nonetheless began to recognize what became a *de facto* main theme.

"As the first season developed," LoDuca explained, "we noticed that there were several 'themes' within the show. [The 'main theme'] is derived from a bass line in 7/4 time, and is used when our band of thieves is 'on the con.' Other themes that appear repeatedly are when we are in the conference room learning who the villains are, or for recurring situations of stealth or action. For the most part, [the show] is scored for an augmented jazz/funk rhythm section."[2]

Quiet drumming sets an infectious, midtempo beat when that main theme kicks off, with multiple keyboards introducing a melodic ostinato punctuated by occasional flashes of a "whistled" 3-2 motif; this invariably signals tricky behavior by our heroes. Caper cues add tasty walking bass, quirky keyboard riffs, vibes, unison brass fanfares and plenty of droll percussion elements.

In early 2010, toward the end of the second season, the show's popularity prompted a soundtrack album containing LoDuca's main theme and 33 underscore cues. Season four's second episode, "The 10 Li'l Grifters Job," takes place during a costumed murder mystery party; in a poignant nod to his father, Timothy Hutton's Nate Ford attends as Ellery Queen.

The Big Screen

Rum cocktails, sandy beaches, scantily clad women and gentle samba rhythms mingle smoothly in 2004's *After the Sunset*, a heist dramedy that takes maximum advantage of its sun-drenched Bahamian setting. The script gets equal mileage from the cat-and-mouse antics that bond seasoned jewel thief Max Burdett (Pierce Brosnan) and his longtime nemesis, FBI Agent Stan Lloyd (Woody Harrelson). Feverish sensuality is supplied by Max's sexy partner/girlfriend, Lola Cirillo (Salma Hayek). Lalo Schifrin supplies a mellow score drenched in Caribbean-style rhythms, although mainstream jazz elements are minimal.

A prologue depicts the clever manner by which Max and Lola steal the second of three fabled Napoleon diamonds, having earlier snatched the first. Despite Stan's ample precautions, this second heist is equally successful; the humiliation ruins the FBI agent's career. Flash-forward six months to Paradise Island, where Max and Lola have retired to a life of sex, sun and sloth. The indolence leaves Max bored, and therefore tempted when Stan appears out of the blue, ostensibly to ensure that his adversary doesn't steal the final Napoleon diamond, which will be exhibited on a cruise ship scheduled to dock at the island for a week. Worse yet, local gangster Henri Mooré (Don Cheadle) "asks" Max to steal the gem for *him*. Matters get more complicated when Stan partners with island police officer Sophie (Naomie Harris), who already has Mooré in her sights. Max's attempt on this third Napoleon is inevitable; the question is how he'll pull off the caper without getting caught by Stan and/or Sophie, or killed by Mooré.

Schifrin's oft-used primary cue, which serves as Max's "heist theme," is a suspenseful blend of double-time percussion and electric keyboard, with a melody that trades between 1-3-4 and 2-2-2-4 motifs. Gentle synth, backed by faintly echoing steel drums, is used for quiet romantic moments shared by Max and Lola; these cues take on a melancholy tone, when Lola grows increasingly worried that Max will "cheat" on her by trying for the diamond. Schifrin minimizes the jazz during the twist-laden third act, relying mostly on bongos, slashing strings, twitchy percussion and nervous keyboard filigrees; everything works out, of course, and a cheerful, steel drum-fueled salsa signals the end credits.

The soundtrack album completely ignores Schifrin's score, in favor of the pop, reggae and ska tunes heard throughout the film. Fans are advised to seek the bootleg promo disc, which isn't too difficult to find via the Internet.

After the Sunset is far more satisfying than 2004's other caper entry. Everybody succumbed to self-indulgence during the making of *Ocean's Twelve*, which too frequently abandons its heist premise for the sort of smug ad-libbing that made its Rat Pack ancestor just as tiresome. Everybody, that is, except for David Holmes, who once again inserts his signature blend of rhythmic funk, cheeky retro-pop, sexy breakbeat and cool combo ostinatos, along with an equally savvy collection of fly source tunes. Many of the latter are drawn from the classic Eurospy school of pulsating chic; Holmes' influences ranged from Italian composers Ennio Morricone and Bruno Nicolai to French musician Serge Gainsbourg.[3] The resulting score gives this film a modicum of suspenseful urgency that compensates for the flaccid pacing.

Things begin when the vengeful Terry Benedict (Andy Garcia), fleeced of $160 million in the previous film, tracks down Danny Ocean (George Clooney) and his buddies, and demands the money be returned—plus $38 million in interest—in lieu of lethal reprisals. With only two weeks to fulfill this impossible ultimatum, the guys head to Europe in hopes of sussing out a target large enough to net the required sum. This puts them in the jealous crosshairs of French master thief François Toulour (Vincent Cassel); additional complications are supplied by Europol detective Isabel Lahiri (Catherine Zeta-Jones), who once had an affair with Rusty Ryan (Brad Pitt). She now relishes the opportunity to put him and his friends behind bars. Everything climaxes with a challenge from Toulour: to see who can steal a priceless Fabergé Imperial Coronation Egg, to earn the designation as "world's best thief." Should Danny and his gang prevail, Toulour promises to settle the debt with Benedict.

Many of Holmes' touches are throbbing ostinatos—fuzz guitar, sleek vibes, thumping double bass, tremulous flute and brass riffs—that never quite become melodies, but nonetheless add nervous tension to all manner of conversations, confrontations and heist-induced jiggery-pokery. A few cues *do* deliver mischievous melodic structure: the bongo- and bass-driven twang of guitar that accompanies the gang's ingenious method of stealing a stock certificate; the sensuous jazz ballad that proclaims Isabel's arrival on the scene (actually a Yellowhammer track aptly titled "Lazy"); and—most notably—the exciting brass, fuzz guitar and pounding rhythm that signal a last-ditch effort to snatch the Fabergé Egg. When Danny and his friends ultimately outwit Toulour, their jubilant celebration is backed with a jazz/rock swinger by Dave Grusin (a cue lifted from his score for 1968's *Candy*, of all things).

The soundtrack album blends the diverse pop tunes with Holmes' longer cues, many of the latter bearing playful titles such as "10:35 Turn Off Camera 3."

In an entirely different genre, mention must be made of writer/director Brad Bird's *The Incredibles*, although at first blush this animated classic seems wholly out of place in these pages. And yet inclusion is essential, because Pixar's superbly structured 2004 superhero saga boasts one of the best action-oriented scores that John Barry never wrote. Composer Michael Giacchino made a stunning big-screen debut on this project, after cutting his teeth on music for computer games and television's *Alias*; he delivered an atmospherically diverse score that captures the story's introspective melancholia, and also propels the suspensefully crafted skirmishes against all manner of super-power villains and robots. Giachinno's rising five-note fanfare—which introduces the main theme—has become as iconic as the retro classics he and Bird deliberately emulated.

The story, set in an alternate version of the 1960s, focuses on a superhero couple—Bob and Helen Parr—forced into civilian "retirement" after public sentiment rebels against the collateral damage resulting from landscape-leveling battles with hyper-powered baddies. After 15 years at a boring white-collar job, Bob jumps at the chance for clandestine super-heroics in his former guise as Mr. Incredible: a "too good to be true" offer that raises Helen's suspicions. Resuming her own identity as Elastigirl—and with unexpected help from children Violet and Dash, and Bob's best friend Lucius Best, formerly known as Frozone—everybody teams up to save Mr. Incredible from the maniacal clutches of a rather unexpected supervillain.

Bird wanted a score that could sound simultaneously 1960s nostalgic and fresh. "I was looking for a specific sound, [that was] keyed in to the design of the movie," Bird explained, "which is kind of the future as seen from the mid-'60s. Sort of. Of a period, but also timeless."[4]

In point of fact, Bird envisioned a vintage-sounding John Barry score by the man himself. "[He] wanted a classic Barry/Bond score," recalled Richard Kraft, Barry's agent at the time. "[Bird] and I talked about tracking down the same mics, amps and guitars Barry had used back in the '60s. Barry and Bird hit it off, and John was onboard. John and I flew to San Francisco, for his first presentation of themes. [He] pulled out his Walkman and hit play. It was one slow, melancholy piece after another. The next day, I got the call from Brad. 'Well, that was interesting. But I sure would like to hear some action music.'

"I was sure Bird was going to fire him, but Brad desperately wanted John to succeed."[5]

Unfortunately, there was a bigger problem. "[John] never had worked in animation. He was never given footage; he was given early storyboards, which are just drawings that don't move. It was very foreign to John's process. He was so frustrated, that it all fell apart."[6]

Ultimately, to the deep regret of all concerned, Barry withdrew from the project.

Bird immediately thought of Giacchino, who turned out to be a kindred spirit. "We quickly realized that he and I both had a love for those 1960s jazz orchestra scores," Giacchino recalled. "Brad's point was, when he was a kid he would hear the theme to *Jonny Quest*, and would want to *be* Jonny Quest. That's what he wanted for *The Incredibles*. He wanted the orchestral jazz energy that they used to have in the Bond movies, Pink Panther movies and everything else [we both enjoyed]."[7]

Giacchino's propulsive, brass-forward score is just the ticket: from the opening notes of the exhilarating title theme, to the lengthy end credits cue ("The Incredits") that weaves all the key themes and motifs into a terrific, seven-minute symphony. In between—along with a wealth of distinct secondary themes—Giacchino includes a big band waltz swinger, with a sax lead and droll trumpet touches ("Life's Incredible Again"); and a rising suspense cue ("Kronos Unveiled") with a strong echo of Barry's "Capsule in Space" theme from *You Only Live Twice*. You also have to love the aptly titled "Lava in the Afternoon," with its sassy mix of vibraphone, toms and high hat.

Best of all, Bird was able to eat his cake *and* have it. The initial two-minute teaser trailer for *The Incredibles*, which debuted in October 2003—more than a year prior to the film's early November 2004 premiere—is spotted with a cover of Barry's title theme for *On Her Majesty's Secret Service*.

* * *

Inside Man (2006) gets its energetic snap from an ingenious original script, which transforms what seems like a bank robbery/hostage drama into an intriguing battle of wits between a criminal mastermind and a veteran police detective. Additional tension is supplied by trumpeter Terence Blanchard's anxiety-laden score, which blends a couple of character themes with plenty of edgy, percussion-laden suspense cues.

The caper begins when four masked intruders burst into a downtown branch of the Manhattan Bank and Trust and order all the employees and customers to surrender their cell phones. Police surround the building, while hostage negotiator Keith Frazier (Denzel Washington) and his partner Bill Mitchell (Chiwetel Ejiofor) assess the situation; Frazier eventually makes contact with Dalton Russell (Clive Owen), who has orchestrated the heist. We get glimpses of Russell's associates doing *something*, but we know not what; Frazier soon deduces that this isn't a conventional bank robbery. The NYPD Emergency Services Unit (ESU) ultimately storms the bank, where they find all the hostages safe … and no trace of the four robbers. Where did they go, and what actually went down?

The opening credits are choreographed to "Chaiyya Chaiyya," a vibrant, dance-ready vocal performed by Sukhwinder Singh and Sapna Awasthi, and orchestrated by Blanchard: a tune that deftly conveys New York's multi-ethnic ambiance, and the similar microcosm of soon-to-be bank hostages. Blanchard then delivers an ominous orchestral blast, laced with slow horn lines, when Dalton and his associates invade the bank. Frazier and Mitchell's subsequent arrival is accompanied by a drum-laden theme with a heavy two-beat; gallant trumpet fanfares amplify Washington's heroic bearing.

"Denzel's character is kind of like an old-school cop," Blanchard explained, "hence the R&B type of groove that you hear under the main theme, in various spots in the film. I tried to draw upon some of the old-school R&B grooves, to give him more of a flavor, because his character reminded me of some of my uncles."[8]

Once the hostages are sequestered in different offices, Blanchard introduces the film's two prominent themes. The first, employed during give-and-take exchanges between Dalton and Frazier—bargaining phone calls, sending food into the bank—is a contemplative, midtempo percussion cue with a recurring horn motif: four descending notes, two ascending notes and a pair of slow single notes. The second cue, more specific to Dalton, features single low-register piano notes with a recurring 2-2-5 motif, backed by some sweet flute comping. Blanchard also supplies an unexpectedly gentle cue—sounding like single notes on a child's xylophone—when Dalton brings pizza to the one youngster among the hostages: isolated from all the others, to minimize his distress.

When the ESU team later enters in force, their increasingly bewildered search is accompanied by ethereal strings and echoplex trumpet bursts (much like the effect Jerry Goldsmith obtained for his primary theme in *Patton*). By now, Frazier has put some of the pieces together: A slow, heavily dramatic reprise of the primary theme is heard when he and Mitchell open a particular safe deposit box several days later.

The soundtrack album features Blanchard's entire score, albeit out of sequence.

On a much lighter note, 2006's *The Pink Panther* reboots the series with a fresh origin story, which brings small-town policeman Jacques Clouseau (Steve Martin) to Paris, to find the villain who killed French soccer coach Yves Gluant (Jason Statham) and stole his fabled Pink Panther diamond ring.

Christophe Beck honors the series' jazz origins with numerous jazz and techno remix arrangements of Henry Mancini's iconic theme. "We surprised ourselves," Beck admitted, "with how we were able to present the theme in some really unexpected ways, both comedically and dramatically."[9] Beck wisely augmented the Hollywood Studio Symphony with Plas Johnson, whose tenor sax solos had been putting the swing in the panther's step since 1963.

As established by long tradition, this famous theme debuts in its entirely during the comic title credits, which splash onto the screen alongside an animated duel between the Pink Panther and Clouseau (the latter a cartoonish version of Steve Martin). Johnson gives Beck's arrangement plenty of swing, backed by cool percussion, lyrical flute work and a huge brass section.

Clouseau's presence in Paris actually is a nasty ploy by Chief Inspector Charles Dreyfus (Kevin Kline), who intends to solve the case himself, but wants to distract the media with a "total idiot" as the investigation's public face. This scheme takes second place to a string of disconnected encounters that show Clouseau at his bumbling best, many of which unfold against variations of the main theme. Bongos and smooth bass licks segue into a ferocious arrangement during Clouseau's chance encounter with British Agent 006, Nigel Boswell (Clive Owen). A techno remix surfaces during the climax at the Presidential Palace, when Clouseau and his capable associate, Gendarme Gilbert Ponton (Jean Reno), surprise Dreyfus by catching the killer and retrieving the Pink Panther.

Beck also contributes plenty of original jazz material: notably a droll bossa nova, when Clouseau and Ponton prepare to interview a suspect; and a sexy, rhythmic blend of vibes, brass and percussion, when Clouseau reveals Nicole's (Emily Mortimer) beauty by removing her glasses. Sharp-eared listeners will recognize Mancini's original version of the main theme, when Clouseau and Ponton dispatch several (apparently) unsavory characters who exit from an elevator.

The soundtrack album is devoted exclusively to Beck's score, along with Mancini's original main theme. (Beck's "Malibu Remix" arrangement can be heard on the anthology album *Pink Panther's Penthouse Party*.)

Martin returned for the disappointing 2009 sequel, *The Pink Panther 2*, but Beck's sophomore score essentially dispenses with jazz, aside from the main theme.

Director Steven Soderbergh and his A-list cast got back to basics with 2007's *Ocean's Thirteen*: a return to Las Vegas, to take down another arrogant mark. The target this time is callous investor Willy Bank (Al Pacino), who ruthlessly breaks a partnership and takes total control of the new Vegas hotel-casino that was to become Reuben's (Elliott Gould) "retirement" dream. The betrayal shocks Reuben into a near-fatal heart attack, which infuriates Danny (George Clooney) and the rest of the crew. They're determined to take Bank down, but the odds are formidable; they're old-school grifters in a world that has gone high-tech, as characterized by the state-of-the-art computer security system—the Greco Player Tracker—that constantly monitors all gamblers' biometric responses while under Bank's roof, as a means of exposing any efforts at cheating or rigging. Danny's scheme relies heavily on momentum to conceal lapses in plot logic, but the effervescent result hits the sweet spot that characterized *Eleven* (and eluded *Twelve*).

Composer David Holmes again draws from obscure movie soundtracks and library cues, but this time fashions a series of themes that give his score a traditional "through line," and are far more melodic than the catchy rhythmic ostinatos that characterized his work in the first two films. ("This one definitely is the most musical score of all three," he acknowledged.)[10] That said, the ensemble's instrumentation remains just as quirky; vibrant brass fanfares and rhythmic bass woodwinds are accompanied by touches on (among others) electric piano, dulcimer, Marxophone, Chamberlin and even "toys." The resulting score is both retro and timeless, with cues that coyly reference 1960s lounge and '70s funk. And—as always—the application of music to on-screen action is flawless.

"Steven [Soderbergh] and [editor] Stephen Mirrione have a lot of rhythm in their editing, which makes it so much easier for us to place a piece of music, and for things to happen at just the right time," Holmes explained. "You start off by putting in the rhythm track, to get the whole feel of the piece, and the energy; then certain editing cuts tell you that something else has to happen: another sound, a change of key, a chord change, or another instrument."[11]

High points include the pulsating bass guitar and bongos that punctuate genius hacker Roman Nagel's (Eddie Izzard) efforts to defeat the Greco; the sparkling jazz waltz heard over a montage, while Danny describes the intricacies of Bank's security system; the aggressive acid jazz that energizes another montage, when Virgil (Casey Affleck) and Turk (Scott Caan) cleverly "spike" the liquid plastic at the Mexico-based manufacturing plant that supplies the casino's dice; and the euphoric, drum-fueled brass swinger that signals the plot's successful execution. Holmes also makes excellent use of other material: none better than Puccio Roelens' wonderfully weird cover of Duke Ellington's iconic "Caravan," heard while Danny and Rusty (Brad Pitt) clandestinely lace a hotel room with bed bugs, bathroom detritus and all manner of other unpalatable messiness. The adventure concludes with Frank Sinatra's grimly ironic "This Town."

Holmes' underscore cues dominate the soundtrack album, with the balance made up by the Sinatra and Roelens tunes, along with Isao Tomita's poetic cover of Debussy's "Claire de Lune." Nobody but Holmes could get away with such an eclectic mix.

Four years passed before the next jazz-inflected caper saga, so 2011's *Tower Heist* marked a welcome genre return. The script is wholly preposterous, but the frothy tone (mostly) excuses the many plot contrivances, particularly when the story's mean-spirited villain gets such a satisfying come-uppance. Christophe Beck contributes a rousing jazz score that greatly enhances the on-screen action.

Josh Kovaks (Ben Stiller) manages The Tower, a massive New York City apartment complex that caters to wealthy residents, chief among them Arthur Shaw (Alan Alda), a Wall Street investor who lives in the top floor penthouse. Josh's closest friends include brother-in-law Charlie (Casey Affleck), who works as the concierge; Lester (Stephen Henderson), the doorman; Enrique (Michael Peña), a newly hired elevator operator; Odessa (Gabourey Sidibe), an immigrant maid from Jamaica; and Miss Iovenko (Nina Arianda), a Slavic receptionist studying to become a lawyer. Josh also is kind to one of the residents: mousy Mr. Fitzhugh (Matthew Broderick), a former Wall Street investor who lost everything in the wake of bankruptcy.

All are surprised one morning, when the Bernie Madoff–style Shaw is arrested by FBI special agent Claire Denham (Téa Leoni) for a Ponzi fraud; worse yet, Josh put everybody's pension fund under the management of the crooked investor. According to report, Shaw is penniless, but the brazenly unrepentant scoundrel is rumored to have hidden at least $20 million somewhere. Believing that these funds must be concealed within Shaw's penthouse—where he has been placed under house arrest—Josh and his friends cook up a crazy scheme to evade building security, Denham and her FBI agents, and even Shaw himself, to locate and steal the loot. But they fail to anticipate the *form* in which the crafty Shaw has concealed his wealth; this leads to a last-minute shift of gears during a heist staged under cover of the Macy's Thanksgiving Day Parade.

"Brett [Ratner] wanted a retro feel to the score; he loves film scores from the 1970s, particularly David Shire's *The Taking of Pelham One Two Three*," Beck recalled. "The challenge was to put in just enough references to that old style, to make it feel cool but not *totally* retro. He also wanted the 'feel' of New York; I tried to capture that by using two drummers in unison, like 1970s prog-rock bands. It creates a really interesting sound, because even if they're great drummers, they'll never play *exactly* the same thing, the same way; there's a little bit of give and take, a little push-pull, which creates a very nice tension and chaos, that I feel represents the hustle and bustle of New York quite well."[12]

The playfully suspenseful main theme and title credits open over a montage of Josh supervising a typical morning's details at The Tower; toe-tapping percussion and smooth walking bass introduce a melody dominated by pairs of rising chords, initially on guitar and then echoed by a wall of horns—short staccato hits—against subtle guitar comping. Later, having decided to go after Shaw, Josh visits Riker's Island to bail out petty criminal Slide (Eddie Murphy)—a long-ago childhood friend—to get some "professional help" for his evolving plan for revenge; this prison outing is spotted by a cacophonous blend of percussion and heavy guitar. The eventual heist unfolds against a series of cues that reprise the main theme, with its sets of rising double chords. Beck varies the intensity as problems occur: cutting back to quiet strings, bass and percussion, during Josh's frantic efforts to think his way past each fresh crisis; and then building to a full-blown orchestral splash each time another improbable "solution" is executed.

"One of the ways I created tension is that the drums and the bass often play in one meter, and the rest of the orchestra plays in a different meter," Beck explained. "So you've got this odd meter groove going, where the bass and drums play in seven, while on top of that, the rest of the orchestra plays in a regular 4/4."[13]

The final triumphant montage is spotted with a spirited, swinging cue that makes ample use of propulsive percussion, aggressive guitar and the wall of horns, along with some playful synth touches. The end credits unspool to an uptempo reprise of the main theme.

The soundtrack album features just about all of Beck's effervescent score.

The musical palette is far less satisfying in *Gangster Squad*, a fictionalized account of the Los Angeles cops who took down mobster Mickey Cohen. It seems a natural for a hard-charging jazz score; the 1949 setting and Dion Beebe's luxuriously *noir* cinematography beg for such treatment. But director Ruben Fleischer and composer Steve Jablonsky had other (lesser) ideas for this 2013 crime drama, giving it a standard-issue synth-and-percussion score that could have been welded to any of the myriad thrillers Hollywood churned out, in the wake of the *Jason Bourne* franchise. The result is as disappointing as the film itself; a terrific cast—Josh Brolin, Ryan Gosling, Nick Nolte, Emma Stone and Sean Penn—is wasted in an overly vicious narrative populated by underdeveloped characters who spout inane dialogue.

That said, music supervisor Steven Baker balances Jablonsky's thumping sonics with plenty of period-appropriate source music from notables such as Stan Kenton ("No Baby, Nobody but You"), The Pied Pipers ("Route 66" and "The Hills of California"), Hoagy Carmichael ("Ole Buttermilk Sky") and Big Jay McNeely ("Blow, Blow, Blow" and "Boogie in Front"). A combo dubbed The Gangster Squad Movie Band—personnel unspecified—also covers classics such as "Early Autumn" and "Chicken Shack Boogie," alongside similarly flavored originals ("Jelly Wiggle Boogie," "Kiss Kiss" and others).

Neither the film nor Jablonsky's score is worth pursuing, but the best source tracks can be found on a solid companion album: *Gangster Squad (Music from and Inspired by the Motion Picture)*.

Every generation is blessed with a fresh version of Alexandre Dumas' *Three Musketeers*, and it appears that every generation is destined to get its own John Shaft. Not quite two decades after Samuel L. Jackson revived the character, the summer of 2019 brought another update, once again simply titled *Shaft*. Rather whimsically assuming that two Shafts hadn't been enough the previous time, this new action comedy offers *three* generations of black private dicks: Richard Roundtree's vintage avenger, Jackson's millennial model, and Jessie T. Usher's John Shaft, Jr. (who more accurately should be John III, given a key plot revelation).

As introduced, the latter is a clean-cut, well-mannered MIT grad newly ensconced as a rookie FBI data analyst: in other words, a profound disappointment to his father, who still struts Harlem's mean streets in a long-outdated suede leather duster (in which Jackson has no trouble looking cool). The estranged father/son dynamic plays for gentle laughs until all three Shafts eventually team up, to bring down a nasty drug operation that—in the first act—claimed the life of John Jr.'s best friend.

Most of Christopher Lennertz's underscore cues are suspenseful synth with minimal jazz elements, but he does make ample use of Isaac Hayes' iconic hit: both as this film's title credits theme, and during action sequences while the story progresses. Those who pay careful attention to such things will smile when Lennertz also references one of Hayes' swinging underscore cues—"Walk from Regio's"—to signal Roundtree's third-act participation in the climactic melee.

The soundtrack album blends Lennertz's contribution with many of the film's rap and classic soul tunes, along with a feisty Math Club remix of Hayes' "Theme from Shaft."

Meanwhile, Across the Pond…

Hustle was one of the brightest stars during the first decade of the UK's 21st century television season: a droll, handsomely mounted spin on the *Mission: Impossible* template with one key twist. The heroes of the BBC's *Hustle* are career con artists who employ equally elaborate schemes to swindle shady bankers, ruthless real estate moguls and all manner of corrupt politicians and condescending aristocrats. The series ran eight effervescent seasons after debuting February 24, 2004, and occasional cast changes didn't slow the momentum a bit.

It's also one of the rare TV shows that successfully applies modern synth touches to classic big band stylings, with a genuinely pleasant result. That starts with Simon Rogers' terrific main theme, heard against the title credits' clever animation montage; it opens on a cigar-smoking "fat cat" tempted by pound notes dangling from half a dozen hooks, who gets hopelessly entangled when he yields to temptation. Rogers' theme begins with rhythmic whistles, knee slaps, finger snaps and hand claps; the melody's rising and falling couplets debut softly on what sounds like harpsichord, then increase in volume and vigor against strings and vibrant horn fanfares, until finally fading when the show's title appears. The theme got a high-intensity makeover in 2009, with the debut of season five; the horns are more prominent, the rhythm section more forceful, and the synth more aggressively drives the beat.

The show's equally lively underscores are by Magnus Fiennes (brother of actors Ralph and Joseph Fiennes). Each episode always includes one or more tightly edited montages, while the crew—initially Mickey (Adrian Lester), Albert (Robert Vaughn), Ash (Robert Glenister), Stacie (Jaime Murray) and Danny (Marc Warren)—prepares an elaborate sting tailored to the mark of the week. These give Fiennes ample space for lengthy cues that include plenty of swing and action jazz: the rhythmic sax and unison brass of "Easy Money"; the bluesy piano of "Old-Timers Get Their Way"; the bongo-backed sax licks of "Casing the Joint"; and even—in a nod to this show's famous predecessor—an updated cover of the *Mission: Impossible* theme, along with a cheeky response titled "Mission Most Possible." The music is just as much fun as everything else about the show.

How disappointing, then, that no soundtrack album ever emerged … at least, not officially.

Hustle is all about payback time: Its larcenous operatives prey on the fraudulent powerful who have long preyed on the powerless. Rarely has television delivered such cheeky satisfaction on a weekly basis; the show's stars frequently pause, during each episode, to break the fourth wall while glancing at us viewers with a wink or a smile.

An "authorized" downloadable bootleg, with several versions of Rogers' title theme and 68 of Fiennes' underscore cues, can be found online. It's a can't-miss treat.

(TNT's *Leverage* obviously was an American response to this British hit show.)

On the big screen, 2012's *The Hot Potato* isn't merely set in 1969, in London's East End; the style and execution feel very much like films made during that period. Much of that ambiance is due to composer Guy Farley's intentionally retro score, which evokes the jazz stylings and orchestrations of that era's scores by John Barry, Henry Mancini, Ron Grainer and Laurie Johnson.

"I loved writing that," Farley enthused, shortly after finishing the assignment, "and I knew what I was writing. I remember saying to [writer/director Tim Lewiston], 'If we were in 1968, and you would have gotten John Barry to write the score, that's what I want it to sound like.' And [Tim] was absolutely crazy about the idea, and let me do my thing."[14]

Indeed, numerous passages sound strikingly like some of Barry's cues for *The Ipcress File*.

Lewiston intentionally evokes the quirky, light-hearted international vibe of British heist classics such as *The Italian Job*, although his film's premise is far more serious. The story gets underway as "salvage entrepreneur" Danny (Jack Huston) drags a large and extremely heavy silver box to the neighborhood metal works shop owned by best mate Kenny (Ray Winstone). After burning their way into what proves to be a lead-lined container, Danny and Kenny find a densely metallic, potato-shaped lump which—after some scrapings are analyzed by a metallurgist friend—proves to be a chunk of solid uranium.

Convinced that they've been exposed to a lethal dose of radiation, the two mopes decide to make the most of a bad situation. Reasoning that the chunk must be valuable, they try to provide financial security for their loved ones, by selling it to an ever-expanding roster of eccentric interested parties: local crime baron Harry (Colm Meaney); German con artist Fritz (Derren Nesbitt) and his nasty companion, Ernst (Jean-Louis Sbille); Harrison (David Harewood), a one-armed American with a disorienting habit of appearing out of nowhere; and Claudia (Maike Billitis), an aristocratic representative of Vatican authorities (!). Fatalistic recklessness makes Kenny braver than he should be—amid such dangerous company—as the stakes get higher, and the ports of call more exotic.

Farley's score is straight out of the 1960s spy jazz playbook, starting with a mischievous primary theme—first heard against the title credits—that opens with *Pink Panther*-esque suspense, and then settles into a midtempo groove; the melody is shared by xylophone and reverbed vibraphone, and punctuated by occasional bursts of brass. Unison trumpets take over for the swing-laden bridge, with Ben Dawson comping cheerily on piano. Geoff Gascoyne's double bass licks power a slightly faster variation of this theme, when Danny and Kenny head to Ostend; a saucy muted trumpet repeats the melody once the gang winds up in Bruges. When our heroes discover that the gun-toting Ernst is following them in another car, the suspenseful, fast-paced cue for the subsequent pursuit could have drifted over from Quincy Jones' chase music in *The Italian Job*. On the gentler side, Farley provides a couple of sweet cues for Kenny's flirty chats with his wife (Louise Redknapp): the first a lyrical flute melody, and the second—several scenes later—a lovely piano anthem.

The soundtrack album features the bulk of Farley's score in film sequence (always a plus).

Proving that fact *can* be stranger than fiction, London's notorious April 2015 Hatton Garden Safe Deposit Company heist—regarded as the largest burglary in English legal history—quickly inspired three film dramatizations. The first two aren't worth even a glimpse, but 2018's *King of Thieves* is a treat: both for its cast of seasoned, scene-stealing British stars; and for composer Benjamin Wallfisch's cheekily retro big band jazz score. Michael Caine stars as Brian Reader, who masterminded the caper and previously had been involved in the 1983 Brinks-Mat robbery; the other cast members—Michael Gambon, Ray Winstone, Jim Broadbent, Tom Courtenay and Charlie Cox—play fictitious characters. Director James Marsh's approach is initially whimsical, with an affectionately comic treatment of old-age pensioners who hope to relive youthful criminality by gathering for one final great job. It might have succeeded, absent the inevitability of thieves falling out; the film's second half, detailing the ultra-efficient police response, turns more serious.

"The movie gave me the opportunity to write a love letter to the '60s," Wallfisch confirmed. "The minute Michael Caine walks on-screen, you hear a certain sound. I've always been a huge fan of Henry Mancini, John Barry, Lalo Schifrin and Quincy Jones. I've always loved the fun, irreverence, color and sense of adventure in that music. This movie gave me a chance to pay my respects to my heroes."[15]

He succeeds brilliantly, starting with the swinging theme that heralds Caine's debut. It opens with cool bass licks and Barry-esque cimbalom, then explodes with sensational blasts of sharply unison brass: four trumpets and an equal number of trombones, with additional shading from a quartet of saxes. A faster, saucier cue—boasting impish jazz flute filigrees—adds zest to the gathering of the gang, as they learn the (frankly brilliant) plan outlined by

Reader and his much younger, tech-savvy apprentice, Basil (Cox). These and several other old-school big band cues evoke the exuberance of the gang's youthful instincts, despite being trapped in elderly bodies debilitated by diabetes, hearing loss and other ailments. Marsh further emphasizes this duality by inserting fleeting clips from classic 1960s- and '70s-era British crime films, most notably those that feature the actors' younger selves (such as a quick glimpse of Caine, from *Get Carter*).

Wallfisch's most audacious cue is a nod to Tchaikovsky's "Dance of the Sugar Plum Fairy," initially teased in its original classical style, within an atmospheric orchestral cue. Once the gang successfully enters the Hatton Garden Safe Deposit vault, Wallfisch shifts into an explosive big band jazz arrangement—dubbed "Sugar Plum Raid"—that turns the heist into a suspensefully exhilarating experience. This sequence, with the on-screen events skillfully choreographed to the music, is breathtaking.

The tone changes abruptly once the police deploy their investigative talents, and Wallfisch responds appropriately. He abandons the old-school jazz ambiance for 21st century touches—twitchy strings and atmospheric synth—by way of acknowledging the fact that these poor crooks, with no comprehension of how the world has changed, are about to be overwhelmed by modern, high-tech surveillance methods. Wallfisch returns to jubilant big band jazz only at the very end, when Reader and his associates trade prison garb for snappy three-piece suits—a defiant last hurrah that hearkens back to their youthful style—in anticipation of the first of many courtroom appearances.

The soundtrack album, highlighted by "Sugar Plum Raid," is a treat.

Epilogue

And where do we go, from here?

Although the current visual mediums remain indifferent—if not downright hostile—to orchestral scores of *any* type, a few outliers remind us that jazz hasn't vanished entirely. Canada's charming *Frankie Drake Mysteries*, which debuted in late 2017 and is set in 1920s Toronto, gives composer Robert Carli plenty of opportunities to affectionately reference the flapper era's old-timey swing ("moldy fig" jazz, today's purists would sniff).

The rise of original programming from streaming services such as Netflix, Amazon Prime and Hulu—and a rapidly increasing number of competitors—naturally included some crime and detective shows. Netflix's *The Good Cop* deserves mention for its score by composer Pat Irwin, who began his music career as a founding member of two avant-garde "No Wave" bands; he then spent two decades with the B-52s, before shifting to composing for independent films. His pleasantly understated, old-school jazz score for *The Good Cop* is deliberately arranged for a small combo that evokes warm memories of bygone days.

That wasn't accidental. "I went for a 'crime jazz' vibe, and pulled from influences like *Bullitt*, *Peter Gunn* and *The Man with the Golden Arm*," Irwin acknowledged. "Anything by Henry Mancini and Lalo Schifrin would point me in the right direction."[1]

The Good Cop debuted September 21, 2018. Josh Groban stars as NYPD Lt. Anthony "TJ" Caruso Jr., a by-the-book investigator who adheres to regulations—even the most trivial—with the fervor of a religious zealot. This frequently puts him at odds with his father, Tony Sr. (Tony Danza), a streetwise ex-cop—recently paroled after serving a seven-year prison stretch for corruption—who's always willing to justify the bending (breaking?) of a few rules, in a good cause. The show's tone owes much to creator/writer/producer Andy Breckman's earlier hit series, *Monk*, which won multiple Emmy Awards during its eight-season run. Although sharing some of Adrian Monk's quirky, detailed-oriented behavior, TJ isn't reclusive or obsessive-compulsive; he's more easily able to navigate everyday society. He listens to bossa nova, and he wakens each morning to "The Girl from Ipanema" (diegetic touches definitely aligned with Irwin's efforts).

Irwin was present during the show's gestation, and therefore helped shape the score's role as it evolved. "Even before I started working, Andy told me that he wanted the score to be driven by piano: specifically, solo piano. He referenced Dave Grusin's score for *The Firm*, [along with] Dave Brubeck's 'Unsquare Dance,' which pointed me in a certain direction. [But] it didn't take us long to figure out that we really needed a bigger sound; the solo piano was just too intimate. We added a double bass and some finger snaps, and some of those cues ended up in the show. [Then] we expanded the band to a quartet, with the drummer doubling on bongos."[2]

The resulting combo featured Jon Cowherd (piano), Tom Beckham (vibes), Tony

Scherr (bass) and Dan Rieser and Kenny Wollesen (drums and bongos). Irwin sat at the piano a few times, and he also contributed an occasional guitar line.

Many of the softly rhythmic cues have an inquisitive, charmingly bemused quality that feels right at home in this quirky police procedural. Irwin wisely avoided the trap of mickey-mousing Groban's affectations: "The humor in the show was able to stand alone; we didn't need to punch [it] up. But when it came to the mystery and the action, the score was essential."[3]

TJ is introduced, in the debut episode, while striding confidently through a police shooting range; Irwin spots this sequence with pairs of rising piano couplets against cheerful rhythmic backing (with plenty of bongos). Whimsical bass and keyboard cues become ubiquitous as this and subsequent episodes proceed, but the musical tone never becomes blatantly comical; even so, it's hard not to smile, during some of Irwin's rhythmic phrases. He never quite develops a specific character theme for TJ, although the debut episode finds Groban shadowed by a rising/falling seven-note motif. Instead, Irwin's cues are suited more specifically to the requirements of each self-contained episode: more in the manner of scoring a minimovie.

Pensive bass and piano often anchor contemplative interludes; leisurely vibes and percussion shadow heavenward glances during moments of frustration. The overall tone more frequently evokes Mancini's *Mr. Lucky* vibe than that of *Peter Gunn*; even so, Irwin cheekily references the "Peter Gunn Theme" bass line in a dynamic cue that spots a restaurant robbery sequence in episode nine ("Why Kill a Busboy?"). Episode 10 ("Who Cut Mrs. Ackroyd in Half?") is highlighted by a terrific—and uncharacteristically lengthy—blend of bass and keyboard filigrees against aggressively rhythmic backing. "I was able to incorporate a little more improvisation toward the end of the run," Irwin acknowledged. "I enjoyed the last two episodes the most, because I had gotten into the rhythm of the show; I was just starting to feel comfortable with the mix of humor, mystery and drama, as the season ended."[4]

Unfortunately, the series was canceled after that 10-episode single season, so Irwin was denied the opportunity to expand on his growing appreciation of the show's tone. None of his music earned official release, although a few cues can be found by Internet sleuths.

Amazon Prime's much grittier *Bosch*, which began its run in early 2014 and is based on Michael Connelly's enormously popular investigative thrillers, often finds star Titus Welliver's Hieronymus "Harry" Bosch researching a case while listening to classic mainstream jazz albums in the comfort of his darkened living room. Unfortunately, the show's title theme—Caught a Ghost's "Can't Let Go"—and underscores don't come within shouting distance of jazz.

Even so, Irwin, Carli, Joseph LoDuca, Guy Farley, Benjamin Wallfisch and others obviously aren't alone in their devotion to the 1960s-era sound. While we're unlikely to enjoy another similarly bountiful era of combo and big band crime and action jazz, I've no doubt that a healthy number of contemporary film and TV score composers—with swing running through their blood—will do their best to honor the genre.

And, perhaps, we'll eventually get a third volume out of the result.

Appendix A: Instrument Abbreviations

ab *acoustic bass*
acc *accordion*
as *alto sax*
b *bass*
bcl *bass clarinet*
bh *baritone horn*
bj *banjo*
bo *bongos*
bs *baritone sax*
bt *bass trombone*
c *cornet*
cbc *contra-bass clarinet*
ce *cello*
cim *cimbalom*
cl *clarinet*
cng *congas*
d *drums*
eb *electric bass*
elg *electric guitar*
ep *electric piano*
f *flute*
Fb *Fender bass*
fh *flugehorn*
Frh *French horn*
g *guitar*
h *harmonica*

HB3 *Hammond B3*
ho *horns*
hps *harpsichord*
key *keyboards*
md *mandolin*
o *oboe*
org *organ*
p *piano*
per *percussion*
pic *piccolo*
r *reeds*
sax *sax*
sg *slide guitar*
ss *soprano sax*
syn *synthesizer*
t *trumpet*
tb *trombone*
timp *timpani*
ts *tenor sax*
tuba *tuba*
v *vocal*
vib *vibraphone*
vtb *valve trombone*
ww *woodwinds*
x *xylophone*

Appendix B: Discography

Films discussed in this book—but not present here—did not generate a soundtrack album or 45 single. If no digital release is cited, one does not (as yet) exist. Participating musicians are cited when known, but in many cases—particularly with session musicians—such records weren't kept. A starred entry (★) is a must-have album that deserves pride of place in a dedicated fan's library. Finally, this discography is limited to soundtracks and scores by the composer(s) who wrote and performed the original title themes and/or underscores and does not include cover albums or singles by different artists, which instead are cited in the text.

* * *

The A-Team
- 45 single by Mike Post: "The A-Team"/"6 Slash 24" (RCA, 1984). Grammy Award nomination for Best Instrumental Composition: 1984.
- *The A-Team: Exciting Music from the Hit Television Series* (Music for Pleasure, 1984; Silva Screen CD, 1990)

Absence of Malice
- *Absence of Malice: Original Motion Picture Soundtrack* (Varèse Sarabande CD, 2019). Chuck Findley and Gary Grant (t); Jim Thatcher (tb); Mitch Holder (g); Dave Grusin (key); Alex Acuña (per).

Across 110th Street
- *Across 110th Street: Original Motion Picture Score* (United Artists, 1972; Rykodisc CD, 1997). Twenty weeks on *Billboard's* Hot 200 album chart, peaking at No. 50 on Jan. 20, 1973.
- 45 single by Bobby Womack and Peace: "Across 110th Street"/"Hang on in There" (United Artists, 1973). Six weeks on *Billboard's* Hot 100 chart, peaking at No. 56 on April 28, 1973.

Action Jackson
- *Action Jackson: Original Motion Picture Soundtrack* (Atlantic LP and CD, 1988).

The Adventurer
- 45 single by John Barry: "The Adventurer"/"Follow, Follow" (Polydor, 1972).

Austin Powers: International Man of Mystery
- *Austin Powers: International Man of Mystery: Original Soundtrack* (Hollywood CD, 1997).
- *Austin Powers: International Man of Mystery & The Spy Who Shagged Me: Original Motion Picture Scores* (RCA Victor CD, 2000). Includes seven tracks from George S. Clinton's underscore for *International Man of Mystery*. Gary Grant and Malcolm McNab (t); Alan Kaplan (tb); Brian O'Connor (Frh); Dan Higgins and Bob Sheppard (r); James Walker (f); Tim May and Bill Pitman (g); Mike Lang (p); Chuck Domanico (ab); Peter Erskine (d); Emil Richards (per).

Austin Powers: The Spy Who Shagged Me
- *Austin Powers: The Spy Who Shagged Me: More Music from the Motion Picture* (Maverick CD, 1999).
- *Austin Powers: International Man of Mystery & The Spy Who Shagged Me: Original Motion Picture Scores* (RCA Victor CD, 2000). Includes 10 tracks from George S. Clinton's underscore for *The Spy Who Shagged Me*.

Baretta
- 45 single by Sammy Davis Jr.: "Baretta's Theme"/"I Heard a Song" (20th Century, 1976).

Barnaby Jones
- *The Quinn Martin Collection, Volume 1: Cop and Detective Series* (La-La Land CDs, 2019). Includes title themes and two episode underscores for *Barnaby Jones*.

The Big Sleep (1978)
- *Jerry Fielding: Film Music* (Bay Cities double-CD, 1990). Includes a 19-minute suite from *The Big Sleep*.
- *The Big Sleep* (Intrada CD, 2009). Fielding's complete score.

The Bill
- 45 single by Charlie Morgan and Andy Pask: "Overkill"/"Rock Steady" (Columbia, 1985).

The Black Bird
- *The Black Bird* (Intrada CD, 2010). Chuck Findley, Maurice Harris, Cappy Lewis, Malcolm McNab, Clarence Sherock, Manny Stevens and Graham Young (t); Francis Howard, Dick Nash, Barrett O'Hara, George Roberts, Lloyd Ulyate and Chauncey Welsch (tb); James Decker, Vince DeRosa, Robert Henderson and Arthur Maebe (Frh); Gene Cipriano, Ronald Langinger, Abe Most and Bud Shank (ww); Al Hendrickson, Mitchell Holder and Tommy Tedesco (g); John Berkman, Artie Kane, Mike Lang and Pete Robinson (p); Charles Domanico, James Hughart, Milt Kestenbaum, Peter Mercurio and Meyer Rubin (b); Sol Gubin and Alvin Stoller (d); Dale Anderson, Larry Bunker and Ken Watson (per).

The Black Windmill
- *The Black Windmill: An Original Soundtrack Recording* (Castle Music/Cinephile CD, 1999). Kenny Baker, Tubby Hays and Ronnie Scott (ho); Roy Budd (key); Daryl Runswick (b); Chris Karan (d, per).

★ Body Heat
- *Body Heat: Original Motion Picture Soundtrack* (Film Score Monthly CDs, 2012). Includes John Barry's original score cues, his approved version of what should have been an earlier soundtrack album, with dozens of bonus tracks. Robert H. Findley, Malcolm McNab, Judd S. Miller and Tony Terran (t); Dick Nash, Thomas Shepard, Lloyd Ulyate and Chauncey Welsch (tb); James Atkinson, Vince DeRosa, Arthur Maebe, Jr., Brian D.A. O'Connor, Richard Perissi and Richard Todd (Frh); Don Ashworth, Gene Cipriano, Dominick Fera, James Kanter, Ronny Lang, John Lowe and Ted Nash (cl); Louise DiTullio, Geraldine Rotella and David J. Shostac (f); Dennis Budimir, Mitch Holder and Thomas A. Rotella (g); Mike Lang and Ian Underwood (key); Peter Mercurio, Susan A. Ranney, Mike Rubin and Robert King Stone (b); Chuck Domanico (Fb); Dale Anderson, John Guerin, Emil Richards and Ken Watson (per).

Bound
- *Bound: Original Motion Picture Soundtrack* (Super Tracks Music Group CD, 1996). Promotional CD never released commercially. Gloria Cheng (p); Chuck Berghofer (ab).

Brannigan
- *Brannigan: Original MGM Motion Picture Soundtrack* (La La Land CD, 2003).

The Cable Car Murder, see *Crosscurrent*.

Cannon
- *The Quinn Martin Collection, Volume 1: Cop and Detective Series* (La-La Land CDs, 2019). Includes title themes and two episode underscores for *Cannon*.

The Carey Treatment
- *Coma/Westworld/The Carey Treatment* (Film Score Monthly CD, 2005). Includes Roy Budd's full score for *The Carey Treatment*, with three bonus tracks.

Catch Me if You Can
- *Catch Me if You Can: Music from the Motion Picture* (DreamWorks CD, 2002). Academy Award nomination for Best Original Score: 2003. Wayne Bergeron and Jon Lewis (t); Andy Malloy (tb); Jim Thatcher (Frh); Dan Higgins (sax); Bill Liston (ww); James Walker (f); Alan Estes (vib); Steve Schaeffer (per).

Chandler
- 45 single by George Romanis: "Theme from *Chandler*"/"The Oracle Speaks" (MGM, 1971).

Chinatown
- *Chinatown: Original Motion Picture Soundtrack* (ABC, 1974; Varèse Sarabande CD, 1995). Academy Award nomination for Best Original Dramatic Score: 1975. Uan Rasey (t); Ralph Grierson, Artie Kane, Pearl Kaufman and Lincoln Mayorga (key); Richard Kelley and Dennis Trembley (b); Joe Porcaro and Emil Richards (per).
- *Chinatown: Music from the Motion Picture* (Intrada CD, 2016). Expanded edition includes Jerry Goldsmith's original score cues.
- *Los Angeles, 1937* (Perseverance CD, 2012). Phillip Lambro's rejected score.

CHiPs
- *CHiPs: Original Television Soundtrack, Volumes 1–3* (Film Score Monthly CDs, 2006–10).

Chopper Squad
- *Chopper Squad: The Original Television Soundtrack* (Grundy, 1977).

Cleopatra Jones
- *Cleopatra Jones: Original Soundtrack from the Motion Picture* (Warner Bros., 1973; Film Score Monthly CD, 2010). Ten weeks on *Billboard*'s Top LPs chart, peaking at No. 109 on Sept. 29 and Oct. 6, 1973. Digital edition includes Dominic Frontiere's score for 1975's *Cleopatra Jones and the Casino of Gold*. Albert Aarons, Bobby Bryant and Buddy Childers (t); Richard Noel, Barrett O'Hara and Chauncey Welsch (tb); Arthur Maebe, Jr., and Alan I. Robinson (Frh); Gene Cipriano, Plas Johnson, Jerome Richardson and Joseph Soldo (ww); Michael J. Anthony and Dennis Budimir (g); Pete Jolly (p); Ian Underwood (key); Chuck Rainey (Fb); Larry Bunker, Victor Feldman, Milt Holland and Emil Richards (d).
- 45 single by Joe Simon: "Theme from *Cleopatra Jones*"/ "Who Was That Lady" (Spring, 1973). Thirteen weeks on *Billboard*'s Hot 100 chart, peaking at No. 18 on Sept. 22, 1973.

★ Cleopatra Jones and the Casino of Gold
- *Cleopatra Jones: Original Soundtrack from the Motion Picture* (Warner Bros., 1973; Film Score Monthly CD, 2010). Digital edition includes the J.J. Johnson/Joe Simon score for 1973's *Cleopatra Jones*. Albert Aarons, Conte Candoli and Buddy Childers (t); Milt Bernhart, Hoyt Bohannon and Dick Nash (tb); James A. Decker, Vince DeRosa and Alan I. Robinson (Frh); Gene Cipriano, Justin Gordon, Harry Klee, Ronny Lang and Wilbur Schwartz (ww); Joseph Robert Gibbons and Tommy Tedesco (g); Artie Kane (key); Chuck Domanico (Fb); Larry Bunker and John Guerin (d); Milt Holland, Joe Porcaro and Emil Richards (per).

Coffy
- *Coffy: Original Motion Picture Soundtrack* (Polydor, 1973; CD, 2001). Three weeks on *Billboard*'s Best-Selling Jazz LPs chart, peaking at No. 31 on Sept. 8 and 15, 1973. Jon Faddis and Cecil

V. Bridgewater (t, fh); Wayne Andre and Garnett Brown (tb); Harry Whitaker (key); Billy Nicholas and Bob Rose (g); Richard Davis (eb, ab); Dennis Davis (d); William King (cng, bng, per).

Come Back Charleston Blue
- *Come Back Charleston Blue: Original Motion Picture Soundtrack* (Atco, 1972; Rhino CD, 2007).
- 45 single by Donny Hathaway and Margie Joseph: "Come Back Charleston Blue"/"Bossa Nova" (Atco, 1972).
- 45 single by Donny Hathaway: "Little Ghetto Boy"/"We're Still Friends" (Atco, 1972).

The Conversation
- *The Conversation: Original Motion Picture Soundtrack* (Intrada CD, 2001). Conte Candoli (t); Don Menza (ts); Jack Nimitz (bs); Pete Jolly and David Shire (p); Ray Brown (b); Shelly Manne (d).

★ *The Cooler*
- *The Cooler: Music from the Film* (Koch/Commotion CD, 2003). Rick Babtist, Wayne Bergeron, Gary E. Grant and Mark Isham (t); Kenneth Kugler and Bob McChesney (tb); Bob Sheppard (sax, cl); Greg Huckins, Joel C. Peskin and Brian Scanlon (sax); Adam Peppers (bs); Gary L. Novack (g); Richard Ruttenberg (key); John Leftwich (b); Ramin Djawidi and Peter Erskine (per).

The Cotton Club
- *The Cotton Club: Original Motion Picture Soundtrack* (Geffen, 1984; CD, 1985). Grammy Award for Best Jazz Instrumental Performance, Big Band: 1986. Dave Brown, Marky Markowitz, Randy Sandke and Lew Soloff (t); Dan Barrett, Joel Helleny and Britt Woodman (tb); Lawrence Feldman, Joe Temperley, Frank Wess, Bob Wilbur and Chuck Wilson (sax, cl); Tony Price and Bob Stewart (tuba); Mike Peters (g, bj); Mark Shane (p); John Goldsby (b); Brian Brake and Chuck Riggs (d); Danny Druckman, Gordon Gottlieb, Dave Samuels and Ronnie Zito (per).

Crosscurrent
- *The Last Run/Crosscurrent/The Scorpio Letters* (Film Score Monthly CD, 2007). Tony Terran (t); Hoyt Bohannon (tb); Carl Fortina (acc); Robert F. Bain and Al Hendrickson (g); William Pitman (Fb); Caesar Giovannini, Artie Kane and Pearl Kaufman (p); Ralph Collier, Frank J. Flynn, Shelly Manne, Joe Porcaro, Emil Richards, Louis Singer and Jerry D. Williams (per).

The Dead Pool
- *The Dead Pool: The Original Score* (Aleph CD, 2009). Chuck Findley, Jerry Hey, Fernando Pullum and Dan Savant (t); Dan Hemwall, Dick Noel, Hans Vidkjer and Bill Watrous (tb); Art Maebe, Brian O'Connor, Henry Sigismonti and Richard Todd (Frh); Don Ashworth, Gary Foster and Steve Kujala (sax); Gary Gray and Jim Kanter (cl); Randy Kerber, Mike Lang, Alan Pasqua and Gary Stockdale (key); Tim Barr, Drew Dembowski, Chuck Domanico, Arni Egilsson, John Hochurch, Bruce Morgenthaler and Sue Ranney (b); Abe Laboriel (eb); Alan Estes, Steve Forman, Harvey Mason and Bob Zimmitti (d, per).

Death of a Corrupt Man, see *Mort d'un pourri*.

★ *Death Wish*
- *Death Wish: Original Soundtrack Recording* (Columbia, 1974; One Way CD, 1996). Grammy Award nomination, for Best Original Score Written for a Motion Picture or Television Show: 1975. Bennie Maupin (sax, cl); Melvin Ragin (g); Herbie Hancock (key); Paul Jackson (b); Harvey Mason (d); Bill Summers (per).

The Destructors, see *The Marseille Contract*.

Devil in a Blue Dress
- *Devil in a Blue Dress: Music from the Motion Picture* (Columbia CD, 1995). Wayne Bergeron (t); and Emil Richards (per).

Appendix B: Discography

The Diamond Mercenaries, see *Killer Force*.

Diamonds
- *Diamonds: The Original Film Soundtrack* (Bradley, 1976; Cinephile CD, 1999). Digital version includes two bonus tracks. Duncan Lamont (sax); Roy Budd (key); Daryl Runswick (b); Chris Karan (d, per).

Diamonds Are Forever
- *Diamonds Are Forever: Original Motion Picture Soundtrack* (United Artists, 1971; EMI CD, 1991). Twelve weeks on *Billboard's* Top LPs & Tape chart, peaking at No. 74 on Feb. 12, 1972.
- 45 single by Shirley Bassey: "Diamonds Are Forever"/"For the Love of Him" (United Artists, 1971). Nine weeks on *Billboard's* Hot 100, peaking at No. 57 on March 11, 1972. Six weeks on the UK's Top Singles chart, peaking at No. 38 on Jan. 15, 1972.
- *Diamonds Are Forever* (EMI/Capitol CD, 2003). Includes nine bonus tracks.

★ *Dirty Harry*
- 45 single by Lalo Schifrin: "Latin Soul"/"Dirty Harry" (Verve, 1972).
- *Sudden Impact and the Best of Dirty Harry!* (Viva LP, 1983). Includes two tracks from *Dirty Harry*.
- *Dirty Harry Anthology* (Aleph CD, 1998). Includes three tracks from *Dirty Harry*.
- *Dirty Harry: The Original Score* (Aleph CD, 2004). Plas Johnson (ts); Jerome Richardson (f); Dennis Budimir and Howard Roberts (g); Max Bennett, Ray Brown, Carol Kaye and Paul Jackson (ab); Larry Bunker and Mel Lewis (d); Emil Richards (per).

Dirty Money, see *Un Flic*.

$ (Dollars)
- *$: Music from the Original Motion Picture Soundtrack* (Reprise, 1972; CD, 2001). Grammy Award nominations for Best Original Arrangement, and Best Original Score Written for a Motion Picture or Television Show: 1973. Clare Fischer, Mike Lang and Billy Preston (key); Arthur Adams and David T. Walker (g); Tommy Johnson (tuba); Ray Brown (ab); Chuck Rainey (Fb); Paul Humphrey and Ronnie Tutt (d); Victor Feldman and Milt Holland (per).
- 45 single by Little Richard: "Money Is"/"Money Runner" (Reprise, 1972).

★ *The Enforcer*
- *Sudden Impact and the Best of Dirty Harry!* (Viva LP, 1983). Includes three tracks from *The Enforcer*.
- *The Enforcer: The Original Score* (Aleph CD, 2007). Chuck Findley, Maurie Harris, Cappy Lewis, Malcolm McNab, Uan Rasey and Bobby Shew (t); Joe Howard, Dick Nash, Phil Teele and Lloyd Ulyate (tb); George Roberts (bt); Jim Decker and Vince DeRosa (Frh); Art Pepper (as); Gene Cipriano, Dominick Fera, Ronnie Lang, Don Menza, Bill Perkins and Bud Shank (ww); Louise DiTullio (f); Ralph Grierson and Mike Lang (key); Ian Underwood (syn); Chuck Domanico and Milt Kestenbaum (ab); Ray Brown (Fb); Larry Bunker and Harvey Mason (d); Joe Porcaro and Ken Watson (per).

Enter the Dragon
- *Enter the Dragon: Original Sound Track from the Motion Picture* (Warner Bros., 1973; CD, 1990). John Audino, Tony Terran and Eugene E. Young (t); Hoyt Bohannon, Dick Nash, Dick Noel and George Roberts (tb); James Decker, Vince DeRosa and Richard Perissi (Frh); John Ellis, Ronnie Lang, Jack Marsh, Jerome Richardson and Sheridon Stokes (r); Clare Rischer, Ralph Grierson and Joe Sample (key); Max Bennett (b); Stix Hooper (d); Francisco Aguabella, Larry Bunker, Joe Porcaro, Emil Richards, Ken Watson and Robert Zimmitti (per).
- 45 single by Lalo Schifrin: "Theme from *Enter the Dragon*"/"The Big Battle" (Warner Bros., 1973).
- *Enter the Dragon: Original Motion Picture Soundtrack Newly Restored and Remastered* (Warner Bros. CD, 1998). Includes seven bonus tracks.

Fallen Angels
- *Fallen Angels: Original Soundtrack Recording* (Verve CD, 1993).

★ Farewell, My Lovely
- *Farewell, My Lovely: Original Motion Picture Soundtrack* (United Artists, 1975; Film Score Monthly CD, 2002). Digital edition includes David Shire's score for 1988's *Monkey Shines*. Cappy Lewis (t); Dick Nash (tb); Ronny Lang (as); Justin Gordon (ts, cl); Don Menza (ss); Al Hendrickson and Tommy Tedesco (g); Artie Kane (p); Chuck Domanico (b); Larry Bunker (d).

Fear Is the Key
- *Fear Is the Key: Original Sound Track Excitement* (Pye, 1972; Cinephile CD, 1999). Kenny Baker (t); Ronnie Scott (ts); Tubby Hayes (ts, f); Roy Budd (p); Jeff Clyne (ab); Chris Karan (d).

★ The Firm
- *The Firm: Original Motion Picture Soundtrack* (MCA/GRP CD, 1993). Academy Award nomination for Best Original Score: 1994. Grammy Award nomination, for Best Sound Track Album: 1994. Dave Grusin (p).
- *The Firm: Music from the Motion Picture* (La-La Land CD, 2015). Expanded edition includes Grusin's complete underscore and numerous bonus tracks .

Un Flic
- 45 single by Michel Colombier: "C'est Ainsi Que Les Choses Arrivent"/"Un Monsieur Distingue" (Barclay, 1972).
- *L'Aîné Des Ferchaux/Un Flic* (Emarcy CD, 2013). Includes Colombier's full score for *Un Flic*.

Foxbat
- *Foxbat* (Bang Bang, 1977; Cinephile CD, 1999). Digital edition includes Roy Budd's scores for 1972's *Something to Hide* and 1974's *The Internecine Project*.

The French Connection
- *The French Connection/The French Connection II* (Film Score Monthly CD, 2001). Grammy Award for Arrangement, Instrumental or A Cappella: 1973. Grammy Award nomination for Best Instrumental Composition: 1973. Stuart L. Blumberg, Jack Caudill, John Clyman, Jack Coan, Jr., Don Ellis, Chuck Findley, Cappy Lewis, Bruce McKay, John Rosenberg and Glenn Stuart (t); Ernest S. Carlson, James V. Sawyer and David Howard Wells (tb); Kenneth L. Sawhill (bt); Vince DeRosa (Frh); Sam Falzone and Ernie Watts (sax); Jon C. Clarke, Abe Most and Fred L. Selden (ww); Jay J. Graydon and Barry K. Zweig (g); Milcho Leviev (p); Chuck Berghofer, Morty Corb, Irving Edelman, Arni Egilsson, Abraham Luboff, Ray Neapolitan, William Plummer, Mike Rubin, Ray Siegel and Robert King Stone (b); Dennis F. Parker (Fb); Ralph S. Humphrey and Franklyn W. Jones (d); Lee Pastora (cng).

French Connection II
- *The French Connection/The French Connection II* (Film Score Monthly CD, 2001). Bud Brisbois, Buddy Childers, Don Ellis, Glenn Stuart and Raymond Triscari (t); Paul V. Keen, Edward Kusby, Charles C. Loper, Lewis Melvin McCreary and Dick Nash (tb); George M. Roberts, Phillip a. Teele and Donald G. Waldrop (bt); James A. Decker, Vince DeRosa, Sinclair Lott, Arthur Maebe, Jr., James M. McGee, Alan I. Robinson and Harry Schmidt (Frh); Thomas A. Rotella and Tommy Tedesco (g); Artie Kane, Roger Kellaway, John Jack Latimer, Clark Spangler and Ian Underwood (key); Arni Egilsson, Paul V. Keen, Milt Kestenbaum and Peter Mercurio (b); John B. Williams Jr. (Fb); Ralph S. Humphrey (d); Francisco Aguabella, Adel Ghattas, Hico Guerrero, Wallace Carl Snow and Tommy Vig (per); Chino Valdes (cng).

The Friends of Eddie Coyle
- *Three Days of the Condor/The Friends of Eddie Coyle* (Film Score Monthly CD, 2012). Includes Dave Grusin's score for 1975's *Three Days of the Condor*. Gene Cipriano, William R. Perkins, Thomas W. Scott and Bud Shank (ww); Dennis Budimir (g); Ralph Grierson, Artie Kane and

Michael R. Wofford (p); Chuck Rainey (Fb); Larry Bunker, John Guerin, Joe Porcaro and Emil Richards (per)

FX2
- *FX2: Original MGM Motion Picture Soundtrack* (Quartet CD, 2013).

Gangster Number One
- *Gangster Number One: Original Motion Picture Score* (4 Music CD, 2000). Martin Shaw (t); Gilad Atzmon (cl, sax).

Gangster Squad
- *Gangster Squad: Music from and Inspired by the Motion Picture* (Sony Classical CD, 2013).

Gangsters
- 45 single by Dave Greenslade: "Gangsters"/"Rubber Face and Lonely Eyes" (Warner Bros., 1976).
- 45 single by Chris Farlowe and Dave Greenslade: "Gangsters"/"Sarah Gant Theme" (Beeb, 1978).

★ The Gauntlet
- *The Gauntlet: Original Sound Track* (Warner Bros., 1978; Perseverance CD, 2012). Jon Faddis (t); Dick Nash and Bill Watrous (tb); Vince DeRosa (Frh); Art Pepper (as); Ronnie Lang and Bud Shank (r); John Berkman and Mike Lang (key); Lee Ritenour (g); Chuck Domanico and Milt Kestenbaum (ab); John Guerin (d); Joe Porcaro and Emil Richards (per).

Get Carter
- 45 single by Roy Budd; "Carter"/"Plaything" (Pye, 1971).
- *Get Carter: Soundtrack Recording* (Odeon, 1971). Brian Daly and Judd Proctor (g); Roy Budd (p); Jeff Cline (ab, eb); Chris Karan (d, per).
- *Get Carter: An Original Soundtrack Recording* (Cinephile LP, 1998; Silva Screen CD, 2010). Digital edition includes six bonus tracks.
- *Get Carter: Deluxe Original Soundtrack* (Cherry Red CDs, 2019). Three-disc package with numerous alternate takes and bonus tracks.

Get Shorty
- *Get Shorty: Original MGM Motion Picture Soundtrack* (Antilles/Verve CD, 1995). Grammy Award nomination for Best Sound Track Album: 1997. Steven Bernstein (t); Art Baron and Curtis Fowlkes (tb); John Lurie (as, key, g); Steve Elson (bs); Michael Blake (ts); John Medeski (key); Danny Blume (g); Tony Garnier and Erik Sanko (b); and Dougie Bowns and Calvin Weston (d); Billy Martin (per).

The Getaway
- 45 single by Quincy Jones: "Love Theme from *The Getaway*" (instrumental)/"Love Theme from *The Getaway*" (vocal) (A&M, 1973).
- *Music for The Getaway: Jerry Fielding's Original [Unused] Score* (Film Score Monthly CD, 2005).

The Good Thief
- *The Good Thief: Original Soundtrack and Music from the Film* (Island CD 2003). Bruce Williamson (sax); Page Hamilton and Mark Stewart (g); Adam Glasser (h); Rufus Reid (b); Jamey Haddad (per).

The Grifters
- *The Grifters: Original Motion Picture Soundtrack* (Varèse Sarabande LP and CD, 1990).

★ Hammett
- *Hammett: Original Motion Picture Soundtrack* (Prometheus CD, 2000). Ronnie Lang (cl); James Walker (f); Mike Lang (p).

The Hanged Man
- *The Hanged Man: Music from the Yorkshire Television Series* (Contour, 1975; D.C. Recordings/

EFA CD, 1998). Alan Parker (g); Alan Hawkshaw (key); Les Hurdle (b); Barry Morgan (d); Frank Ricotti (per).
- *The Hanged Man: Alan Tew's Music from the Television Series* (Vocalion CD, 2011). Includes four bonus tracks.

Harry in Your Pocket
- *Harry in Your Pocket: Original MGM Motion Picture Soundtrack* (Quartet CD, 2011). Dennis Budimir (g); Ralph Grierson (p); Ray Brown (b); Larry Bunker (d).

Hawkins
- *Hawkins on Murder/Winter Kill/Babe* (Film Score Monthly CD, 2003). Includes the title theme and roughly 16 minutes of underscore from the *Hawkins* pilot film, "Death and the Maiden." Manny Stevens and George Werth (t); Richard Noel and Phillip A. Teele (tb); Sinclair Lott and Arthur Maebe, Jr. (Frh); Louise DiTullio and Sheridon W. Stokes (f); Laurindo Almeida and Al Hendrickson (g); Pearl Kaufman (p); Arni Egilsson and Milt Kestenbaum (b); Larry Bunker, Joe Porcaro and Jerry D. Williams (per).
- *Zigzag/The Super Cops* (Film Score Monthly CD, 2006). Includes Jerry Fielding's underscores for three episodes of *Hawkins*.

Hill Street Blues
- 45 single by Mike Post: "Theme from *Hill Street Blues*"/"Aaron's Tune" (Elektra, 1981). Twenty-two weeks on *Billboard*'s Hot 100 chart, peaking at No. 10 on Nov. 14 and 21, 1981. Eleven weeks on the UK Singles chart, peaking at No. 25 on Jan. 16, 1982. Emmy Award nomination for Outstanding Music Composition for a Series: 1981. Grammy Awards for Best Pop Instrumental Performance, and Best Instrumental Composition: 1982.
- *Hill Street Blues: Music from the Original Television Score* (Indiana, 1985; Silva Screen CD, 1990).

The Hot Potato
- *The Hot Potato: Original Motion Picture Soundtrack* (MovieScore Media CD, 2012). John Barclay (t); Ben Dawson (p); Geoff Gascoyne (ab); Ralph Salmins (d).

The Hot Rock
- *The Hot Rock: Original Motion Picture Soundtrack and More* (Atlantic, 1972).
- Clark Terry (t); Frank Rosolino (tb); Gerry Mulligan (bs); Jerome Richardson (sax); Carol Kaye and Chuck Rainey (Fb); Ray Brown (ab); Grady Tate (d); Bobbi Porter (cng, bng); Emil Richards (per).
- 45 single by Quincy Jones: "Listen to the Melody"/"Hot Rock Theme" (Atlantic, 1972).

★ The Hot Spot
- *The Hot Spot: Original Motion Picture Soundtrack* (Antilles LP and CD, 1990). Miles Davis (t); John Lee Hooker (g); Taj Mahal (acoustic g); Roy Rogers (sg); Tim Drummond (b); Bradford Ellis (key); Earl Palmer (d).

★ I, The Jury (1982)
- *I, The Jury: Original Motion Picture Soundtrack* (La-La Land CD, 2013). Includes eight bonus tracks. Bob Findley, Chuck Findley and Walt Fowler (t); Jim Thatcher (tb); Dennis Budimir (g); Emil Richards (per).

The Incredibles
- *The Incredibles* (Walt Disney CD, 2004). Rick Baptist, Wayne Bergeron, Jeff Bunnell, John Fumo, Larry Hall, Jon Lewis, Maurice Murphy and Paul Salvo (t); Roger Argente, Bill Booth, Alex Iles, Alan Kaplan, Charlie Loper, Charlie Moriallas, Dick Nash, Bill Reichenbach and Phillip A. Teele (tb); Steve Becknell, David Duke, Steve Durnin, Jerry Folsom, Joe Meyer, Todd Miller, Yvonne S. Moriarty, Diane Mueller, Brian O'Connor, John Reynolds, Kurt Snyder, James Thatcher, Richard Todd, Brad Warnaar and Phillip Yao (Frh); Dan Higgins, Don Markese, Dick

Mitchell, John Mitchell, Joe Stone, Michael Vaccaro and John Yoakum (sax); Norman Ludwin (b); Larry Bunker, M.B. Gordy, Emil Richards and Steve Schaeffer (per).

Inside Man
- *Inside Man: Original Motion Picture Soundtrack* (Varèse Sarabande CD, 2006). Terence Blanchard, Jon Lewis and Malcolm McNab (t); James Walker and Geri Rotella (f); Brice Winston (sax); Lionel Loueke (g); Aaron Parks (p); Derrick Hodge (b); Kendrick Scott and Oscar Seaton (d).

The Internecine Project
- *Something to Hide: An Original Soundtrack Recording* (Castle Music CD, 2001). Includes seven tracks from *The Internecine Project*. Kenny Baker and Tubby Hayes (ho); Paul Fishman (ARP 2600); Judd Proctor (g); Jeff Clyne (b); Frank Barber and Tristan Fry (per).
- *The Internecine Project* (Jambo Records digital download, 2019). Debut release of the entire score.

Jason King
- 45 single by Laurie Johnson: "The Jason King Theme"/"There Comes a Time" (Columbia, 1971).
- *Jason King Original Soundtrack* (Network CDs, 2009). Includes the title theme and all of Johnson's cues, alternate takes and unused bits.

★ *Johnny English*
- *Johnny English: Original Motion Picture Soundtrack* (Decca CD, 2003).

★ *Kansas City*
- *Kansas City: Original Motion Picture Soundtrack* (Verve CD, 1996). Nicholas Payton and James Zollar (t); Curtis Fowlkes and Clark Gayton (tb); James Carter, Craig Handy, David Murray and Joshua Redman (ts); Jesse Davis and David "Fathead" Newman (as); Don Byron (bs, cl); Olu Dara (c); Russell Malone and Mark Whitfield (g); Geri Allen and Cyrus Chestnut (p); Ron Carter, Tyrone Clarke and Christian McBride (b); Victor Lewis (d).
- *KC After Dark: More Music from Kansas City* (Verve CD, 1997). Same personnel as above.

Killer by Night
- *Nightwatch/Killer by Night* (Film Score Monthly CD, 2011). Frank Beach and Maurie Harris (t); Jack Cave, James A. Decker, Sinclair Lott, Arthur Maebe, Jr., Richard Perissi and Henry Sigismonti (Frh); John Lowe (cl); William E. Green (f); Allen Reuss, Tony Rizzi and Howard Roberts (g); Artie Kane (p); Abe Luboff and Joe Mondragon (b); Frank J. Flynn (d); Shelly Manne, Jerry D. Williams and John F. Williams (per).

Killer Force
- *Killer Force: Original Sound Track* (Audio Fidelity, 1976; Music Box CD, 2013). Digital edition includes George Garvarentz's score from 1967's *The Corrupt Ones*.

★ *King of Thieves*
- *King of Thieves: Original Motion Picture Soundtrack* (Milan CD, 2018). Simon Gardner, Tom Rees Roberts, Pat White and Craig Wild (t); Mark Nightingale, Alistair White, Richard Wigley and Andy Wood (tb); Sammy Mayne, Nick Moss, Jamie Talbot and Martin Williams (sax); Andy Findon and Gareth Lockrane (alto f); Ed Cervenka (cim); Adam Goldsmith (g); Christopher Egan (key); Phil Mulford (eb); Chris Hill (ab); Ralph Salmins (d).

L.A. Confidential
- *L.A. Confidential* (Restless CD, 1997). Academy Award nomination for Best Original Score: 1998. Malcolm McNab and Chris Tedesco (t); Jim Thatcher (Frh); Emil Richards and Steve Schaeffer (per).
- *L.A. Confidential: Original Motion Picture Score* (Varèse Sarabande CD, 1997). Jerry Goldsmith's complete score.

L.A. Law
- 45 single by Mike Post: "Theme from *L.A. Law*"/"Jenny's Ayre" (Polydor, 1987). Grammy Award for Best Instrumental Composition: 1988.
- *Music from L.A. Law and Otherwise* (Polydor CD, 1988). Grammy Award nomination for Best Pop Instrumental Performance: 1988. Dave Boruff (sax); Jim Atkinson, Vince DeRosa, David Duke, Ronn Kaufmann and Brian O'Connor (Frh); Philip Ayling (o); James Kanter (cl); James Walker (f); John Goux (g); Pete Robinson (synesizer); Steve Edelman, Arni Egilsson and Jim Hackman (ab); Leland Sklar (eb); Willie Ornelas (d); Gary Coleman and Jeffrey Gerson (per).

The Last Seduction
- *The Last Seduction: Original Motion Picture Soundtrack* (Pure CD, 1995). Jeff Beal and Walt Fowler (t); Les Pierce (as); Steve Tavaglione (cl); Joseph Vitarelli (key); John Pattitucci (b); Kurt Wortman (d, per).

Leverage
- *Leverage: Soundtrack from the Original Television Series* (La La Land CD, 2010).

The Living Daylights
- *The Living Daylights: Original Motion Picture Soundtrack* (Warner Bros. LP and CD, 1987). The first film score—in this book—simultaneously released on analog and digital. Six weeks on the UK's Top LPs chart, peaking at No. 57 on Aug. 1, 1987.
- 45 single by a-ha: "The Living Daylights"/"The Living Daylights" (instrumental) (Warner Bros., 1987). Nine weeks on the UK's Top Singles chart, peaking at No. 5 on July 4, 1987.
- 45 single by The Pretenders: "If There Was a Man"/"Into Vienna" (Real, 1987). Six weeks on the UK's Top Singles chart, peaking at No. 49 on Aug. 15, 1987.
- *The Living Daylights: Original MGM Motion Picture Soundtrack* (Rykodisc CD, 1998). Includes nine bonus tracks.

The Long Goodbye
- *Fitzwilly/The Long Goodbye* (Varèse Sarabande CD, 2004). Includes seven tracks from *The Long Goodbye*.
- *The Long Goodbye: Original Motion Picture Soundtrack* (Quartet CD, 2015). Tommy Tedesco (g); Dave Grusin and John Williams (p); Carol Kaye (ab); Nick Ceroli (d); Emil Richards (per).

Mafia Junction, see *Si può essere più bastardi dell'ispettore Cliff?*

Magnum Force
- *Sudden Impact and the Best of Dirty Harry!* (Viva LP, 1983). Includes one track from *Magnum Force*.
- *Dirty Harry Anthology* (Aleph CD, 1998). Includes five tracks from *Magnum Force*.
- *Magnum Force: The Original Score* (Aleph CD, 2005). Bud Shank (r); Dennis Budimir, Howard Roberts and Tommy Tedesco (g); Max Bennett (ab); Carol Kaye (eb); Emil Richards (per).

Magnum P.I.
- 45 single by Mike Post: "Theme from *Magnum P.I.*"/"Gumbus Red" (Elektra, 1982). Seventeen weeks on *Billboard*'s Hot 100 chart, peaking at No. 25 on May 8 and 15, 1982.

The Manhunter
- *The Quinn Martin Collection, Volume 1: Cop and Detective Series* (La-La Land CDs, 2019). Includes the title theme for *The Manhunter*.

The Marseille Contract
- 45 single by Roy Budd: "Theme Generique Marseille Contrat"/"Contrat" (Warner Bros. France, 1974).
- *The Marseille Contract* (Cinephile CD, 1999). Roy Budd (key); Paul Fishman (electronics); Chris Karan (d, per).

McQ
- *McQ: Original Motion Picture Soundtrack* (Film Score Monthly CD, 2003). John Audino, William B. Peterson and Tony Terran (t); Harold Diner, Barrett O'Hara and Thomas Shepard (tb); Vince DeRosa, Richard E. Perissi, Alan I. Robinson and Gale H. Robinson (Frh); Buddy Collette, Carole Levine and Sylvia Ruderman (f); Justin Gordon, James Kanter and Hugo Raimondi (cl); Al Hendrickson and Alfred Viola (g); Ralph Grierson, Artie Kane and Pearl Kaufman (p); Milt Kestenbaum, Peter Mercurio and Joe Mondragon (b); Max R. Bennett (Fb); Shelly Manne and Mark Z. Stevens (d); Dale L. Anderson, Thomas D. Raney, Louis Singer and Ken Watson (per).

The Mechanic (1972)
- *The Mechanic: Original Motion Picture Soundtrack* (Intrada CD, 2007).

The Men
- 45 single by Isaac Hayes: "Theme from *The Men*"/"Type Thang" (Enterprise, 1972). Nine weeks on *Billboard*'s Hot 100 chart, peaking at No. 38 on Dec. 9, 1972.

La Menace
- *La Menace: Featuring the Music for the Original Soundtrack* (CBS, 1977; DRG CD, 1999). (Digital edition is retitled *Watching and Waiting*.) Gerry Mulligan (ss, bs, key); Dave Grusin and Derek Smith (p); Tom Fay (p and Fender Rhodes); Peter Levin (Moog synthesizer); Edward Walsh (Oberheim synthesizer); Jay Leonhart and Jack Six (b); Michael Di Pasqua and Bobby Rosengarden (d).

The Midnight Man
- 45 single Yvonne Elliman: "Come on Back Where You Belong (Mono)"/"Come on Back Where You Belong (Stereo)" (MCA, 1974).

Mr. Majestyk
- *Mr. Majestyk: Original Motion Picture Soundtrack* (Intrada CD, 2009). Tony Terran (t); Peter Andrews, Dennis Budimir and David Cohen (g); Tommy Morgan (h); Ralph Grierson, Lincoln Mayorga and Clark Spangler (key); Stephens LaFever (b); Gary L. Coleman, Gene P. Estes, Joseph T. Porcaro and Mark Z. Stevens (d, per).

Monty Nash
- 45 single by The Good Stuff: "Theme from *Monty Nash*"/"Theme from *Monty Nash*" (Quad, 1971).

★ Mort d'un pourri
- *Mort d'un pourri: Bande originale du film* (Melba, 1977; Universal Music Jazz CD, 2002). Both LP and CD include unique tracks. Stan Getz (ts); Andrew Laverne (p); Rick Laird (b); Billy Cobham and Billy Hart (d); Efrain Toro (per).

Most Wanted
- 45 single by Lalo Schifrin: "Theme from *Most Wanted*"/"Roller Coaster" (CTI, 1977).
- *The Quinn Martin Collection, Volume 1: Cop and Detective Series* (La-La Land CDs, 2019). Includes the title theme and one episode underscore from *Most Wanted*.

Mulholland Falls
- *Mulholland Falls: Original MGM Motion Picture Soundtrack* (Edel America CD, 1996).
- *Mulholland Falls: Original MGM Motion Picture Soundtrack* (Kritzerland CD, 2011). Expanded edition with Dave Grusin's complete underscore. George Dillon, Warren Luening and Malcolm McNab (t); Charlie Loper, Dick Nash and Bill Reichenbach (tb); Steve Becknell, David Duke, Brian O'Connor, Jim Thatcher and Rick Todd (Frh); Louise DiTullio and James Walker (f); Phil Ayling, Emily Bernstein, Gary Bovyer, Dan Higgins, Jim Kanter, Tom Scott and Sheridon Stokes (ww); Randy Kerber (key); Nico Abondolo, Drew Dembowski, Chuck Domanico, Steve

Edelman, Arni Egilsson, Oscar Hidalgo, Ed Meares, Bruce Morganthaler and Sue Ranney (ab); Greg Goodall, Joe Porcaro and Emil Richards (per).

NBC Mystery Movie
- 45 single by Henry Mancini: "Theme from *Cade's County*"/"*Mystery Movie* Theme" (RCA, 1971). Graham Young (t); Clare Fischer (org).

The New Avengers
- 45 single by Laurie Johnson: "*The New Avengers* Theme"/"A Flavour of *The New Avengers*" (EMI, 1976).
- *Original Television Scores: The Avengers* (Unicorn-Kanchana, 1980). Includes three underscore tracks from *The New Avengers*.
- *The Music of Laurie Johnson, Volume 3: The New Avengers* (Edsel CD box set, 2009). Includes the title themes, complete scores from three episodes, and other incidental cues.

Ocean's Eleven (2001)
- *Ocean's Eleven: Music from the Motion Picture* (Warner Bros. CD, 2001). Ron King (t); Steve Tavaglione (sax, f); Chris Dawkins (g); Brad Dutz (vib, per); Stephen Hilton, Scott Kinsey and Jim Watson (key); Bob Hurst (ab, eb); Zach Danziger (d, per).

Ocean's Twelve
- *Ocean's Twelve: Music from and Inspired by the Motion Picture* (Warner Bros. CD, 2004). Chris Tedesco (t); Bruce Fowler, Walt Fowler and Steve Tavaglione (ho); Leo Abrahams, George Doering and Woody Jackson (g); Jason Faulkner (bg); Robert Hurst and Tim LeFebvre (ab); Zach Danziger (d); Luis Conte, Michael Fisher and Darryl Munyungo Jackson (per).

Ocean's Thirteen
- *Ocean's Thirteen: Music from the Motion Picture* (Warner Sunset CD, 2007). Walt Fowler (t); Bruce Fowler (tb); Steve Tavaglione (sax, f); Tommy Morgan (h); Scott Kinsey (ep); Zac Rae (key); George Doering (g, dulcimer); Jason Falkner and Woody Jackson (bg); Robert Hurst and Tim LeFebvre (ab); Zach Danziger (d); Davey Chegwidden, Luis Conte and Hugo Nicolson (per).

Ordeal by Innocence
- *Ordeal by Innocence: An Original MGM Motion Picture Soundtrack* (Kritzerland CD, 2011). Pino Donaggio's rejected initial score.

The Organization
- *The Organization: Original MGM Motion Picture Soundtrack* (Intrada CD, 2010). John Audino, Conte Candoli, Jay J. Daversa and James C. Zito (t); Gilbert M. Falco, George M. Roberts, Thomas M. Shepart and Lloyd Ulyate (tb); Vince DeRosa, William Hinshaw, Richard L. Mackey, Arthur N. Maebe and Richard Perissi (Frh); Gene Cipriano, Robert W. Cooper, Bernard Fleischer, Jules Jacob, John E. Lowe, Don Menza and Bud Shank (ww); Charles Domanico (b); John Guerin, Paul N. Humphrey, Emil Richards, Mark Stevens and Tommy Vig (d, per).

The Osterman Weekend
- *The Osterman Weekend: Original Motion Picture Soundtrack* (Varèse Sarabande, 1983; Aleph CD, 1999). Digital edition includes six bonus tracks. Malcolm McNab (t); Ernie Watts (sax); Paulinho Da Costa and Emil Richards (per).

Out of Sight
- *Out of Sight: Music from the Motion Picture* (Jersey/MCA CD, 1998). Darren Morris (key); Phil Mossman (g, b); and Tim Goldsworthy (d).

★ Out of Time
- *Out of Time: Original Motion Picture Soundtrack* (Varèse Sarabande CD, 2003). Oscar Brashear

and Harry Kim (t); Alex Iles, Alan Kaplan and Bill Reichenbach (tb); Rick Todd (Frh); Mike Lang (p); Ed Meares (ab); Peter Erskine (d); Alex Acuña, Lenny Castro, Luis Conte, Paulinho Da Costa and Emil Richards (per).

The Outfit
- *Point Blank/The Outfit* (Film Score Monthly CD, 2002). Maurie Harris and Cappy Lewis (t); Joe Howard, Dick Nash, George M. Roberts, Thomas Shepard and Lloyd Ulyate (tb); Vince DeRosa, Arthur Maebe, Jr., and Henry Sigismonti (Frh); Bud Shank and Sheridon W. Stokes (f); Gene Cipriano, Dominick Fera and Joseph Soldo (cl); Artie Kane (p); Ralph Grierson (key); Larry G. Muhoberac Jr. (org); Suzanne Ailman, Chuck Domanico, Arni Egilsson, Milt Kestenbaum, Abe Luboff and Peter Mercurio (b); Larry Bunker, Emil Richards and Ken Watson (per).

Payback
- *Payback: Original Motion Picture Soundtrack* (Varèse Sarabande CD, 1999).
- *Payback: Original Film Score* (Icon Productions CD, 1999). Promo album devoted exclusively to Chris Boardman's underscore. Jerry Hey and Malcolm McNab (t); Alan Kaplan and Charlie Morillas (tb); Jim Thatcher (Frh); Tom Boyd (o); Dan Higgins and Plas Johnson (ww); John Goux (g); Norman Ludwin (ab).

The Persuaders
- 45 single by John Barry: "Theme from *The Persuaders*"/"The Girl with the Sun in Her Hair" (CBS, 1971). Fifteen weeks on the British Singles chart, peaking at No. 13 on Dec. 11, 1971.
- *The Music of ITC* (Network CD, 2009). Includes Barry's title theme and two Ken Thorne underscore cues from *The Persuaders*.

The Pink Panther (2006)
- *The Pink Panther: Original Motion Picture Soundtrack* (Varèse Sarabande CD, 2006). Wayne Bergeron, Walt Fowler, Gary Grant, Jon Lewis, Warren Luening and Malcolm McNab (t); Bill Booth, Charlie Loper, Bill Reichenbach, Phil Teele and George Thatcher (tb); Jim Thatcher (Frh); Plas Johnson (ts); Joel Peskin and James Walker (f); Dan Higgins and Bob Sheppard (cl); George Doering (g); Mike Lang, Richard Ruttenberg and Mike Watts (key); Michael Valerio (ab); Peter Erskine (d); Alan Estes and Mike Fisher (per).

Police Story
- *Police Story: Original Soundtrack Recording* (Prometheus CD, 2000). Emmy Award nomination for Outstanding Music Composition for a Series: 1977.

The Pope of Greenwich Village
- *The Pope of Greenwich Village: Original MGM Motion Picture Soundtrack* (Quartet CD, 2012).

Pretty Maids All in a Row
- *Pretty Maids All in a Row* (Film Score Monthly CD, 2011). Gary A. Barone, Bobby Bryant and Tony Terran (t); Dick Hyde, Dick Nash, Richard Noel and Benny Powell (tb); Vince DeRosa, William A. Hinshaw and Richard Perissi (Frh); Gene Cipriano, Buddy Collette, Dominick Fera, Plas Johnson, John J. Kelson, Ronny Lang, Ted Nash and Jack Nimitz (sax); Donald G. Peake, Howard Roberts, Tommy Tedesco and David T. Walker (g); Ralph Grierson, Artie Kane and Lincoln Mayorga (p); Max R. Bennett and Ray Brown (b); John Guerin and Jerry D. Williams (d); Jack Arnold, Joe Porcaro and Emil Richards (per).

The Professionals
- *Original Television Scores: The Avengers* (Unicorn-Kanchana, 1980). Includes seven tracks from *The Professionals*.
- 45 single by Laurie Johnson: "*The Professionals* (Main Title Theme)"/"On Target" (Unicorn-Kanchana, 1980).
- *The Music of Laurie Johnson, Volume 2: The Professionals* (Edsel CD box set, 2008). Includes the title theme and underscore cues from 10 episodes.

The Protector
- *The Protector: Original Motion Picture Soundtrack* (Easy Street, 1985; Dragon's Domain CD, 2018).

The Protectors
- 45 single by Tony Christie: "Avenues and Alleyways"/"I Never Was a Child" (MCA, 1972). Four weeks on the UK Singles chart, rising to No. 37 on Feb. 10, 1973.
- *The Protectors: Original Soundtrack* (Network CDs, 2009). Five-disc set with the roughly 400 surviving cues and alternate takes.

The Public Eye
- *The Public Eye: Original Motion Picture Soundtrack* (Varèse Sarabande CD, 1992). Plas Johnson (ts); Jim Walker (f); Rich Ruttenberg and Gerald Wiggins (p); Chuck Domanio (b); Kurt Wortman (d).

Puppet on a Chain
- *Puppet on a Chain: An Original Soundtrack Recording* (D.C. Recordings LP and CD, 2001).

Quiller (TV series)
- 45 single by Richard Denton and Martin Cook: "Quiller"/"General Direction" (BBC, 1975).

The Rainmaker
- *The Rainmaker* (Hollywood CD, 1997). Wayne Bergeron, Warren Luening and Malcolm McNab (t); Jim Thatcher (Frh); Tommy Johnson (tuba); Dan Higgins (ww); Tom Boyd (o); George Doering (g); Mike Lang (HB3).

The Return of the Pink Panther
- *The Return of the Pink Panther: Original Motion Picture Soundtrack* (RCA Victor, 1975; CD, 1991). Grammy Award nomination for Best Original Score Written for a Motion Picture or Television Show: 1976. Tony Coe (ts); Adrian Brett (f); Henry Mancini (p); Kenny Clare (d).

Return of The Saint
- 45 single by Brian Dee and Irving Martin: "*Return of The Saint* Theme"/"Funko" (Pye, 1978).
- *The Music of ITC* (Network CD, 2009). Includes eight tracks from *Return of The Saint*.

The Rockford Files
- 45 single by Mike Post: "The Rockford Files"/"Dixie Lullabye" (MGM, 1974). Sixteen weeks on *Billboard*'s Top 100 chart, peaking at No. 10 on Aug. 9 and 16, 1975. Grammy Award for Arrangement, Instrumental or A Cappella: 1976. Grammy Award nominations for Best Instrumental Composition, and Best Pop Instrumental Performance: 1976.

★ Rough Cut
- *Rough Cut: Music from the Motion Picture* (Quartet CD, 2019). Bob Findley (t); Bill Watrous (tb); Plas Johnson (ts); Emil Richards (per).

★ Rounders
- *Rounders: Music from the Miramax Motion Picture* (Varèse Sarabande CD, 1998). Wayne Bergeron (t); Alex Iles (tb); Brandon Fields (sax, f); Bill Liston (ts, bs); Gary Gray (cl); Gary Nesterux (p); Mike Lang (org); Dean Parks (g); Karl Vincent-Wickliff (ab); M.B. Gordy (d); John Fitzgerald (per).

Rush Hour
- *Rush Hour: Original Film Score* (Aleph CD, 1998). Grammy Award nomination for Best Sound Track Album—Background Score from a Motion Picture or Television: 1999. Rick Baptist, Jon Lewis, Warren Luening, Carl Saunders and Frank Szabo (t); Alan Kaplan, Charlie Loper and Andy Martin (tb); Rick Todd and Brad Warnaar (Frh); Steve Kujala and Joel Peskin (f); Gene Cipriano and Steve Tavaglione (ww); George Doering (g); Alex Acuña and Emil Richards (per).

★ The Russia House
- *The Russia House: The Motion Picture Soundtrack* (MCA LP and CD, 1990). Branford Marsalis (ss); Billy Childs and Mike Lang (p); Tony Dumas and John Patitucci (b); Ralph Penland (d).
- *The Russia House: Original MGM Motion Picture Soundtrack* (Quartet CD, 2017). Includes eight bonus tracks.

The Saint (1989)
- *The Saint: Original Television Soundtrack* (Music Box CDs, 2016).

The Score
- *The Score: Original Motion Picture Soundtrack* (Varèse Sarabande CD, 2001). Does not include any of the film's jazz source cues.

Sea of Love
- *Sea of Love: Original Motion Picture Soundtrack* (Mercury LP and CD, 1989). Malcolm McNab (t); Tom Scott (sax).

The Seven-Ups
- *The Seven-Ups/The Verdict* (Intrada CD, 2007).
- *The Verdict/The Seven-Ups/M.A.S.H.* (Kritzerland CD, 2018). Includes Johnny Mandel's complete unused score for *The Seven-Ups*.

★ Shaft (1971 film)
- *Shaft: Music from the Soundtrack* (Enterprise 1971; Stax CD, 1986). Sixty weeks on *Billboard*'s Hot 200 album chart, peaking at No. 1 on Nov. 6, 1971. Academy Award for Best Original Song: 1972. Academy Award nomination for Best Original Score: 1972. Grammy Awards for Best Engineered Recording, Best Instrumental Arrangement, and Best Original Score Written for a Motion Picture or Television Special: 1972. Grammy Award nominations for Album of the Year, Best Instrumental Composition, Best Rhythm and Blues Performance, and Record of the Year: 1972. Richard "Johnny" Davis (t); John Fonville (f); Isaac Hayes (key); Lester Snell (ep); Michael Toles (g); James Alexander (bg); Willie Hall (d); Gary Jones (cng, bng).
- 45 single by Isaac Hayes: "Theme from *Shaft*"/"Café Regios" (Enterprise, 1971). Thirteen weeks on *Billboard*'s Hot 100 chart, peaking at No. 1 on Nov. 20 and 27, 1971.
- 45 single by Isaac Hayes: "Do Your Thing"/"Ellie's Love Theme" (Enterprise, 1972). Eleven weeks on *Billboard*'s Hot 100 chart, parking at No. 30 on April 8, 1972.
- *Shaft Anthology: His Big Score and More* (Film Score Monthly CDs, 2008). Includes Hayes' original score cues (as opposed to the LP reorchestrations).

Shaft (1973 TV series)
- *Shaft Anthology: His Big Score and More* (Film Score Monthly CDs, 2008). Includes all of Johnny Pate's work on the TV series.

Shaft (2000 film)
- *Shaft: Still the Man* (Big Apple CD, 2000). Includes tracks from the three 1970s *Shaft* films.
- *Shaft: Music from the Motion Picture* (La-La Land CD, 2014). David Arnold's complete 2000 underscore, along with five bonus tracks.

Shaft (2019 film)
- *Shaft: Original Motion Picture Soundtrack* (Watertower CD, 2019).

Shaft in Africa
- *Shaft in Africa: Original Music from the MGM Film* (ABC, 1973; Hip-O Select/Geffen CD, 2005).
- 45 single by the Four Tops: "Are You Man Enough"/"Peace of Mind" (Dunhill, 1973). Thirteen weeks on *Billboard*'s Hot 100 chart, peaking at No. 15 on Sept. 8, 1973.

★ Shaft's Big Score
- *Shaft's Big Score: Original Motion Picture Soundtrack* (MGM, 1972).

- *Shaft Anthology: His Big Score and More* (Film Score Monthly CDs, 2008). Includes the contents of the MGM album, along with nine bonus tracks. Albert Aarons, Bobby Bryant, Freddie Hubbard and Tony Terran (t); James Cleveland, Grover Mitchell, Dick Nash, Maurice Spears and Britt Woodman (tb); William A. Hinshaw and Arthur Maebe, Jr. (Frh); Buddy Collette, Wilton L. Felder, Norman Foster, William E. Green, Plas Johnson, Jerome Richardson and Marshall Royal (sax); Louise DiTullio (f); David H. Cohen, Joe Passalaqua and Tommy Tedesco (g); Douglas Clare Fischer, Caesar Giovannini and Joseph L. Sample (p); Max R. Bennett and Ray Brown (b); Wilton L. Felder (Fb); Dale L. Anderson, Colin Bailey, Larry Bunker, Gene Paul Estes, Victor Feldman, Paul N. Humphrey and Emil Richards (d).
- 45 single by Isaac Hayes: "Theme from *The Men*"/"Type Thang" (Enterprise, 1972). Nine weeks on *Billboard's* Hot 100 chart, peaking at No. 38 on Dec. 9, 1972.

★ *Sharky's Machine*
- *The Soundtrack Music from Sharky's Machine* (Warner Bros., 1981; Varèse Sarabande CD, 2014). Pete Candoli, Doc Severinsen and Snooky Young (t); Jimmy Cleveland, Carl Fontana and Bill Watrous (tb); Art Pepper and Marshall Royal (as); Eddie Harris and Bill Perkins (ts); Buddy De Franco (cl); Pete Jolly (key); Terry Gibbs (vib); Barney Kessel and Tommy Tedesco (g); Ray Brown and Bob Magnusson (b); Shelly Manne (d); Gene Estes and Emile Richards (per).

Shiner
- *Shiner: Original Motion Picture Soundtrack* (Decca CD, 2001). Guy Barker and Phil Slater (t); Lachlan Davidson (b cl); Ren Walters (g); Paul Grabowsky (key); Mike Grabowsky (b); Niko Schauble (d); Alex Pertout (per).

Shoestring
- 45 single by George Fenton: "Shoestring"/"Tumpy" (BBC, 1979).

★ *Si può essere più bastardi dell'ispettore Cliff?*
- 45 single by Riz Ortolani: "L'Intoccabile Mr. Cliff"/"Love Break" (Cam, 1973).
- *Si può essere più bastardi dell'ispettore Cliff?: Colonna Sonora Originale del Film* (Four Flies LP, 2017).
- *Si può essere più bastardi dell'ispettore Cliff?* (Chris' Soundtrack Corner CD, 2018). Includes eight bonus tracks.

★ *The Silent Partner*
- *The Silent Partner* (Pablo, 1979). Clark Terry (t); Benny Carter (as); Zoot Sims (ts); Oscar Peterson (key); Milt Jackson (vib); John Heard (b); Grady Tate (d).

Sneakers
- *Sneakers: Original Motion Picture Soundtrack Album* (Columbia CD, 1992). Branford Marsalis (ts); Alan Kaplan (tb); Jim Thatcher (Frh); Joel Peskin (ww); James Walker (f); James Horner and Ralph Grierson (p); Ian Underwood (key); Mike Fisher (per).

The Specialist
- *The Specialist: Original Motion Picture Score* (Epic CD, 1994).

Starsky & Hutch
- 45 single by Tom Scott: "Gotcha (Theme from *Starsky & Hutch*)"/"Smoothin' on Down" (Epic/Ode, 1977).

A Step Out of Line
- *The Brotherhood of the Bell/A Step Out of Line* (Intrada CD, 2010). Includes Jerry Goldsmith's score for 1970's *The Brotherhood of the Bell*. Pete Candoli (t); Buddy Collette (r); Bobby Bain and Al Viola (g); Ralph Grierson and Artie Kane (p); Ray Brown, Milt Kestenbaum and Peter Mercurio (b); Shelly Manne (d).

★ The Stone Killer
- 45 single by Roy Budd: "Main Theme from Stone Killer"/"Jazz Theme from Stone Killer" (Seven Seas, 1973).
- *The Stone Killer: L'Assassino Di Pietra* (Fonit Cetra International, 1974; Legend CD, 1991).
- *The Stone Killer: Original Motion Picture Soundtrack* (Cinephile CD, 1999).
- *The Stone Killer* (Jambo Records digital download, 2019). Includes 13 bonus tracks.

Stormy Monday
- *Stormy Monday: Original Soundtrack Album* (Atlantic CD, 1988). Mike Figgis (t); Davey Payne (ts); Paul Jolly and Ray Warleigh (as); Ed Dean (g); Mel Davis (p); Alex Dankworth and Charlie Hart (b); Clark Tracey (d); Terry Day (per).

The Streets of San Francisco
- 45 single by Patrick Williams: "Theme from *The Streets of San Francisco*"/"California Love Story" (Capitol, 1975). Emmy Award nomination for Outstanding Music Composition for a Series: 1975.

Sudden Impact
- *Sudden Impact and the Best of Dirty Harry!* (Viva LP, 1983). Includes four tracks from *Sudden Impact*.
- *Dirty Harry Anthology* (Aleph CD, 1998). Includes eight tracks from *Sudden Impact*.
- *Sudden Impact: The Original Score* (Aleph CD, 2008). Chuck Findley, Gary Grant and Jerry Hey (t); Herbie Harper, Dick Nash, Dick Noel, Bob Payne, Ken Shroyer and Phil Teele (tb); Vince DeRosa and Richard Perissi (Frh); Gene Cipriano, Louise DiTullio, Bob Efford, Bob Hardaway, Gary Herbig, Ronnie Lang, Ted Nash, Dave Pell, Joe Peskin and Ernie Watts (ww); Randy Kerber, Mike Lang, Bill Mays and Ian Underwood (key); Anita Priest (org); Ray Brown and Chuck Domanico (ab); Abe Laboriel (eb, ab); Alex Acuña, Larry Bunker, Alan Estes, Paul Leim, Harvey Mason, Emil Richards and Ken Watson (d, per).

★ The Super Cops
- *Zigzag/The Super Cops* (Film Score Monthly CD, 2006). Includes Oliver Nelson's score for 1970's *Zig Zag*. David Gale, Ralph Mazer, Bob McCoy and Bob Millikan (t); Bob Alexander (tb); Charles Urbont (b).

The Sweeney
- 45 single by Harry South: "The Sweeney (Closing Version)"/"The Sweeney (Opening Version)" (EMI, 1975).
- *Shut It: The Music of The Sweeney* (Sanctuary CD, 2001).

★ The Taking of Pelham One Two Three (1974)
- *The Taking of Pelham One Two Three: Original Motion Picture Soundtrack* (Retrograde/Film Score Monthly CD, 1996). Chuck Findley, Malcolm McNab, Edward Allen Sheftel and Tony Terran (t); Dick Nash, George M. Roberts and Lloyd Ulyate (tb); Vince DeRosa, David A. Duke, Arthur Maebe, Jr., Richard Perissi and Gale H. Robinson (Frh); David H. Cohen (g); Artie Kane and Clark Spangler (key); Charles L. Domanico, Milt Kestenbaum, Joe Mondragon and Mike Rubin (b); Larry Bunker, Milt Holland, Shelly Manne and Emil Richards (per).

The Talented Mr. Ripley
- *The Talented Mr. Ripley: Music from the Motion Picture* (Sony Classical CD, 1999). Academy Award nomination for Best Original Score: 2000. Guy Barker (t); Byron Wallen (c); Pete King and Perico Sambeat (as); Rosario Giuliuni and Jean Toussaint (ts); Eddie Palermo (g); Carlo Negroni and Bernardo Sassetti (p); Geoff Gascogne and Joseph Lepore (ab); Gene Calderazzo and Clark Tracey (d).

Taxi Driver
- *Taxi Driver: Original Soundtrack Recording* (Arista, 1976; CD, 1985). Academy Award nomination

for Best Original Score: 1977. Grammy Award nomination for Best Original Score Written for a Motion Picture or Television Show: 1977.
- *Taxi Driver: Original Soundtrack Recording* (Arista CD, 1998). Expanded edition with Bernard Herrmann's original score cues. Warren Luening, Malcolm McNab and Uan Rasey (t); Charlie Loper (tb); Ronnie Lang and Tom Scott (as); Emil Richards (per).

Tequila Sunrise
- *Tequila Sunrise: Original Motion Picture Soundtrack* (Capitol LP and CD, 1988). Chuck Findley (t); Alan Kaplan (tb); David Sanborn (sax); Lee Ritenour (g); Paulinho Da Costa (per).

The Thief Who Came to Dinner
- *The Thief Who Came to Dinner: Original Motion Picture Soundtrack* (Warner Bros., 1973; Film Score Monthly CD, 2009). Digital edition includes 17 bonus tracks. Albert Aarons, Oscar Brashear, Bud Brisbois, Raymond Triscari and Graham Young (t); Dick Nash, James Priddy, Terry C. Woodson (tb); Vince DeRosa, Richard E. Perissi, Alan I. Robinson and Marilyn Robinson (Frh); Hoyt Bohannon, Dick Hyde, Lewis Melvin McCreary and David Howard Wells (bh); Ronny Lang, Don Menza, Ted Nash, Ray Pizzi and Ethmer Roten (ww); Douglas Clare Fischer, Ralph Grierson, Artie Kane, Larry G. Muhoberac Jr., Jimmy Rowles, Clark Spangler (key); John Montenegro (syn); Shelly Manne (d); Tommy Vig (per).
- 45 single by Henry Mancini: "Theme from *The Thief Who Came to Dinner*"/"Charade" (RCA Victor, 1973).

Three Days of the Condor
- *Three Days of the Condor: Original Soundtrack Recording* (Capitol, 1975; Film Score Monthly CD, 2012). Digital edition includes eight bonus tracks, along with Dave Grusin's score for 1973's *The Friends of Eddie Coyle*. Tom Bahler, Chuck Findley and Paul T. Hubinon (t); Joe Howard, Charles C. Loper and Frank Rosolino (tb); Vince DeRosa and Richard Perissi (Frh); Jules Jacob, John Neufeld, Jerome Richardson, Thomas W. Scott and Bud Shank (ww); Hugh McCracken and Lee Ritenour (g); Artie Kane and Ian Underwood (key); Ray Brown and Chuck Rainey (b); Ralph MacDonald, Harvey Mason, Joe Porcaro and Emil Richards (d).
- 45 promo single by Dave Grusin: "Condor! (mono)"/"Condor! (stereo)" (Capitol, 1975).

Tower Heist
- *Tower Heist: Original Motion Picture Soundtrack* (Varèse Sarabande CD, 2011). Tony Kadleck, Raymond Riccomini, Jim Ross and John Sheppard (t); Demian Austin, Mike Davis, George Flynn, Patrick Herb and Jim Markey (tb); Lawrence Feldman and Andy Snitzer (sax); Wade Culbreath (vib); George Doering (g); Randy Kerber (key); Rachel Calin, Shawn Conley, Jacqui Danilow, Satoshi Okamoto, John Patitucci, Michael Valerio and Kingsley Wood (b); Matt Chamberlain, Peter Erskine and John Robinson (d); Erik Charlston, Gordon Gottlieb, Roland Morales, Joe Passaro and Kevin Ricard (per).

★ *Trouble Man*
- *Trouble Man: Motion Picture Soundtrack* (Tamla, 1972; Motown CD, 1994). Twenty-one weeks on *Billboard*'s Top LPs chart, peaking at No. 14 on Feb. 3, 1973. Trevor Lawrence (as, ts, bs); Eli Fountain (as); Marty Montgomery (ss); James Anthony Carmichael and Dale Oehler (ho); Don Peake and Louis Shelton (g); Larry Mizell and Bob Ragland (p); Wilton Felder (b); Earl Palmer (d).
- 45 single by Marvin Gaye: "Trouble Man"/"Don't Mess with Mr. T" (Tamla, 1972). Twelve weeks on *Billboard*'s Hot 100 chart, peaking at No. 7 on Feb. 3, 1973.
- *Trouble Man: 40th Anniversary Expanded Edition* (Motown/Hip-O Select CD, 2012). Includes Gaye's original score cues, the 1972 LP contents and numerous bonus tracks.

Twin Peaks (1990)
- *Soundtrack from Twin Peaks* (Warner Bros. CD, 1990). Grammy Award for Best Pop Instrumental Performance: 1991. Grammy Award nomination, for Best Sound Track Album: 1991. Emmy

Award nominations for Outstanding Main Title Theme, Outstanding Original Music and Lyrics, and Outstanding Music Composition for a Series: 1990.
- 45 single by Julee Cruise and Angelo Badalamenti: "Falling"/"*Twin Peaks* Theme" (Warner Bros., 1990).
- *Twin Peaks: Season Two Music and More* (David Lynch Music Co. CD, 2007).

Twin Peaks (2017)
- *Twin Peaks: Limited Event Series Soundtrack* (Rhino CD, 2017).

Twin Peaks: Fire Walk with Me
- *Twin Peaks: Fire Walk with Me (Music from the Motion Picture Soundtrack)* (Warner Bros. CD, 1992).

The Yakuza
- *The Yakuza: Original Motion Picture Soundtrack* (Film Score Monthly CD, 2005). Vince DeRosa, David Duke and Alan I. Robinson (Frh); Richard H. Anderson, Gene Cipriano, Dominick Fera, John Neufeld and Bud Shank (ww); Lee Ritenour (g); Ralph Grierson and Artie Kane (p); Chuck Berghofer and Peter Mercurio (b); Chuck Berghofer (Fb); Kayoko Wakita (koto); Larry Bunker, Joe Porcaro, Emil Richards and Jerry D. Williams (per).

Appendix C: Cover Artists, Compilation Albums and Box Sets

In the wake of Henry Mancini's success with *Peter Gunn*—and, a few years later, the brass-heavy spy jazz John Barry delivered for James Bond—various jazz artists and band leaders began to cover the most popular themes and interior cues with their own ensembles. A few turned this practice into quite successful cottage industries, releasing multiple albums as the years passed. Compilation albums took a different approach, bundling original and/or cover versions of TV and movie themes according to subject or era; although such albums debuted in the 1960s, they didn't really take off until the 1990s and beyond, fueled by the rising nostalgia for classic action and spy jazz. (Repetition became ubiquitous; some classics—such as Lalo Schifrin's original "Mission: Impossible" theme—found their way onto *every single release*.) Lavish box sets gave the genre even more respect as the 21st century dawned.

This list is limited to must-have releases. The first section is arranged alphabetically by cover artist's last name, after which the compilation albums and box sets are arranged alphabetically by title. As is the case with the discography of soundtrack albums, some of the following have yet to be digitized.

* * *

Count Basie and His Orchestra
- *Basie Meets Bond* (United Artists, 1966; Capitol CD, 2002). Digital edition includes a bonus track.

Al Caiola
- *Sounds for Spies and Private Eyes* (United Artists, 1965).

Ray Davies and the Button Down Brass
- *Firedog!* (DJM, 1976).

Brian Fahey and His Orchestra
- *Time for T.V.* (Studio 2 Stereo, 1967; CD, 1999). Digital edition includes Alan Hawkshaw's *27 Top TV Themes and Commercials*.

The Jason Frederick Cinematic Sound
- *Mods and Coppers* (Lomax CD, 2015). Marvelous "little big band" arrangements of film and TV themes, including clever mash-ups (notably the blend of "S.W.A.T." and "The New Avengers").

John Gregory and His Orchestra
- *TV Thriller Themes* (Philips, 1961; él CD, 2015). Digital edition includes Gregory's *Channel West*.
- *Chaquito Plays the Themes from TV Thrillers* (Philips, 1972; Vocalion CD, 2010).

- *Spies and Dolls* (Philips, 1972; Vocalion CD, 2010).
- *The Detectives* (Philips, 1976).
- *Mission: Impossible and Other TV Themes* (Mercury CD, 1996).

Mundell Lowe and His All Stars
- *TV Action Jazz* (RCA, 1959).
- *Themes from Mr. Lucky, The Untouchables and Other TV Action Jazz* (RCA, 1960).
- *Complete TV Action Jazz!* (Lone Hill Jazz CD, 2005). Gathers all tracks from both LPs.

Ralph Marterie and His Marlboro Men
- *Music for a Private Eye: Swinging Themes of Famous TV Whodunits* (Mercury, 1959).

Skip Martin and the Video All-Stars
- *TV Jazz Themes* (Somerset, 1958).

Hugo Montenegro and His Orchestra
- *Come Spy with Me* (RCA, 1966; CD, 2002).

Norrie Paramor and His Orchestra
- *Law Beat* (Contour, 1974).

The Roland Shaw Orchestra
- *Themes from the James Bond Thrillers* (London, 1964).
- *More Themes from James Bond Thrillers* (London, 1965).
- *Themes from the James Bond Thrillers: Vol. 3* (London, 1966).
- *Themes for Secret Agents* (London, 1966).
- *The Return of James Bond: Diamonds Are Forever and Other Secret Agent Themes* (London, 1971).
- *James Bond in Action: Themes for Secret Agents* (Cherry Red, 2008). Gathers all tracks from the five LPs. (Be advised: The mastering of this two-disc package is seriously suboptimal.)

Keith Williams and His Orchestra
- *Big Band Jazz Themes from Television & Motion Pictures* (Edison International, 1960).

Si Zentner and His Orchestra
- *From Russia with Love* (Liberty, 1964; Vocalion CD, 2012). Digital edition includes Zentner's cover score of 1967's *Warning Shot*.

* * *

Come Spy with Us: The Secret Agent Songbook (Ace CD, 2014). A blend of original and obscure cover versions of TV and film themes.

Crime Jazz: Music in the First Degree (Rhino CD, 1997). A blend of original and cover versions.

Crime Jazz: Music in the Second Degree (Rhino CD, 1997). Includes numerous obscure tracks from lesser-known thrillers.

Crime Scene: Ultra-Lounge Volume Seven (Capitol CD, 1996). A solid blend of original and cover TV and film themes.

Jazz Noir: 60 Menacing Masterpieces of Mystery, Murder and Mayhem (Not Now Music CDs, 2014). A wide-ranging three-disc set that includes foreign and lesser-known American thriller themes and cues.

Jazzwise Magazine: Beat, Square & Cool (Jazz on Film CDs, 2012). A five-disc set with full or partial scores from eight films.

Jazzwise Magazine: Chet Baker—Italian Movies (Jazz on Film CDs, 2013). A three-disc set with full or partial scores from five films.

Jazzwise Magazine: Crime Jazz! (Jazz on Film, 2014). An eight-disc set with full soundtracks from 13 1950s and early '60s TV shows.

Jazzwise Magazine: Film Noir (Jazz on Film CDs, 2011). A five-disc set with full scores from seven films.

Jazzwise Magazine: French New Wave (Jazz on Film CDs, 2013). A five-disc set with full or partial scores from seven films.

Jazzwise Magazine: The New Wave II (Jazz on Film CDs, 2015). An eight-disc set with full or partial scores from 25 films (many of which don't qualify as crime or action jazz).

Mission Accomplished: Themes for Spies & Cops (Hip-O CD, 1996). Mostly TV title themes, with a bit o' Bond.

Mission Accomplished, Too: More Themes for Spies & Cops (Hip-O CD, 1998). Almost entirely TV titles themes, along with some obscure covers.

Shaken Not Stirred: 45 Classic Agents, Spies, Cops & PIs Movie Themes (Sony CDs, 2001). The title notwithstanding, a terrific two-disc blend of TV and movie themes: the most comprehensive compilation in this list.

This Is ... Cult Fiction Royale (Virgin CDs, 1997). A two-disc set that also slides toward sci-fi and fantasy TV.

Thriller Jazz (Verve CD, 2008). A good mix of TV and film covers and originals.

Watching the Detectives: Themes and Music from Classic TV Crime Shows and Movies (Jasmine CD, 2015). The title notwithstanding, focuses mostly on 1950s and early '60s TV themes.

Chapter Notes

Preface

1. Charles Gompertz, interview with the author, Feb. 8, 2010.
2. Selwyn Harris, booklet notes for *The Sweet Smell of Success*, in the box set *Film Noir* (Jazz on Film, 2011), 29.

Chapter 1

1. Jonathan Etter, *Quinn Martin, Producer* (Jefferson, NC: McFarland, 2008), 127.
2. "Columbo: Just One More Thing," accessed Aug. 8, 2019, http://www.columbo-site.freeuk.com/murderplay.htm.
3. Jon Burlingame, *TV's Biggest Hits* (New York: Schirmer, 1996), 55.
4. Jon Burlingame, "Caught in the Crosscurrent," booklet notes for the soundtrack compilation *The Last Run/Crosscurrent/The Scorpio Letters* (Film Score Monthly, 2007), 12.
5. Rob Bowman, *Soulsville USA: The Story of Stax Records* (New York: Music Sales, 1997), 233.
6. Isaac Hayes, archive interview in Karen Michel's "Can Ya Dig It? Still Down with Shaft," National Public Radio's *Morning Edition*, December 21, 2000, accessed Aug. 8, 2019, https://www.npr.org/2000/12/21/1115821/the-npr-100-isaac-hayes-shaft.
7. Bowman, *Soulsville USA: The Story of Stax Records*, 230.
8. Douglass Fake, "*The Organization*: Tech Talk," accessed Aug. 8, 2019, http://store.intrada.com/s.nl/it.A/id.6742/.f.
9. Lalo Schifrin, *Music Composition for Film and Television* (Boston: Berklee, 2011), 26.
10. Ibid., 2.
11. Jon Burlingame, "Dirty Harry Makes Day," *The Film Music Society*, Aug. 6, 2004, accessed Aug. 8, 2019, http://www.filmmusicsociety.org/news_events/features/2004/080604.html.
12. Scott Harris, "Life in 13/8," *Film Score Monthly*, March 2001, 22.
13. Burlingame, *TV's Biggest Hits*, 212.
14. Jon Burlingame, "Jon Leach, English Cimbalom Player, Dead at 82," *The Film Music Society*, July 14, 2014, accessed Aug. 8, 2019, http://www.filmmusicsociety.org/news_events/features/newsprint.php?ArticleID=071414.
15. Ibid.
16. "The Official Roy Budd Website," accessed Aug. 8, 2019, http://www.roybudd.com.
17. Phil Johnson, "Sight and Sound," *NewStatesman*, March 5, 1999, accessed Aug. 8, 2019, https://www.newstatesman.com/node/148771.
18. Paul Fishman, "Get Carter," booklet notes for the digital reissue of the album *Get Carter: Original Motion Picture Soundtrack* (Silva Screen, 2010), 7.
19. Allan Bryce, "A Conversation with Roy Budd," *Soundtrack Magazine*, Vol. 3, No. 11, 1984, accessed Aug. 8, 2019, https://cnmsarchive.wordpress.com/2014/06/21/roy-budd-2/.
20. Johnson, "Sight and Sound," March 5, 1999.
21. Alan Burton, *Historical Dictionary of British Spy Fiction* (Lanham, MD: Rowman & Littlefield, 2016), 425–27.

Chapter 2

1. Jon Burlingame, *TV's Biggest Hits* (New York: Schirmer, 1996), 52.
2. David Ritz, *Divided Soul: The Life of Marvin Gaye* (Lebanon, IN: Hachette, 2009), 164.
3. Marvin Gaye, interview by Paul Gambaccini, BBC Radio 1, late 1976, accessed Aug. 8, 2019, https://www.dialogues.org/interview/01/01/1976/marvin-gaye-interview-with-paul-gambaccini-bbc-radio-one-1976-part-1-4-/1437331850.
4. Nick Redman, "The One That Got Away," booklet notes for the album *Music for The Getaway: Jerry Fielding's Original Score* (Film Score Monthly, 2005), 7.
5. Garner Simmons, *Peckinpah: A Portrait in Montage* (Milwaukee, WI: Hal Leonard, 1998), 165–66.
6. Lukas Kendall, correspondence with the author, Sept. 5, 2017.
7. "The Standard Music Library," accessed Aug. 8, 2019, http://www.standardmusiclibrary.com/about/.

Chapter 3

1. Mike Post, video interview by Stephen

J. Abramson on May 25, 2005, accessed Aug. 8, 2019, https://interviews.televisionacademy.com/interviews/mike-post#interview-clips.

2. Paul Vitello, "Tony Musante, Actor Known for Role in *Toma*, Dies at 77," *The New York Times*, Nov. 27, 2013, accessed Aug. 8, 2019, https://www.nytimes.com/2013/11/28/arts/tony-musante-actor-known-for-role-in-toma-dies-at-77.html.

3. Lee Goldberg, *Unsold Television Pilots: 1955–1989* (CreateSpace, 2015), entry 1183.

4. Vincent Terrace, *Encyclopedia of Television Pilots, 1937–2012* (Jefferson, NC: McFarland, 2008), 131–32.

5. Lalo Schifrin, *Music Composition for Film and Television* (Boston: Berklee, 2011), 45.

6. *Ibid.*, 47.

7. Charles Fox, *Killing Me Softly: My Life in Music* (Lanham, MD: Scarecrow, 2010), 158.

8. Johnny Mandel, video interview by Linda Danly on Aug. 1, 2007, accessed July 31, 2019, https://www.filmmusicfoundation.org/interviews.html.

9. Peter Yates, audio commentary on DVD of *The Friends of Eddie Coyle* (Criterion, 2015)

10. Mitchell Zuckoff, *Robert Altman: The Oral Biography* (New York: Vintage, 2010), 250.

11. John Caps, *Henry Mancini ... Reinventing Film Music* (Chicago: University of Illinois Press, 2012), 151.

Chapter 4

1. Mike Post, video interview by Stephen J. Abramson on May 25, 2005, accessed Aug. 8, 2019, https://interviews.televisionacademy.com/interviews/mike-post#interview-clips.

2. Jonathan Etter, *Quinn Martin, Producer* (Jefferson, NC: McFarland, 2008), 167.

3. Jon Burlingame, *TV's Biggest Hits* (New York: Schirmer, 1996), 51.

4. Kevin Courrier, "Notes and Frames II: Interview with Composer Jerry Goldsmith," *Critics At Large*, May 17, 2014, accessed Aug. 9, 2019, https://www.criticsatlarge.ca/2014/05/notes-and-frames-ii-interview-with.html.

5. "Jerry Goldsmith discusses his score for *Chinatown*," video interview broadcast in June 2000 by BBC Arts, accessed Aug. 9, 2019, https://www.bbc.co.uk/programmes/p02jn92b.

6. Courrier, "Notes and Frames II," 2014.

7. Charles Bernstein, quoted by Daniel Schweiger in the booklet notes for the album *Mr. Majestyk: Original Motion Picture Soundtrack* (Intrada, 2009), 4.

8. *Ibid.*

9. Herbie Hancock and Lisa Dickey, *Herbie Hancock: Possibilities* (London: Penguin, 2014), 187–88.

10. David Shire, video interview by Jon Burlingame on April 6, 2018, accessed Aug. 9, 2019, https://www.filmmusicfoundation.org/interviews.html.

11. David Shire, "Scoring the Conversation," booklet notes for the album *The Conversation: Original Motion Picture Soundtrack* (Intrada, 2001), 1.

12. Shire, video interview, 2018.

13. *Ibid.*

14. David Shire, podcast interview by Movie Geeks United, February 5, 2013, accessed Aug. 9, 2019, https://www.youtube.com/watch?v=Q-YOTikHOEY.

15. Shire, video interview, 2018.

Chapter 5

1. Jon Burlingame, *TV's Biggest Hits* (New York: Schirmer, 1996), 60.

2. *Ibid.*

3. Dave Grusin, "Baretta," *The Dave Grusin Archive*, accessed Aug. 9, 2019, http://www.grusin.net/tv_series_a_f.htm.

4. Mark Snow, video interview by Adrienne Faillace on March 24, 2016, accessed Aug. 9, 2019, https://interviews.televisionacademy.com/interviews/mark-snow#about.

5. *Ibid.*

6. Barry DeVorzon, video interview July 13, 2011, accessed Aug. 9, 2019, https://www.youtube.com/watch?v=CIDQgt_tneg&frags=pl%2Cwn.

7. Dominic Frontiere, 2006 (?), accessed Aug. 9, 2019, http://www.pteforums.com/viewtopic.php?f=29&t=1158.

8. Lukas Kendall, "Night Moves," *Film Score Monthly Message Board*, June 15, 2008, accessed Aug. 9, 2019, https://www.filmscoremonthly.com/board/posts.cfm?threadID=51408&forumID=1&archive=0.

9. David Shire, video interview by Jon Burlingame on April 6, 2018, accessed Aug. 9, 2019, https://www.filmmusicfoundation.org/interviews.html.

10. Dave Grusin, video interview by Jon Burlingame on March 22, 2011, accessed Aug. 9, 2019, https://www.filmmusicfoundation.org/interviews.html.

11. *Ibid.*

Chapter 6

1. Lalo Schifrin, video interview by Jon Burlingame in December 2008, accessed Aug. 9, 2019, https://www.filmmusicfoundation.org/interviews.html.

2. Jon Burlingame, *TV's Biggest Hits* (New York: Schirmer, 1996), 59.

3. Eric Malnic, "Legendary LAPD Detective 'Jigsaw John' St. John Dies," *Los Angeles Times*, May 4, 1995, accessed Aug. 9, 2019, https://www.latimes.com/archives/la-xpm-1995-05-04-mn-62350-story.html.

4. Doug Payne, "John Blair: Southern Love," *Sound Insights*, May 23, 2009, accessed Aug. 9, 2019, http://dougpayne.blogspot.com/2009/05/john-blair-southern-love.html.

5. Martin Scorsese, "On Bernard Herrmann," booklet notes for the album *Taxi Driver: Original Soundtrack Recording* (Arista, 1998), 1.

6. Martin Scorsese, Directors Guild of America discussion of the 35th anniversary Blu-ray restoration of *Taxi Driver*, March 10, 2011, accessed Aug. 9, 2019, https://www.youtube.com/watch?v=zrU4QT_gmRk.

7. Royal S. Brown, "An Interview with Bernard Herrmann," *High Fidelity*, September 1976, accessed Aug. 9, 2019, http://www.bernardherrmann.org/articles/an-interview-with-bernard-herrmann/.

8. David Meeker, "Jazz on the Screen: Taxi Driver," Library of Congress, accessed Aug. 9, 2019, https://www.loc.gov/item/jots.200019880/.

9. Staff writers, "Peeper," *Variety*, Dec. 31, 1974, accessed Aug. 9, 2019, https://variety.com/1974/film/reviews/peeper-1200423410/.

10. Laurie Johnson, *Noises in the Head* (New Romney, UK: Bank House, 2003), 131.

Chapter 7

1. Mark R. Hasan, "Oscar Peterson on *The Silent Partner*," *Music from the Movies*, Fall 1994, accessed Aug. 10, 2019, http://www.kqek.com/exclusives/Exclusives_Peterson_1.htm.

2. *Ibid.*

3. "Partners in Crime: Brian Clemens and Laurie Johnson," bonus feature interview included in the DVD set *The Professionals CI 5: Dossier 2* (Umbrella Entertainment, 2006).

4. Ian Dickerson, *The Saint on TV* (London: Hirst, 2011), 207–208.

5. Sanford Josephson, *Jeru's Journey: The Life and Music of Gerry Mulligan* (Milwaukee, WI: Hal Leonard, 2015), 152.

Chapter 8

1. Jon Burlingame, booklet notes for the album *Body Heat: Original Motion Picture Soundtrack* (Film Score Monthly, 2012), 5.

2. Mike Post, video interview by Stephen J. Abramson on May 25, 2005, accessed Aug. 8, 2019, https://interviews.televisionacademy.com/interviews/mike-post#interview-clips.

3. *Ibid.*

4. Nelson Riddle, *Arranged by Nelson Riddle* (Van Nuys, CA: Alfred, 1985), 143.

5. Burlingame, *Body Heat*, 6.

6. John Barry, "*Body Heat*: The Post-Production," bonus feature included in the deluxe edition DVD release of the film (Warner Bros., 2006).

7. Tim Greiving, booklet notes from the album *Absence of Malice: Original Motion Picture Soundtrack* (Varèse Sarabande, 2018), 6.

8. "Shoestring: George Fenton," *The Story of Euston Films*, Sept. 30, 2017, accessed Aug. 10, 2019, http://eustonfilms.blogspot.com/2017/09/shoestring-george-fenton.html.

Chapter 9

1. Mike Post, video interview by Stephen J. Abramson on May 25, 2005, accessed Aug. 8, 2019, https://interviews.televisionacademy.com/interviews/mike-post#interview-clips.

2. Bill Conti, video interview by Jon Burlingame on Sept. 20, 2010, accessed Aug. 11, 2019, https://interviews.televisionacademy.com/interviews/bill-conti#interview-clips.

3. Post, video interview, May 25, 2005.

4. Bruce Webber, "Earle Hagen, Who Composed Noted TV Tunes, Dies at 88," *The New York Times*, May 28, 2008, accessed Aug. 11, 2019, https://www.nytimes.com/2008/05/28/arts/television/28hagen.html.

5. Earle Hagen, video interview by Jon Burlingame on Nov. 17, 1997, accessed Aug. 4, 2019, https://interviews.televisionacademy.com/interviews/earle-hagen.

6. Associated Press, "Stacy Keach Out of Prison, Promises War on Drug Use," *Los Angeles Times*, June 7, 1975, accessed Aug. 11, 2019, https://www.latimes.com/archives/la-xpm-1985-06-07-mn-15982-story.html.

7. Max Allan Collins and James L. Traylor, *Mickey Spillane on Screen* (Jefferson, NC: McFarland, 2012), 153.

8. Ford A. Thaxton, "John Barry on Scoring the *Enigma*," *Soundtrack Magazine*, Vol. 20, No. 79, 2001, accessed Aug. 11, 2019, https://cnmsarchive.wordpress.com/2013/07/08/john-barry-on-scoring-the-enigma/.

9. Daniel Schweiger, booklet notes for the album *The Pope of Greenwich Village: Original MGM Motion Picture Soundtrack* (Quartet, 2012), 8.

Chapter 10

1. Jeff Bond, "Shagging a Sequel Score," *Film Score Monthly*, July 1999, 25.

2. Mike Post, video interview by Stephen J. Abramson on May 25, 2005, accessed Aug. 11, 2019, https://interviews.televisionacademy.com/interviews/mike-post#interview-clips.

3. Ashley Kahn, "A Conversation on Jazz & Hollywood," *JazzTimes*, April 1, 2016, accessed Aug. 11, 2019, https://jazztimes.com/features/interviews/a-conversation-on-jazz-hollywood/.

4. Sam Weisberg, "A Snake Pit Gig: The Making (and Undoing) of Abel Ferrara's *Cat Chaser*, *Hidden Films*, Sept. 9, 2015, accessed Aug. 11, 2019, https://hidden-films.com/2015/09/09/a-snake-pit-gig-the-making-and-undoing-of-abel-ferraras-cat-chaser/.

5. Geoff Leonard, Pete Walker and Gareth Bramley, *John Barry: The Man with the Midas Touch* (Bristol, UK: Redcliffe, 2008), 93.

6. Eddi Fiegel, *John Barry: A Sixties Theme* (London: Constable, 1998), 240.

Chapter 11

1. Stephen Pitalo, "Indie Film Pioneer John Sayles Talks about His New Film *Amigo*," *The Golden Age of Music Video*, Aug. 19, 2011, accessed Aug. 11, 2019, http://goldenageofmusicvideo.com/indie-film-pioneer-john-sayles-talks-about-his-new-film-amigo-and-directing-the-born-in-the-u-s-a-im-on-fire-and-glory-days-videos-for-the-boss/.
2. Jon Burlingame, "Wynton Marsalis: Scoring *Shannon's Deal*," *Soundtrack: The Collector's Quarterly*, September 1989, 18.
3. Elmer Bernstein, interview clip on his involvement with *The Grifters*, Elmer Bernstein: The Official Site, accessed Aug. 11, 2019, https://elmerbernstein.com/bio/.
4. Ibid.
5. Daniel Schweiger, "Jerry Goldsmith on Scoring *Basic Instinct*," *Soundtrack Magazine*, Vol. 11, No. 42, 1992, accessed Aug. 11, 2019, https://cnmsarchive.wordpress.com/2013/06/25/jerry-goldsmith-on-scoring-basic-instinct/.
6. "*The Public Eye*: Rejected Score," *Film Cue Database*, accessed Aug. 11, 2019, http://filmcues.blogspot.com/2013/04/the-public-eye-rejected.html.
7. Dave Grusin, video interview by Jon Burlingame on March 22, 2011, accessed Aug. 11, 2019, https://www.filmmusicfoundation.org/interviews.html.
8. Jeff Bond, "Shoot the Piano Player," booklet notes for the album *The Firm: Music from the Motion Picture* (La-La Land, 2015), 8.
9. Geoff Leonard, "The John Barry Interview: 1994," *johnbarry.org.uk*, accessed Aug. 11, 2019, https://johnbarry.org.uk/index.php/lyrics/item/327-the-john-barry-interview-1994.
10. Geoff Leonard, Pete Walker and Gareth Bramley, *John Barry: The Man with the Midas Touch* (Bristol, UK: Redcliffe, 2008), 156.

Chapter 12

1. Gwen Thompkins, "David Torkanowsky," *Music Inside Out*, accessed Aug. 11, 2019, http://musicinsideout.wwno.org/david-torkanowsky/.
2. Geraldine Wyckoff, "David Torkanowsky," *Offbeat Magazine*, Oct. 1, 2001, accessed Aug. 11, 2019, http://www.offbeat.com/articles/david-torkanowsky/.
3. Robert Fontenot, Jr., "Profile: Film score composer David Torkanowsky," *FrugalFun.com*, accessed Aug. 11, 2019, https://www.frugalfun.com/torkanowsky.html.
4. David Sterritt, "Director Builds Metaphor for Jazz in *Kansas City*," *The Christian Science Monitor*, Aug. 13, 1996, accessed Aug. 11, 2019, https://www.questia.com/read/1P2-33413964/director-builds-metaphor-for-jazz-in-kansas-city.
5. Ibid.
6. Richard Davis, *Complete Guide to Film Scoring* (Boston: Berklee, 1999), 260.
7. Gail Mitchell, "Quincy Jones' *Q: Soul Bossa Nostra* Track-By-Track," *Billboard*, Nov. 4, 2010, accessed Aug. 11, 2019, https://www.billboard.com/articles/news/952995/quincy-jones-q-soul-bossa-nostra-track-by-track.
8. Jeff Bond, "Shagging a Sequel Score," *Film Score Monthly*, July 1999, 22–23.
9. Steven Soderbergh, *Steven Soderbergh: Interviews* (Jackson: University Press of Mississippi, 2002), 109.
10. Ambrose Heron, "David Holmes on *Ocean's Thirteen*," *FilmDetail* podcast, Aug. 6, 2007, accessed Aug. 11, 2019, http://www.filmdetail.com/2007/06/08/david-holmes-on-oceans-thirteen/.
11. Doug Adams, "Schifrin Rushes In," *Film Score Monthly*, September 1998, 20.
12. Ibid., 24.
13. Ibid.
14. Bond, *Film Score Monthly*, 24.
15. "Same Story, Different Movie," bonus featurette included with the DVD/Blu-ray release of *Payback Straight Up: The Director's Cut* (Paramount, 2007).
16. Ibid.
17. Fred Topel, "*Edge of Tomorrow*: Christophe Beck on Over-Scoring, *Frozen* and *Buffy*," *Mandatory*, accessed Aug. 11, 2019, https://www.mandatory.com/fun/698309-edge-of-tomorrow-christophe-beck-on-over-scoring-frozen-and-buffy.

Chapter 13

1. "Music on Film: Elmer Bernstein in Conversation with Ken Barnes," bonus feature video included with the 50th anniversary DVD and Blu-ray release of *The Man with the Golden Arm* (Hart Sharp Video, 2005).
2. Tim Greiving, "Can You Dig It?," booklet notes for the album *Shaft: Music from the Motion Picture* (La-La Land, 2014), 11–12.
3. Ambrose Heron, "David Holmes on *Ocean's Thirteen*," *FilmDetail* podcast, Aug. 6, 2007, accessed Aug. 12, 2019, http://www.filmdetail.com/2007/06/08/david-holmes-on-oceans-thirteen/.
4. Dan Goldwasser, "Goldenthal's Frida Fantasy," *Soundtrack.net*, Nov. 2, 2002, accessed Aug. 12, 2019, https://www.soundtrack.net/content/article/?id=99.
5. Daniel Schweiger, "Playing It Cooler," *Film Score Monthly*, October/November 2003, 22.
6. Paul Grabowsky, booklet notes for the album *Shiner: Original Motion Picture Soundtrack* (Decca, 2001), 5.
7. Christine Blanc, "Big Movie—Epic Movie: Interview du compositeur Edward Shearmur," *Inter-Activities*, Feb. 5, 2008, accessed Aug. 12, 2019, http://inter-activities.blogspot.com/2008/02/big-movie-epic-movie-interview-du.html.

Chapter 14

1. Joseph LoDuca, "A Note from Composer Joseph LoDuca," booklet notes for the album *Leverage: Soundtrack from the Original Television Series* (La-La Land, 2009), 2–3.
2. Chad Walker, "Composer Interview: Joseph LoDuca," fandomania, Jan. 22, 2010, accessed Aug. 12, 2019, http://fandomania.com/composer-interview-joseph-loduca/.
3. David Holmes, "David Holmes: Music Supervisor, Ocean's 13," 2007 Warner Bros. promotional video produced for the release of *Ocean's 13*, accessed Aug. 12, 2019, https://www.youtube.com/watch?v=pejOtxuczJQ.
4. Brad Bird, "More Making of *The Incredibles*: Music," bonus feature video included with the two-disc collector's edition of *The Incredibles* (Disney/Pixar, 2005).
5. Richard Kraft, "The Beyondness of Things: My Bittersweet Relationship with Barry, John Barry," *Film Score Monthly* discussion board, May 25, 2016, accessed Aug. 12, 2019, https://www.filmscoremonthly.com/board/posts.cfm?threadID=115332&forumID=1&archive=0.
6. "Talking John Barry: Richard Kraft Interview," James Bond Radio podcast, Sept. 7, 2018, accessed Aug. 12, 2019, http://jamesbondradio.com/talking-john-barry-richard-craft-interview-the-music-of-bond-015/.
7. Dan Goldwasser, "Incredibly Lost with Michael Giacchino," *Soundtrack.net*, November 11, 2004, accessed Aug. 12, 2019, https://www.soundtrack.net/content/article/?id=132.
8. Farai Chideya, "Terence Blanchard on Scoring Spike Lee Joints," *National Public Radio News & Notes*, Feb. 15, 2008, accessed Aug. 12, 2019, https://www.npr.org/templates/story/story.php?storyId=19084952.
9. Jon Burlingame, "Teaching an Old Cat a New Song," *The New York Times*, June 12, 2005, accessed Aug. 12, 2019, https://www.nytimes.com/2005/06/12/movies/teaching-an-old-cat-a-new-song.html.
10. Holmes, "David Holmes: Music Supervisor, Ocean's 13," 2007.
11. *Ibid.*
12. Tim Horemans, "Interview: Christophe Beck," *Film Music Site* podcast, Dec. 8, 2011, accessed Aug. 12, 2019, https://www.filmmusicsite.com/en/composers.cgi?go=interview&coid=18&firstname=Christophe&lastname=Beck.
13. *Ibid.*
14. Stephan Eicke, "Given Freedom, I Can Write Good Music," Guy Farley's web site, March 3, 2012, accessed Aug. 12, 2019, http://www.guy-farley.com/interviews/interview_2012.htm.
15. Benjamin Wallfisch, "Behind the Scenes with Benjamin Wallfisch," 2018 video produced by Milan Records to promote the release of the soundtrack for *King of Thieves*, accessed Aug. 12, 2019, https://www.youtube.com/watch?v=RrOeHgnoUYA.

Epilogue

1. Brooke Yunis, "Composer Pat Irwin Talks The Good Cop and Rocko's Modern Life," *Broadway World*, Oct. 2, 2018, accessed Aug. 31, 2019, https://www.broadwayworld.com/bwwtv/article/BWW-Interview-Composer-Pat-Irwin-Talks-THE-GOOD-COP-and-ROCKOs-MODERN-LIFE-20181002.
2. "The Good Cop: Interview with Composer Pat Irwin," spoilertv.com, Oct. 30, 2018, accessed Aug. 31, 2019, https://www.spoilertv.com/2018/10/the-good-cop-interview-with-composer.html.
3. Pat Irwin, correspondence with the author, Aug. 21, 2019.
4. *Ibid.*

Bibliography

Books

Bowman, Rob. *Soulsville USA: The Story of Stax Records.* New York: Music Sales, 1997.

Brooks, Tim, and Earle Marsh. *The Complete Directory to Prime-Time Network and Cable TV Shows,* Ninth Ed. New York: Ballantine, 2007.

Burlingame, Jon. *TV's Biggest Hits.* New York: Schirmer, 1996.

Burton, Alan. *Historical Dictionary of British Spy Fiction.* Lanham, MD: Rowman & Littlefield, 2016.

Caps, John. *Henry Mancini … Reinventing Film Music.* Chicago: University of Illinois Press, 2012.

Collins, Max Allan, and James L. Traylor. *Mickey Spillane on Screen.* Jefferson, NC: McFarland, 2012.

Davis, Richard. *Complete Guide to Film Scoring.* Boston: Berklee, 1999.

Dickerson, Ian. *The Saint on TV.* London: Hirst, 2011.

Etter, Jonathan. *Quinn Martin, Producer.* Jefferson, NC: McFarland, 2008.

Fiegel, Eddi. *John Barry: A Sixties Theme.* London: Constable, 1998.

Goldberg, Lee. *Unsold Television Pilots: 1955–1989.* CreateSpace, 2015.

Hancock, Herbie, and Lisa Dickey. *Herbie Hancock: Possibilities.* London: Penguin, 2014.

Johnson, Laurie. *Noises in the Head.* New Romney, UK: Bank House, 2003.

Josephson, Sanford. *Jeru's Journey: The Life and Music of Gerry Mulligan.* Milwaukee, WI: Hal Leonard, 2015.

Leonard, Geoff, Pete Walker and Gareth Bramley. *John Barry: The Man with the Midas Touch.* Bristol, UK: Redcliffe, 2008.

Riddle, Nelson. *Arranged by Nelson Riddle.* Van Nuys, CA: Alfred, 1985.

Ritz, David. *Divided Soul: The Life of Marvin Gaye.* Lebanon, IN: Hachette, 2009.

Schifrin, Lalo. *Music Composition for Film and Television.* Boston: Berklee, 2011.

Simmons, Garner. *Peckinpah: A Portrait in Montage.* Milwaukee, WI: Hal Leonard, 1998.

Soderbergh, Steven. *Steven Soderbergh: Interviews.* Jackson: University Press of Mississippi, 2002.

Terrace, Vincent. *Encyclopedia of Television Pilots, 1937–2012.* Jefferson, NC: McFarland, 2008.

Interviews

Beck, Christophe. "Interview: Christophe Beck," *Film Music Site* podcast, December 8, 2011. https://www.filmmusicsite.com/en/composers.cgi?go=interview&coid=18&firstname=Christophe&lastname=Beck.

Conti, Bill. Video interview by Jon Burlingame, September 20, 2010. https://interviews.televisionacademy.com/interviews/bill-conti#interview-clips.

DeVorzon, Barry. Video interview, July 13, 2011. https://www.youtube.com/watch?v=CIDQgt_tneg&frags=pl%2Cwn.

Grusin, Dave. Video interview by Jon Burlingame, March 22, 2011. https://www.filmmusicfoundation.org/interviews.html.

Hagen, Earle. Video interview by Jon Burlingame, November 17, 1997. https://interviews.televisionacademy.com/interviews/earle-hagen.

Kraft, Richard. "Talking John Barry: Richard Kraft Interview," *James Bond Radio* podcast, September 7, 2018. http://jamesbondradio.com/talking-john-barry-richard-craft-interview-the-music-of-bond-015/.

Mandel, Johnny. Video interview by Linda Danly, August 1, 2007. https://www.filmmusicfoundation.org/interviews.html.

Post, Mike. Video interview by Stephen J. Abramson, May 25, 2005. https://interviews.televisionacademy.com/interviews/mike-post#-interview-clips.

Schifrin, Lalo. Video interview by Jon Burlingame, December 2008. https://www.filmmusicfoundation.org/interviews.html.

Shire, David. Podcast interview by Movie Geeks United, February 5, 2013. https://www.youtube.com/watch?v=Q-YOTikHOEY.

Shire, David. Video interview by Jon Burlingame, April 6, 2018. https://www.filmmusicfoundation.org/interviews.html.

Snow, Mark. Video interview by Adrienne Faillace, March 24, 2016. https://interviews.televisionacademy.com/interviews/mark-snow#about.

Index

Numbers in ***bold italics*** indicate pages with illustrations

The A-Team 49, 136–137, 222
Abbott, John 95
The ABC Mystery Movie 12, 152–153
Absence of Malice 93, 130–131, 222
Acree, Neal 162
Across 110th Street 35–36, 222
Action Jackson 83, 159, 222
Adams, Don 127, 155–156
Adams, Dorothy 105
Adams, Maud 107
Adderley, Cannonball 11
The Adventurer 29, 42–43, 222
Affleck, Casey 212
After the Sunset 207–208
Aiello, Danny 156
Albert, Eddie 73
Alda, Alan 212
Alias 208
Allaman, Eric 140
Allen, Geri 185, 230
Allen, Jonelle 35
Allison, Mose 199
The Alpha Caper 50–51
Altman, Robert 62, 184–185
Altruda, Joey 169
Ames, Morgan 62, 83
Ammons, Gene 40
The Anderson Tapes 17–18
Andre, Wayne 18, 225
Andress, Ursula 188, 191
Andrews, Dana 43
Andrews, Harry 81
The Andrews Sisters 114
Anholt, Tony 43
Arbus, Allan 56
Arianda, Nina 212
Armchair Cinema 95
Armstrong, Louis 7
Arneric, Neda 55
Arnold, David 163, 196–197, 236
Ashby, Linden 180
Assante, Armand 141–142
Assault in Paradise 111–112
Assignment: Vienna 31
Astley, Edwin 43, 162
Atkinson, Rowan 204
Aubert, Isabelle 45
Audran, Stéphane 95, 120
Austin Powers in Goldmember 199
Austin Powers: International Man of Mystery 187–188, 222

Austin Powers: The Spy Who Shagged Me 190–191, 223
The Avengers 24, 41, 106, 180
Avery, Val 17
Awasthi, Sapna 210
Ayers, Roy 56–57
Aykroyd, Dan 173
Aznavour, Charles 108

B.A.D. Cats 123–124
Bad Company 182–183
Badalamenti, Angelo 165–166, 240
Bagley, Don 123
Bailey, Pearl 155
Baker, Chet 130, 186, 192
Baker, Diane 32
Baker, Joe Don 15, 53, 61, 123, 163
Baker, Stanley 43
Baker, Steven 213
Balaban, Bob 130
Baldwin, Alec 183, 202
Bale, Christian 197
Balfe, Lorne 96
Ball of Fire 7
Balmer, Jean-François 118
Balsam, Martin 17, 59, 77
Banacek 30
Banyon 31–32, 68
Baretta 48, 83–84, 223
Barker, Guy 192, 203, 237, 238
Barkin, Ellen 159, 179, 183
Barnaby Jones 49, 223
Barri, Steve 11
Barry, Gene 12, 42
Barry, John 2–4, 9, 23, 26–29, 42, 44, 117, 122, ***128***–129, 134, 140–141, 145, 162–163, 171, 176–177, 188, 190, 200, 204, 206, 208–209, 215, 216, 222–224, 241
Barth, Ed 48
Bassey, Shirley 26, 226
Beach, Michael 183
Beacham, Stephanie 65
Beals, Jennifer 181
Bean, Sean 164
Beatty, Warren 18
Bechet, Sidney 7
Beck, Christophe 180, 206, 210, 212
Beck, Michael 151
Beckham, Tom 218
Beebe, Dion 213
Beery, Noah, Jr. 66

Belafonte, Harry 185
Bell, David 152
Bellman, Gina 206
Bello, Maria 202
Beltran, Robert 168
Benedict, Dirk 71, 136
Bening, Annette 170
Benjamin, Paul 36
Bennett, Richard Rodney 114
Benoit, David 167
Benson, George 139–140
Berg, Peter 176
Berghofer, Chuck 31, 185–186, 223, 227, 240
Bernard, Ed 36, 70
Bernsen, Corbin 148
Bernstein, Charles 55, 74
Bernstein, Elmer 2, 8, 9, 29, 73, 88, 101, 169, 170, 180, 181, 187, 195
Bernstein, Leonard 186, 200
Bernstein, Peter 169
Bernstein, Steven 153, 228
Bettany, Paul 203
Beyoncé 199
The Big Easy (TV series) 179
The Big Sleep ***113***–114, 223
Bikel, Theodore 33
The Bill 146, 223
Billboard 1, 15, 27, 66, 84–86, 100, 125–126, 133, 222, 224, 226, 229, 231, 232, 235–239
Billitis, Maike 216
Binder, Maurice 26, 138
Bird, Brad 208–209
Birney, David 101
Bisset, Jacqueline ***63***–64, 104
B.L. Stryker 152–153
Black, Karen 61
Black Belt Jones 70
The Black Bird 95, 223
Black Moon Rising 157
The Black Windmill 80–81, 223
Blair, John 101
Blake, Robert 83–84
Blakely, Colin 96, 114
Blanchard, Terence 210, 230
Blanchett, Cate 192
Bloodsport 132
Bloom, Lindsay 139
Blow-Up 74
The Blue Knight 86
Blume, Danny 182, 228

253

Index

Blume, Dave 102
Boardman, Chris 192–194, 234
Bob Le Flambeur 200
Bobo, Willie 48, 189
Bochco, Steve 125–126, 148
Boddicker, Michael 173
Bodelsen, Anders 112
Body Heat 4, 122, **128**–129, 140, 171, 176, 183, 223
Bolden, Buddy 7
Bonanza 13
Bond, James 2, 3, 9, 26–27, 57, 134, 162–163, 168, 177, 197, 241
Booker T. 182
Bookwalter, DeVeren 102
Boone, Richard 114
Boothe, Powers 137
Bosch 219
Bosco, Philip 172
Bound 185–186, 223
Bouton, Jim 62
Bowns, Dougie 182, 228
Boyle, Peter 141
Bozzuffi, Marcel 22
Brady, Scott 18
Brandauer, Klaus Maria 171
Brando, Marlon 198
Brandt, Carl **56**-57
Brannigan 89, 223
Brauner, Asher 123
Brauss, Arthur 18
Breckman, Andy 218
Brett, Adrian 94, 235
Bridgewater, Denise 56
The Brink's Job 114
Broadbent, Jim 216
Broderick, Matthew 160, 212
Brolin, Josh 151, 213
Bronk 86–87
Bronson, Charles 38, 68, 73–75, 104
Brooks, Avery 153–154
Brooks, Richard 18–19
Brosnan, Pierce 133–134, 207
Broughton, Bruce 49
Brown, Bryan 172, 194
Brown, Clifford 169
Brown, Garnett 18, 225
Brown, George Stanford 29
Brown, Ray 38, 226, 229, 234, 237–239
Brubeck, Chris 147
Brubeck, Dave 147, 218
Brynner, Yul 39
Budd, Roy 24–**25**, 41, 44, 59, 61, 66, 80–82, 97–98, 118, 120–121, 223, 224, 226–228
Buddy Faro 180–181
Budimir, Dennis 38, 104, 223, 224, 226, 227, 229, 231, 232
Bullitt 1, 19, 22, 40, 58, 73, 103, 218
Burke, James Lee 183
Burns, Ralph 4
Burr, Raymond 9
Burton, Norman 27
Burwell, Carter 182–183
Byers, Billy 30, 123
Byrd, Charlie 174
Byron, Don 185, 230

Caan, Scott 212
Cacavas, John 12, 48, 112, 123
Cagney & Lacey 134–135
Cain, Dean 201
Cain, Marie 135
Caine, Daniel 126, 137
Caine, Michael **25**–26, 80–82, 105, 199, 203, 216–217
Cairns, Rob 196
Callahan, "Dirty" Harry 20, 54, 59, 102, 142–143, 158
Cambridge, Godfrey 35
Cameron, John 42–43, 138
Camillo, Tony 70
Campbell, Bill 168
Candy 208
Cannell, Stephen J. 49, 66, 136–137
Cannon 2, 10, 150, 224
Cannon, Dyan 62
Capri, Ahna 52
Carey, Michele 123
The Carey Treatment 40–41, 224
Carli, Robert 218–219
Carlisle, John 42
Carlton, Larry 124, 126
Carmichael, Hoagy 213
Caron, Leslie 22
Carpenter, John 157
Carpenter, Pete 6, 46–47, 66–67, 109, 124–125, 136–137
Carrera, Barbara 141
Carson, John David 20
Carter, Benny 169, 237
Carter, James 185, 230
Carter, Ron 84
A Case of Need 40
Casey, Bernie 57, 130
Cassel, Vincent 208
Cassie & Co. 136
Cat Chaser 161
Catch Me If You Can 200, 224
Catenacci, Luciano 65
Cather, Orrie 195
CBS Summer Playhouse 117
Chamberlin, Lee 122
Chamota, Anthony 158
Champlin, Bill 152
Chan, Jackie 156, 189–190
Chan, Shen 92
Chandler 22–23, 224
Chandler, Raymond 31, 40, 61, 62, 67, 90, 91, 99, 113, 137, 166, 169, 184
Chaplin, Geraldine 43
Chapman, Michael 102
Charley Varrick 53
Charlie's Angels 99–100, 109, 123
Charteris, Leslie 116, 161–162
Chase 49–50
Chaumette, François 120
Chaykin, Maury 195
Cheadle, Don 181, 198, 207
Cheng, Gloria 185, 223
Chermak, Cy 109
Chestnut, Cyrus 185, 230
The Chevy Mystery Show 12
Chianese, Dominic 174
Chiao, Roy 156

Childers, Buddy 18, 224, 227
Childs, Billy 138, 236
Chinatown 3, 71–**72**, **91**, 99, 138, 157, 224
CHiPs 109–110, 224
Chopper One 71
Chopper Squad 108, 224
Chow, Michael 141
Christie, Agatha 146
Christie, Tony 43, 235
Christine Cromwell 153
CI5: The New Professionals 115–116
Cimino, Leonardo 35
The Cincinnati Kid 188
Cioffi, Charles 63
City of Angels 99, 138
Clark, Candy 114
Clarke, Andrew 117
Clarke, Patrick James 156
Clarke, Stanley 153–154
Clarkson, Patricia 159
Clay, Paul B. 42
Clayburgh, Jill **63**
Clayton, Merry 84, 127
Clemens, Brian 115
Clément, René 191
Clements, Richard 105
Cleopatra Jones 57, 224
Cleopatra Jones and the Casino of Gold 92, 224
Cleyndert, Andrew 164
Cline, Jeff 26, 228
Clinton, George S. 187–188, 190–191, 199, 222, 223
Clooney, George 189, 198, 208, 211
Coburn, James 40, 53, 81
Coe, Tony 94, 235
Coffy 56–57, 224–225
Colaiuta, Vinnie 161
Colbourne, Maurice 105
Cole, Nat King 169
Coleby, Robert 108
Coleman, Cy 160
Colla, Richard A. 39
Collette, Toni 197
Colley, Dana 183
Colley, Don Pedro 13
Collins, Joan 114
Collins, Lewis 115
Colombier, Michel 45, 227
Columbo 11–12, 49, 152–153
Come Back, Charleston Blue 35, 225
Connelly, Jennifer 171, 184
Connelly, Michael 219
Connery, Sean 17, 26, 160, 171–172
Conrad, Robert 31, 123
Conrad, William 10, 149–150
Constantine, Michael 105
Conti, Bill 135, 141, 172
The Conversation 75–**77**, 225
Coogan's Bluff 12
Cook, Martin 97, 235
Cool Hand Luke 19, 40
The Cooler 202, 245
Cooper, Gary 7
Cop Hater 39
Coppola, Carmine 72

Coppola, Francis Ford 75–76, 140, 145, 187
Corbett, Gretchen 66
Corea, Chick 161
Corneau, Alain 118
Corniche 110
The Cotton Club 145–146, 225
Cotton Comes to Harlem 35
Count Basie 34–35, 180, 184, 185, 241
Courage, Alexander 175
Courtenay, Tom 216
Covell, James J. 156
Cowherd, Jon 218
Cox, Charlie 216–217
Crane, Tony 179
Crawford, John 90
Crawford, Randy 130
Crenna, Richard 45, 129
Crichton, Michael 40–41
Crime 50
Crime Story 151
Cristal, Linda 74
Cromwell, James 186
Crosby, Bing 114
Crosby, Gary 50
Crosscurrent 13, 225
Crowe, Russell 186
Cruise, Tom 175
Culp, Robert 180
Cumbuka, Ji-Tu 123
Curse of the Pink Panther 94
Curtis, Tony 23–24
Cusack, John 170
Cutter, John 176

d'Abo, Maryam 163
Da Costa, Paulinho 144, 233, 234, 239
Daddo, Cameron 194
Dallamano, Massimo 64
D'Alton, Hugo 23
Dalton, Timothy 162–163
Daly, Tyne 103, 134
Damon, Matt 187, 188, 191, 198
Dandrea, Ron 156
Danes, Claire 187
Dankworth, Alex 164, 238
Dankworth, John 203–204
Danson, Ted 129
D'Antoni, Philip 58
Danza, Tony 218
Darc, Mireille 120
Darin, Bobby 158
Darmon, Gérard 200
Darren, James 134
Darrow, Henry 67
David, Thayer 105
Davies, Ray 48, 70
Davis, Charlie 183
Davis, Desmond 146
Davis, Don 185–186
Davis, John E. 134
Davis, Miles 111, 170–171, 174, 192, 203, 229
Davis, Ossie 152
Davis, Sammy, Jr. 84, 223
Dawson, Ben 216, 229

Day, Rolf 105
The Dead Pool 158, 225
Deakins, Roger 164
Dean, Jimmy 26
De Anda, Peter 35
de Angelis, Guido 116
de Angelis, Maurizio 116
Death of a Corrupt Man 119–120
The Death Squad 71
Death Wish 74–75, 113, 225
DeBenedictis, Dick 12–13, 150, 152
Dee, Brian 116, 235
De Franco, Buddy 130, 169, 237
D'Egidilo, Nick 202
De Jesus, Luchi 13, 69
Delon, Alain 45, 119–120, 191
Delon, Nathalie 28
The Delphi Bureau 31
Deneuve, Catherine 45
De Niro, Robert 102, 198
Dennehy, Brian 194
Denton, Richard 97, 235
Department S 24
Dern, Bruce 58
Desmond, Paul 128
DeSoto, Rosana 160
The Destructors 82
Detroit 9000 70
Devil in a Blue Dress 181, 225
De Vorzon, Barry 85–86, 123–124
Dey, Susan 148
The Diamond Mercenaries 107–108
Diamonds 97–98, 226
Diamonds Are Forever 26–27, 226
DiCaprio, Leonardo 200
Dickinson, Angie 20, 70, 136
Diehl, William 129
Dierkop, Charles 70
Dignam, Mark 107
Dillon, Melinda 130–131
Dinner with Friends 4
Dintenfass, Andrew 166
Dirty Harry 1, 19–20, 40, 52, 54, 71, 103, 143, 158–159, 189, 226
Dirty Money 45
Les Discrets 24
Dixon of Dock Green 42
Dobson, Kevin 138, 194
Dobson, Tamara 57, 92
Dr. No 187
Doering, George 151, 233–235, 239
$ (Dollars) 18–19, 226
Domanico, Chuck 128, 222–228, 232–234, 238
Donaggio, Pino 147
Donaldson, Norma 36
DoQui, Robert 56
Dorff, Steve 153
Double Indemnity 128
Dougherty, Mac 152
Douglas, Michael 30
Down, Lesley-Anne 126
Drasnin, Robert 10, 29, 46, 87
Dreier, Alex 23
The Drowning Pool 89–90
Drummond, Tim 171, 229
Dubois, Marie 118

Duke, Bill 159
Dumont, Jack 138
Dunaway, Faye 72, 93, 146
Duncan, Robert 86
Durkin, Fred 195
Durning, Charles 161
Dutton, Simon 162
Duvall, Robert 61
Dysart, Richard 148

Eastwood, Clint 19–20, 59, 68, 71, 102, 111, 142, 158
Edwards, Blake 40, 94, 155
Edwards, Glynn 25
Edwards, Jennifer 155
Edwards, Teddy 169
Egleton, Clive 80
Eischied 122–123
Eisler, Fil 110
Ejiofor, Chiwetel 210
El Chicano 84
Eldridge, Roy 174
Elizalde, John 10, 30
Elizondo, Hector 77
Elkind, Mort W. 81
Ellery Queen 87–88
Elliman, Yvonne 78, 232
Ellington, Duke 4, 7, 34, 77, 126–127, 138, 145, 155, 160, 167, 181, 185, 212
Elliott, Don 19, 38
Elliott, Jack 29, 70, 100
Ellis, Bradford 171, 229
Ellis, Don 1, 22, 58–59, 88, 111–112, 227
Ellroy, James 169, 186
The Enforcer 102–103, 226
Enter the Dragon 51–**52**, 156, 190, 226
Eshkeri, Ilan 205
Estrada, Eric 109–110
Eve, Trevor 131

The Fabulous Baker Boys 4
Faddis, Jon 111, 224, 228
Falk, Peter 12, 14, 49, 114, 152
Fallen Angels 169, 227
Family Business 160–161
Fann, Al 80
Farewell, My Lovely **91**–92, 227
Fargas, Antonio 36, 57, 84
Fargo, James 103
Farina, Dennis 180, 182
Farley, Guy 206, 215–216, 219
Farlowe, Chris 106, 228
Fawcett-Majors, Farrah 67, 100
Fear Is the Key 44, 227
Feldman, Victor 136, 224, 226, 237
Feldon, Barbara 127, 155–156
Fenn, Sherilyn 166
Fenton, George 131–132, 183–184, 237
Ferguson, Allyn 29, 70, 100
Ferrara, Abel 161
Ferrer, José 13
Ferrer, Mel 89
Ferrer, Miguel 169
Field, Sally 15, 130

Fielding, Jerry 13, 37–**39**, 61, 66, 70, **80**, 87, 95, 103, 111, **113**–114, 223, 228, 229
Fiennes, Magnus 214
Figgis, Mike 163–164, 238
Film Score Monthly 165
Finlay, Frank 55
Fiorentino, Linda 176
The Firm 175–176, 227
Fischer, Clare 11, 38, 226, 233, 237, 239
Fischer, Günther 162
Fishburne, Laurence 182
Fisher, Terry Louise 148
Fishman, Jack 25–26
Fishman, Paul 82, 230, 231
Fitzpatrick, Frank 183
Flack, Roberta 90, 143
Fleischer, Richard 74
Fleischer, Rubin 213
Un Flic 45, 227
Flick, Vic 163, 188
Flores, Ramon 161
Flynn, John 61
Fonda, Henry 50
Fonda, Peter 107
Fong, Brian 50
Ford, Mick 132
Foreman, Jamie 204
Forrest, Frederic 75, 141, 161
Forrest, Steve 85
Forster, Robert 31, 71
Forsythe, John 99–100
Fortune Dane 149
Foster, Jodie 102
Foster, Meg 135, 143
Fotonjy, Richard 174
Four in One 13
The Four Tops 55, 236
Fox, Charles 58, 90
Fox, Colin 195
Fox, Edward 114
Fox, James 171
Foxbat 82, 120–121, 227
Franciosa, Tony 32, 36, 87, 89
Francis, Clive 42
Francis, Dick 132
Franciscus, James 9
Frankenheimer, John 88–89
Frankie Drake Mysteries 218
Franklin, Carl 181
Franklin, Richard 172
Franklin, Rodney 126
Franklin, Serge 162
Fraser, Douglas 149
Frazier, Sheila 80
Frears, Stephen 170
Freebairn-Smith, Ian 124
Freed, Bert 11
Freedgood, Morton 77
The French Connection 1, 22, 58, **59**, 111, 227
French Connection II 88–89, 227
Fresson, Bernard 88
Friedkin, William 22, 88, 114
The Friends of Eddie Coyle **60**–61, 94, 227
Fröbe, Gert 18

Frontiere, Dominic 32, 71, 89, 92, 224
Frost, Mark 105, 165–166
The Fugitive 10
Fuller, Penny 149
Fuzz 39–40
F/X 172
F/X: The Series 194
F/X2 172–173, 228

Gainsbourg, Serge 208
Gambon, Michael 216
Gangster Number One 203–204, 228
Gangster Squad 213–214, 228
Gangsters 105–106, 228
Garcia, Andy 198, 208
Gardner, Craig 50
Gardner, John 59
Garfield, Brian 74
Garfield, Wayne 56
Garner, Erroll 200
Garner, James 66–67
Garnier, Tony 182, 228
Garrett, Snuff 129, 153
Garvarentz, Georges 107–108, 230
Gascoyne, Geoff 216, 229
Gassman, Vittorio 127, 130
The Gauntlet 111, 228
Gautier, Dick 155
Gaye, Marvin 33–34, 239
Gelbart, Larry 126
Gentry, Minnie 35
George, Melissa 196
Gere, Richard 145
Gershon, Gina 185
Get Carter 24–26, 81, 164, 203, 217, 228
Get Christie Love! 69–70
Get Shorty 181–182, 228
Get Smart 127, 179
Get Smart, Again! 155–156
The Getaway 37–**38**, 228
Getz, Stan 119–120, 169, 200, 232
Giacchino, Michael 206, 208–209
Gibson, Henry 62
Gibson, Mel 157, 192–193
Gideon Oliver 152–153
Gilberto, Joao 200
Gillespie, Dizzy 188
Gilstrap, Jim 83–84
Ging, Jack 55
Glanville, Maxwell 35
Glaser, Paul Michael 84
Gleason, Joanna 173
Gleason, Michael 110
Glenister, Robert **215**
Gless, Sharon 135
Glickenhaus, James 156
Glover, Bruce 26
Glover, Danny 169
The Golden Spiders 195
Goldenberg, Billy 12, 13, 30, 48, 67–68
Goldeneye 163
Goldenthal, Elliot 86, 200–201
Goldman, William 36
Goldsmith, Jerry 2, 3, 5, 13–14, 41, 46–**47**, 48, 49, 61–62, 71–**72**, **91**, 138, 165, 171–172, 175, 186–187, 210, 224, 237
Golson, Benny 10
Gompertz, Charles 7
The Good Cop 218–219
The Good Stuff 11, 232
The Good Thief 200–201, 228
Goodall, Howard 205
Goodman, Benny 160
Gordon, Justin 91, 224, 227, 232
Gosling, Ryan 213
Gottlieb, Stan 17
Gould, Elliott 62, 112–113, 211
Goux, John 193, 231, 234
Grabowsky, Mike 203, 237
Grabowsky, Paul 203, 237
Grady, James 92
Graham, Heather 191
Grainer, Ron 215
Grant, Lee 81
Grant, Simon 203
Graves, Teresa 55
Gray, Charles 26
Green, Lorne 49
Greenslade, David 105–106, 228
Gregg, Julie 31–32
Gregory, John 10, 28, 30, 48, 70, 241–242
Grier, Pam 56
Griffith, Melanie 90, 164, 184
The Grifters 170, 228
Grisham, John 175, 187
Groban, Josh 218–219
Grosvenor, Dennis 108
Grusin, Dave 2, 4, 9, 12, 14, 31, 38, 39, **60**–61, 62, 71, 78, **79**, 83–84, 92–94, 119, 130–131, 144–145, 148, 157–**158**, 175–176, 184, 206, 208, 218, 222, 227, 231, 232, 239
Guaraldi, Vince 7
Guardino, Harry 11, 104
Guerin, John 30, 31, 128, 223, 224, 228, 233, 234
Gunn, Moses 15, 34, 36
Gunsmoke 10
Gwilym, Mike 132
Gwynne, Michael C. 103

Hackman, Gene 22, 40, 75–**76**, 88, 90, 182
Hagans, Tim 199
Hagen, Earle 6, 9, 138–140
Hagman, Larry 50
Haig, Sid 56
Hall, Jim 18
Hall, Vondie Curtis 183
Halloween 157
Hamilton, Donald 87
Hamilton, Linda 157
Hamilton, Murray 89
Hamlin, Harry 148
Hammett 140–141, 228
Hammett, Dashiell 31, 95, 169, 184
Hancock, Herbie 66, 74–75, 139, 148, 159, 225
Handy, Craig 185, 230
The Hanged Man 96, 228–229

Index

Hanks, Steve 123
Hanks, Tom 200
Hanna, Jake 140
Hannah, Daryl 144
Hannon, Neil 203
Hardin, Jerry 170
Harewood, David 216
Harper 89
Harper, Frank 203
Harrelson, Woody 207
Harris, Jo Ann 101
Harris, Julius 33
Harris, Max 42
Harris, Naomie 207
Harry in Your Pocket 53–54, 229
Harry O 67–68
Hart, Billy 120, 232
Hart, Cecilia 122
Hatch, Richard 30
Hathaway, Donny 35, 225
Hauer, Rutger 143
Hawaii Five-O 1, 2, 70, 87, 124–125
Hawkins 48–49, **80**, 229
Hawkins, Jack 28
Hawkins, Jim 182
Hawkshaw, Alan 96, 229, 241
Hawn, Goldie 18
Hayden, Sterling 62
Hayek, Selma 207
Hayes, Bill 86
Hayes, Helen 49
Hayes, Isaac 1–3, 5, 15–17, 29, 31, 34–35, 48, 56, 197, 214, 232, 236–237
Hayes, Patricia 65
Hayes, Tubby 44, 227, 230
Haynes, Linda 90
Hazard, Richard 67, 87
Heaven's Prisoners 183–184
Heffron, Richard T. 141
Helgeland, Brian 192–193
Henderson, Bill 34
Henderson, Don 107, 117
Henderson, Scott 161
Henderson, Stephen 212
Hendry, Ian 25, 81
Henner, Marilu 141
Henry, Gregg 193
Herbig, Gary 149, 238
Herman, Woody 160
Herrmann, Bernard 102, 239
Hershey, Barbara 97, 174
Higgins, Dan 150, 200, 222, 224, 229, 232, 234, 235
Higgins, George V. 60
Highsmith, Patricia 191
Hill Street Blues 125–126, 134, 148, 229
Hillerman, John 124
Hindman, Earl 77
Hines, Earl "Fatha" 7
Hines, Gregory 145
Hingle, Pat 170
Hitchcock, Alfred 102
Hoblit, Gregory 126, 148
Hodge, Aldis 206
Hodges, Johnny 138
Hodges, Mike 24

Hodges, Teenie 176
Hoffman, Dustin 160
Hoffman, Philip Seymour 192
Holden, William 86
Holdridge, Lee 153
Holiday, Billie 40, 169
Holliman Earl 70
Holmes, David 189, 198, 208, 211–212
Hong, James 40
Hooker, John Lee 170–171, 229
Hooks, Robert 13, 33
Hooper, Les 123
Hopkins, Anthony 28
Hopkins, Bo 37
Hopper, Dennis 143
Horner, James 5, 173–174, 237
Hornung, E.W. 63
The Hot Potato 215–216, 229
The Hot Rock 36–37, 229
The Hot Spot 170–171, 229
Houseman, John 104
Houston Knights 151
Howard, Andrea 128
Howard, Ken 68
Howard, Susan 69
Hubbard, Freddie 18, 34–35, 237
Huddleston, David 73
Hudson, Rock 13, 20
Humperdinck, Engelbert 203
Hunt, Gareth 106
Hunter 50–51
Hunter, Evan 169
Hunters Are for Killing 113
Hurdle, Les 96, 229
Hurley, Elizabeth 188
Hurt, John 143
Hurt, William 129
Hustle 214–**215**
Huston, Anjelica 170
Huston, Jack 215
Huston, John 72
Hutchins, Peter 27
Hutton, Jim 88
Hutton, Timothy 88, 195, 206–207
Hynde, Chrissie 162–163

I Spy 9
I, the Jury (1982) 141–142, 229
Ihnat, Steve 39, 51
Imbruglia, Natalie 204
Immel, Jerrold 87
Imrie, Kathy 34
In the Frame 132
In the Heat of the Night (TV series) 152
The Incredibles 208–209, 229
Innocent Bystanders 43–44
Inside Man 210, 230
The Internecine Project 81–82, 121, 230
Intrada 165
Intveld, James 169
The Ipcress File 23, 215
Irvin, John 203
Irwin, Pat 218–219
Isham, Mark 161, 174, 202, 225
The Isley Brothers 189

It Takes a Thief 32, 110, 196
The Italian Job 215–216
Izzard, Eddie 212

Jablonsky, Steve 213
Jackson, Gordon 115
Jackson, Joe 151
Jackson, Kate 100
Jackson, Millie 57
Jackson, Milt 18, 237
Jackson, Samuel L. 86, 196–197, 214
Jackson, Sherry 155
Jaeckel, Richard 31, 89, 157
Jaffrey, Saeed 105
Jake and the Fatman 149–150
James Taylor Quartet 85
Janssen, David 67
Jason King 24, 41, 230
Jayston, Michael 81, 97
Jensen, Karen 41
Jigsaw 31
Jigsaw John 100–101
Jobim, Antonio Carlos 200
Johnny English 204–205, 230
Johnny English Reborn 204
Johnny English Strikes Again 205
Johnson, Anne-Marie 152
Johnson, Ben 37
Johnson, Don 170
Johnson, Emil Richard 14
Johnson, James P. 7
Johnson, J.J. 2, 35–36, **56**–57, 84, 92, 109, 139, 169
Johnson, Kevin 136
Johnson, Laurie 6, 24, 106, 115–116, 215, 230, 233
Johnson, Plas 94, 127, 174, 211, 224, 226, 234–237
Johnston, Kristen 191
Jones, James Earl 122
Jones, Quincy 2, 9, 17, 33, 35–**38**, 61, 78, 188, 191, 198, 206, 216, 228, 229
Jones, Randy 147
Jones, Tommy Lee 157, 164
Jones, Trevor 160
Jonny Quest 209
Joplin, Scott 7
Jordan, Neil 200
Jordan, Richard 60
Jurasik, Peter 155
Justin, John 114

Kamen, Michael 159, 163
Kane, Artie 21, 150, 223–225, 227, 230, 232, 234, 237–240
Kane, Christian 206
Kansas City 184–185, 230
Kaper, Bronislau 41
Kaplan, Alan 157, 222, 229, 234, 235, 237, 239
Kaproff, Dana 135
Karan, Chris 24–26, 81, 82, 97, 223, 226–228, 231
Karina, Anna 41
Karlen, John 135
Karlin, Fred 41, 110–111, 122

Index

Karvelas, Robert 155
Kasdan, Lawrence 122, *128*–129
Katsaros, Doug 154
Kaye, Carol 30, 36, 226, 229, 231
Kaye, Danny 7
Kaz 110–111
Kazama, Ken 56
Keach, Stacy 138–141
Keating, John(ny) 24, 43
Keats, Steven 61
Keitel, Harvey 102
Keith, Brian 79, 130
Kelly, Jim 51
Kelly, Paula 34
Kendall, Suzy 44
Kennedy, George 86
Kent, Rolfe 4
Kenton, Stan 68, 213
Kenyatta, Caro 57, 92
Kerber, Randy 184, 225, 232, 238, 239
Kershaw, Doug 19
Kerwin, Maureen 82
Ketchum, Dave 155
Kieling, Wolfgang 19
Kien, Shih 51
Killer by Night 32–33, 230
Killer Force 107, 230
Kim, Harry 161, 234
King, Alan 17, 141
King, B.B. 164, 175, 187, 193
King, Clydie 62
King, Earl 179
King of Thieves 216, 230
Kingsley, Ben 173
Kinski, Klaus 120
Kishi, Keiko 79
Kitchen, Michael 171
Kline, Kevin 211
Klugh, Earl 84
Knox, Alexander 27
Koffman, Moe 138
Kojak 15, 48, 107, 153
Kopell, Bernie 156
Koslo, Paul 60, 74
Kotto, Yaphet 36
Krabbé, Jeroen 162
Kraft, Richard 209
Krakow Jazz Ensemble 164
Kral, Irene 62
Krall, Diana 199, 202
Kristofferson, Kris 192–193
Kritzerland 165
Krüger, Christiane 81
Kujala, Steve 161, 225, 235
Kukhianidze, Nutsa 200
Kulik, Buzz 61–62
Kurtz, David 149

L.A. Confidential 5, *91*, 186–187, 230
L.A. Law 148–149, 231
Lââm 24
Laborde, Jean 119
Laboriel, Abe 136, 142, 225, 238
Laboriel, Abraham 142
La-La Land 165
Lambert, Derek 126

Lambro, Phillip 3, 71–72, 224
Lamont, Duncan 97, 226
Lancaster, Burt 78, 143
Lancaster, William 78
Landau, Martin 203
Landon, Laurene 141
Lane, Diane 145
Lang, Mike 128–129, 141, 172, 199, 222, 223, 225, 226, 228, 234–236
Lang, Ronnie 90, 102, 128, 141, 226, 228, 238, 239
Langella, Frank 183
Lansing, Robert 32
Larson, Glen A. 13, 70, 110
The Last Seduction 176, 231
Laszlo, Andrew 141
Latham, Jim 168
Lathan, Sanaa 201
The Laughing Policeman 57–58
Laumer, Keith 104
Laure, Carole 118
Lautner, Georges 119
Laverne, Andrew 120, 232
Law, Jude 192
Lawford, Peter 14
Laws, Hubert 18
The Lawyer 69
Leach, John 23
Le Carré, John 171
Lee, Bruce 9, 51–*52*
Lee, Peggy 130, 202
Lee, Robert 105
Lee, Will 101
Legrand, Michel 15, 191
Lei, Lydia 141
Leibman, Ron 36, 80, 110
Leigh, Barbara 20
Leigh, Jennifer Jason 185
Lennertz, Christopher 214
Lenny 4
Leonard, Elmore 73, 161, 181, 189
Leoni, Téa 212
Le Roy, Gloria 110
Lester, Adrian 215
Lett, Bruce 140
Lettieri, Al 37, 73, 74
Leung, Ken 190
Leverage 88, 206–207, 215, 231
Levin, Stewart 149
Lewis, Geoffrey 142
Lewis, Ted 25
Lewiston, Tim 215
Libertini, Richard 130
Licence to Kill 163
Linder, Cec 65
Lindo, Delroy 182
Little Richard 18, 226
Liu, Lucy 193
The Living Daylights 27, 162–163, 231
Llewelyn, Desmond 27
Llosa, Luis 176–177
Lloyd, Michael 11
Lloyd, Sue 43
Lo Bianco, Tony 22, 58
Locke, Sondra 111, 143
Lockett, Willie 179
Locklear, Heather 134

LoDuca, Joseph 206–207, 219
Loggia, Robert 154
Lom, Herbert 94
Lomez, Celine 112
The Long Goodbye 62–63, 231
Longstreet 2, 9–10, *92*
Lopez, Jennifer 189
The Lounge Lizards 182
Lowe, Mundell 84, 242
Luckinbill, Laurence 31
Lui, James Yi 120
Lumet, Sidney 17–18, 161
Lumley, Joanna 106
Lupus, Peter 180
Lurie, John 182, 228
Lynch, David 105, 165–166
Lynch, Kelly 183
Lynley, Carol 13

M Squad 180
Ma, Tzi 190
MacDonald, John D. 152
Macdonald, Ross 89
MacGraw, Ali 37
MacInnes, Helen 41
MacLachlan, Kyle 165
MacLean, Alistair 27–28, 44, 82
Macnee, Patrick 106, 180
Macy, William H. 202
Madsen, Michael 184
Madsen, Virginia 170–171
Mafia Junction see *Si può essere più bastardi dell'ispettore Cliff?*
Magee, Patrick 127
Maggs, Hywel 116
Mancini, Henry 9, 11, 41, *63*–64, 70, 86, 94, 100, 133–134, 142, 155, 180, 182, 188, 211, 215, 216, 218, 219, 233, 235, 239, 241
The Mancini Generation 64
Mancuso, FBI 154
Mandel, Johnny 32, 58–59, 236
Manetti, Larry 124
Mangione, Chuck 125
The Manhattan Transfer 130
The Manhunter 68, 231
Manni, Ettore 65
Mao, Angela 51
The Marcus-Nelson Murders 48
Margin for Murder 138
Margolin, Stuart 66
Markowitz, Richard 46, 101
Marlowe, Philip 62, 90–*91*, 104, *113*–114, 137–138, 169
Marsalis, Branford 171–172, 173, 236, 237
Marsalis, Delfeayo 167–168
Marsalis, Wynton 166–167
Marsan, Eddie 204
Marsden, Matthew 203
Marsden, Roy 118
The Marseille Contract 82, 231
Marsh, James 216
Martin, Dean 87, 189, 193
Martin, Irving 116, 235
Martin, Steve 94, 210–211
Martin, Tony 169
Marvin, Lee 40

Mascolo, Joseph 34
Mason, Harvey 38, 136, 225, 226, 238, 239
Mason, James 82
Mason, Marlyn 9
Masterson, Mary Stuart 183
Matchett, Kari 195
Matt Helm 87
Matthau, Walter 53, 57–58, 77–78
Matthews, Al 127
Maunder, Wayne 50
May, Billy 109
Maybach, Christiane 18
Mayo, Virginia 7
McBain, Ed 39
McBride, Christian 185, 230
McCarthy, Dennis 151
McCloud 11–13, 77
McClure, Doug 32
McCoy, Noel 183
McDowall, Roddy 20
McDowell, Malcolm 203
McEachin, James 39, 49, 50
McEveety, Bernard 14
McGillis, Kelly 161
McGraw, Charles 23
McGuigan, Paul 203
McKee, Lonette 145
McManus, Mark 117
McMillan, Lannie 176
McMillan and Wife 11, 13
McMullan, Jim 71
McNab, Malcolm 102, 160, 222, 223, 226, 230, 232–236, 238, 239
McNeely, "Big" Jay 213
McNeely, Joel 180–181
McNeil, Willie 169
McPartland, Marian 96
McQ 73, 232
McQueen, Steve 37
McShane, Ian 132
Meaney, Colm 216
The Mechanic 38–39, 61, 232
Medeski, John 182, 228
Medford, Don 17
Mellé, Gil 12, 17, 49, 168
Melnick, Peter Rodgers 156
Melville, Jean-Pierre 45, 200
Melville, Sam 29
Melvoin, Michael 15
The Men 30–31, 232
La Menace 118–119, 232
Mendes, Eva 201
Menten, Dale 178–179
Menza, Don 17, 225–227, 233, 239
Meredith, Burgess 32
Meriwether, Lee 49
Miami Vice 133, 151, 161
Mickey Spillane's Mike Hammer 139–140
The Midnight Man 78
Mike Hammer, Private Eye 140
Miles, Sarah 113
Miles, Sylvia 91
Milian, Tomas 161
Miller, Ben 204
Minghella, Anthony 191

Mission: Impossible 1–3, 50–51, 53, 157, 214–215, 241
Mr. and Mrs. North 13
Mr. Majestyk 73–74, 232
Mr. T 33–34, 136–137
Mitchell, Cameron 78
Mitchell, Gwenn 16
Mitchell, Jake 122
Mitchell, James 43
Mitchell, Thomas 12
Mitchum, Robert 60, 79, 90, **113**
The Mod Squad 29
Moffat, Geraldine 26
Moffet, Charnett 199
Mol, Gretchen 189
Mongo's Back in Town 14–15
Monk 218
Monk, Debra 195
Monk, Thelonious 181
Montand, Yves 118
Monty Nash 2, 11, 232
Moon Over Miami 167–168
Moonlighting 167, 196
Moore, Robin 22
Moore, Roger 23–24, 26–27, 116–117, 162
Moran, Mike 107, 117, 132
More Than Murder 139
Morgan, Barry 96, 229
Morgan, Charlie 146, 223
Morgan, Pete 24
Morgan, Tommy 74, 232
Morley, Angela 28
Morley, Robert 28
Morricone, Ennio 208
Morris, Butch 153–154
Morris, Garrett 17
Morris, Greg 32
Morris the Cat 61
Morrow, Vic 14, 123
Mort D'un Pourri 119–120, 232
Mortimer, Emily 211
Morton, Jelly Roll 7
Mosely, Roger E. 124
Mosely, Walter 181
Mosley, Bryan 25
Most Wanted 101, 232
Mostel, Zero 37
Mower, Patrick 116
The Mugger 39
Mulholland Falls 184, 232
Mullen, Jim 182
Mulligan, Gerry 37, 118–119, 186, 229, 232
Mulroney, Dermot 185
Murder Me, Murder You 138
Murphy, Eddie 213
Murray, Jaime 215
Musante, Tony 47–48
Muti, Ornella 120
Myers, Mike 187–188, 191, 199, 204
Myers, Peter T. 150
Myhre, John 192

Nakamura, Masatoshi 55
The Name of the Game 32, 68
Nash, Dick 90, 128, 223, 224, 226–229, 232, 234, 237, 238, 239

Natwick, Mildred 49
The NBC Mystery Movie 11–13, 64, 233
The NBC Sunday Mystery Movie 11
The NBC Wednesday Mystery Movie 11
Neeson, Liam 158
Nelson, Craig T. 143, 159
Nelson, Oliver 2, 9–10, 50, 80, 238
A Nero Wolfe Mystery 195–196
Nesbit, Derren 43, 216
Neville, Aaron 184
The New Avengers 106, 233
The New CBS Friday Movie 13
The New Centurions 46
The New Mike Hammer 139–140
New Scotland Yard 41–42, 95
Newell, Patrick 106
Newley, Anthony 203
Newman, Barry 41, 44, 69
Newman, Paul 89, 130
Newman, Randy 137
Newman, Thomas 163
Nicholson, Jack 72
Nicolai, Bruno 208
Night Games 69
Night Moves 90
Nimoy, Leonard 50
Niven, David 126
Noble, Ray 138, 140
Nolte, Nick 184, 200, 213
Norton, Edward 188, 199
Novack, Shelly 101
The Nude Bomb 127–128, 155
N.Y.P.D. 13

Oates, Warren 22, 64
O'Brien, Hugh 32
Ocean's Eleven 198, 233
Ocean's Thirteen 211–212, 233
Ocean's Twelve 208, 233
O'Connor, Carroll 152
O'Connor, Kevin J. 172
Ogilvy, Ian 116, 162
O'Halloran, Jack 91
Ohno, Yuki 110
Okada, Eiji 79
Oldfield, Eric 108
O'Leary, John 91
O'Loughlin, Gerald S. 29
On Her Majesty's Secret Service 23, 209
O'Neal, Patrick 110
O'Neal, Ryan 63–64
O'Neill, Jennifer 41
Ontkean, Michael 29
Ordeal by Innocence 146–147, 233
The Organization 2, 17, 233
Ortega, Anthony 141–142
Ortolani, Riz 64–65, 237
The Osmonds 20
The Osterman Weekend 143–144, 233
Our Man Flint 14, 187
Out of Sight 189, 233
Out of Time 195, 201–202, 233
The Outfit 61, 234
Owen, Clive 210, 211

Pacino, Al 101, 159, 211
Palance, Jack 86–87
Palmer, Earl 171, 229, 239
Palminteri, Chazz 184
Paltrow, Gwyneth 192
Panic in the Streets 32
Pantoliano, Joe 186
Panzer, Saul 195
Paré, Michael 151
Paris 122
Paris Blues 4
Parker, Alan 96, 229
Parker, Charlie 169, 192
Parker, John Carl 10–11, 31, 109–110, 149
Parker, Mary 181
Parker, Robert 153
Parkins, Barbara 27
Parks, Gordon 1, 15–16, 34–35, 79–80
Parrish, Robert 82
Parsons, Alibe 105
Pask, Andy 146, 223
Pate, Johnny 48, 55
Patitucci, John 161, 236, 239
Paulsen, Albert 58
Payback 192–194, 234
Pearce, Guy 186
Peckinpah, Sam 37, 143
Peeper 105
Peña, Michael 110, 212
Pendleton, Austin 64
Penn, Chris 184
Penn, Sean 213
Penny, Joe 150
Peppard, George 30, 136
Pepper, Art 103, 111, 226, 228, 237
Peppers, Adam 202, 225
Perjanik, Mike 108
Perry, Felton 54
The Persuaders 23–24, 42, 234
Pesci, Joe 174
Peter Gunn (1989 TV movie) 155
Peter Gunn (TV series) 9, 41, 63, 133–134, 142, 151, 180, 218–219, 241
Peterson, Oscar 112–113, 237
Petrocelli 69
Pfeiffer, Michelle 123–124, 157, 171
Philip Marlowe, Private Eye 137–138
Phillips, Michelle 71
Phillips, Stu 13, 70, 110
Phoenix, River 173
Piccioni, Piero 27–28
Pidgeon, Walter 53
The Pied Pipers 213
The Pink Panther (2006) 210–211, 234
The Pink Panther Strikes Again 94
The Pink Panther 2 211
Pitt, Brad 198, 208, 212
Pitts, Charles 16
Pizzi, Ray 135, 239
Playing by Heart 4
Pleasance, Donald 43, 81
Plein Soleil 191
Plimpton, George 195

Plummer, Christopher 94, 112, 147
The Pointer Sisters 159
Pointman 178–179
Poitier, Sidney 13, 17, 173
Polanski, Roman 72
Police Story 46–47, 70, 234
Police Woman 70–71
Pollack, Sydney 79, 92–**93**, 130–131, 175
The Pope of Greenwich Village 144–145, 234
Popwell, Albert 57, 92
Porter, Bobbi 37, 229
Porter, Cole 172
Porter, Nyree Dawn 43
Portnow, Richard 155
Post, Mike 5, 6, 46, 66, 109, 124, 125–126, 133, 136–137, 148, 152, 179, 222, 229, 235
Post, Ted 54
The Postman Always Rings Twice 128
Powers, Stefanie 69
Prescription: Murder 12
Presencer, Gerard 182
Preston, J.A. 129
The Pretenders 162, 231
Pretty Maids All in a Row 2, 20–*21*, 234
Prime Cut 40
Prince, Robert 30
Private Eye 151
Probe 32
The Professionals 115, 234
The Protector 156, 235
The Protectors 42–43
The Public Enemy 203
The Public Eye 174–175, 235
Pullman, Bill 176
Puppet on a Chain 27–28, 235
Purple Noon 191
The Pusher 39
Pyne, Mick 164

Qin, Shaobo 198
Quantum of Solace 163
Quartet 165
Queen, Ellery 87–88, 207
Quiller 97, 235
The Quiller Memorandum 97
Quinn, Anthony 36, 82
Quinn Martin Productions 10, 30, 68

The Racing Game 132
Raffin, Deborah 112
Rainey, Chuck 38, 224, 226, 228, 229, 239
The Rainmaker 187, 235
Rambo, Dack 110
Ramin, Ron 135, 140, 149
Ramirez, Frank 122
Rampling, Charlotte 91
Randolph, John 13
Random Hearts 4
Ransom for a Dead Man 12
Rappaport, David 155
Rasey, Uan 72, 224, 226, 239

Rassimov, Ivan 65
Ratner, Brett 190, 213
Rawls, Lou 193
Rayner, Adam 162
Rebhorn, James 192
Redford, Robert 36, 92, 173
Redgrave, Corin 28
Redknapp, Louise 216
Redman, Joshua 185, 230
Reed, Oliver 112, 114
Reeve, Geoffrey 27
Reid, R.D. 195
Reiner, Carl 198
Remar, James 145
Remington Steele 133–134
Reno, Jean 211
The Return of Maxwell Smart 127–128
The Return of Mickey Spillane's Mike Hammer 139
The Return of the Pink Panther 94
Return of the Saint 116–117
Revell, Graeme 201
Revenge of the Pink Panther 94
Rey, Fernando 22, 88
Reynolds, Burt 39, 61, 126, 129–130, 152–153
Rhames, Ving 48
Rhythm Heritage 84, 85, 86
Rich, Buddy 95
Richards, Dick 91
Richards, Emil 15, 93, 127, 144, 222–226, 228–231, 233–235, 237–240
Richardson, Michael 50
Richardson, Miranda 185
Riddle, Nelson 86, 99, 109, 126–127, 135–136, 138
Rieser, Dan 219
Riesgraf, Beth 206
Rifkin, Ron 195
Rigsby, Clarke 153
Ritchie, Michael 40
Ritenour, Lee 136, 157–158, 167, 228, 239, 240
Rivers, Johnny 11
Roach, Jay 148
Roberts, Eric 144, 177, 183
Roberts, Julia 198
Roberts, Tanya 139
Robicheaux, Coco 179
Robinson, Andy 19, 53
Robinson, Laura 168
Rocco, Alex 60
The Rockford Files 47, 66–67, 131, 189, 235
Roddenberry, Gene 20–21
Rogers, Roy 171, 229
Rogers, Shorty 29, 84, 151, 174
Rogers, Simon 214–215
Rogers, Wayne 99
Rollins, Howard 152
Rollins, Sonny 192
Romanis, George 23, 87, 224
Ronet, Maurice 119
The Rookies 2, 29, 85
Ros, Edmundo 203
Rose, David 13

Index

Rosenbaum, Joel 150
Rosenberg, Stuart 58, 90
Rosenman, Leonard 32
Rosenzweig, Barney 135
Ross, Annie 95
Rough Cut 126–127, 235
Rounders 188–189, 235
Roundtree, Richard 15–16, 34, 48–49, 54, 97, 214
Rourke, Mickey 144
Royce, Kenneth 107
Ruffins, Kermit 179
Rugolo, Pete 29, 47, 70, 100–101
Rumble in the Bronx 189
Rush Hour 189–190, 235
Rush Hour 2 190
Rush Hour 3 190
Rushmore 148
Russell, Kurt 157
The Russia House 171–172, 236
Ryan, Mitchell 23, 50
Ryan, Robert 61
Rydell, Mark 62

The Saint (1989 TV series) 161–162
The Saint in Manhattan 117
St. Ives 104
St. Jacques, Raymond 35
St. James, Susan 13
St. John, Christopher 15
St. John, Jill 26
St. John, John P. 100–101
Salmi, Albert 69
The Salzburg Connection 41
Samuels, Dave 199, 225
Sanborn, David 125, 149, 157–158, 239
Sanchez, Antonio 182
The Sandbaggers 118
Sanders, Lawrence 17
Sandman, Mark 183
Sanford, Isabel 140
Sanko, Erik Norse 183, 228
Santamaria, Mongo 189
Santos, Joe 66
Sarandon, Chris 143
Sarde, Philippe 119
Sargent, Joseph 77
Sarrazin, Michael 53
Savalas, Telly 15, 20, 48, 107, 153
Saxon, John 51
Sayles, John 166–167
Sbille, Jean-Louis 216
Scalia, Jack 178–179
Schaeffer, Steve 199, 224, 230
Scharf, Sabrina 51
Scheider, Roy 22, 58, 171
Scheiwiller, Fred 53
Schell, Catherine 94
Scherr, Tony 219–220
Schifrin, Lalo 1–3, 9, 19–21, 22, 40, 50–51, **52**–54, 65, 69, 78, 84, 87, 92, 99, 101, 103–104, 108, 127, **142**–144, 151, 156–159, 172–173, 188–190, 206–208, 216, 218, 226, 232, 241
Schoenberg, Arnold 78
Schultz, Dwight 136–137

Schwartz, Nan 152
The Score 198–199, 236
Scorsese, Martin 102
Scott, Jacqueline 53
Scott, John 116
Scott, Judson 141
Scott, Ronnie 44, 223, 227
Scott, Tom 10, 30, 31, 84, 85, 93, 102, 159, 167, 232, 236, 237, 239
Screen Archives Entertainment 165
Sea of Love 159–160, 236
Search 32
Segal, George 36, 95, 97
Segall, Bernardo 12
Selby, David 80
Selleck, Tom 5, 101, 124–125
Sellers, Peter 94
Serkis, Andy 203
Serpico (1976 TV series) 101
Serra, Eric 163
The Seven-Ups 58–**59**, 236
Severinsen, Doc 130, 237
Seyrig, Delphine 81
Shaft (1971 film) 5, 15–17, 236
Shaft (1973 TV series) 48–49, 236
Shaft (2000 film) 196–197, 236
Shaft (2019 film) 214, 236
Shaft in Africa 54–55, 236
Shaft's Big Score 34–35, 236
Shamus 61–62
Shank, Bud 79, 104, 139, 223, 226–228, 231, 233, 234, 239, 240
Shannon's Deal 166–167
Shapiro, Theodore 85
Sharky's Machine 129–130, 237
Shatner, William 134
Shaw, Martin 115
Shaw, Robert 77, 97
Shearmur, Edward 204
Sheen, Martin 15
Sheldon, Jack 62, 140
Shepherd, Cybill 102, 103
Sheridan, Jamey 166
Sheybal, Vladek 27, 43
Shiner 202–203, 237
Shire, David 13, 66, 75–76, **77**–78, 90–**91**, 92, 213, 225, 227
Shoestring 131–132, 237
Shore, Dinah 40
Shore, Howard 198–199
Shores, Richard 46–47, 70, 87
Si può essere più bastardi dell'ispettore Cliff? 64–65, 237
Sideways 4
Sidibe, Gabourey 212
Siegel, Don 19–20
The Silent Partner 112–113, 237
Silla, Felix 95
Silva, Henry 120, 130
Silvestri, Alan 109–110, 137
Simon, Joe 57, 92, 224
Simpson, Dudley 116
Sinatra, Frank 144, 200, 202, 212
Singh, Sukhwinder 210
Sjöwall, Maj 57
Skerritt, Tom 39
Skyfall 163

Slate, Jeremy 13
Slaughter 70
Slim, Memphis 181
Sloan, P.F. 11
Small, Michael 89, 90, 195
Smalley, Jack 100
Smile, Jenny, You're Dead 67
Smith, Allison 180
Smith, Bill 147
Smith, Jaclyn 100, 153
Smith, Jimmy 18
Smith, Norman "Hurricane" 43
Smith, O.C. 34–35
Smith, Putter 26
Smith, Reid 50
Smithers, Bill 33
Smitrovich, Bill 195
Smits, Jimmy 148
Sneakers 173–174, 237
Snider, Barry 141
Snow, Mark 29, 85, 117, 134, 135
Soderbergh, Steven 189, 198, 211–212
Sohmer, Steve 154
Son of the Pink Panther 94
A Song Is Born 7
Sonnenfeld, Barry 182
Sorvino, Paul 141
Soul, David 84
South, Harry 95
Spacek, Sissy 40
Spacey, Kevin 186
Special Delivery 103–104
The Specialist 176–177, 237
Spectre 163
Spenser: For Hire 153
Spielberg, Steven 12
Spillane, Mickey 138, 141, 169
Sprague, Peter 161
Spy Game 180
Staccato 101, 180
Stack, Robert 101
Stafford, Jill 169
Stallone, Sylvester 176–177
Stambler, Scott 192–194
Stamos, John 196
Standard Music Library 42
Stanwyck, Barbara 7
Starsky & Hutch 84–85, 237
Statham, Jason 210
Steiger, Rod 177
A Step Out of Line 14, 237
Stern, Leonard 128
Stevens, Mort(on) 2, 3, 70, 87, 150
Stevens, Stella 92
Stewart, James 48, 49, 113
Stiller, Ben 85, 212
Sting 164
Stipe, Debra 155
Stoller, Kevin 153
Stone, Emma 213
Stone, Sharon 159, 176
The Stone Killer 59–60
Stormy Monday 163–164, 238
Storyboard 146
Stott, Walter 28
Stradling, Harry, Jr. 104
Strangers 117

Strathairn, David 173, 186
Strauss, Peter 155
The Streets of San Francisco 29–30
Strickland, Gail 90
Stuart, Giacomo Rossi 65
Stuart, Mark 200
Such Dust as Dreams Are Made On 67
Sudden Impact 142–143, 238
Summer of '42 15
The Super Cops 79–**80**, 238
Sutherland, Donald 146
Sutton, Tierney 202
Suzman, Janet 81
Svenson, Bo 103
S.W.A.T. 85–86
The Sweeney 95–96, 115, 116, 117, 238
Swit, Loretta 135
Sword of Justice 110
Szathmary, Irving 127, 155–156

Taj Mahal 171, 229
Takakura, Ken 79
The Taking of Pelham One Two Three 4, 77–78, 213, 238
The Talented Mr. Ripley 191–192, 238
Tamahori, Lee 184
Target 116
Tartaglia, John Andrew 110
Tate, Grady 18, 229, 237
Tate, Phil 24
Tatro, Duane 68
Taube, Sven-Bertil 27
Taxi Driver 102, 238–239
Taylor, James 153
Taylor, Mark 164
Taylor, Stephen James 153
Taylor, Wally 34
Tee, Richard 85, 136
Telfair, Richard 11
Tenafly 49
The 10th Victim 188
Tequila Sunrise 157–**158**, 239
Terran, Tony 74, 223, 225, 226, 232, 234, 237, 238
Terry, John 163
Tew, Alan 96
That Man Bolt 55–56
Thaw, John 95
Thewlis, David 203
They Only Come Out at Night 100
The Thief Who Came to Dinner **63**–64, 239
Thielemans, Toots 18, 38
Thieves 196
The Thin Man 13, 134
Thomas, Ross 104, 182
The Thomas Crown Affair 191
Thompson, Jim 37, 169, 170
Thorne, Ken 24, 156, 234
Thorson, Linda 106
The Threat 118
Three Days of the Condor 31, 61, 71, 92–94, 119, 239
Three Degrees 98
Thunderball 44

Ticotin, Rachel 172
Tien, Ni 92
Tiffany Memorandum 64–65
Tilly, Jennifer 186
T.J. Hooker 134
Toma 47
Tomorrow Never Dies 163
Tompkins, Angel 32
Tompkins, Ross 140
Torkanowsky, David 179
Tormé, Mel 68
Torn, David 199
Toro, Efrain 120, 161, 232
Torres, Jacqueline 194
Touch of Evil 182
Tower Heist 212–213, 239
Towne, Robert 72, 157
Tracey, Clark 164, 238
Trail of the Pink Panther 94
Travanti, Daniel J. 125
Travolta, John 181–182
Trevor, Elleston 97
Tripplehorn, Jeanne 175
Trouble Man 33–34, 239
Troyer, Verne 199
Tuchner, Michael 44
Tucker, Chris 189–190
Turner, Charles 80
Turner, Kathleen 122, 129
Turner, Michael 42
Turner, Simon Fisher 204
Twelve-tone compositional structure 68, 78
Twice Shy 132
Twin Peaks 165–166
Twin Peaks: Fire Walk with Me 166
Tyner, Charles 78

Udenio, Fabiana 188
The Umbrella 24
Unger, Deborah Kara 193
Urbont, Jacques 87
Urich, Robert 153
Usher, Jessie T. 214

Vadim, Roger 20
Van Devere, Trish 53
Vanishing Point 44
Vanity 159
van Pallandt, Nina 62
Vaughan, Sarah 95, 130, 169
Vaughn, Robert 42–43, 157, 215
The Ventures 70, 85, 100
Vernon, John 44, 51, 81, 89
Veronica Clare 168
Vincent, Jan-Michael 38
Visser, Edward 140
Vitarelli, Joseph 176, 231
Voight, Jon 187

Wagner, Robert 13, 32
Wahlöö, Per 57
Wainwright, James 31
Waite, Ralph 33
Walcot, Gregory 40
Walden, Lynette 169
Waldman, Randy 100
Walk on the Wild Side 187

Walken, Christopher 17, 200
Walker, Ally 167
Walker, T-Bone 176, 181
Wall, Robert 51
Waller, Fats 7
Walley, Moira 140
Wallfisch, Benjamin 206, 216, 219
Walsh, John 172
Walters, Susan 179
Wambaugh, Joseph 46–47, 86
Wanderly, Walter 189
Wannberg, Ken 112–113
Ward, Janet 90
Ward, Rachel 130
Ward, Richard 36
Warden, Jack 100–101
Warren, Jennifer 90
Warren, Marc 215
Warren, Michael 122
Warren, Richard Lewis 134
Washington, Denzel 181, 201, 210
Washington, Dinah 169
Washington, Grover, Jr. 136
Waterman, Dennis 95
Waters, Oren 174
Watson, Ken 31, 223, 226, 232, 234, 238
Watts, Ernie 135, 143, 227, 233, 238
Wayne, David 88
Wayne, John 72–73, 89
Weathers, Carl 149, 159
Weaver, Dennis 12–13
Webb, Doug 169
Webber, Robert 18
Welch, Raquel 39
Weller, Don 164
Weller, Peter 161
Wenders, Wim 140
West, Timothy 127
Westlake, Donald E. 36, 61, 170, 192
Weston, Jack 39
Wexler, Haskell 184
Whaley, Frank 180
When Eight Bells Toll 28
Whirry, Shannon 140
Whitaker, Jim 202
Whitman, Stuart 112
Whittemore, L.H. 80
Widelitz, Stacy 110
Wiggins, Gerald 174, 235
Wilcox, Larry 109–110
Wilcox, Ralph 80
Wilkinson, Geoff 182
Williams, Barbara 155
Williams, Charles 170
Williams, Cindy 75
Williams, David 149
Williams, Dick Anthony 17
Williams, Joe 130
Williams, John 5–7, 33, 62, 109, 137, 175, 200, 231
Williams, Patrick 12, 29–30, 101, 122, 123, 238
Williams, Richard 94
Williams, Vanessa L. 197
Williamson, Fred 55
Wilson, Cassandra 199

Wilson, John 28
Wilson, Owen 85
Winfield, Paul 33
Winn, Kitty 105
Winner, Michael 75, 113
Winstone, Ray 96, 215, 216
Winter, Chris 116
Winters, Shelley 57
Winterstein, Richard 78
Wisniewski, Andreas 163
Witherspoon, Jimmy 95, 179, 181
Wollesen, Kenny 219
Womack, Bobby 35–36, 222
Wood, Natalie 105
Woods, James 177
Woods, Michael 151

Woodvine, John 42
Woodward, Edward 115
Woodward, Joanne 89
Woodward, Morgan 78
Woolrich, Cornell 169
Wyngarde, Peter 24
Wynn, Keenan 20

The XYY Man 107

The Yakuza **79**, **93**, 240
Yardley, Stephen 107
Yared, Gabriel 192
Yates, Peter 36, **60**–61
Yerkovich, Anthony 151
Yeung, Bolo 51

York, Susannah 112–113
Yorkin, Bud 63
You Only Live Twice 191, 209
Young, Christopher 188
Young, Red 169
Young, Snooky 18, 237
Young, Terence 120
Yulin, Harris 78, 104

Zamprogna, Dominic 172
Zawinul, Joe 117
Zerbe, Anthony 67, 91
Zeta-Jones, Catherine 208
Zimbalist, Stephanie 133–134
Zmed, Adrian 134

www.ingramcontent.com/pod-product-compliance
Lightning Source LLC
Chambersburg PA
CBHW080802300426
44114CB00020B/2796